THE ART CRITICISM OF JOHN RUSKIN

THE ART CRITICISM
of
JOHN RUSKIN

SELECTED, EDITED, AND
WITH AN INTRODUCTION BY
ROBERT L. HERBERT

A DA CAPO PAPERBACK

Library of Congress Cataloging in Publication Data

Ruskin, John, 1819-1900.
   The art of criticism of John Ruskin.

   (A Da Capo paperback)
   Reprint. Originally published: New York: Doubleday,
1964.
   Bibliography: p.
   1. Art criticism. I. Herbert, Robert L. II. Title.
N7445.2.R77   1987   709   87-13496
ISBN 0-306-80310-0

Published by Da Capo Press, Inc.
A Subsidiary of Plenum Publishing Corporation
233 Spring Street, New York, N.Y. 10013

To the memory of
E. T. COOK *and* ALEXANDER WEDDERBURN

INTRODUCTION

*Et comme on a dit de Ruskin tant de choses
contraires, on en a conclu qu'il était contradic-
toire.*

MARCEL PROUST[1]

"One no longer wants gods," he cried, "yet gods are essential to our imagination. We can't get around it, modern
rationalism, if it is able to satisfy the learned, is a way of
thinking incompatible with any conception of art . . . Ma-
chinism, the division of labor, have transformed the worker
into a simple automaton and have killed the joy of working. In the factory, the worker, tied to a machine which
asks nothing of his brain, sadly accomplishes a monotonous
task of which he feels only the fatigue."

A typical Ruskin statement? In one sense, yes, but in
fact the words are Renoir's.[2] It is only surprising because
we have warped the nineteenth century to suit the values
of the twentieth. Thus Renoir is universally accepted as a
painters' painter and his repeated statements of an arts-
and-crafts morality are ignored. Ignored, because we ourselves separate morality from what we regard as "pure
art," and therefore insist on the same separation in artists
of the past. And thus Ruskin is regarded as the arch moral-
izer of the past century, which leads us to conclude, from
the same prejudice, that he was unaware of artistic values.

The irony of this incorrect assessment is that Ruskin is
the one critic of the nineteenth century who, more than

[1] *Pastiches et Mélanges* (Paris, 1919), p. 153.
[2] Letter to Henry Mottez, editor, Cennino Cennini, *Le Livre
de l'Art* (Paris, 1911), pp. x and xi.

any other, based his life's work upon visual sensations, and provided the twentieth century with the most compendious discussion of the "abstract" components of art. That this is imbedded in the matrix of naturalism and the evangelical style of Victorian writing in no way denies its import. On the contrary, returning to Ruskin with the intention of being at best condescending, the modern observer will instead be struck by the incorporation of so many contemporary values in a vast and harmonious system. He will discover a man who finds no contradiction between naturalism and formal values, nor between fidelity to nature as a principle of apprenticeship, and disdain of natural detail as the sign of mastery.

VISION AND ABSTRACTION. In his famous confessional letter to Rossetti (MP III, xliii),[3] Ruskin places first among his several pleasures that of *seeing*. So much of his thought can be traced to experiences in seeing, that his vision is simultaneously its source and its ultimate arbitrator. Despite the depth of his early religious and moral convictions, his eye, seduced by the sheer beauty of Veronese, Titian, and Tintoretto, led him to place the seemingly amoral and irreligious Venetians at the very top of his pyramid of quality. Vision became the arbitrator of knowledge so that, when discussing science (ENest 210), he tells us that one day Turner, working out of doors, omitted to draw the portholes of a ship in the distance though he knew full well they were there, answering to the objections of a naval officer that "my business is to draw what I see, and not what I know is there."

The beauty of Ruskin's descriptions of nature and of works of art depends upon this same vision, and we are tempted to believe that his persuasive word-pictures are what helped him most to teach the British to see. Ruskin was perfectly aware of the fact that vision is not a neutral or passive experience, that if a person is to become educated in the visual arts, his eye and his mind must be exercised together. "You do not see *with* the lens of the eye.

[3] For all references to Ruskin see below, the *Key to Abbreviations*.

You see *through* that, and by means of that, but you see with the soul of the eye." (ENest 194). Much of his writing was accordingly devoted to analyzing the character of the artist's mind since his vision was interdependent with it, and also the character of the artist's society since, in turn, his mind was interdependent with that. Hence his analysis of Turner's styles and subjects in relation to his youthful environment, or his discussion of Venetian art in relation to her maritime and independent character.

Ruskin's own vision has this same dual nature, interlocked in complete health and harmony. He can see the purely visual, the purely abstract, but though he may for a moment separate this element for the sake of exposition, he also "sees" it as the external sign of the poetic mind. To be yet closer to Ruskin's vision we must, finally, from our vantage point, recognize that his vision is that of a painter rather than of an architect or sculptor, and consequently much of what *we* must discern in the soul of *his* eye will be a painterly sight born of a passion for light and color.

For these reasons, Ruskin begins a discussion of naturalism in the Gothic mind (SV II, 215 ff) by first emphasizing the primacy of pure color. After reminding us, as Baudelaire might, that "the arrangement of colours and lines is an art analogous to the composition of music, and entirely independent of the representation of facts," he states that "Good colouring does not necessarily convey the image of anything but itself." An artist may, with strokes of grey and purple, convey to us the image of a dove's neck, "But the good colouring does not consist in that imitation, but in the abstract qualities and relations of the grey and purple." Because "the noblest art is an exact unison of the abstract value, with the imitative power, of forms and colours," Ruskin finds it no dilemma to insist upon the analysis of both abstraction and imitation. On the contrary, he points toward the dichotomy of twentieth-century criticism when he concludes that "the human mind cannot in general unite the two perfections: it either pursues the fact to the neglect of the composition, or pursues the composition to the neglect of the fact."

When Ruskin is willing to suspend his concern for subject matter, as in his brilliant discussion of the form of a common breakfast plate (ArP 205 ff), he strikes us as very "modern." When he insists that, essential as they are, the formal components of art are truly significant only as exponents of "other and higher things" (Lamps 151), we no longer follow him, for fear we will be trapped into moral judgments. Amusingly enough, these "higher things" are often formal properties such as motion and repose, which he finds embodied in the differing structure of Greek and Gothic drapery (Lamps 150 f). Instead of casting Ruskin out, modern formalists could have found comfort in his constant attention to the language of art. Of course this would also be a distortion, but the defenders of Abstract Expressionism, feeling obliged to prove that pure color and form have significance because they can communicate states of emotionality (Ruskin would have said "soul"), should really have delighted in his conviction that "in these various differences from reality," the painting has its highest power (MP III, 187). Mere imitation gives us nothing of the artist's own self, nor therefore of Divine power vested in the artist, because these are found only in the language of art standing as intercessor between ourselves and the highest beauty, that of the spiritual order of the universe as revealed by artistic imagination.

It is not the tree that expresses "the power and intelligence of a companionable human soul" (MP III, 187), but the degree to which the image of the tree departs from reality by accepting the stamp of the artist's imagination. Ruskin delights in pointing out the mysterious way in which emotional states have their counterparts in formal qualities. "You need not be in the least afraid of pushing these analogies too far. They cannot be pushed too far; they are so precise and complete, that the farther you pursue them, the clearer, the more certain, the more useful you will find them." Hence "conditions of line and colour" have the ability to embody every nuance of human feeling: "Affection and discord, fretfulness and quietness, feebleness and firmness, luxury and purity, pride and mod-

esty . . ."—words for which there are exact equivalents in
the criticism of abstract art.

Ruskin borrows from Locke (MP I, 91 f) in assigning
the status of *idea* to the intellectual and sensual pleasures derived from consulting the abstract language of art.
Therefore his famous dictum (MP I, 92) "that the art is
greatest which conveys to the mind of the spectator, by
any means whatsoever, the greatest number of the greatest
ideas," does not elevate moral and literary qualities high
above the purely formal, but ennobles the latter by giving
them the rank of idea. The formal components of art are
placed on a par with morality and other, supposedly non-
formal qualities.

THE PREFERRED "CONDITION OF CHILDHOOD." Ruskin was
so far taken by the abstract elements of the arts that he
preferred the early and less polished work of each period
he loved: archaic and fifth-century Greek sculpture to Hel-
lenistic; early Byzantine sculpture and mosaic to later;
early to High Gothic; Giotto to Masaccio; Pisano to Ghiberti; Florentine quattrocento painting to High Renaissance; cinquecento Venetian to Baroque. The very apex,
beyond which decline sets in, is the same for Gothic sculpture (the Madonna at the south transept door, Amiens) as
for the Renaissance (Michelangelo): the culmination and
perfection of the earlier stages of a style but, through that
perfection, a devotion to naturalism for its own sake, a kind
of exhibitionism resulting from hubris, in which the abstract and the vital are lost. The two are found together
only in a "condition of childhood," because "The feebleness
of childhood is full of promise and interest,—the struggle
of imperfect knowledge full of energy and continuity . . ."
(Lamps 194). The maturity following upon vital childhood
has a bittersweet taste, because if it does state more fully
the early ideals, it is at the cost of the approaching decline.
The "purest architectural abstractions," Ruskin insists, "are
expressions of the mind of manhood by the hands of childhood" (SV I, 290), a compromise in which he comes closest to resolving the dilemma. A mature architect supplies
the main elements of the design, but the detailed work is
left to the initiative of the workmen who, uneducated by

comparison, are in the proper condition of childhood to give vitality to the visible surfaces of the building.

In painting, Ruskin finds several ways in which the rich energies of childhood can be retained. The artist must try to see like a child and think like one, especially in coloring, which for Ruskin is decidedly the highest instinctual gift. The modern artist must recognize that the Renaissance suppressed the instinctive sense of color the Gothic era enjoyed. It is not a case of returning to a state of historical infancy, against which we are warned, but of liberating the essential instincts by recognizing the repressive role played by the Renaissance urge for cruel perfection. The sketch is thus preferred to the finished picture because, being less than perfect, it is the exterior repository of inner searching and change, and is closer to the state of instinct. Moreover, being "imperfect," the sketch taxes the viewer's imagination more and forces *him* to seek in the manner of a child, rather than affirm in the manner of an adult (MP III, 186 ff; SV II, 199 ff).

That this doctrine is central to Ruskin is clear from its relevance to his strictures upon the nineteenth century. Aged, irregular Venetian glass is shown to be superior to modern, uniform glassware *because* of its imperfections, its childlike richness (SV II, 199 ff). The uniformity of modern art production is his target also because it suppresses the individuality of the workman, who becomes a mere robot. Renoir and Pissarro later agreed, which suggests not only that Ruskin's social views were hardly parochial, but that the "condition of childhood" underpinning them had singular significance for the Impressionists. In our century we have simply given a new name to Ruskin's concept: "primitivism."

COLOR. Like most writers of the nineteenth century, Ruskin attributed to form, divorced from color, the most basic role of recording images in imaginary space and, like them, wrote that color showed the fleeting, the passionate, and the most intimate aspects of artistic sensibility. But more than any other writer of his period, he exalted color for its own sake. While art's most essential requisite is form, its highest calling is color, so that his greatest painters are so because of their color, and his preferred architectural styles are marked by colored surfaces.

Given his fascination with science, it is no surprise that he had a highly developed theory of color. Partly because of his own apprenticeship in British watercolor methods, his theory emphasizes reflected and refracted color-light brought about by stippling, that is, by the admixture of multiple strokes of pure color, with white showing between to exalt the whole. Reckoned by the standards of later French art, this was the most advanced part of his color theory, and was made generally available by 1881 in the French translation of Ogden Rood's *Modern Chromatics*.[4] The generous sections on color from the *Elements of Drawing* that Rood included were highly influential in the development of Neo-Impressionism, and Monet told a British journalist in 1900 that "ninety percent of the theory of impressionist painting is . . . in 'Elements of Drawing.'"[5] Actually Ruskin's color is more bound together with light and shade than is true of French painting, but that was easy to overlook given his constant stress upon the inherent abstraction of "the flat stains of colour" (ED 27, footnote) and the necessity of seizing upon visual appearances without the interference of memory knowledge. He went so far as to admit that the artist would probably violate the laws of science, but "his very transgressions will be admirable" (MP I, 509).

Ruskin's exaltation of prismatic color had to do with painting directly out of doors and was directed primarily to sketching in watercolor, when the goal was the rapid rendering of nature's most lovely truths of light and color. Turner was the model for such paintings. In finished oils there had to be more of a balance with form, but the variety and richness of prismatic color must be retained, even

[4] First published in New York in 1879, translated two years later as *Théorie scientifique des couleurs*. Despite the unquestioned importance of these texts, they are seldom included in anthologies of Ruskin (not a single excerpt, for example, in Miss Evans' recent selection mentioned in the bibliography below).

[5] Cited by Wynford Dewhurst, "What Is Impressionism?" *The Contemporary Review*, 99 (March, 1911), p. 296.

if subdued. William Henry Hunt was his model here. The greatest art of the present day, however, like that of the past, rises above naturalism to a superior level and exposes the supreme order of the universe in the grandness of the artist's imagination. For this purpose naturalistic color is not a requisite, and other, more abstract considerations enter, based upon a straightforward concept of the effectiveness and the emotional powers of pure color. Here again, Turner was the ideal painter. The greatest art of the past, after the advent of Renaissance naturalism, is exemplified by Titian, Tintoretto, and Veronese, whose color has nearly the depths of nature itself, due to layers of glazes and flickering brushwork.

Color by the juxtaposition of flat patches, on the other hand, marks the greatest art of the past *before* Renaissance naturalism. Here Ruskin's favorites are medieval illuminators, Fra Angelico, and Giovanni Bellini. Allied to his love of colored surfaces in architecture, the predilection for flat areas of color seems to dominate Ruskin's sense of color after about 1870 and is further supported then by his special love for Giotto, for quattrocento painting, especially Carpaccio and Botticelli, and for Greek vase painting. The doctrine of prismatic color seems to us now to have characterized the 1840s, the time of his greatest passion for Turner, and the 1850s, when he was the chief defender of the Pre-Raphaelites' painting directly from nature.

The two, apparently contrasting types of color harmony are not, however, in conflict. Ruskin could assimilate a love for what was then deemed primitive art, with its flat patches of color, and for high Venetian art and Turner, graced by delicate veils of indescribable hues, just as Pre-Raphaelitism meant simultaneously the preference for quattrocento art and for the most painstaking, literal imitation of nature. In Ruskin's case, he consistently relates the color to the purpose, so that an art of essentially symbolic content, like that of Angelico, has the more abstract structure, while an art of greater naturalism, say Turner, has the more interlaced color.

Regardless of the type of color Ruskin is discussing, he finds so much sheer release in its sensory power that he comes to love it for its own sake. His belief that color is separate from form goes so far, in painting, as to assert that it disguises form, that it has an infinitely greater power than form (and is therefore the greater gift), and that the color of a given object is not its local property, not sensation itself, but the active power of producing sensation in the observer. In architecture, he insists that color have a system entirely separate from the pattern of ornament so that, for example, instead of giving sculpted leaves one color and their background another, both are incorporated in a color harmony unrelated to their separate forms. In such discussions the modern reader thinks of Léger and other artists of our century who have made color float independently of the form because they, too, have wanted to grant it autonomy.

SCIENCE AND ANTI-SCIENCE. Ruskin's theory of color is often expressed in quasi-scientific language, and was even included in Rood's treatise. But this, and his still more prominent devotion to the natural sciences, including whole books on geology, minerology, plant and animal life, often bring consternation to the casual reader, since just as often he roundly condemns science. The resolution is not hard to find. Any science that adds to the *descriptive* knowledge of nature, and thus acts as the artist's servant, is all to the good; any science that deals with *analytical* knowledge, is only bad. This is because for artists "only the imaginative truth is precious," and "all mathematical, and arithmetical, and generally scientific truth, is, in comparison, truth of the husk and surface, hard and shallow . . ." (MP IV, 44 f). Scientific knowledge, save for description, will positively interfere with the free play of imagination, which is instinctive. Hence the technical skills of late Gothic architecture permitted the substitution of linear for massive structure, and the knowledge of anatomy of the High Renaissance led to the triumph of prideful naturalism. In each case science overcame feeling, and resulted in decadence.

This is why, of course, he considered "perfection," which is merely the same enemy on a different mount, the very sign of accomplished decadence, for it meant the triumph of uniformity, rational knowledge, of the *known* and *learned* over life-imbued irregularity, instinctive knowledge, the *felt* and the *dreamed.* The artist can only consummate his role in life by exposing the supreme order of the universe, and this he does by way of his imagination, the unique bond with the spiritual (anti-science) as opposed to the material (science). Science, therefore, if it can be turned to value at all, must act as a squire to the knight of imagination, and arm him with a description of the battleground, after which he is best away from the field.

The natural sciences preoccupied Ruskin from earliest youth, it is true, not only because they were the dominant sciences of the nineteenth century and hence absorbed by a precocious boy, but because they suited his powers of observation and description. They could become an essential part of his painter's temperament, unlike the theoretical sciences, because they helped plunge him all the more thoroughly into an absorption with the visible exterior of nature, that nature which was the only thing that might rival artistic imagination. Nevertheless, much as he was often seduced by the natural sciences, and nature herself, he always returned to the dictum that "Only natural phenomena in their direct relation to humanity" were the fit subjects in landscape, because "Rocks and water and air may no more be painted for their own sakes, than the armour carved without the warrior" (Land 17). It was entirely possible to paint a scene devoid of human beings and of their artifacts, but it was not possible to deny to the scene the feelings of the painter. In painting, even the wildest bit of nature bears the imprint of the artistic mind and, since nature is thus inconceivable without the intercession of the human imagination, so are the sciences that describe her.

For once it is possible to point to a specific passage that makes this relationship entirely clear. In the final paragraph of his essay of 1851, *Pre-Raphaelitism* (below, pp. 34 f), he contrasts two observers of the same mountainous country, one a scientist who has thoroughly explored it, the other, an "unlearned spectator." Against the dessication resulting from scientific inquiry, he places the awe coming from blissful ignorance. If he had stopped there, he would have had only a simplistic view of science, but in one of his rare attacks on his beloved Wordsworth (in the footnote attached to the paragraph) he warns us against such shortsightedness. He knows that the innocence of childhood cannot be retained, and that fine science can rise even to the heights he would like to reserve to art, a sense of the unifying order of the universe. Fortunately, the scientist can win back some of the lost innocence, by turning to the ideal artist who will give "the facts of science" their true vocation by providing them with the palpable flesh of feeling.

This ideal confluence of science and art, terminating, we should note, in the broad current of human feeling, makes it clear that Ruskin could accept at least the natural sciences if they were recognized as of a different, and subordinate category to art. Much of his derision of science stems from his instinctive disdain for the Victorian marriage of science and material progress. Besides, he believed that the artist and the art-minded layman to whom he addressed himself, being in no way scientists, would benefit far more from assaying the world about them as poets, and he wished to attack head-on the amateur "science" which was the obligatory, but superficial acquirement of every gentleman of his day. Some of his finest, and most amusing discussions occur when he is thinking of the amateur, for then his real respect for the natural sciences leads him almost unwillingly into a defense of them as properly studied. In *Deucalion*, his major treatise on earth and mineral structure, he defends the then radical, now accepted theory of James David Forbes that a glacier is essentially a slowly moving river of ice. He was literally in the forward ranks of science in this one instance, and uses Forbes' theory to demolish his rival Viollet-le-Duc's book, *Le Massif du Mont Blanc* (Paris, 1876), which accepted the now outmoded theories championed by Agassiz and Tyndall. Amending General Pelissier's famous statement, he says of Viollet-le-Duc's science, *"C'est magnifique;—mais ce n'est pas la géologie"* (*Works* XXVI, 223).

FIDELITY TO NATURE. Especially because of Ruskin's extensive writings in the natural sciences, and his own careful watercolors, his insistence upon the literal imitation of nature has come to be his best-known test of excellence. Faced nonetheless by his lavishly expressed admiration for Turner or Tintoretto, who can hardly be associated with such literalness, too many observers have deduced that Ruskin is woefully inconsistent. The pre-eminence he gave to the imagination should alone make it apparent that, like science, the literal copying of nature is best the servant of the higher forms of art. For *all* modern artists, the devotion to copying is a vital apprenticeship, and provides the artist with a type of knowledge similar to that afforded by the natural sciences. The rare great artist, like Turner, will soar above and beyond this stage, retaining its lessons in the certain knowledge that, though not actually represented in detail, underlies the completed work. Young artists, like the Pre-Raphaelites, have not yet reached their maturity, and therefore their literalness is for them, and for English art, a necessary purgative and temporarily a good in itself. Ultimately, since such faithfulness to nature "is Mirror's work, not Man's" (Acad 1859, 237), a new school must rise from the Pre-Raphaelites' endeavors. Meanwhile, this same faithfulness will be the highest goal for those amateurs who can never aspire to greatness. At least they will be storing up knowledge and dealing with one order, albeit an inferior one, of truth. Depending upon where Ruskin stands on this scale of diminishing aspirations, he will put forth apparently different, but actually interrelated, ideas of the imitation of nature.

Ruskin applies the same scale of values to art of the past, although the balance of his analysis is shifted to imaginative art. That is, much of his emphasis upon direct copying from nature is included in advice to beginners, and has less a place in discussions of historical art since even Ruskin stops short of giving dead men advice. Copying nature in past art becomes also an essential apprenticeship, not so much in the life of any one artist as in the youthful stage of a given period. If such imitation of nature proves to have been the goal, it means that the artists were mediocre, and then Ruskin feels the same loss of innocence he attributed to the geologist on the mountain. He repeatedly asserts, for each era, that the sign of decline is the triumph of "scientific naturalism."

Still, the reader aware of Ruskin's role as the ardent defender of Pre-Raphaelitism is apt at this point to shake his head, for he remembers that before the founding of the Brotherhood, Ruskin had become famous partly for clothing himself in the lion's skin of precise naturalism, and that afterward he announced that their clean river of faithful realism was cleaning out the stables of musty eclecticism. The fact that his first major defense of Pre-Raphaelitism, the essay of 1851 (PRB), is really yet another song of praise to Turner, is sufficient evidence that there was no conflict in Ruskin's mind. It is vital to see in how many ways he insisted upon departing from precise imitation of nature.

Certainly he was drawn all his life to grandness of conception, and to the sketch, more than to the manner of realizing the conceptions, or to the completed work. He insisted that only the very greatest artists could provide the perfect finish, without imprisoning themselves in the chains of "perfection." The vast majority of artists, being lower than these few, would err only in such detailed finish, and their virtues are best displayed in rougher form. "Rather choose rough work than smooth work, so only that the practical purpose be answered, and never imagine there is reason to be proud of anything that may be accomplished by patience and sand-paper" (SV III, 199). The less-than-great artist must retain "the sacredness of the truth of *Impression*" [sic] (MP IV, 36), and must not impose over it any arbitrary concept of what is right, for the intuitive is truer than the carefully reasoned.

Parallel to his love of the sketch (which, in combination with his color theory, brings him so close to the Impressionists), Ruskin was also so far attracted by the "mystery" of nature that he elaborated an entire, rather unique theory of mystery, or unclearness, versus clarity (below, pp. 39 f). The human eye simply cannot see all of nature, and in the mystery of what we do *not* see with precision, is found the essence of nature's great joys, the source of our impressions of space and depth. Transcribed into painterly terms, it is the source of the highest esthetic pleasures. "A single dusty roll of Turner's brush is more truly expressive of the infinity of foliage, than the niggling of Hobbima could have rendered his canvas, if he had worked on it till doomsday" (MP I, 339). Hence the Venetians are infinitely greater than the Dutch, because the latters' "niggling" detail is devoid of imaginative qualities. The Dutch, and any painter who believes precise imitation to be the goal of art, commit the very worst sin in Ruskin's view, the "scientific" error of drawing what one knows, rather than what one actually sees.

Ruskin's rules can be readily summarized, as he did himself (ENest 221):

First, to represent visual appearances only, never memory knowledge. This is what placed him in opposition to conventional art circles and allied him, unknowingly, with progressive French art.

Second, to test these appearances only by the aspect of knowledge that pertains to visual appearances so that, for example, one would avoid the error of drawing each lash of an eye because one can't really see them as individual hairs.

Third, "Having learned to represent actual appearances faithfully, if you have any human faculty of your own, visionary appearances will take place to you which will be nobler and more true than any actual or material appearances; and the realization of these is the function of every fine art, which is founded absolutely, therefore, in truth, and consists absolutely in imagination."

One must not, he repeats again and again, depart from the truth of appearances an iota, if not guided by the pure play of imagination. Any principle of generalization or synthesis is disastrous, for it would be based upon preconceived notions. It is the imagination, enflamed by the absorption of the purely visual, and untrammeled by scientific knowledge, which will carry the artist beyond mere appearances. That is (MP I, 137), Ruskin wants both the thoughts, and the feelings of the artist. Thoughts arise from knowing the truth of nature's appearances, and feelings from contemplating those truths until a kind of exaltation results. The

superior works of art that come from this state of exaltation
will not be exactly like nature, because the observer is
looking through the artist's mind. "We do not want his
mind to be like a badly blown glass, that distorts what we
see through it, but like a glass of sweet and strange colour,
that gives new tones to what we see through it; and a glass
of rare strength and clearness too, to let us see more than
we could ourselves . . ." We therefore return again to that
central precept: the artistic imagination as the source of
great art.

Ruskin's great lament is that by his day man had cast
out spirituality and substituted a purely mechanical, materialistic universe, so that his contemporaries were driven
to nature as a *substitute for,* rather than a revelation of,
the divine unity of purpose, the divine sense of order. This
new dialectic between man and nature is the "pathetic fallacy," one of Ruskin's most original and significant critical
concepts. It pointed to a terrible loss for mankind, because
nature was not seen as a manifestation of God. Such an
idea today makes us rather uncomfortable, because upon
reflection we realize that it exposes much of our solipsism.
Art for us is rigorously separate from nature, and is superior
because it has a sense of purpose nature lacks; for Ruskin
art and nature are united by the powers of artistic imagination. Art for us is invested with human significance, but it
does not require nature; art for Ruskin not only requires
nature, but "the majesty of nature depends upon the force
of the human spirit . . ." (MP III, xix). We find more
sympathetic the nature concepts of Jean-Jacques or other,
"purer" romantics, who permit us to lose ourselves in solitary reverie, divorced from the problems of man's society.
The fundamental moralism of Ruskin's view of nature is
that by looking we act upon her; we do not register nature
in any passive manner, but *seek* her. Were we able to share
the vitality of Ruskin's vision, we too could see mountains
as the earth's "muscular action," and clouds as "sculptured
mist" (MP I, 427, and ED 130).

ARCHITECTURE, IRON, AND THE NINETEENTH CENTURY.
From the same wholeness of his view of nature, and from
the same poetic feelings, Ruskin thought of iron and its use

in architecture in a way forbidden the twentieth century. In a most beautiful lecture of 1858 (TwoP 375 ff) he sketches the geological history of iron from earliest times, and remarks upon its essential values to man. It is nourishment to the plants which provide his food, it is an essential ingredient of his blood and helps give its color, it is the ochre stain of soil and rock which caresses his eye with beauty. When not in its purely natural state, it is best thought of in the form of the plow which turns the earth but, alas, it must be consulted also in the form of fetters and sword. When Ruskin then carries us to iron laws, prisons and wars that so debase humankind, we have a superb example of the interwoven texture of his thought. He found myriad associations in thinking of iron, and was incapable of viewing it as an inert architectural substance. He does grudgingly acknowledge the potentialities of iron when used according to its nature (in flat sheets, cut and twisted), but cast iron had become one of the most prevalent forms of ornament, and violently offended Ruskin on several counts: It displayed the worst of debased taste by imitating other art forms; it therefore was the veritable symbol of unlettered, crass materialism; it was cast separately, and applied, rather than being made an integral part of architecture; it did not bear the impress of man's living hand nor, because of its imitative origin, of his mind.

In all of this we recognize as usual Ruskin's romantic nostalgia for the past (although a glance back at the iron ornament of his era makes us feel more sympathetic to him). He felt forced to acknowledge that "the time is probably near when a new system of architectural laws will be developed, adapted entirely to metallic construction" (Lamps 66), and urged that if industrial architecture were left to itself it would be far better than applying to it "fine arts" standards. Nonetheless, he frankly confessed that he and his contemporaries derived their pleasures from, and based their judgments upon, traditional materials, and since these would be used for the foreseeable future, he had best address himself to them. He also admitted that earlier materials provided ties with the past, and we today realize how desperately he and his contemporaries needed such continuity, assaulted as they were by the first maturity of the new urban-industrial revolution. Ostensibly innocent remarks, such as lamenting in 1849 that his time "has been lately occupied in taking drawings from one side of buildings, of which masons were knocking down the other" (Lamps 3) are actually important clues. Ruskin had a morbid fear, obviously justified, that many of the values he held were being destroyed by cataclysmic change.

In his second decade of life (he was born in 1819, just after the Luddite riots, and died in 1900), he witnessed both the coming of the railroad, that most awesome instrument and veritable symbol of industrial change, and the climax of the Chartist movement, embodiment of social upheaval. He lived in the London of Dickens, Mayhew, and the Chadwick report, of rampant growth which seemed more certainly characterized by festering wound than by "progress." *The Seven Lamps of Architecture* of 1848–49, with all its anger, its intemperate rhetoric, its evangelical disdain for materialism and middle-class optimism, is unthinkable unless we realize how intimately it is allied to the revolutions which swept Europe while it was being written. Ruskin, like most artists of the nineteenth century, tried desperately to retain values of the past in the midst of revolution, for he saw nothing worthy of replacing the old order. "We have the misfortune to live in an epoch of transition from irrational dulness to irrational excitement; and while once it was the highest courage of science to question anything, it is now an agony to her to leave anything unquestioned." (ENest 168). Science is included in his malediction because it fortifies change and is used by the simple-minded to buttress their confidence in the urban-industrial order. He would reserve the word science "for the acquaintance with things long since discovered, and established as true" (ENest 168).

Ruskin's role as one of the principal spokesmen for social reform is adequate proof that he was not a mere escapist and that, constantly as he opposed to the present the beauties of nature and of the past, he had no hope that by marching backward man could find salvation. As far as that goes, in his most Cassandra-like moods he still looks forward to our elders, like Frank Lloyd Wright, and to our contemporaries who find the source of their art in their revulsion for the noise and pace of urban-industrial life. He will sound surprisingly modern to the readers of Lewis Mumford and David Riesman when he debates (ENest 163) the effects upon city dwellers. His dislike of the machine and rejection of technological optimism will not appear out-of-date to the artists who came into prominence after World War II, his love of natural materials and a feeling of the hand of man will not offend those who love Scandinavian furniture.

To the degree Ruskin proposed nature and the past as a solution, it was in *principles,* not in forms. The architect should not imitate the past, but determine its essential values and offer them to the present (below, 163–71). Ruskin was too much a part of his generation to make a full separation of principle and form, so that he could insist the pointed window was a principle of good building, not just a Gothic form. But he consistently maintained that the early styles he admired were the natural products of their societies and "cannot be recovered by a voluntary condescension" (Lamps 184). He spoke out regularly against conventional revivalism and in all the arts permitted the use of the past only when directly relevant to the present. This is more obvious in painting than in architecture. As the chief defender first of Turner, then of the Pre-Raphaelites, he was the most progressive critic of painting in the mid-century. In architecture his eclecticism is more obvious because he addressed himself primarily to mending the abuses of his day, dominated by Victorian revivalism. It is therefore not to his discredit that he had a taste for past styles, but to his honor that out of his writings came some of the most important and progressive developments in modern architecture. In his lengthy discussions of architectural ornament, his vision was admittedly that of a painter concerned with surface, but then that is a characteristic of much mid-century architecture itself. The fact that he paid attention to ornament at all makes him seem out of date to us, but against the background of his day, Ruskin's writings were nearly unique in their demands for *simplification* of ornament. He always maintained, for example, that the finest embellishment of architecture was the use of bands of naturally colored stones, and that the decadence of late Gothic was due to the substitution of linear for massive elements. As a guiding principle he said ornament must be part of structure, not fastened on, and ideally in association with massive, solid wall. He was attracted most by Italian Romanesque and Gothic architecture because of his instinctive preference for flat and abstract patterns which had a "childlike" vitality devoid of the complexity of late Gothic. He is far from the mere defender of the Gothic revival he is so often made out to be.

RUSKIN THE MORALIST. Much of the difficulty of assessing Ruskin's real morality is in overcoming the pejorative overtones that our era has added to the word "moralism." We so hate being preached to that we can hardly imagine how it was that the Victorian era loved to be harangued. Carlyle, Arnold, Dickens, Ruskin: the language of moral judgment was then a common means of communication. Certain points can therefore be gained from assessing the language. Modern artists and critics would never knowingly confess their true ancestry, but Ruskin's doctrine of honesty of materials and structure, cast down in thunderbolts of moral rage, is nonetheless the major forebear of a universally accepted principle.

Ruskin was the very last to let moral judgment interfere with *seeing*. Far from the typical Evangelical Protestant, far from the puritan, he indulged his sensual appetite for art to the point that Pater and Whistler are in this one sense his heirs. His vision led his mind, his sensual passions led his reason, vision and passion entwined in the most profound love of art and nature. "The business of a painter is *to paint* [sic]," he insists (SV I, 448 f).

> Now it is well, when we have strong moral or poetical feeling manifested in painting, to mark this as the best part of the work; but it is not well to consider as a thing of small account, the painter's language in which that feeling is conveyed; for if that language be not good and lovely, the man may indeed be a just moral-

ist or a great poet, but he is not a *painter*, and it was
wrong of him to paint . . . On the other hand, if the
man be a painter indeed, and have the gift of colours
and lines, what is in him will come from his hand
freely and faithfully; and the language itself is so difficult and so vast, that the mere possession of it argues
the man is great, and that his works are worth reading.
So that I have never yet seen the case in which this
true artistical excellence, visible by the eye-glance,
was not the index of some true expressional worth in
the work.

This is not to say that Ruskin denies morality, of course,
but instead that morality is expressed in the forms as well
as the subjects of art. Ruskin believes that merely to look
at nature is a purposive act. How much more, then, is the
act of painting one of purpose, not just the individual artist's but, because the exercise of his imagination joins him
to the larger order of the universe, also the supreme purpose of divine unity. One of Ruskin's most original beliefs
is that though ultimately man must see beyond the merely
sensual, the "language of art" embodies the most fundamental morality. This language, even when divorced from
the representation of fact, confesses the individual and his
society.

Morality in the observer is based upon the comprehension of artistic morality, because it is the necessary revelation of spiritual order. Ruskin's countless lectures, his
many books, and his entire life, were directed to this principal end: that viewing a work of art is a moral obligation,
a truly creative participation. This is the moral position toward which he urged the nineteenth century. In an almost
"existential" manner he cries out against the kind of living
stupor in which a man merely accepts what is there without choosing to act himself. He finds that man is a "double
creature," having both a true and a false life (Lamps
191 f).

His true life is like that of lower organic beings, the
independent force by which he moulds and governs
external things; it is a force of assimilation which con-

verts everything around him into food, or into instruments; and which, however humbly or obediently it
may listen to or follow the guidance of superior intelligence, never forfeits its own authority as a judging
principle, as a will capable either of obeying or rebel-
ling. His false life is, indeed, but one of the conditions
of death or stupor . . . It is that life of custom and accident in which many of us pass much of our time in
the world; that life in which we do what we have not
proposed, and speak what we do not mean, and assent
to what we do not understand . . .

It is more commonly the grown man who lives the false
life. In childhood, man is instinctively in a more moral condition and because Ruskin means not just the individual
man, but his whole society as well, "childhood" also means
the early phase of a given period. Early Gothic therefore
has more of the quintessential vitality than later Gothic,
and the entire Gothic period more than the Renaissance.
Every work of art must be placed somewhere on this scale
of maturity, for one of the reasons why Ruskin indulges in
the value judgments that offend us, is that he identifies
merit with the stamp of youthful energy. This spirit of
growth, this morality, this "true life," which permitted the
Gothic workmen more initiative than did the false life of
the Renaissance, is ultimately associated with change and
movement in nature. The whole concept, of course, is typical of the nineteenth century's habit of superimposing a
biological model over history, but only Ruskin interweaves
burgeoning growth in organic life, the cycle of art history,
man's purposive vision, artistic imagination, both the forms
and subjects of art—all these into a higher morality. Once
plunged into this pulsating stream of passion and thought,
the modern observer begins to feel jealous of Ruskin's freedom in interlocking man's modes of creation and thought,
in thinking of art not in isolation, but in live union with
society and history. We finally become aware that, judged
from Ruskin's vantage point, our freedom from "morality"
would be a frightening prison.

RUSKIN THE CRITIC. The love of art and life which was

Ruskin's motive power made him more of a critic, in the modern sense of the word, than an historian, whom we feel should have more "objectivity." Such objectivity is actually a curious bias, for we all have our passions and our prejudices, and to suppress them for the sake of an historical standard is somehow to believe that passion and history cannot mix. Ruskin's prejudices have, even for the modern historian, a large claim to forgiveness because they are those of an *artist,* from whom we expect feeling. Ruskin is ever the pamphleteer, the charging warrior of words who turned to new enemies as soon as the old had been wounded, leaving others to panse the victim or raise the victorious standard. He is something like his contemporary Dickens: Both were brilliant stylists who could manipulate words with great beauty, especially when indulging their superb powers of description; both were missionaries in their writings, both became lecturers of almost mesmerizing gifts, with few rivals in all of nineteenth-century England; both wrote serially for, and lectured to, the same audience, the newly enfranchised middle class; both wrote also for the working class, although neither was a proponent of "democracy" because they appealed to the ruling classes as the holders of knowledge and power, and hence were really Tory radicals; both saw rampant industrialization as the chief evil; both were great reformers in whose wake varied reading groups and societies were established, and these were able to perpetuate beyond death some of their messianic qualities. Perhaps the most important of the differences as critics is that Ruskin preached more directly, since he believed that ideas had to lead immediately to behavior.

For all that he is an artist and a critic, Ruskin had a marvelous sense of history, of history as an organic, living continuity, "like the flow of a lava stream, first bright and fierce, then languid and covered, at last advancing only by the tumbling over and over of its frozen blocks" (Lamps 193). Some of his most rewarding discoveries result from his giving way to an immersion in this life of the past, so that today his *Stones of Venice,* in both method and content, remains one of the handful of superlative historical studies. Today also, we accept as fundamental history his thesis that Greco-Etruscan qualities are a constant in later Italic art, and essential to the understanding of Giotto or Botticelli. We do not balk when the Bardi chapel is described as a Greco-Etruscan vase, "upside down, and outside in" (MorFlor 341), and Botticelli's frescoed Zipporah as a reincarnation of ancient Pallas (below, 272 ff).

Among critics contemporary to him, Ruskin is most easily distinguished by his great stature. He rears far above their heads, although he shared many of his ideas with the generation before his as well as his own. It is very well to trace the origin of one of Ruskin's concepts to another thinker, but typically that concept will be the whole of this other man, whereas Ruskin will strike fire from it by rubbing it against his other ideas, until finally it will take its place as part of a cohesive unity, welded by the passion of his genius.

During his lifetime, his role as a critic seems to have altered in the most maddening way, but it was entirely constant, only the targets and, accordingly, the weapons were changed. In 1843, with the first volume of *Modern Painters,* he determined that people should see Turner and, more generally, that they should *see.* He therefore assaulted the bastions of classical landscape, for its lack of truth, and of Lowlands painting, for its lack of imagination. In *The Seven Lamps of Architecture,* he chose as enemy the sham materialism of contemporary architecture, with its cheap, cast-iron ornament, its picturesque quotations from the past, its impersonal slickness, and rallied against it the spiritual forces of "rude and infantine" building of rough surface and blocky mass. Coming in 1849, one year after the revolutions that had swept across the Continent, Ruskin's cry for "audacity of treatment" and the "sweeping sacrifice of precedent" (below, 171) could have been accepted only as revolutionary. In the next decade, as usual siding with what was modern, he defended the Pre-Raphaelites by attacking the canons of the High Renaissance. Fidelity to nature was his lance, and quattrocento primitivism, his shield. And toward the end of the 1850's, though still regarded as the major defender of the Brotherhood, he had so grown in his love for Tintoretto and the Venetians that the arms of nature imitation and pre-Renaissance style were temporarily couched. The 1860's were given almost entirely to writings on political economy, and early in the next decade he began the last phase of his life, devoted largely to art before the High Renaissance, particularly to the period of Giotto, and to the work of Carpaccio and Botticelli.

In the five decades of his public career, Ruskin was the principal pioneer in all these arts of past and present. Almost singlehandedly he removed the cataract of indifference from British eyes. It is admittedly difficult to separate his role entirely from that of William Morris, his principal disciple, especially in the flowering of the vast Arts and Crafts movement and its principal manifestation, the Art Nouveau. Morris was much more accessible to the public and may, for example, have been more important than his master to the young Roger Fry in 1912, as he was organizing the Omega Workshops, dedicated to the decorative arts. Lest we think Ruskin's role was insular, we need only recall that his fear of the modern city and compensatory love of nature is also found in Monet's cathedrals and garden pools, as it is found later in the buildings of Frank Lloyd Wright and the writing of Lewis Mumford; that Patrick Geddes carried his ideas to cities in the Near and Far East, where Gandhi owned himself a Ruskin disciple; or that Marcel Proust became one of his major translators and a devoted admirer.

But in the most profound sense of history, Ruskin is like his contemporaries Marx and Darwin, and we need not travel along the routes of the many tributaries in order to discover the principal source. His was one of the most beautiful and fertile rivers of imagination the history of art has known, which merged into one turbulent stream the highest qualities of the eye and the mind and the heart.

BIBLIOGRAPHICAL NOTE

Ruskin's literary criticism is the subject of a forthcoming Anchor book, edited by my colleague Harold Bloom. The idea for these anthologies is his, and he accepted the task of providing a biographical sketch in the introduction to his volume. He also analyzes Ruskin's theory of imagination, permitting me to give it rather short shrift here. In addition to these dispensations, I have willfully eliminated many other aspects of Ruskin's thought in order to concentrate upon some of those that are neglected or misunderstood. With no remorse whatsoever, I have forsaken any mention of his unconsummated marriage and what could be called his Lolita complex, which have prompted analyses that stress the origin of his ideas in his libido. I believe that much may be gained by looking at the ideas for themselves and not at their exfoliation within his life. On the other hand, it is with regret that I chose not to deal with Ruskin's position in the history of architecture, but in this case I believe him to be better dealt with and not in need of much reinterpretation. To redress the balance, the reader might select from the following:

Derrick Leon's *Ruskin the Great Victorian* (London, 1949) remains the unrivaled biography, despite more recent monographs characterized by enthusiasm but lacking real insight. In her anthology *The Lamp of Beauty* (London, 1959), Joan Evans provides a strict chronological method of selection. Henry Needham's passages on Ruskin in his *Développement de l'esthétique sociologique* (Paris, 1926) form the most pithy interpretation, and I have also found these three indispensable: Graham Hough, *The Last Romantics* (London, 1949); L. C. Dolk, *The Aesthetics of*

John Ruskin in Relation to the Aesthetics of the Romantic Era (Urbana, 1941), and F. G. Townsend, *Ruskin and the Landscape Feeling* . . . (Urbana, 1951). Among the numerous essays of high quality, I would cite F. D. Curtin, *Aesthetics in English Social Reform: Ruskin and his Followers* (Ithaca, 1940) and H. A. Ladd, *The Victorian Morality of Art* . . . (New York, 1932). As samples of Ruskin's relevance to the twentieth century, one might read Mr. Hough's "Ruskin and Roger Fry," *The Cambridge Journal*, I (October, 1947), pp. 14–27, and Marcel Proust, *Pastiches et Mélanges* (Paris, 1919).

GUIDE TO THE SELECTIONS

The introductory essay will have prepared the reader for the rather unorthodox method of selecting from Ruskin's vast output. The evolution of his ideas, rather than the ideas themselves, has so long intrigued scholars that nearly all anthologies have attempted to present the heart of each major book, in chronological order. I have used a topical method which disregards chronology (although all excerpts can be dated by using the *Key to Abbreviations*, which follows), and which does not attempt to keep together the portions of any one book. I have focused still more sharply on ideas *qua* ideas by selecting succinct passages in preference to those embellished by extended example or by the sheer beauty of the prose. For each category I have chosen the clearest, not necessarily the most famous passages. The undoubted sacrifices of this method are compensated for, I believe, by the rich number of ideas that can be represented in a single volume. Among the surprises produced by using the topical categories as starting points, I discovered that despite the impressions absorbed by reading straight through Ruskin's major works, he wrote astonishingly little on Fra Angelico, and almost as little on domestic architecture and handicrafts, although they are frequently mentioned in passing. On the other hand, he wrote much more on color theory than has been generally assumed, and so much on Greek vases, sculpture, ornament and literature that a rather full, separate anthology could be compiled.

All passages have been collated with Cook and Wedderburn's *Library Edition* of Ruskin's works, and explained in the *Key to Abbreviations*. The selections are directed to painting (about 40% of the whole) since Ruskin's output is clearly in that balance, despite the larger fame of his writings on architecture. The separate headings are not at all exclusive, but are merely conveniences. Thus Tintoretto is best included in the section on Michelangelo and Tintoretto, and under his name will be found only supplemental passages. The subheadings are not Ruskin's although sometimes the words are his, in which case quotation marks are supplied. Any letters or words in brackets, and all uses of three successive periods (. . .) indicate that words have been omitted. The word "omit" in the footnote means that entire sentences or paragraphs have been omitted from the page or pages indicated, the succession of Ruskin's words otherwise undisturbed. Paragraphing of the *Library Edition* has therefore been changed, but spelling and punctuation, even when inconsistent, have not been modernized. I have felt free to include his own footnotes only when I considered the material essential, and they are always from his first editions unless otherwise dated. Internal references, such as Biblical or other literary sources, are given in parentheses, followed by the customary citation of the appropriate page and volume of the *Library Edition.* The material for these internal references comes largely from the editorial commentaries provided by Cook and Wedderburn. Present locations of works of art are my doing, and are normally given within brackets.

This anthology is dedicated to the memory of the editors of the magnificent collected works. I would like to thank Harry P. Harrison of the Sterling Memorial Library, Yale University, for placing these and other materials at my disposal with the most perfect grace and efficiency.

Yale University, September 1963

R. L. H.

KEY TO ABBREVIATIONS

All volume and page references are to the *Library Edition, The Works of John Ruskin,* edited by E. T. Cook and Alexander Wedderburn, published in London from 1903–10 by George Allen, Ruskin's friend and associate. The firm of George Allen and Unwin, Ltd., retains the copyright for unpublished Ruskin materials. The dates given are those of first editions, or of public lectures, in the latter case followed by the date of first publication. For those published serially, over a span of years, the specific year is provided in the footnotes. Only those essays and volumes that figure in the anthology have been included in this key. Roman numerals within the abbreviations refer to volumes of one title. The appropriate volumes of the *Library Edition* are indicated by roman numerals at the end of each listing.

Acad 1855–59, and 1875. *Academy Notes.* XIV

AFlor Delivered 1872, published 1873–76. *Ariadne Florentina.* XXII

ArP Delivered 1870, published 1872 with the exception of the essay "The School of Florence" (pp. 355–67), not published until 1905. *Aratra Pentelici.* XX

ArtEng Delivered 1883, published 1883–84. *The Art of England.* XXXIII

Bequest 1857. 'The Turner Bequest,' *Catalogue of the Turner Sketches in the National Gallery.* XIII

Cestus 1865–66. *The Cestus of Aglaia.* XIX

Colours 1878. *The Three Colours of Pre-Raphaelitism.* XXXIV

ED 1857. *The Elements of Drawing.* XV

ENest 1872. *The Eagle's Nest.* XXII

Flamb Delivered 1869, published 1905. *The Flamboyant Architecture of the Valley of the Somme.* XIX

Fors 1871–84. *Fors Clavigera.* XXVII (1871–73); XXVIII (1874–76); XXIX (1877–84)

Harb 1856. *The Harbours of England.* XIII

Lamps 1849. *The Seven Lamps of Architecture.* VIII

Land Delivered 1871, published 1897. *Lectures on Landscape.* XXII

LAP Delivered 1853, published 1854. *Lectures on Architecture and Painting.* XII

Laws 1877–79. *The Laws of Fésole* XV

Lect 1870. *Lectures on Art.* XX

MorFlor 1875–77. *Mornings in Florence.* XXIII

MP I 1843. *Modern Painters,* vol. one. III

MP II 1846. *Modern Painters,* vol. two. IV

MP III 1856. *Modern Painters,* vol. three. V

MP IV 1856. *Modern Painters,* vol. four. VI

MP V 1860. *Modern Painters,* vol. five. VII

MTint Delivered 1871, published 1872. *The Relation between Michael Angelo and Tintoret.* XXII

Omit See above, "Guide to the Selections."

Padua 1853–60. *Giotto and his Works in Padua.* XXIV

PRB. 1851. *Pre-Raphaelitism.* XII

Rest 1877–84. *St. Mark's Rest.* XXIV

ReyHolb 1860. *Sir Joshua and Holbein.* XIX

SchFlor Delivered 1874, published 1906. *The Schools of Florence* (Not to be confused with the essay in ArP). XXIII

SV I 1851. *The Stones of Venice,* vol. one. IX

SV II 1853. *The Stones of Venice,* vol. two. X

SV III 1853. *The Stones of Venice,* vol. three. XI

TwoP Delivered 1858–59, published 1859. *The Two Paths.* XVI

Val Delivered 1873, published 1874. *Val d'Arno.* XXIII

CONTENTS

PART III. SCULPTURE AND ORNAMENT

PART IV. PAINTING

THE ART CRITICISM OF JOHN RUSKIN

INTRODUCTORY APHORISMS

"Please paint me my white cat," said little Imelda. "Child," answered the Bolognese Professor, "in the grand school, all cats are grey."

Never, if you can help it, miss seeing the sunset and the dawn. And never, if you can help it, see anything but dreams between them.

A fine picture, you say? "The finest possible; St. Jerome, and his lion, and his arm-chair. St. Jerome was painted by a saint, and the Lion by a hunter, and the chair by an upholsterer." My compliments. It must be very fine; but I do not care to see it.

Every light is a shade, compared to higher lights, till you come to the sun; and every shade is a light, compared to deeper shades, till you come to the night.

You will be told that shadow is grey. But Correggio, when he has to shade with one colour, takes red chalk.

"I can do what I like with my colours, now," said the proud young scholar. "So could I, at your age," answered the master; "but now, I can only do what other people like."[1]

I want you to begin with colour in the very outset, and to see everything as children would see it. For, believe me,

[1] Laws 361–64, omit. To the *Laws of Fésole* Ruskin appended a short section of aphorisms (several of them here included), the origin of the idea for this introductory section.

the final philosophy of art can only ratify their opinion that the beauty of a cock-robin is to be red, and of a grass-plot to be green; and the best skill of art is in instantly seizing on the manifold deliciousness of light, which you can only seize by precision of instantaneous touch.[2]

The whole technical power of painting depends on our recovery of what may be called the *innocence of the eye;* that is to say, of a sort of childish perception of these flat stains of colour, merely as such, without consciousness of what they signify,—as a blind man would see them if suddenly gifted with sight.[3]

Everything that you can see in the world around you, presents itself to your eyes only as an arrangement of patches of different colours variously shaded.[4]

Give me some mud off a city crossing, some ochre out of a gravel pit, a little whitening, and some coal-dust, and I will paint you a luminous picture . . .[5]

[T]he arrangement of colours and lines is an art analogous to the composition of music, and entirely independent of the representation of facts.[6]

[T]he student may be led into folly by philosophers, and into falsehood by purists; but he is always safe, if he holds the hand of a colourist.[7]

All good drawing consists merely in dirtying the paper delicately.[8]

The sculptor must paint with his chisel: half his touches are not to realize, but to put power into, the form: they

[2] Land 54
[3] ED 27, footnote
[4] ED 27
[5] ED 149
[6] SV II, 215 f
[7] MP IV, 72
[8] Letter of 1855, in *Works*, XV, 489.

are touches of light and shadow; and raise a ridge, or sink a hollow, not to represent an actual ridge or hollow, but to get a line of light, or a spot of darkness.[9]

[Giovanni Pisano:] He is the Canova of the thirteenth century.[10]

[A]ll the architectural arts begin in the shaping of the cup and the platter, and they end in a glorified roof.[11]

His eye must be delicate indeed, who would desire to see the Pitti palace polished.[12]

Railroad architecture has, or would have, a dignity of its own if it were only left to its work. You would not put rings on the fingers of a smith at his anvil.[13]

And in exactly measured and inevitable degree, as architecture is more ingenious, it is less passionate.[14]

For, whatever infinity of fair form there may be in the maze of the forest, there is a fairer, as I think, in the surface of the quiet lake; and I hardly know that association of shaft or tracery, for which I would exchange the warm sleep of sunshine on some smooth, broad, human-like front of marble.[15]

All classicality, all middle-aged patent-reviving, is utterly vain and absurd; if we are now to do anything great, good, awful, religious, it must be got out of our own little island, and out of these very times, railroads and all . . .[16]

[9] Lamps 215
[10] Val 108
[11] Lect 96
[12] Lamps 115
[13] Lamps 160
[14] Flamb 255
[15] Lamps 109
[16] MP I, 231

All the pleasure which the people of the nineteenth century take in art, is in pictures, sculpture, minor objects of virtù, or mediaeval architecture, which we enjoy under the term picturesque: no pleasure is taken anywhere in modern buildings, and we find all men of true feeling delighting to escape out of modern cities into natural scenery: hence . . . that peculiar love of landscape, which is characteristic of the age.[17]

And the whole difference between a man of genius and other men, it has been said a thousand times, and most truly, is that the first remains in great part a child, seeing with the large eyes of children, in perpetual wonder, not conscious of much knowledge,—conscious, rather, of infinite ignorance, and yet infinite power; a fountain of eternal admiration, delight, and creative force within him, meeting the ocean of visible and governable things around him.[18]

[F]or one person who can recognize the loveliness of a look, or the purity of a colour, there are a hundred who can calculate the length of a bone.[19]

[I]n higher fields of thought increasing knowledge means increasing sorrow, and every art which has complete sympathy with humanity must be chastened by the sight and oppressed by the memory of pain.[20]

But, accurately speaking, no good work whatever can be perfect, and *the demand for perfection is always a sign of a misunderstanding of the ends of art.*[21]

[A]ny man who can reason at all, does it instinctively, and takes leaps over intermediate syllogisms by the score, yet never misses his footing at the end of the leap; but he

[17] SV II, 207
[18] SV III, 66
[19] MTint 97
[20] Land 56
[21] SV II, 202

who cannot instinctively argue, might as well, with the gout in both feet, try to follow a chamois hunter by the help of crutches . . .[22]

[T]he feeling induced by what is called a "liberal education" is utterly adverse to the understanding of noble art; and the name which is given to the feeling,—Taste, Goût, Gusto,—in all languages indicates the baseness of it, for it implies that art gives only a kind of pleasure analogous to that derived from eating by the palate.[23]

[22] MP III, 8
[23] MP III, 96

PART I

THEORY AND PRACTICE

1

CREATIVITY

There is no moral vice, no moral virtue, which has not its *precise* prototype in the art of painting; so that you may at your will illustrate the moral habit by the art, or the art by the moral habit. Affection and discord, fretfulness and quietness, feebleness and firmness, luxury and purity, pride and modesty, and all other such habits, and every conceivable modification and mingling of them, may be illustrated, with mathematical exactness, by conditions of line and colour; and not merely these definable vices and virtues, but also every conceivable shade of human character and passion, from the righteous or unrighteous majesty of the king to the innocent or faultful simplicity of the shepherd boy.[1]

Yet although in all our speculations on art, language is thus to be distinguished from, and held subordinate to, that which it conveys, we must still remember that there are certain ideas inherent in language itself, and that, strictly speaking, every pleasure connected with art has in it some reference to the intellect. The mere sensual pleasure of the eye, received from the most brilliant piece of colouring, is as nothing to that which it receives from a crystal prism, except as it depends on our perception of a certain meaning and intended arrangement of colour, which has been the subject of intellect. Nay, the term idea, according to Locke's definition of it, will extend even to the sensual impressions themselves as far as they are "things which the mind occupies itself about in thinking;" that is, not as they are felt by the eye only, but as they are received by the mind through the eye. So that, if I say that the greatest

[1] ED 118

picture is that which conveys to the mind of the spectator the greatest number of the greatest ideas, I have a definition which will include as subjects of comparison every pleasure which art is capable of conveying. If I were to say, on the contrary, that the best picture was that which most closely imitated nature, I should assume that art could only please by imitating nature; and I should cast out of the pale of criticism those parts of works of art which are not imitative, that is to say, intrinsic beauties of colour and form, and those works of art wholly, which, like the Arabesques of Raffaelle in the Loggias, are not imitative at all. Now, I want a definition of art wide enough to include all its varieties of aim. I do not say, therefore, that the art is greatest which gives most pleasure, because perhaps there is some art whose end is to teach, and not to please. I do not say that the art is greatest which teaches us most, because perhaps there is some art whose end is to please, and not to teach. I do not say that the art is greatest which imitates best, because perhaps there is some art whose end is to create and not to imitate. But I say that the art is greatest which conveys to the mind of the spectator, by any means whatsoever, the greatest number of the greatest ideas; and I call an idea great in proportion as it is received by a higher faculty of the mind, and as it more fully occupies, and in occupying, exercises and exalts, the faculty by which it is received.

If this, then, be the definition of great art, that of a great artist naturally follows. He is the greatest artist who has embodied, in the sum of his works, the greatest number of the greatest ideas.[2]

Imitation of nature

First,—Imitation can only be of something material, but truth has reference to statements both of the qualities of material things, and of emotions, impressions, and thoughts. There is a moral as well as material truth,—a truth of impression as well as of form,—of thought as well as of mat-

2 MP I, 91 f

ter; and the truth of impression and thought is a thousand times the more important of the two. Hence, truth is a term of universal application, but imitation is limited to that narrow field of art which takes cognizance only of material things.

Secondly,—Truth may be stated by any signs or symbols which have a definite signification in the minds of those to whom they are addressed, although such signs be themselves no image nor likeness of anything. Whatever can excite in the mind the conception of certain facts, can give ideas of truth, though it be in no degree the imitation or resemblance of those facts. If there be—we do not say there is,—but if there be in painting anything which operates, as words do, not by resembling anything, but by being taken as a symbol and substitute for it, and thus inducing the effect of it, then this channel of communication can convey uncorrupted truth, though it do not in any degree resemble the facts whose conception it induces. But ideas of imitation, of course, require the likeness of the object. They speak to the perceptive faculties only: truth to the conceptive.

Thirdly, and in consequence of what is above stated, an idea of truth exists in the statement of *one* attribute of anything, but an idea of imitation requires the resemblance of as many attributes as we are usually cognizant of in its real presence. A pencil outline of the bough of a tree on white paper is a statement of a certain number of facts of form. It does not yet amount to the imitation of anything. The idea of that form is not given in nature by lines at all, still less by black lines with a white space between them. But those lines convey to the mind a distinct impression of a certain number of facts, which it recognizes as agreeable with its previous impressions of the bough of a tree; and it receives, therefore, an idea of truth. If, instead of two lines, we give a dark form with the brush, we convey information of a certain relation of shade between the bough and sky, recognizable for another idea of truth: but we have still no imitation, for the white paper is not the least like air, nor the black shadow like wood. It is not until after a certain number of ideas of truth have been collected together, that we arrive at an idea of imitation.[3]

The artist's prerogatives

We saw [already] . . . with what kind of feeling an artist ought to regard the character of every object he undertakes to paint. The next question is, what objects he *ought* to undertake to paint; how far he should be influenced by his feelings in the choice of subjects; and how far he should permit himself to alter, or in the usual art language, improve, nature. For it has already been stated that all great art must be inventive; that is to say, its subject must be produced by the imagination. If so, then great landscape art cannot be a mere copy of any given scene; and we have now to inquire what else than this it may be.[4]

First, he receives a true impression from the place itself, and takes care to keep hold of that as his chief good; indeed, he needs no care in the matter, for the distinction of his mind from that of others consists in his instantly receiving such sensations strongly, and being unable to lose them; and then he sets himself as far as possible to reproduce that impression on the mind of the spectator of his picture.

And the aim of the great inventive landscape painter must be to give the far higher and deeper truth of mental vision, rather than that of the physical facts, and to reach a representation which, though it may be totally useless to engineers or geographers, and, when tried by rule and measure, totally unlike the place, shall yet be capable of producing on the far-away beholder's mind precisely the impression which the reality would have produced, and putting his heart into the same state in which it would have been . . .

Now observe; if in his attempt to do this the artist does not understand the sacredness of the truth of *Impression*, and supposes that, once quitting hold of his first thought,

[3] MP I, 104 f
[4] MP IV, 27

he may by Philosophy compose something prettier than he saw and mightier than he felt, it is all over with him. Every such attempt at composition will be utterly abortive, and end in something that is neither true nor fanciful; something geographically useless, and intellectually absurd.

But if, holding fast his first thought, he finds other ideas insensibly gathering to it, and, whether he will or not, modifying it into something which is not so much the image of the place itself, as the spirit of the place, let him yield to such fancies, and follow them wherever they lead.

The kind of mental chemistry by which the dream summons and associates its materials, I have already endeavoured, not to explain, for it is utterly inexplicable, but to illustrate . . . [W]ith all those whom I have carefully studied (Dante, Scott, Turner, and Tintoret) it seems to me to hold absolutely; their imagination consisting, not in a voluntary production of new images, but an involuntary remembrance, exactly at the right moment, of something they had actually seen.

Imagine all that any of these men had seen or heard in the whole course of their lives, laid up accurately in their memories as in vast storehouses, extending, with the poets, even to the slightest intonations of syllables heard in the beginning of their lives, and with the painters, down to minute folds of drapery, and shapes of leaves or stones; and over all this unindexed and immeasurable mass of treasure, the imagination brooding and wandering, but dream-gifted, so as to summon at any moment exactly such groups of ideas as shall justly fit each other: this I conceive to be the real nature of the imaginative mind, and this, I believe, it would be oftener explained to us as being, by the men themselves who possess it, but that they have no idea what the state of other persons' minds is in comparison; they suppose every one remembers all that he has seen in the same way, and do not understand how it happens that they alone can produce good drawings or great thoughts.

So that I am more and more convinced of what I had to state respecting the imagination, now many years ago, viz., that its true force lies in its marvellous insight and foresight,—that it is, instead of a false and deceptive faculty, exactly the most accurate and truth-telling faculty which the human mind possesses; and all the more truth-telling, because in *its* work, the vanity and individualism of the man himself are crushed, and he becomes a mere instrument or mirror, used by a higher power for the reflection to others of a truth which no effort of his could ever have ascertained; so that all mathematical, and arithmetical, and generally scientific truth, is, in comparison, truth of the husk and surface, hard and shallow; and only the imaginative truth is precious. Hence, whenever we want to know what are the chief facts of any case, it is better not to go to political economists, nor to mathematicians, but to the great poets; for I find they always see more of the matter than any one else; and in like manner those who want to know the real facts of the world's outside aspect, will find that they cannot trust maps, nor charts, nor any manner of mensuration; the most important facts being always quite immeasurable, and that, (with only some occasional and trifling inconvenience, if they form too definite anticipations as to the position of a bridge here, or a road there) the Turnerian topography is the only one to be trusted.

One or two important corollaries may be drawn from these principles, respecting the kind of fidelity which is to be exacted from men who have no imaginative power. It has been stated, over and over again, that it is not *possible* to draw the whole of nature, as in a mirror. Certain omissions must be made, and certain conventionalities admitted, in all art. Now it ought to be the instinctive affection of each painter which guides him to the omissions he is to make, or signs he is to use; and his choice of this or the other fact for representation, his insistence upon this or the other character in his subject, as that which to him is impressive, constitutes, when it is earnest and simple, part of the value of his work.[5]

[5] MP IV, 33–45, omit.

2

SCIENCE AND ART

You observe, I hope, that I always use the term "science," merely as the equivalent of "knowledge." I take the Latin word, rather than the English, to mark that it is knowledge of constant things, not merely of passing events: but you had better lose even that distinction, and receive the word "scientia" as merely the equivalent of our English "knowledge," than fall into the opposite error of supposing that science means systematization or discovery. It is not the arrangement of new systems, nor the discovery of new facts, which constitutes a man of science; but the submission to an eternal system, and the proper grasp of facts already known.

And, at first, to-day, I use the word "art" only of that in which it is my special office to instruct you; graphic imitation; or, as it is commonly called, Fine art. Of course, the arts of construction,—building, carpentering, and the like, are directly dependent on many sciences, but in a manner which needs no discussion, so that we may put that part of the business out of our way. I mean by art, to-day, only imitative art; and by science, to-day, not the knowledge of general laws, but of existent facts.[6]

Once again, therefore, I must limit my application of the word science with respect to art. I told you that I did not mean by "science" such knowledge as that triangles on equal bases and between parallels are equal, but such knowledge as that the stars in Cassiopeia are in the form of a W. But, farther still, it is not to be considered as science, for an artist, that they are stars at all. What *he* has to know is that they are luminous points which twinkle

[6] ENest 150 f

in a certain manner, and are pale yellow, or deep yellow, and may be quite deceptively imitated at a certain distance by brass-headed nails. This he ought to know, and to remember accurately, and his art knowledge—the science, that is to say—of which his art is to be the reflection, is the sum of knowledges of this sort; his memory of the look of the sun and moon at such and such times, through such and such clouds; his memory of the look of the mountains,—of the look of sea,—of the look of human faces. Perhaps you would not call that "science" at all. It is no matter what either you or I call it. It *is* science of a certain order of facts.[7]

Science vs. art

Science and art are commonly distinguished by the nature of their actions; the one as knowing, the other as changing, producing, or creating. But there is a still more important distinction in the nature of the things they deal with. Science deals exclusively with things as they are in themselves; and art exclusively with things as they affect the human sense and human soul. Her work is to portray the appearances of things, and to deepen the natural impressions which they produce upon living creatures. The work of science is to substitute facts for appearances, and demonstrations for impressions. Both, observe, are equally concerned with truth; the one with truth of aspect, the other with truth of essence. Art does not represent things falsely, but truly as they appear to mankind. Science studies the relations of things to each other: but art studies only their relations to man: and it requires of everything which is submitted to it imperatively this, and only this, —what that thing is to the human eyes and human heart, what it has to say to men, and what it can become to them: a field of question just as much vaster than that of science, as the soul is larger than the material creation.

Take a single instance. Science informs us that the sun is ninety-five millions of miles distant from, and 111 times

[7] ENest 209

broader than, the earth: that we and all the planets re-
volve round it; and that it revolves on its own axis in 25
days, 14 hours, and 4 minutes. With all this, art has nothing whatsoever to do. It has no care to know anything of
this kind. But the things which it does care to know are
these: that in the heavens God hath set a tabernacle for
the sun, "which is as a bridegroom coming out of his chamber, and rejoiceth as a strong man to run a race. His going
forth is from the end of the heaven, and his circuit unto
the ends of it, and there is nothing hid from the heat
thereof."[8]

This, then, being the kind of truth with which art is
exclusively concerned, how is such truth as this to be ascertained and accumulated? Evidently, and only, by perception and feeling. Never either by reasoning or report.
Nothing must come between Nature and the artist's sight;
nothing between God and the artist's soul. Neither calculation nor hearsay,—be it the most subtle of calculations,
or the wisest of sayings,—may be allowed to come between
the universe, and the witness which art bears to its visible
nature. The whole value of that witness depends on its
being *eye*-witness; the whole genuineness, acceptableness,
and dominion of it depend on the personal assurance of
the man who utters it. All its victory depends on the veracity of the one preceding word, "Vidi."

The whole function of the artist in the world is to be
a seeing and feeling creature; to be an instrument of such
tenderness and sensitiveness, that no shadow, no hue, no
line, no instantaneous and evanescent expression of the
visible things around him, nor any of the emotions which
they are capable of conveying to the spirit which has been
given him, shall either be left unrecorded, or fade from the
book of record. It is not his business either to think, to
judge, to argue, or to know. His place is neither in the
closet, nor on the bench, nor at the bar, nor in the library.
They are for other men, and other work. He may think,
in a by-way; reason, now and then, when he has nothing
better to do; know, such fragments of knowledge as he

[8] (Psalm xix: 5, 6.) SV III, 47–49

can gather without stooping, or reach without pains; but none of these things are to be his care. The work of his life is to be two-fold only; to see, to feel.

Nay, but, the reader perhaps pleads with me, one of the great uses of knowledge is to open the eyes; to make things perceivable which never would have been seen, unless first they had been known.

Not so. This could only be said or believed by those who do not know what the perceptive faculty of a great artist is, in comparison with that of other men. There is no great painter, no great workman in any art, but he sees more with the glance of a moment than he can learn by the labour of a thousand hours.

And in this respect, observe, there is an enormous difference between knowledge and education. An artist need not be a *learned* man; in all probability it will be a disadvantage to him to become so; but he ought, if possible, always to be an *educated* man: that is, one who has understanding of his own uses and duties in the world, and therefore of the general nature of the things done and existing in the world; and who has so trained himself, or been trained, as to turn to the best and most courteous account whatever faculties or knowledge he has. The mind of an educated man is greater than the knowledge it possesses; it is like the vault of heaven, encompassing the earth which lives and flourishes beneath it: but the mind of an uneducated and learned man is like a caoutchouc band, with an everlasting spirit of contraction in it, fastening together papers which it cannot open, and keeps others from opening.

Half our artists are ruined for want of education, and by the possession of knowledge; the best that I have known have been educated, and illiterate. The ideal of an artist, however, is not that he should be illiterate, but well read in the best books, and thoroughly high bred, both in heart and in bearing. In a word, he should be fit for the best society, *and should keep out of it.*[9]

9 (Ruskin note "Society always has a destructive influence upon an artist: first, by its sympathy with his meanest powers; secondly, by its chilling want of understanding of his greatest;

There are, indeed, some kinds of knowledge with which
an artist ought to be thoroughly furnished; those, for instance, which enable him to express himself: for this knowledge relieves instead of encumbering his mind, and permits
it to attend to its purposes instead of wearying itself about
means. The whole mystery of manipulation and manufacture should be familiar to the painter from a child. He
should know the chemistry of all colours and materials
whatsoever, and should prepare all his colours himself, in
a little laboratory of his own. Limiting his chemistry to this
one object, the amount of practical science necessary for
it, and such accidental discoveries as might fall in his way
in the course of his work, of better colours or better methods of preparing them, would be an infinite refreshment to
his mind; a minor subject of interest, to which it might
turn when jaded with comfortless labour, or exhausted
with feverish invention, and yet which would never interfere with its higher functions, when it chose to address
itself to them.

And yet even this, to the painter, the safest of sciences,
and in some degree necessary, has its temptations, and
capabilities of abuse. For the simplest means are always
enough for a great man; and when once he has obtained a
few ordinary colours which he is sure will stand, and a
white surface that will not darken, nor moulder, nor rend,
he is master of the world, and of his fellow-men.

Within its due limits, however, here is one branch of
science which the artist may pursue; and, within limits still
more strict, another also, namely, the science of the appearances of things as they have been ascertained and
registered by his fellow-men. For no day passes but some
visible fact is pointed out to us by others, which, without
their help, we should not have noticed; and the accumulation and generalization of visible facts have formed, in the
succession of ages, the sciences of light and shade, and
perspective, linear and aerial: so that the artist is now at
once put in possession of certain truths respecting the ap-

and, thirdly, by its vain occupation of his time and thoughts.
Of course a painter of men must be *among* men; but it ought
to be as a watcher, not as a companion.") SV III, 49–53, omit.

pearances of things, which, so pointed out to him, any
man may in a few days understand and acknowledge; but
which, without aid, he could not probably discover in his
lifetime.

"Well but," still answers the reader, . . . "the fact is,
that a picture of the Renaissance period, or by a modern
master, does indeed represent Nature more faithfully than
one wrought in the ignorance of old times." No, not one
whit; for the most part, less faithfully. Indeed, the outside
of Nature is more truly drawn; the material commonplace,
which can be systematized, catalogued, and taught to all
painstaking mankind,—forms of ribs and scapulæ, of eyebrows and lips, and curls of hair. Whatever can be measured and handled, dissected and demonstrated,—in a word,
whatever is of the body only,—that the schools of knowledge do resolutely and courageously possess themselves of,
and portray. But whatever is immeasurable, intangible,
indivisible, and of the spirit, that the schools of knowledge
do as certainly lose, and blot out of their sight: that is to
say, all that is worth art's possessing or recording at all;
for whatever can be arrested, measured, and systematized,
we can contemplate as much as we will in Nature herself.
But what we want art to do for us is to stay what is fleeting, and to enlighten what is incomprehensible, to incor-
porate the things that have no measure, and immortalize
the things that have no duration. The dimly seen, momentary glance, the flitting shadow of faint emotion, the
imperfect lines of fading thought, and all that by and
through such things as these is recorded on the features of
man, and all that in man's person and actions, and in the
great natural world, is infinite and wonderful; having in it
that spirit and power which man may witness, but not
weigh; conceive, but not comprehend; love, but not limit;
and imagine, but not define;—this, the beginning and the
end of the aim of all noble art, we have, in the ancient
art, by perception; and we have *not*, in the newer art, by
knowledge. Giotto gives it us: Orcagna gives it us; Angelico, Memmi, Pisano,—it matters not who,—all simple and
unlearned men, in their measure and manner,—give it us;
and the learned men that followed them give it us not, and

we, in our supreme learning, own ourselves at this day farther from it than ever.

[T]he real animating power of knowledge is only in the
moment of its being first received, when it fills us with
wonder and joy; a joy for which, observe, the previous
ignorance is just as necessary as the present knowledge.
That man is always happy who is in the presence of something which he cannot know to the full, which he is always
going on to know. This is the necessary condition of a finite
creature with divinely rooted and divinely directed intelligence; this, therefore, its happy state,—but observe, a
state, not of triumph or joy in what it knows, but of joy
rather in the continual discovery, of new ignorance, continual self-abasement, continual astonishment. Once thoroughly our own, the knowledge ceases to give us pleasure.
It may be practically useful to us, it may be good for
others, or good for usury to obtain more; but, in itself,
once let it be thoroughly familiar, and it is dead, the wonder is gone from it, and all the fine colour which it had
when first we drew it up out of the infinite sea.[10]

Science and 'progress'

That modern science, with all its additions to the com-
forts of life, and to the fields of rational contemplation, has
placed the existing races of mankind on a higher platform
than any that preceded them, none can doubt for an instant; and I believe the position in which we find ourselves
is somewhat analogous to that of thoughtful and laborious
youth succeeding a restless and heedless infancy. Not long
ago, it was said to me by one of the masters of modern
science: "When men invented the locomotive, the child
was learning to go; when they invented the telegraph, it
was learning to speak." He looked forward to the manhood of mankind as assuredly the nobler in proportion to
the slowness of its development. What might not be expected from the prime and middle strength of the order of
existence whose infancy had lasted six thousand years? And

[10] SV III, 53–65, omit.

indeed, I think this the truest, as well as the most cheering, view that we can take of the world's history. Little progress has been made as yet. Base war, lying policy, thoughtless cruelty, senseless improvidence,—all things which, in nations, are analogous to the petulance, cunning, impatience, and carelessness of infancy,—have been, up to this hour, as characteristic of mankind as they were in the earliest periods; so that we must either be driven to doubt of human progress at all, or look upon it as in its very earliest stage.

It seems to me, then, that the whole human race, so far as their own reason can be trusted, may at present be regarded as just emergent from childhood; and beginning for the first time to feel their strength, to stretch their limbs, and explore the creation around them. If we consider that, till within the last fifty years, the nature of the ground we tread on, of the air we breathe, and of the light by which we see, were not so much as conjecturally conceived by us; that the duration of the globe, and the races of animal life by which it was inhabited, are just beginning to be apprehended; and that the scope of the magnificent science which has revealed them is as yet so little received by the public mind, that presumption and ignorance are still permitted to raise their voices against it unrebuked . . .

On the other hand, a power of obtaining veracity [i.e., photography] in the representation of material and tangible things, which, within certain limits and conditions, is unimpeachable, has now been placed in the hands of all men, almost without labour. The foundation of every natural science is now at last firmly laid, not a day passing without some addition of buttress and pinnacle to their already magnificent fabric. Social theorems, if fiercely agitated, are therefore the more likely to be at last determined, so that they never can be matters of question more. Human life has been in some sense prolonged by the increased powers of locomotion, and an almost limitless power of converse. Finally, there is hardly any serious mind in Europe but is occupied, more or less, in the investigation of the questions which have so long paralyzed the strength of religious feeling, and shortened the dominion of religious faith. And we may therefore at least look upon ourselves as so far in a definite state of progress, as to justify our caution in guarding against the dangers incident to every period of change, and especially to that from childhood into youth.[11]

Optics

I will not delay you by any defence of the arrangement of sciences I have chosen. Of course we may at once dismiss chemistry and pure mathematics from our consideration. Chemistry can do nothing for art but mix her colours, and tell her what stones will stand weather; (I wish, at this day, she did as much;) and with pure mathematics we have nothing whatever to do; nor can that abstract form of high mathesis stoop to comprehend the simplicity of art. To a first wrangler at Cambridge, under the present conditions of his trial, statues will necessarily be stone dolls, and imaginative work unintelligible. We have, then, in true fellowship with art, only the sciences of light and form (optics and geometry). If you will take the first syllable of the word "geometry" to mean earth in the form of flesh, as well as of clay, the two words sum every science that regards graphic art, or of which graphic art can represent the conclusions.

To-day we are to speak of optics, the science of seeing; —of that power, whatever it may be, which (by Plato's definition), "through the eyes, manifests colour to us." Hold that definition always, and remember that "light" means accurately the power that affects the eyes of animals with the sensation proper to them. The study of the effect of light on nitrate of silver is chemistry, not optics; and what is light to *us* may indeed shine on a stone; but is not light to the stone. The "fiat lux" of creation is, therefore, in the deep sense of it, "fiat anima." We cannot say that it is merely "fiat oculus," for the effect of light on living organism, even when sightless, cannot be separated from its influence on sight. A plant consists essentially of

[11] SV III, 196–200, omit.

two parts, root and leaf: the leaf by nature seeks light, the root by nature seeks darkness: it is not warmth or cold, but essentially light and shade, which are to them, as to us, the appointed conditions of existence.

And you are to remember still more distinctly that the words "fiat lux" mean indeed "fiat anima," because even the power of the eye itself, as such, is *in* its animation. You do not see *with* the lens of the eye. You see *through* that, and by means of that, but you see with the soul of the eye. A great physiologist said to me the other day—it was in the rashness of controversy, and ought not to be remembered, as a deliberate assertion, therefore I do not give his name [Huxley], still he did say—that sight was "altogether mechanical." The words simply meant, if they meant anything, that all his physiology had never taught him the difference between eyes and telescopes. Sight is an absolutely spiritual phenomenon; accurately, and only, to be so defined . . .[12]

[As an example, Turner] was one day making a drawing of Plymouth harbour, with some ships at the distance of a mile or two, seen against the light. Having shown this drawing to a naval officer, the naval officer observed with surprise, and objected with very justifiable indignation, that the ships of the line had no port-holes. "No," said Turner, "certainly not. If you will walk up to Mount Edge-cumbe, and look at the ships against the sunset, you will find you can't see the port-holes." "Well, but," said the naval officer, still indignant, "you know the port-holes are there." "Yes," said Turner, "I know that well enough; but my business is to draw what I see, and not what I know is there."

Now, that is the law of all fine artistic work whatsoever; and, more than that, it is, on the whole, perilous to you, and undesirable, that you *should* know what is there. If, indeed, you have so perfectly disciplined your sight that it cannot be influenced by prejudice;—if you are sure that none of your knowledge of what is there will be allowed to assert itself; and that you can reflect the ship as

12 ENest 193–95

simply as the sea beneath it does, though you may know
it with the intelligence of a sailor,—then, indeed, you may
allow yourself the pleasure, and what will sometimes be
the safeguard from error, of learning what ships or stars,
or mountains, are in reality; but the ordinary powers of
human perception are almost certain to be disturbed by
the knowledge of the real nature of what they draw: and,
until you are quite fearless of your faithfulness to the appearances of things, the less you know of their reality the
better.

And it is precisely in this passive and naïve simplicity
that art becomes, not only greatest in herself, but most
useful to science. If she *knew* anything of what she was
representing, she would exhibit that partial knowledge
with complacency; and miss the points beside it, and beyond it. Two painters draw the same mountain; the one
has got unluckily into his head some curiosity about glacier marking; and the other has a theory of cleavage. The
one will scratch his mountain all over;—the other split it to
pieces; and both drawings will be equally useless for the
purposes of honest science.

Superiority of artistic truth

Any of you who chance to know my books cannot but
be surprised at my saying these things; for, of all writers
on art, I suppose there is no one who appeals so often as
I do to physical science. But observe, I appeal as a critic
of art, never as a master of it. Turner made drawings of
mountains and clouds which the public said were absurd.
I said, on the contrary, they were the only true drawings
of mountains and clouds ever made yet: and I proved this
to be so, as only it could be proved, by steady test of physical science: but Turner had drawn his mountains rightly,
long before their structure was known to any geologist in
Europe; and has painted perfectly truths of anatomy in
clouds which I challenge any meteorologist in Europe to
explain at this day.

And indeed I was obliged to leave *Modern Painters* incomplete, or, rather, as a mere sketch of intention, in analy-

sis of the forms of cloud and wave, because I had not scientific data enough to appeal to. Just reflect for an instant how absolutely whatever has been done in art to represent these most familiar, yet most spectral forms of cloud—utterly inorganic, yet, by spiritual ordinance, in their kindness fair, and in their anger frightful,—how all that has yet been done to represent them, from the undulating bands of blue and white which give to heraldry its nebule bearing, to the finished and deceptive skies of Turner, has been done without one syllable of help from the lips of science.

For all his own purposes, merely graphic, we say, if an artist's eye is fine and faithful, the fewer points of science he has in his head, the better. But for purposes *more* than graphic, in order that he may feel towards things as he should, and choose them as *we* should, he ought to know something about them; and if he is quite sure that he can receive the science of them without letting himself become uncandid and narrow in observation, it is very desirable that he should be acquainted with a little of the alphabet of structure,—just as much as may quicken and certify his observation, without prejudicing it. Cautiously, therefore, and receiving it as a perilous indulgence, he may venture to learn, perhaps as much astronomy as may prevent his carelessly putting the new moon wrong side upwards; and as much botany as will prevent him from confusing, which I am sorry to say Turner did, too often, Scotch firs with stone pines. He may concede so much to geology as to choose, of two equally picturesque views, one that illustrates rather than conceals the structure of a crag: and perhaps, once or twice in his life, a portrait painter might advantageously observe how unlike a skull is to a face. And for you, who are to use your drawing as one element in general education, it is desirable that physical science should assist in the attainment of truth which a real painter seizes by practice of eye.[13]

Here is a bit of Greek sculpture, with many folds; here is a bit of Christian sculpture with few. From the many,

[13] ENest 210–14, omit.

not one could be removed without harm, and to the few, not one could be added. This alone is art, and no science will ever enable you to do this, but the poetic and fabric instincts only.

Nevertheless, however far above science, your work must comply with all the requirements of science. The first thing you have to ask is, Is it scientifically right? That is still nothing, but it is essential. In modern imitations of Gothic work the artists think it religious to be wrong, and that Heaven will be propitious only to saints whose stoles or petticoats stand or fall into incredible angles. All that nonsense I will soon get well out of your heads by enabling you to make accurate studies from real drapery, so that you may be able to detect in a moment whether the folds in any design are natural and true to the form, or artificial and ridiculous. But this, which is the science of drapery, will never do more than guard you in your first attempts in the art of it. Nay, when once you have mastered the elements of such science, the most sickening of all work to you will be that in which the draperies are all right,—and nothing else is.

Finally, observe that what is true respecting these simple forms of drapery is true of all other inorganic form. It must become organic under the artist's hand by his invention. As there must not be a fold in a vestment too few or too many, there must not, in noble landscape, be a fold in a mountain, too few or too many. As you will never get from real linen cloth, by copying it ever so faithfully, the drapery of a noble statue, so you will never get from real mountains, copy them never so faithfully, the forms of noble landscape. Anything more beautiful than the photographs of the Valley of Chamouni, now in your print-sellers' windows, cannot be conceived. For geographical and geological purposes they are worth anything; for art purposes, worth—a good deal less than zero. You may learn much from them, and will mislearn more. But in Turner's "Valley of Chamouni" the mountains have not a fold too much, nor too little. There are no such mountains at Chamouni: they are the ghosts of eternal mountains, such as have been, and shall be, for evermore.

So now in sum, for I may have confused you by illustration,—

I. You are, in drawing, to try only to represent the appearances of things, never what you know the things to be.

II. Those appearances you are to test by the appliance of the scientific laws relating to aspect; and to learn, by accurate measurement, and the most fixed attention, to represent with absolute fidelity.

III. Having learned to represent actual appearances faithfully, if you have any human faculty of your own, visionary appearances will take place to you which will be nobler and more true than any actual or material appearances; and the realization of these is the function of every fine art, which is founded absolutely, therefore, in truth, and consists absolutely in imagination. And once more we may conclude with, but now using them in a deeper sense, the words of our master—"The best in this kind are but shadows."[14]

Darwinism

Some animals have to dig with their noses, some to build with their tails, some to spin with their stomachs: their dexterities are usually few—their awkwardnesses numberless;—a lion is continually puzzled how to hold a bone; and an eagle can scarcely pull the meat off one, without upsetting himself.

Respecting the origin of these variously awkward, imperfectly, or grotesquely developed phases of form and power, you need not at present inquire: in all probability the race of man is appointed to live in wonder, and in acknowledgment of ignorance; but if ever he is to know any of the secrets of his own or of brutal existence, it will assuredly be through discipline of virtue, not through inquisitiveness of science. I have just used the expression, "had Darwinism been true," implying its fallacy more positively than is justifiable in the present state of our knowledge; but very positively I can say to you that I have never

[14] ENest 219–21, omit.

heard yet one logical argument in its favour, and I have heard, and read, many that were beneath contempt. For instance, by the time you have copied one or two of your exercises on the feather of the halcyon, you will be more interested in the construction and disposition of plume-filaments than heretofore; and you may, perhaps, refer, in hope of help, to Mr. Darwin's account of the peacock's feather. I went to it myself, hoping to learn some of the existing laws of life which regulate the local disposition of the colour. But none of these appear to be known; and I am informed only that peacocks have grown to be pea-cocks out of brown pheasants, because the young feminine brown pheasants like fine feathers. Whereupon I say to myself, "Then either there was a distinct species of brown pheasants originally born with a taste for fine feathers; and therefore with remarkable eyes in their heads,—which would be a much more wonderful distinction of species than being born with remarkable eyes in their tails,—or else all pheasants would have been peacocks by this time!" And I trouble myself no more about the Darwinian theory.

When you have drawn some of the actual patterns of plume and scale with attention, I believe you will see rea-son to think that spectra of organic species may be at least as distinct as those of metals or gases; but learn at all events what they are now, and never mind what they have been.[15]

[15] ENest 247 f

3

NATURE

[A]lthough it is possible to reach what I have stated to be the first end of art, the representation of facts, without reaching the second, the representation of thoughts, yet it is altogether impossible to reach the second without having previously reached the first. I do not say that a man cannot think, having false basis and material for thought; but that a false thought is worse than the want of thought, and therefore is not art. And this is the reason why, though I consider the second as the real and only important end of all art, I call the representation of facts the first end; because it is necessary to the other and must be attained before it. It is the foundation of all art; like real foundations, it may be little thought of when a brilliant fabric is raised on it; but it must be there. And as few buildings are beautiful unless every line and column of their mass have reference to their foundation, and be suggestive of its existence and strength, so nothing can be beautiful in art which does not in all its parts suggest and guide to the foundation . . . And thus, though we want the thoughts and feelings of the artist as well as the truth, yet they must be thoughts arising out of the knowledge of truth, and feelings arising out of the contemplation of truth. We do not want his mind to be like a badly blown glass, that distorts what we see through it, but like a glass of sweet and strange colour, that gives new tones to what we see through it; and a glass of rare strength and clearness too, to let us see more than we could ourselves, and bring nature up to us and near to us.[16]

[16] MP I, 136 f, omit.

'Truth' in nature

It is just as impossible to generalize granite and slate, as
it is to generalize a man and a cow. An animal must be
either one animal or another animal: it cannot be a general animal, or it is no animal; and so a rock must be either
one rock or another rock; it cannot be a general rock, or
it is no rock. If there were a creature in the foreground
of a picture of which he could not decide whether it were
a pony or a pig, the *Athenæum* critic[17] would perhaps
affirm it to be a generalization of pony and pig, and consequently a high example of "harmonious union and simple effect." But *I* should call it simple bad drawing. And so
when there are things in the foreground of Salvator of
which I cannot pronounce whether they be granite, or
slate, or tufa, I affirm that there is in them neither harmonious union, nor simple effect, but simple monstrosity.
There is no grandeur, no beauty of any sort or kind, nothing but destruction, disorganization, and ruin, to be obtained by the violation of natural distinctions.

It is true that the distinctions of rocks and plants and
clouds are less conspicuous, and less constantly subjects of
observation, than those of the animal creation; but the
difficulty of observing them proves not the merit of over-
looking them. It only accounts for the singular fact, that
the world has never yet seen anything like a perfect school
of landscape. For just as the highest historical painting is
based on perfect knowledge of the workings of the human
form and human mind, so must the highest landscape
painting be based on perfect cognizance of the form, functions, and system of every organic or definitely structured
existence which it has to represent. This proportion is self-
evident to every thinking mind; and every principle which
appears to contradict it is either misstated or misunderstood. For instance, the *Athenæum* critic calls the right
statement of generic difference "*Denner*-like portraiture."

[17] (In reviewing MP I: No. 850, February 10, 1844.) MP I,
34 f, preface 2nd edition, 1844.

If he can find anything like Denner in what I have advanced as the utmost perfection of landscape art, the recent works of Turner, he is welcome to his discovery and his theory. No; Denner-like portraiture would be the endeavour to paint the separate crystals of quartz and felspar in the granite, and the separate flakes of mica in the mica slate; an attempt just as far removed from what I assert to be great art (the bold rendering of the generic characters of form in both rocks), as modern sculpture of lace and buttonholes is from the Elgin marbles.

This is the difference between the mere botanist's knowledge of plants, and the great poet's or painter's knowledge of them. The one notes their distinctions for the sake of swelling his herbarium, the other, that he may render them vehicles of expression and emotion. The one counts the stamens, and affixes a name, and is content; the other observes every character of the plant's colour and form; considering each of its attributes as an element of expression, he seizes on its lines of grace or energy, rigidity or repose; notes the feebleness or the vigour, the serenity or tremulousness of its hues; observes its local habits, its love or fear of peculiar places, its nourishment or destruction by particular influences; he associates it in his mind with all the features of the situations it inhabits, and the ministering agencies necessary to its support. Thenceforward the flower is to him a living creature, with histories written on its leaves, and passions breathing in its motion. Its occurrence in his picture is no mere point of colour, no meaningless spark of light. It is a voice rising from the earth, a new chord of the mind's music, a necessary note in the harmony of his picture, contributing alike to its tenderness and its dignity, nor less to its loveliness than its truth.[18]

Not every casual idea caught from the flight of a shower or the fall of a sunbeam, not every glowing fragment of harvest light, nor every flickering dream of copse-wood coolness is to be given to the world as it came, unconsidered, incomplete, and forgotten by the artist as soon as it

[18] *Ibid.*, 35–37, omit.

has left his easel. That only should be considered a picture, in which the spirit, not the materials, observe, but the animating emotion, of many such studies is concentrated and exhibited by the aid of long studied, painfully chosen forms; idealized in the right sense of the word, not by audacious liberty of that faculty of degrading God's works which man calls his "imagination," but by perfect assertion of entire knowledge of every part and character and function of the object, and in which the details are completed to the last line compatible with the dignity and simplicity of the whole, wrought out with that noblest industry which concentrates profusion into point, and transforms accumulation into structure. Neither must this labour be bestowed on every subject which appears to afford a capability of good, but on chosen subjects in which nature has prepared to the artist's hand the purest sources of the impression he would convey. These may be humble in their order, but they must be perfect of their kind. There is a perfection of the hedgerow and cottage, as well as of the forest and the palace; and more ideality in a great artist's selection and treatment of roadside weeds and brook-worn pebbles, than in all the struggling caricature of the meaner mind, which heaps its foreground with colossal columns, and heaves impossible mountains into the encumbered sky.[19]

And if painters would only go out to the nearest common, and take the nearest dirty pond among the furze, and draw that thoroughly; not considering that it is water that they are drawing, and that water must be done in a certain way, but drawing determinedly what they *see;*— that is to say, all the trees, and their shaking leaves, and all the hazy passages of disturbing sunshine; and the bottom seen in the clearer little bits at the edge, and the stones of it; and all the sky, and the clouds far down in the middle, drawn as completely as the real clouds above; —they would come home with such a notion of water-painting as might save me and every one else all trouble of writing about the matter.[20]

[19] *Ibid.,* 47
[20] MP I, 497

Constant and eager watchfulness, and portfolios filled with actual statements of water-effect, drawn on the spot and on the instant, are worth more to the painter than the most extended optical knowledge. Without these all his knowledge will end in a pedantic falsehood; with these it does not matter how gross or how daring here and there may be his violations of this or that law; his very transgressions will be admirable.[21]

Science dessicates nature

Every archæologist, every natural philosopher, knows that there is a peculiar rigidity of mind brought on by long devotion to logical and analytical inquiries. Weak men, giving themselves to such studies, are utterly hardened by them, and become incapable of understanding anything nobler, or even of feeling the value of the results to which they lead. But even the best men are in a sort injured by them, and pay a definite price, as in most other matters, for definite advantages. They gain a peculiar strength, but lose in tenderness, elasticity, and impressibility. The man who has gone, hammer in hand, over the surface of a romantic country, feels no longer, in the mountain ranges he has so laboriously explored, the sublimity or mystery with which they were veiled when he first beheld them, and with which they are adorned in the mind of the passing traveller. In his more informed conception, they arrange themselves like a dissected model: where another man would be awe-struck by the magnificence of the precipice, he sees nothing but the emergence of a fossiliferous rock, familiarised already to his imagination as extending in a shallow stratum, over a perhaps uninteresting district; where the unlearned spectator would be touched with strong emotion by the aspect of the snowy summits which rise in the distance, he sees only the culminating points of a metamorphic formation, with an uncomfortable web of fan-like fissures radiating, in his imagination,

[21] MP I, 508 f

through their centres.[22] That in the grasp he has obtained
of the inner relations of all these things to the universe,
and to man, that in the views which have been opened to
him of natural energies such as no human mind would
have ventured to conceive, and of past states of being,
each in some new way bearing witness to the unity of
purpose and everlastingly consistent providence of the
Maker of all things, he has received reward well worthy
the sacrifice, I would not for an instant deny; but the sense
of the loss is not less painful to him if his mind be rightly
constituted; and it would be with infinite gratitude that
he would regard the man, who, retaining in his delineation
of natural scenery a fidelity to the facts of science so rigid
as to make his work at once acceptable and credible to
the most sternly critical intellect, should yet invest its
features again with the sweet veil of their daily aspect;
should make them dazzling with the splendour of wandering light, and involve them in the unsearchableness of
stormy obscurity; should restore to the divided anatomy
its visible vitality of operation, clothe the naked crags with
soft forests, enrich the mountain ruins with bright pastures,
and lead the thoughts from the monotonous recurrence of
the phenomena of the physical world, to the sweet interests and sorrows of human life and death.[23]

[22] (Ruskin note: "This state of mind appears to have been
the only one which Wordsworth had been able to discern in
men of science; and in disdain of which, he wrote that short-
sighted passage in the *Excursion*, Book III. l. 165–190, which is,
I think, the only one in the whole range of his works which his
true friends would have desired to see blotted out. What else has
been found fault with as feeble or superfluous, is not so in the
intense distinctive relief which it gives to his character. But these
lines are written in mere ignorance of the matter they treat; in
mere want of sympathy with the men they describe: for, observe, though the passage is put into the mouth of the Solitary,
it is fully confirmed, and even rendered more scornful, by the
speech which follows.") PRB, 391–92
[23] PRB, 392–93

Aspects of nature: mountains

Mountains are to the rest of the body of the earth, what violent muscular action is to the body of man. The muscles and tendons of its anatomy are, in the mountain, brought out with force and convulsive energy, full of expression, passion, and strength; the plains and the lower hills are the repose and the effortless motion of the frame, when its muscles lie dormant and concealed beneath the lines of its beauty, yet ruling those lines in their every undulation. This, then, is the first grand principle of the truth of the earth. The spirit of the hills is action, that of the lowlands repose; and between these there is to be found every variety of motion and of rest, from the inactive plain, sleeping like the firmament, with cities for stars, to the fiery peaks, which, with heaving bosoms and exulting limbs, with the clouds drifting like hair from their bright foreheads, lift up their Titan hands to heaven, saying, "I live for ever!"

But there is this difference between the action of the earth, and that of a living creature; that while the exerted limb marks its bones and tendons through the flesh, the excited earth casts off the flesh altogether, and its bones come out from beneath. Mountains are the bones of the earth, their highest peaks are invariably those parts of its anatomy which in the plains lie buried under five and twenty thousand feet of solid thickness of superincumbent soil, and which spring up in the mountain ranges in vast pyramids or wedges, flinging their garment of earth away from them on each side. The masses of the lower hills are laid over and against their sides, like the masses of lateral masonry against the skeleton arch of an unfinished bridge, except that they slope up to and lean against the central ridge: and, finally, upon the slopes of these lower hills are strewed the level beds of sprinkled gravel, sand, and clay, which form the extent of the champaign. Here then is another grand principle of the truth of earth, that the mountains must come from under all, and be the support of all; and that everything else must be laid in their arms, heap

above heap, the plains being the uppermost. Opposed to
this truth is every appearance of the hills being laid upon
the plains, or built upon them.[24]

Clouds

Clouds, it is to be remembered, are not so much local
vapour, as vapour rendered locally visible by a fall of
temperature. Thus a cloud, whose parts are in constant motion, will hover on a snowy mountain, pursuing constantly
the same track upon its flanks, and yet remaining of the
same size, the same form, and in the same place, for half a
day together. No matter how violent or how capricious
the wind may be, the instant it approaches the spot where
the chilly influence of the snow extends, the moisture it
carries becomes visible, and then and there the cloud
forms on the instant, apparently maintaining its shape
against the wind, though the careful and keen eye can see
all its parts in the most rapid motion across the mountain.
The outlines of such a cloud are of course not determined
by the irregular impulses of the wind, but by the fixed lines
of radiant heat which regulate the temperature of the atmosphere of the mountain. It is terminated, therefore, not
by changing curves, but by steady right lines of more or
less decision, often exactly correspondent with the outline
of the mountain on which it is formed, and falling therefore
into grotesque peaks and precipices. I have seen the
marked and angular outline of the Grandes Jorasses, at
Chamonix, mimicked in its every jag by a line of clouds
above it. Another resultant phenomenon is the formation
of cloud in the calm air to leeward of a steep summit; cloud
whose edges are in rapid motion, where they are affected
by the current of the wind above, and stream from the
peak like the smoke of a volcano, yet always vanish at a
certain distance from it as steam issuing from a chimney.
When wet weather of some duration is approaching, a
small white spot of cloud will sometimes appear low on
the hill flanks; it will not move, but will increase gradually

[24] MP I, 427 f

for some little time, then diminish, still without moving; disappear altogether, reappear ten minutes afterwards, exactly in the same spot . . .[25]

But the clouds, though we can hide them with smoke, and mix them with poison, cannot be quarried nor built over, and they are always therefore gloriously arranged; so gloriously, that unless you have notable powers of memory you need not hope to approach the effect of any sky that interests you. For both its grace and its glow depend upon the united influence of every cloud within its compass: they all move and burn together in a marvellous harmony; not a cloud of them is out of its appointed place, or fails of its part in the choir: and if you are not able to recollect (which in the case of a complicated sky it is impossible you should) precisely the form and position of all the clouds at a given moment, you cannot draw the sky at all; for the clouds will not fit if you draw one part of them three or four minutes before another.

You must try therefore to help what memory you have, by sketching at the utmost possible speed the whole range of the clouds; marking, by any shorthand or symbolic work you can hit upon, the peculiar character of each, as transparent, or fleecy, or linear, or undulatory; giving afterwards such completion to the parts as your recollection will enable you to do.

Now clouds are not as solid as flour-sacks; but, on the other hand, they are neither spongy nor flat. They are definite and very beautiful forms of sculptured mist; sculptured is a perfectly accurate word; they are not more *drifted* into form than they are *carved* into form, the warm air around them cutting them into shape by absorbing the visible vapour beyond certain limits; hence their angular and fantastic outlines, as different from a swollen, spherical, or globular formation, on the one hand, as from that of flat films or shapeless mists on the other.[26]

[25] MP I, 371 f
[26] ED 129 f, omit.

Mystery vs. clarity in nature

But not only is there a *partial* and variable mystery thus caused by clouds and vapours throughout great spaces of landscape; there is a continual mystery caused throughout *all* spaces, caused by the absolute infinity of things. WE NEVER SEE ANYTHING CLEARLY. Thus: throwing an open book and an embroidered handkerchief on a lawn, at a distance of a quarter of a mile we cannot tell which is which; that is the point of mystery for the whole of those things. They are then merely white spots of indistinct shape. We approach them, and perceive that one is a book, the other a handkerchief, but cannot read the one, nor trace the embroidery of the other. The mystery has ceased to be in the whole things, and has gone into their details. We go nearer, and can now read the text and trace the embroidery, but cannot see the fibres of the paper, nor the threads of the stuff. The mystery has gone into a third place. We take both up and look closely at them; we see the watermark and the threads, but not the hills and dales in the paper's surface, nor the fine fibres which shoot off from every thread. The mystery has gone into a fourth place, where it must stay, till we take a microscope, which will send it into a fifth, sixth, hundredth, or thousandth place, according to the power we use. When, therefore, we say, we see the book *clearly*, we mean only that we know it is a book.

Everything in the field of sight is equally puzzling, and can only be drawn rightly on the same difficult conditions. Try it fairly. Take the commonest, closest, most familiar thing, and strive to draw it verily as you see it. Be sure of this last fact, for otherwise you will find yourself continually drawing, not what you *see*, but what you *know*.

Then try to draw a bank of grass, with all its blades; or a bush, with all its leaves; and you will soon begin to understand under what a universal law of obscurity we live, and perceive that all *distinct* drawing must be *bad* drawing, and that nothing can be right, till it is unintelligible.

"How! and Pre-Raphaelitism and Dürerism, and all that you have been talking to us about for these five hundred pages!" Well, it is all right; Pre-Raphaelitism is quite as unintelligible as need be (I will answer for Dürerism farther on). Examine your Pre-Raphaelite painting well, and you will find it is the precise fulfilment of these laws. You can make out your plantain head and your pine, and see entirely what they are; but yet they are full of mystery, and suggest more than you can see. So also with Turner, the true head of Pre-Raphaelitism. You shall see the spots of the trout lying dead on the rock in his foreground, but not count them. It is only the Germans and the so-called masters of drawing and defining that are wrong, not the Pre-Raphaelites.

Not, that is to say, so far as it is *possible* to be right. No human skill can get the absolute truth in this matter; but a drawing by Turner of a large scene, and by Holman Hunt of a small one, are as close to truth as human eyes and hands can reach.

"Well, but how of Veronese and all the firm, fearless draughtsmen of days gone by?" They are indeed firm and fearless, but they are all mysterious. Not one great man of them, but he will puzzle you, if you look close, to know what he means. Distinct enough, as to his general intent, indeed, just as Nature is distinct in her general intent, but examine his touches, and you will find in Veronese, in Titian, in Tintoret, in Correggio, and in all the great *painters,* properly so called, a peculiar melting and mystery about the pencilling, sometimes called softness, sometimes freedom, sometimes breadth; but in reality a most subtle confusion of colours and forms, obtained either by the apparently careless stroke of the brush, or by careful retouching with tenderest labour; but always obtained in one way or another; so that though, when compared with work that has no meaning, all great work is *distinct,*—compared with work that has narrow and stubborn meaning, all great work is *in*distinct; and if we find, on examining any picture closely, that it is all clearly to be made out, it can-

not be, as painting, first-rate. There is no exception to this
rule. EXCELLENCE OF THE HIGHEST KIND, WITHOUT OBSCU-
RITY, CANNOT EXIST.[27]

[27] MP IV, 75–81, omit.

4

LIGHT AND SHADE

I wish now only to speak of those great principles of chiaroscuro, which nature observes, even when she is most working for effect; when she is playing with thunderclouds and sunbeams, and throwing one thing out and obscuring another, with the most marked artistical feeling and intention: even then, she never forgets her great rule, to give both the deepest shade and highest light in small quantities: points of the one answering to points of the other, and both vividly conspicuous, and separated from the rest of the landscape.

And it is most singular that this separation, which is the great source of brilliancy in nature, should not only be unobserved, but absolutely forbidden, by our great writers on art, who are always talking about connecting the light with the shade by *imperceptible gradations*. Now so surely as this is done, all sunshine is lost, for imperceptible gradation from light to dark is the characteristic of objects seen out of sunshine, in what is, in landscape, shadow. Nature's principle of getting light is the direct reverse. She will cover her whole landscape with middle tint, in which she will have as many gradations as you please, and a great many more than you can paint; but on this middle tint she touches her extreme lights, and extreme darks, isolated and sharp, so that the eye goes to them directly, and feels them to be keynotes of the whole composition.[28]

You will often indeed see in Leonardo's work, and in Michael Angelo's, shadow wrought laboriously to an extreme of fineness; but when you look into it, you will find that they have always been drawing more and more form

[28] MP I, 313

within the space, and never finishing for the sake of added texture, but of added fact. And all those effects of transparency and reflected light, aimed at in common chalk drawings, are wholly spurious. For since, as I told you, all lights are shades compared to higher lights, and lights only as compared to lower ones, it follows that there can be no difference in their quality as such; but that light is opaque when it expresses substance, and transparent when it expresses space; and shade is also opaque when it expresses substance, and transparent when it expresses space. But it is not, even then, transparent in the common sense of that word; nor is its appearance to be obtained by dotting or cross hatching, but by touches so tender as to look like mist. And now we find the use of having Leonardo for our guide. He is supreme in all questions of execution, and in his 28th chapter, you will find that shadows are to be "dolce è sfumose," to be tender, and look as if they were exhaled, or breathed on the paper. Then, look at any of Michael Angelo's finished drawings, or of Correggio's sketches, and you will see that the true nurse of light is in art, as in nature, the cloud; a misty and tender darkness, made lovely by gradation.[29]

"Well, but," it is still objected, "if this be so, why is it necessary to insist, as you do always, upon the most minute and careful renderings of form?" Because, though these gradations of light are indeed, as an object dies in distance, the only things it can retain, yet as it lives its active life near us, those very gradations can only be seen properly by the effect they have on its character. You can only show how the light affects the object, by knowing thoroughly what the object is; and noble mystery differs from ignoble, in being a veil thrown between us and something definite, known, and substantial; but the ignoble mystery is a veil cast before chaos, the studious concealment of Nothing.[30]

Understand, therefore, at once, that no detail can be as strongly expressed in drawing as it is in reality; and

[29] Lect 158
[30] MP IV, 94

strive to keep all your shadows and marks and minor markings on the masses, lighter than they appear to be in Nature; you are sure otherwise to get them too dark. You will in doing this find that you cannot get the projection of things sufficiently shown; but never mind that; there is no need that they should appear to project, but great need that their relations of shade to each other should be preserved. All deceptive projection is obtained by partial exaggeration of shadow; and whenever you see it, you may be sure the drawing is more or less bad: a thoroughly fine drawing or painting will always show a slight tendency towards flatness.[31]

Reflected light

Take a sheet of note-paper, and holding it edgewise, as you hold your hand, wave it up and down past the side of your hand which is turned from the light, the paper being of course farther from the window. You will see, as it passes, a strong gleam of light strike on your hand, and light it considerably on its dark side. This light is *reflected* light. It is thrown back from the paper (on which it strikes first in coming from the window) to the surface of your hand, just as a ball would be if somebody threw it through the window at the wall and you caught it at the rebound.

Next, instead of the note-paper, take a red book, or a piece of scarlet cloth. You will see that the gleam of light falling on your hand, as you wave the book, is now reddened. Take a blue book, and you will find the gleam is blue. Thus every object will cast some of its own colour back in the light that it reflects.

Now it is not only these books or papers that reflect light to your hand: every object in the room on that side of it reflects some, but more feebly, and the colours mixing all together form a neutral light, which lets the colour of your hand itself be more distinctly seen than that of any object which reflects light to it; but if there were no re-

[31] ED 66

flected light, that side of your hand would look as black
as a coal.

Objects are seen therefore, in general, partly by direct
light, and partly by light reflected from the objects around
them, or from the atmosphere and clouds. The colour of
their light sides depends much on that of the direct light,
and that of the dark sides on the colours of the objects
near them. It is therefore impossible to say beforehand
what colour an object will have at any point of its surface, that colour depending partly on its own tint, and
partly on infinite combinations of rays reflected from other
things. The only certain fact about dark sides is, that their
colour will be changeful, and that a picture which gives
them merely darker shades of the colour of the light sides
must assuredly be bad.[32]

"Shadow abstracts"

You will find it of great use, whatever kind of landscape
scenery you are passing through, to get into the habit of
making memoranda of the shapes of shadows. You will
find that many objects of no essential interest in themselves, and neither deserving a finished study, nor a
Düreresque one, may yet become of singular value in consequence of the fantastic shapes of their shadows; for it
happens often, in distant effect, that the shadow is by
much a more important element than the substance. A
perfectly great painter, throughout his distances, continually reduces his objects to these shadow abstracts; and the
singular, and to many persons unaccountable, effect of the
confused touches in Turner's distances, is owing chiefly to
this thorough accuracy and intense meaning of the shadow
abstracts.[33]

[32] ED 55 f
[33] ED 105 f, omit.

5

COLOUR AND COLOUR-LIGHT

Everything that you can see in the world around you, presents itself to your eyes only as an arrangement of patches of different colours variously shaded.[34] The perception of solid Form is entirely a matter of experience. We *see* nothing but flat colours; and it is only by a series of experiments that we find out that a stain of black or grey indicates the dark side of a solid substance, or that a faint hue indicates that the object in which it appears is far away. The whole technical power of painting depends on our recovery of what may be called the *innocence of the eye;* that is to say, of a sort of childish perception of these flat stains of colour, merely as such, without consciousness of what they signify,—as a blind man would see them if suddenly gifted with sight.

For instance: when grass is lighted strongly by the sun in certain directions, it is turned from green into a peculiar and somewhat dusty-looking yellow. If we had been born blind, and were suddenly endowed with sight on a piece of grass thus lighted in some parts by the sun, it would appear to us that part of the grass was green, and part a dusty yellow (very nearly of the colour of primroses); and, if there were primroses near, we should think that the sunlighted grass was another mass of plants of the same sulphur-yellow colour. We should try to gather some of them, and then find that the colour went away from the grass when we stood between it and the sun, but not from the primroses; and by a series of experiments we should find out that the sun was really the cause of the colour in the one,—not in the other. We go through such processes of

[34] ED 27

experiment unconsciously in childhood; and having once come to conclusions touching the signification of certain colours, we always suppose that we *see* what we only know, and have hardly any consciousness of the real aspect of the signs we have learned to interpret. Very few people have any idea that sunlighted grass is yellow.

Now, a highly accomplished artist has always reduced himself as nearly as possible to this condition of infantine sight. He sees the colours of nature exactly as they are, and therefore perceives at once in the sunlighted grass the precise relation between the two colours that form its shade and light. To him it does not seem shade and light, but bluish green barred with gold.[35]

And this is the reason for the somewhat singular, but very palpable truth that the Chinese, and Indians, and other semi-civilized nations, can colour better than we do, and that an Indian shawl and China vase are still, in invention of colour, inimitable by us. It is their glorious ignorance of all rules that does it; the pure and true instincts have play, and do their work,—instincts so subtle, that the least warping or compression breaks or blunts them; and the moment we begin teaching people any rules about colour, and make them do this or that, we crush the instinct, generally for ever. Hence, hitherto, it has been an actual necessity, in order to obtain power of colouring, that a nation should be half savage: everybody could colour in the twelfth and thirteenth centuries; but we were ruled and legalized into grey in the fifteenth;—only a little salt simplicity of their sea natures at Venice still keeping their precious, shell-fishy purpleness and power; and now that is gone; and nobody can colour anywhere, except the Hindoos and Chinese; but that need not be so, and will not be so long; for, in a little while, people will find out their mistake, and give up talking about rules of colour, and then everybody will colour again, as easily as they now talk.[36]

[35] ED 27 f, Ruskin note attached to first sentence this section.
[36] MP III, 123

Light and colour

When you have got a little used to the principal combinations [of colours], place yourself at a window which the
sun does not shine in at, commanding some simple piece
of landscape: outline this landscape roughly; then take a
piece of white cardboard, cut out a hole in it about the
size of a large pea . . . Then you will see the landscape,
bit by bit, through the circular hole. Match the colours of
each important bit as nearly as you can, mixing your tints
with white, beside the aperture. When matched, put a
touch of the same tint at the top of your paper, writing
under it: "dark tree colour," "hill colour," "field colour,"
as the case may be. Then wash the tint away from beside
the opening, and the cardboard will be ready to match
another piece of the landscape. When you have got the
colours of the principal masses thus indicated, lay on a
piece of each in your sketch in its right place, and then
proceed to complete the sketch in harmony with them,
by your eye.

In the course of your early experiments, you will be
much struck by two things: the first, the inimitable brilliancy of light in sky and in sun-lighted things; and the
second, that among the tints which you can imitate, those
which you thought the darkest will continually turn out
to be in reality the lightest. Darkness of objects is estimated by us, under ordinary circumstances, much more
by knowledge than by sight; thus, a cedar or Scotch fir, at
200 yards off, will be thought of darker green than an elm
or oak near us; because we know by experience that the
peculiar colour they exhibit, at that distance, is the *sign* of
darkness of foliage. But when we try them through the
cardboard, the near oak will be found, indeed, rather dark
green, and the distant cedar, perhaps, pale grey-purple.
The quantity of purple and grey in Nature is, by the way,
another somewhat surprising subject of discovery.

Well, having ascertained thus your principal tints, you
may proceed to fill up your sketch; in doing which observe
these following particulars:

(1.) Many portions of your subject appeared through the aperture in the paper brighter than the paper, as sky, sun-lighted grass, etc. Leave these portions, for the present, white; and proceed with the parts of which you can match the tints.

(2.) As you tried your subject with the cardboard, you must have observed how many changes of hue took place over small spaces. In filling up your work, try to educate your eye to perceive these differences of hue without the help of the cardboard, and lay them deliberately, like a mosaic-worker, as separate colours, preparing each carefully on your palette, and laying it as if it were a patch of coloured cloth, cut out, to be fitted neatly by its edge to the next patch; so that the *fault* of your work may be, not a slurred or misty look, but a patched bed-cover look, as if it had all been cut out with scissors. For instance, in drawing the trunk of a birch tree, there will be probably white high lights, then a pale rosy grey round them on the light side, then a (probably greenish) deeper grey on the dark side, varied by reflected colours, and, over all, rich black strips of bark and brown spots of moss. Lay first the rosy grey, leaving white for the high lights *and for the spots of moss,* and not touching the dark side. Then lay the grey for the dark side, fitting it well up to the rosy grey of the light, leaving also in this darker grey the white paper in the places for the black and brown moss; then prepare the moss colours separately for each spot, and lay each in the white place left for it. Not one grain of white, except that purposely left for the high lights, must be visible when the work is done, even through a magnifying-glass, so cunningly must you fit the edges to each other. Finally, take your background colours, and put them on each side of the tree trunk, fitting them carefully to its edge.[37]

[37] ED 142–45, omit.

"Gradated colour"

(3.) Whenever you lay on a mass of colour, be sure that however large it may be, or however small, it shall be gradated. No colour exists in Nature under ordinary circumstances without gradation. If you do not see this, it is the fault of your inexperience: you will see it in due time, if you practise enough. But in general you may see it at once. In the birch trunk, for instance, the rosy grey *must* be gradated by the roundness of the stem till it meets the shaded side; similarly the shaded side is gradated by reflected light. Accordingly, whether by adding water, or white paint, or by unequal force of touch (this you will do at pleasure, according to the texture you wish to produce), you must, in every tint you lay on, make it a little paler at one part than another, and get an even gradation between the two depths.

And it does not matter how small the touch of colour may be, though not larger than the smallest pin's head, if one part of it is not darker than the rest, it is a bad touch; for it is not merely because the natural fact is so, that your colour should be gradated; the preciousness and pleasantness of the colour itself depends more on this than on any other of its qualities, for gradation is to colours just what curvature is to lines, both being felt to be beautiful by the pure instinct of every human mind, and both, considered as types, expressing the law of gradual change and progress in the human soul itself.

You will not, in Turner's largest oil pictures, perhaps six or seven feet long by four or five high, find one spot of colour as large as a grain of wheat ungradated: and you will find in pratice, that brilliancy of hue, and vigour of light, and even the aspect of transparency in shade, are essentially dependent on this character alone; hardness, coldness, and opacity resulting far more from *equality* of colour than from nature of colour. Give me some mud off a city crossing, some ochre out of a gravel pit, a little whitening, and some coal-dust, and I will paint you a luminous picture, if you give me time to gradate my mud,

and subdue my dust: but though you had the red of the
ruby, the blue of the gentian, snow for the light, and amber for the gold, you cannot paint a luminous picture, if
you keep the masses of those colours unbroken in purity,
and unvarying in depth.

Next, note the three processes by which gradation and
other characters are to be obtained:

A. Mixing while the colour is wet.

You may be confused by my first telling you to lay on
the hues in separate patches, and then telling you to mix
hues together as you lay them on: but the separate masses
are to be laid, when colours distinctly oppose each other
at a given limit; the hues to be mixed, when they palpitate
one through the other, or fade one into the other. It is
better to err a little on the distinct side. Thus I told you
to paint the dark and light sides of the birch trunk separately, though, in reality, the two tints change, as the trunk
turns away from the light, gradually one into the other;
and, after being laid separately on, will need some farther
touching to harmonise them: but they do so in a very
narrow space, marked distinctly all the way up the trunk,
and it is easier and safer, therefore, to keep them separate
at first. Whereas it often happens that the whole beauty
of two colours will depend on the one being continued well
through the other, and playing in the midst of it: blue and
green often do so in water; blue and grey, or purple and
scarlet, in sky: in hundreds of such instances the most
beautiful and truthful results may be obtained by laying
one colour into the other while wet; judging wisely how
far it will spread, or blending it with the brush in somewhat thicker consistence of wet body-colour; only observe,
never mix in this way two *mixtures;* let the colour you lay
into the other be always a simple, not a compound tint.

B. Laying one colour over another.

If you lay on a solid touch of vermilion, and after it is
quite dry, strike a little very wet carmine quickly over it,
you will obtain a much more brilliant red than by mixing
the carmine and vermilion. Similarly, if you lay a dark
colour first, and strike a little blue or white body-colour
lightly over it, you will get a more beautiful grey than by

mixing the colour and the blue or white. In very perfect painting, artifices of this kind are continually used; but I would not have you trust much to them: they are apt to make you think too much of quality of colour. I should like you to depend on little more than the dead colours, simply laid on, only observe always this, that the *less* colour you do the work with, the better it will always be: so that if you had laid a red colour, and you want a purple one above, do not mix the purple on your palette and lay it on so thick as to overpower the red, but take a little thin blue from your palette, and lay it lightly over the red, so as to let the red be seen through, and thus produce the required purple; and if you want a green hue over a blue one, do not lay a quantity of green on the blue, but a *little* yellow, and so on, always bringing the under colour into service as far as you possibly can. If, however, the colour beneath is wholly opposed to the one you have to lay on, as, suppose, if green is to be laid over scarlet, you must either remove the required parts of the under colour daintily first with your knife, or with water; or else, lay solid white over it massively, and leave that to dry, and then glaze the white with the upper colour. This is better, in general, than laying the upper colour itself so thick as to conquer the ground, which, in fact, if it be a transparent colour, you cannot do. Thus, if you have to strike warm boughs and leaves of trees over blue sky, and they are too intricate to have their places left for them in laying the blue, it is better to lay them first in solid white, and then glaze with sienna and ochre, than to mix the sienna and white; though, of course, the process is longer and more troublesome. Nevertheless, if the forms of touches required are very delicate, the after glazing is impossible. You must then mix the warm colour thick at once, and so use it: and this is often necessary for delicate grasses, and such other fine threads of light in foreground work.[38]

[38] ED 146–51, omit.

Optical mixture: divided colour

C. Breaking one colour in small points through or over another.

This is the most important of all processes in good modern[39] oil and water-colour painting, but you need not hope to attain very great skill in it. To do it well is very laborious, and requires such skill and delicacy of hand as can only be acquired by unceasing practice. But you will find advantage in noting the following points:

(*a.*) In distant effects of rich subject, wood, or rippled water, or broken clouds, much may be done by touches or crumbling dashes of rather dry colour, with other colours afterwards put cunningly into the interstices. The more you practise this, when the subject evidently calls for it, the more your eye will enjoy the higher qualities of colour. The process is, in fact, the carrying out of the principle of separate colours to the utmost possible refinement; using atoms of colour in juxtaposition, instead of large spaces. And note, in filling up minute interstices of this kind, that if you want the colour you fill them with to show brightly, it is better to put a rather positive point of it, with a little white left beside or round it in the interstice, than to put a pale tint of the colour over the whole interstice. Yellow or orange will hardly show, if pale, in small spaces; but they show brightly in firm touches, however small, with white beside them.

(*b.*) If a colour is to be darkened by superimposed portions of another, it is, in many cases, better to lay the uppermost colour in rather vigorous small touches, like finely chopped straw, over the under one, than to lay it on as a tint, for two reasons: the first, that the play of the two colours together is pleasant to the eye; the second, that much expression of form may be got by wise administration of the upper dark touches. In distant mountains they

[39] (Ruskin note: "I say *modern,* because Titian's quiet way of blending colours, which is the perfectly right one, is not understood now by any artist. The best colour we reach is got by stippling; but this is not quite right.") ED 151

may be made pines of, or broken crags, or villages, or stones, or whatever you choose; in clouds they may indicate the direction of the rain, the roll and outline of the cloud masses; and in water, the minor waves. All noble effects of dark atmosphere are got in good water-colour drawing by these two expedients, interlacing the colours, or retouching the lower one with fine darker drawing in an upper. Sponging and washing for dark atmospheric effect is barbarous, and mere tyro's work, though it is often useful for passages of delicate atmospheric light.

(c.) When you have time, practise the production of mixed tints by interlaced touches of the pure colours out of which they are formed, and use the process at the parts of your sketches where you wish to get rich and luscious effects.[40]

White and black

I say, first, [make] the white precious. I do not mean merely glittering or brilliant: it is easy to scratch white sea-gulls out of black clouds, and dot clumsy foliage with chalky dew; but when white is well managed, it ought to be strangely delicious,—tender as well as bright,—like inlaid mother of pearl, or white roses washed in milk. The eye ought to seek it for rest, brilliant though it may be; and to feel it as a space of strange, heavenly paleness in the midst of the flushing of the colours. This effect you can only reach by general depth of middle tint, by absolutely refusing to allow any white to exist except where you need it, and by keeping the white itself subdued by grey, except at a few points of chief lustre.

Secondly, you must make the black conspicuous. However small a point of black may be, it ought to catch the eye, otherwise your work is too heavy in the shadow. All the ordinary shadows should be of some *colour*,—never black, nor approaching black, they should be evidently and always of a luminous nature, and the black should look strange among them; never occurring except in a black

[40] ED 151 f

object, or in small points indicative of intense shade in the very centre of masses of shadow. Shadows of absolutely negative grey, however, may be beautifully used with white, or with gold; but still though the black thus, in subdued strength, becomes spacious, it should always be conspicuous; the spectator should notice this grey neutrality with some wonder, and enjoy, all the more intensely on account of it, the gold colour and the white which it relieves. Of all the great colourists Velasquez is the greatest master of the black chords. His black is more precious than most other people's crimson.[41]

Harmonies of colour

As to the choice and harmony of colours in general, if you cannot choose and harmonise them by instinct, you will never do it at all. If you need examples of utterly harsh and horrible colour, you may find plenty given in treatises upon colouring, to illustrate the laws of harmony; and if you want to colour beautifully, colour as best pleases yourself at *quiet times,* not so as to catch the eye, nor look as if it were clever or difficult to colour in that way, but so that the colour may be pleasant to you when you are happy or thoughtful. Look much at the morning and evening sky, and much at simple flowers—dog-roses, wood-hyacinths, violets, poppies, thistles, heather, and such like, —as Nature arranges them in the woods and fields. If ever any scientific person tells you that two colours are "discordant," make a note of the two colours, and put them together whenever you can. I have actually heard people say that blue and green were discordant; the two colours which Nature seems to intend never to be separated, and never to be felt, either of them, in its full beauty without the other!—a peacock's neck, or a blue sky through green leaves, or a blue wave with green lights through it, being precisely the loveliest things, next to clouds at sunrise, in this coloured world of ours.[42]

[41] ED 154
[42] ED 155 f

Colour separate from form

Take care also never to be misled into any idea that colour can help or display *form;* colour always disguises form, and is meant to do so.[43] That is to say, local colour inherent in the object. The gradations of colour in the various shadows belonging to various lights exhibit form, and therefore no one but a colourist can ever draw *forms* perfectly; but all notions of explaining form by superimposed colour, as in architectural mouldings, are absurd. Colour adorns form, but does not interpret it. An apple is prettier because it is striped, but it does not look a bit rounder; and a cheek is prettier because it is flushed, but you would see the form of the cheek bone better if it were not. Colour may, indeed, detach one shape from another, as in grounding a bas-relief, but it always diminishes the appearance of projection, and whether you put blue, purple, red, yellow, or green, for your ground, the bas-relief will be just as clearly or just as imperfectly relieved, as long as the colours are of equal depth. The blue ground will not retire the hundredth part of an inch more than the red one.[44]

It is a favourite dogma among modern writers on colour that "warm colours" (reds and yellows) "approach," or express nearness, and "cold colours" (blue and grey) "retire," or express distance. So far is this from being the case, that no expression of distance in the world is so great as that of the gold and orange in twilight sky. Colours, as such, are ABSOLUTELY inexpressive respecting distance. It is their quality (as depth, delicacy, etc.) which expresses distance, not their tint. A blue bandbox set on the same shelf with a yellow one will not look an inch farther off, but a red or orange cloud, in the upper sky, will always appear to be beyond a blue cloud close to us, as it is in reality. It is quite true that in certain objects, blue is a *sign* of distance; but that is not because blue is a retiring col-

[43] ED 157
[44] ED 157, Ruskin note attached to first sentence this section.

our, but because the mist in the air is blue, and therefore any warm colour which has not strength of light enough to pierce the mist is lost or subdued in its blue: but blue is no more, on this account, a "retiring colour," than brown is a retiring colour, because, when stones are seen through brown water, the deeper they lie the browner they look; or than yellow is a retiring colour, because, when objects are seen through a London fog, the farther off they are the yellower they look. Neither blue, nor yellow, nor red, can have, as such, the smallest power of expressing either nearness or distance: they express them only under the peculiar circumstances which render them at the moment, or in that place, *signs* of nearness or distance. Thus, vivid orange in an orange is a sign of nearness, for if you put the orange a great way off, its colour will not look so bright; but vivid orange in sky is a sign of distance, because you cannot get the colour of orange in a cloud near you.[45]

Colour-light

[I]t is only the white light, the perfect unmodified group of rays, which will bring out local colour perfectly; and if the picture, therefore, is to be complete in its system of colour, that is, if it is to have each of the three primitives in their purity, it *must* have white for its highest light, otherwise the purity of one of them at least will be impossible. And this leads us to notice the second and more frequent quality of light (which is assumed if we make our highest representation of it yellow), the positive hue, namely, which it may itself possess, of course modifying whatever local tints it exhibits, and thereby rendering certain colours necessary, and certain colours impossible. Under the direct yellow light of a descending sun, for instance, pure white and pure blue are both impossible; because the purest whites and blues that nature could produce would be turned in some degree into gold or green by it; and when the sun is within half a degree of the horizon, if the sky be clear, a rose light supersedes the golden one, still

[45] ED 157 f

more overwhelming in its effect on local colour. I have seen the pale fresh green of spring vegetation in the gardens of Venice, on the Lido side, turned pure russet, or between that and crimson, by a vivid sunset of this kind, every particle of green colour being absolutely annihilated. And so under all coloured lights (and there are few, from dawn to twilight, which are not slightly tinted by some accident of atmosphere), there is a change of local colour, which, when in a picture it is so exactly proportioned that we feel at once both what the local colours are in themselves, and what are the colour and strength of the light upon them, gives us truth of tone.[46]

I happened to be sitting by one of our best living modern colourists, watching him at his work, when he said, suddenly, and by mere accident, after we had been talking of other things, "Do you know I have found that there is no *brown* in Nature? What we call brown is always a variety either of orange or purple. It never can be represented by umber, unless altered by contrast."

Let not, however, the reader confuse the use of brown, as an expression of a natural tint, with its use as a means of *getting other tints*. Brown is often an admirable ground, just because it is the only tint which is *not* to be in the finished picture, and because it is the best basis of many silver greys and purples utterly opposite to it in their nature. But there is infinite difference between laying a brown ground as a representation of shadow,—and as a base for light: and also an infinite difference between using brown shadows, associated with coloured lights—always the characteristic of false schools of colour,—and using brown as a warm neutral tint for general study. I shall have to pursue this subject farther hereafter, in noticing how brown is used by great colourists in their studies, not as colour, but as the pleasantest negation of colour, possessing more transparency than black, and having more pleasant and sunlike warmth.[47]

[46] MP I, 270 f
[47] MP III, 301 f, omit.

Preferred ground-colours

But the absolutely best, or centrally, and entirely *right* way of painting is as follows:—

A light ground, white, red, yellow, or gray, not brown, or black. On that an entirely accurate, and firm black outline of the whole picture, in its principal masses. The outline to be exquisitely correct as far as it reaches, but not to include small details; the use of it being to limit the masses of first colour. The ground-colours then to be laid firmly, each on its own proper part of the picture, as inlaid work in a mosaic table, meeting each other truly at the edges: as much of each being laid as will get itself into the state which the artist requires it to be in for his second painting, by the time he comes to it. On this first colour, the second colours and subordinate masses laid in due order, now, of course, necessarily without previous outline, and all small detail reserved to the last, the bracelet being not touched, nor indicated in the least, till the arm is finished.

This is, as far as it can be expressed in a few words, the right, or Venetian way of painting; but it is incapable of absolute definition, for it depends on the scale, the material, and the nature of the object represented, *how much* a great painter will do with his first colour; or how many after processes he will use. Very often the first colour, richly blended and worked into, is also the last; sometimes it wants a glaze only to modify it; sometimes an entirely different colour above it. Turner's storm-blues, for instance, were produced by a black ground with opaque blue, mixed with white, struck over it.[48] The amount of detail given in the first colour will also depend on convenience. For instance, if a jewel *fastens* a fold of dress, a

[48] (Ruskin note: "In cleaning the 'Hero and Leander' [National Gallery, London], these upper glazes were taken off, and only the black ground left. I remember the picture when its distance was of the most exquisite blue. I have no doubt the 'Fire at Sea' [National Gallery, London] has had its distance destroyed in the same manner.") MP V, 245 f

Venetian will lay probably a piece of the jewel colour in its place at the time he draws the fold; but if the jewel *falls upon* the dress, he will paint the folds only in the ground colour, and the jewel afterwards. For in the first case his hand must pause, at any rate, where the fold is fastened; so that he may as well mark the colour of the gem: but he would have to check his hand in the sweep with which he drew the drapery, if he painted a jewel that fell upon it with the first colour. So far, however, as he can possibly use the under colour, he will, in whatever he has to superimpose. There is a pretty little instance of such economical work in the painting of the pearls on the breast of the elder princess, in our best Paul Veronese (Family of Darius). The lowest is about the size of a small hazelnut, and falls on her rose-red dress. Any other but a Venetian would have put a complete piece of white paint over the dress, for the whole pearl, and painted into that the colours of the stone. But Veronese knows beforehand that all the dark side of the pearl will reflect the red of the dress. He will not put white over the red, only to put red over the white again. He leaves the actual dress for the dark side of the pearl, and with two small separate touches, one white, another brown, places its high light and shadow. This he does with perfect care and calm; but in two decisive seconds. There is no dash, nor display, nor hurry, nor error. The exactly right thing is done in the exactly right place, and not one atom of colour, nor moment of time spent vainly. Look close at the two touches,—you wonder what they mean. Retire six feet from the picture —the pearl is there![49]

After many years' study of the various results of fresco and oil painting in Italy, and of body-colour and transparent colour in England, I am now entirely convinced that the greatest things that are to be done in art must be done in dead colour. The habit of depending on varnish or on lucid tints for transparency, makes the painter comparatively lose sight of the nobler translucence which is obtained by breaking various colours amidst each other:

[49] MP V, 246 f

and even when, as by Correggio, exquisite play of hue is joined with exquisite transparency, the delight in the depth almost always leads the painter into mean and false chiaroscuro; it leads him to like dark backgrounds instead of luminous ones, and to enjoy, in general, quality of colour more than grandeur of composition, and confined light rather than open sunshine: so that the really greatest thoughts of the greatest men have always, so far as I remember, been reached in dead colour, and the noblest oil pictures of Tintoret and Veronese are those which are likest frescoes.[50]

Colour seen in water

The more you look down into the water, the better you see objects through it; the more you look along it, the eye being low, the more you see the reflection of objects above it. Hence the colour of a given space of surface in a stream will entirely change while you stand still in the same spot, merely as you stoop or raise your head; and thus the colours with which water is painted are an indication of the position of the spectator, and connected inseparably with the perspective of the shores. The most beautiful of all results that I know in mountain streams is when the water is shallow, and the stones at the bottom are rich reddish-orange and black, and the water is seen at an angle which exactly divides the visible colours between those of the stones and that of the sky, and the sky is of clear, full blue. The resulting purple, obtained by the blending of the blue and the orange-red, broken by the play of innumerable gradations in the stones, is indescribably lovely.

All this seems complicated enough already; but if there be a strong colour in the clear water itself, as of green or blue in the Swiss lakes, all these phenomena are doubly involved; for the darker reflections now become of the colour of the water. The reflection of a black gondola, for instance, at Venice, is never black, but pure dark green. And, farther, the colour of the water itself is of three kinds:

[50] ED 138 f

one, seen on the surface, is a kind of milky bloom; the next is seen where the waves let light through them, at their edges; and the third, shown as a change of colour on the objects seen through the water. Thus, the same wave that makes a white object look of a clear blue, when seen through it, will take a red or violet-coloured bloom on its surface, and will be made pure emerald green by transmitted sunshine through its edges.[51]

"Geneva, 21st April, morning. The sunlight falls from the cypresses of Rousseau's island straight towards the bridge. The shadows of the bridge and of the trees fall on the water in leaden purple, opposed to its general hue of aquamarine green. This green colour is caused by the light being reflected from the bottom, though the bottom is not seen; as is evident by its becoming paler towards the middle of the river, where the water shoals, on which pale part the purple shadow of the small bridge falls most forcibly; which shadow, however, is still only apparent, being the absence of this reflected light, associated with the increased reflective power of the water, which in those spaces reflects blue sky above. A boat swings in the shoal water; its reflection is cast in a transparent pea-green, which is considerably darker than the pale aquamarine of the surface at the spots. Its shadow is detached from it just about half the depth of the reflection, which, therefore, forms a bright green light between the keel of the boat and its shadow; where the shadow cuts the reflection, the reflection is darkest and something like the true colour of the boat; where the shadow falls out of the reflection, it is of a leaden purple, pale. Another boat, nearer, in deeper water, shows no shadow whatsoever, and the reflection is marked by its transparent green, while the surrounding water takes a lightish blue reflection from the sky."[52]

[51] ED 126 f
[52] Inserted by Ruskin in later edition of MP I, 504, from his notebook of 1846.

Superiority of colour

Hence, as I have said elsewhere, the business of a painter is to paint. If he can colour, he is a painter, though he can do nothing else; if he cannot colour, he is no painter, though he may do everything else. But it is, in fact, impossible, if he can colour, but that he should be able to do more; for a faithful study of colour will always give power over form, though the most intense study of form will give no power over colour. The man who can see all the greys, and reds, and purples in a peach, will paint the peach rightly round, and rightly altogether; but the man who has only studied its roundness, may not see its purples and greys, and if he does not, will never get it to look like a peach; so that great power over colour is always a sign of large general art-intellect. Expression of the most subtle kind can be often reached by the slight studies of caricaturists; sometimes elaborated by the toil of the dull, and sometimes by the sentiment of the feeble; but to colour well requires real talent and earnest study, and to colour perfectly is the rarest and most precious power an artist can possess. Every other gift may be erroneously cultivated, but this will guide to all healthy, natural, and forcible truth; the student may be led into folly by philosophers, and into falsehood by purists; but he is always safe, if he holds the hand of a colourist.[53]

[53] MP IV, 72

6

COMPOSITION

In the composition I have chosen for our illustration ["Ehrenbreitstein and the Bridge at Coblentz," a Turner drawing once in Ruskin's collection], . . . reduplication is employed to a singular extent. The tower, or leading feature, is first repeated by the low echo of it to the left; put your finger over this lower tower, and see how the picture is spoiled. Then the spires of Coblentz are all arranged in couples (how they are arranged in reality does not matter; when we are composing a great picture, we must play the towers about till they come right, as fearlessly as if they were chessmen instead of cathedrals). The dual arrangement of these towers would have been too easily seen, were it not for the little one which pretends to make a triad of the last group on the right, but is so faint as hardly to be discernible; it just takes off the attention from the artifice, helped in doing so by the mast at the head of the boat, which, however, has instantly its own duplicate put at the stern. Then there is the large boat near, and its echo beyond it. That echo is divided into two again, and each of those two smaller boats has two figures in it; while two figures are also sitting together on the great rudder that lies half in the water, and half aground. Then, finally, the great mass of Ehrenbreitstein, which appears at first to have no answering form, has almost its *facsimile* in the bank on which the girl is sitting; this bank is as absolutely essential to the completion of the picture as any object in the whole series. All this is done to deepen the effect of repose.[54]

[T]he towers of Ehrenbreitstein . . . appear at first in-

[54] ED 168 f

dependent of each other; but when I give their profile, on a larger scale, the reader may easily perceive that there is a subtle cadence and harmony among them. The reason of this is, that they are all bounded by one grand curve, traced by the dotted line; out of the seven towers, four precisely touch this curve, the others only falling back from it here and there to keep the eye from discovering it too easily.[55]

Now, there are two kinds of harmonies of lines. One in which, moving more or less side by side, they variously, but evidently with consent, retire from or approach each other, intersect or oppose each other; currents of melody in music, for different voices, thus approach and cross, fall and rise, in harmony; so the waves of the sea, as they approach the shore, flow into one another or cross, but with a great unity through all; and so various lines of composition often flow harmoniously through and across each other in a picture. But the most simple and perfect connexion of lines is by radiation; that is, by their all springing from one point, or closing towards it; and this harmony is often, in Nature almost always, united with the other; as the boughs of trees, though they intersect and play amongst each other irregularly, indicate by their general tendency their origin from one root. An essential part of the beauty of all vegetable form is in this radiation; it is seen most simply in a single flower or leaf, as in a convolvulus bell, or chestnut leaf; but more beautifully in the complicated arrangements of the large boughs and sprays. For a leaf is only a flat piece of radiation; but the tree throws its branches on all sides, and even in every profile view of it, which presents a radiation more or less correspondent to that of its leaves, it is more beautiful, because varied by the freedom of the separate branches.[56]

This law of radiation, then, enforcing unison of action in arising from, or proceeding to, some given point, is perhaps, of all principles of composition, the most influential in producing the beauty of groups of form. Other laws make them forcible or interesting, but this generally is chief

[55] ED 177
[56] ED 180 f

in rendering them beautiful. In the arrangement of masses in pictures, it is constantly obeyed by the great composers; but, like the law of principality, with careful concealment of its imperativeness, the point to which the lines of main curvature are directed being very often far away out of the picture. Sometimes, however, a system of curves will be employed definitely to exalt, by their concurrence, the value of some leading object, and then the law becomes traceable enough.

In the instance before us, the principal object being, as we have seen, the tower on the bridge, Turner has determined that his system of curvature should have its origin in the top of this tower. One curve joins the two towers, and is continued by the back of the figure sitting on the bank into the piece of bent timber. This is a limiting curve of great importance, and Turner has drawn a considerable part of it with the edge of the timber very carefully, and then led the eye up to the sitting girl by some white spots and indications of a ledge in the bank; then the passage to the tops of the towers cannot be missed.

The next curve is begun and drawn carefully for half an inch of its course by the rudder; it is then taken up by the basket and the heads of the figures, and leads accurately to the tower angle. The gunwales of both the boats begin the next two curves, which meet in the same point; and all are centralised by the long reflection which continues the vertical lines.

Subordinated to this first system of curves there is another, begun by the small crossing bar of wood inserted in the angle behind the rudder; continued by the bottom of the bank on which the figure sits, interrupted forcibly beyond it, but taken up again by the water-line leading to the bridge foot, and passing on in delicate shadows under the arches, not easily shown in so rude a diagram, towards the other extremity of the bridge. This is a most important curve, indicating that the force and sweep of the river have indeed been in old times under the large arches; while the antiquity of the bridge is told us by a long tongue of land, either of carted rubbish, or washed down by some minor stream, which has interrupted this curve, and is now used as a landing-place for the boats, and for embarkation of merchandise, of which some bales and bundles are laid in a heap, immediately beneath the great tower. A common composer would have put these bales to one side or the other, but Turner knows better; he uses them as a foundation for his tower, adding to its importance precisely as the sculptured base adorns a pillar; and he farther increases the aspect of its height by throwing the reflection of it far down in the nearer water. All the great composers have this same feeling about sustaining their vertical masses: you will constantly find Prout using the artifice most dexterously . . . and Veronese, Titian, and Tintoret continually put their principal figures at bases of pillars. Turner found out their secret very early, the most prominent instance of his composition on this principle being the drawing of Turin from the Superga, in Hakewill's Italy. I chose ["Sheep-Washing, Windsor from Slough," a drawing now in the National Gallery, London] to illustrate foliage drawing, chiefly because, being another instance of precisely the same arrangement, it will serve to convince you of its being intentional. There, the vertical, formed by the larger tree, is continued by the figure of the farmer, and that of one of the smaller trees by his stick. The lines of the interior mass of the bushes radiate, under the law of radiation, from a point behind the farmer's head; but their outline curves are carried on and repeated, under the law of continuity, by the curves of the dog and boy—by the way, note the remarkable instance in these of the use of darkest lines towards the light—all more or less guiding the eye up to the right, in order to bring it finally to the Keep of Windsor, which is the central object of the picture, as the bridge tower is in the Coblentz. The wall on which the boy climbs answers the purpose of contrasting, both in direction and character, with these greater curves; thus corresponding as nearly as possible to the minor tongue of land in the Coblentz. This, however, introduces us to another law, which we must consider separately.

Of course the character of everything is best manifested by Contrast. Rest can only be enjoyed after labour; sound to be heard clearly, must rise out of silence; light is exhibited by darkness, darkness by light; and so on in all things. Now in art every colour has an opponent colour, which, if brought near it, will relieve it more completely than any other; so, also, every form and line may be made more striking to the eye by an opponent form or line near them . . . Thus in the rock of Ehrenbreitstein, the main current of the lines being downwards, in a convex swell, they are suddenly stopped at the lowest tower by a counter series of beds, directed nearly straight across them. This adverse force sets off and relieves the great curvature, but it is reconciled to it by a series of radiating lines below, which at first sympathise with the oblique bar, then gradually get steeper, till they meet and join in the fall of the great curve.[57]

[57] ED 188–92, omit.

7

"FINISH AND INCOMPLETION"

The fact is, that both finish and impetuosity, specific minuteness and large abstraction, may be the signs of passion, or of its reverse; may result from affection or indifference, intellect or dulness. Some men finish from intense love of the beautiful in the smallest parts of what they do; others in pure incapability of comprehending anything but parts; others to show their dexterity with the brush, and prove expenditure of time. Some are impetuous and bold in their handling, from having great thoughts to express which are independent of detail; others because they have bad taste or have been badly taught; others from vanity, and others from indolence. Now both the finish and incompletion are right where they are the signs of passion or of thought, and both are wrong, and I think the finish the more contemptible of the two, when they cease to be so.[58]

And thus it is, that, for the most part, imperfect sketches, engravings, outlines, rude sculptures, and other forms of abstraction, possess a charm which the most finished picture frequently wants. For not only does the finished picture excite the imagination less, but, like nature itself, it *taxes* it more. None of it can be enjoyed till the imagination is brought to bear upon it; and the details of the completed picture are so numerous, that it needs greater strength and willingness in the beholder to follow them all out; the redundance, perhaps, being not too great for the mind of a careful observer, but too great for a casual or careless observer. So that, although the perfection of art will always consist in the utmost *acceptable* completion, yet, as every added idea will increase the difficulty of ap-

[58] MP I, 176 f

prehension, and every added touch advance the dangerous realism which makes the imagination languid, the difference between a noble and ignoble painter is in nothing more sharply defined than in this,—that he first wishes to put into his work as much truth as possible, and yet to keep it looking *un*-real; the second wishes to get through his work lazily, with as little truth as possible, and yet to make it look real; and, so far as they add colour to their abstract sketch, the first realizes for the sake of the colour, and the second colours for the sake of the realization.

And then, lastly, it is another infinite advantage possessed by the picture, that in these various differences from reality it becomes the expression of the power and intelligence of a companionable human soul. In all this choice, arrangement, penetrative sight, and kindly guidance, we recognize a supernatural operation, and perceive, not merely the landscape or incident as in a mirror; but, besides, the presence of what, after all, may perhaps be the most wonderful piece of divine work in the whole matter —the great human spirit through which it is manifested to us. So that, although with respect to many important scenes, it might, as we saw above, be one of the most precious gifts that could be given us to see them with *our own eyes,* yet also in many things it is more desirable to be permitted to see them with the eyes of others; and although, to the small, conceited, and affected painter displaying his narrow knowledge and tiny dexterities, our only word may be, "Stand aside from between that nature and me:" yet to the great imaginative painter—greater a million times in every faculty of soul than we—our word may wisely be, "Come between this nature and me—this nature which is too great and too wonderful for me; temper it for me, interpret it to me; let me see with your eyes, and hear with your ears, and have help and strength from your great spirit."[59]

[59] MP III, 186 f

8

EXHIBITING WORKS OF ART

All large pictures should be on walls lighted from above; because light, from whatever point it enters, must be gradually subdued as it passes further into the room. Now, if it enters at either side of the picture, the gradation of diminishing light to the other side is generally unnatural; but if the light falls from above, its gradation from the sky of the picture down to the foreground is never unnatural, even in a figure piece, and is often a great help to the effect of a landscape. Even interiors, in which lateral light is represented as entering a room, and none as falling from the ceiling, are yet best seen by light from above: for a lateral light contrary to the supposed direction of that in the picture will greatly neutralize its effect; and a lateral light in the same direction will exaggerate it. The artist's real intention can only be seen fairly by light from above.

Every picture should be hung so as to admit of its horizon being brought on a level with the eye of the spectator, without difficulty, or stooping. When pictures are small, one line may be disposed so as to be seen by a sitting spectator, and one to be seen standing, but more than two lines should never be admitted. A *model* gallery should have one line only; and some interval between each picture, to prevent the interference of the colours of one piece with those of the rest—a most serious source of deterioration of effect.

If pictures were placed thus, only in one low line, the gorgeousness of large rooms and galleries would be lost, and it would be useless to endeavour to obtain any imposing architectural effect by the arrangement or extent of the rooms. But the far more important objects might be attained, of making them perfectly comfortable, securing good light in the darkest days, and ventilation without draughts in the warmest and coldest.

And if hope of architectural effect were thus surrendered, there would be a great advantage in giving large upright pictures a room to themselves. For as the perspective horizon of such pictures cannot always be brought low enough even for a standing spectator, and as, whether it can or not, the upper parts of great designs are often more interesting than the lower, the floor at the further extremity of the room might be raised by the number of steps necessary to give full command of the composition; and a narrow lateral gallery carried from this elevated daïs, to its sides. Such a gallery of close access to the flanks of pictures like Titian's Assumption or Peter Martyr would be of the greatest service to artists.

It is of the highest importance that the works of each master should be kept together. No great master can be thoroughly enjoyed but by getting into his humour, and remaining long enough under his influence to understand his whole mode and cast of thought. The contrast of works by different masters never brings out their merits; but their defects: the spectator's effort (if he is kind enough to make any) to throw his mind into their various tempers, materially increases his fatigue—and the fatigue of examining a series of pictures carefully is always great, even under the most favourable circumstances. The advantage thus gained in peace of mind and power of understanding, by the assemblage of the works of each master, is connected with another, hardly less important, in the light thrown on the painter's own progress of intellect and methods of study.

Whatever sketches and studies for any picture exist by its master's hand, should be collected at any sacrifice; a little reciprocal courtesy among Governments might easily bring this about: such studies should be shown under glass (as in the rooms appropriated to drawings in the Louvre), in the centre of the room in which the picture itself is placed. The existing engravings from it, whatever their merit or demerit (it is often a great point in art education to demonstrate the *last*), should be collected and exhibited in a similar manner.

As the condition that the pictures should be placed at the level of sight would do away with all objections to glass as an impediment of vision (who is there who cannot see the Perugino in the National Gallery?), *all* pictures should be put under glass, firmly secured and made airtight behind. The glass is an important protection, not only from dust, but from chance injury. All drawings should be glazed, simply framed in wood, and enclosed in sliding grooves in portable cases. For the more beautiful ones, golden frames should be provided at central tables; turning on a swivel, with grooves in the thickness of them, into which the wooden frame should slide in an instant, and show the drawing framed in gold. The department for the drawings should be, of course, separate, and like a beautiful and spacious library, with its cases of drawings ranged on the walls (as those of the coins are in the Coin-room of the British Museum), and convenient recesses, with pleasant lateral light, for the visitors to take each his case of drawings into. Lateral light is best for drawings, because the variation in intensity is small, and of little consequence to a small work; but the shadow of the head is inconvenient in looking close at them, when the light falls from above.

I think the collections of Natural History should be kept separate from those of Art. Books, manuscripts, coins, sculpture, pottery, metal-work, engravings, drawings, and pictures, should be in one building; and minerals, fossils, shells, and stuffed animals (with a perfect library of works on natural history), in another, connected, as at Paris, with the Zoological Gardens.[60]

[60] Bequest 176–81, omit. The separation of natural history from art was accomplished in 1880–83 when the scientific exhibits were moved from the British Museum to South Kensington.

PART II

ARCHITECTURE

1

PRINCIPLES AND PROHIBITIONS

Architecture is the art which so disposes and adorns the edifices raised by man, for whatsoever uses, that the sight of them may contribute to his mental health, power, and pleasure.

It is very necessary, in the outset of all inquiry, to distinguish carefully between Architecture and Building.

To build,—literally, to confirm,—is by common understanding to put together and adjust the several pieces of any edifice or receptacle of a considerable size. Thus we have church building, house building, ship building, and coach building. That one edifice stands, another floats, and another is suspended on iron springs, makes no difference in the nature of the art, if so it may be called, of building or edification. The persons who profess that art, are severally builders, ecclesiastical, naval, or of whatever other name their work may justify: but building does not become architecture merely by the stability of what it erects; and it is no more architecture which raises a church, or which fits it to receive and contain with comfort a required number of persons occupied in certain religious offices, than it is architecture which makes a carriage commodious, or a ship swift. I do not, of course, mean that the word is not often, or even may not be legitimately, applied in such a sense (as we speak of naval architecture); but in that sense architecture ceases to be one of the fine arts, and it is therefore better not to run the risk, by loose nomenclature, of the confusion which would arise, and has often arisen, from extending principles which belong altogether to building, into the sphere of architecture proper.

Let us, therefore, at once confine the name to that art which, taking up and admitting, as conditions of its working, the necessities and common uses of the building, impresses on its form certain characters venerable or beautiful, but otherwise unnecessary.[1]

Architecture as sacrifice

It has been said—it ought always to be said, for it is true,—that a better and more honourable offering is made to our Master in ministry to the poor, in extending the knowledge of His name, in the practice of the virtues by which that name is hallowed, than in material presents to His temple. Assuredly it is so: woe to all who think that any other kind or manner of offering may in any wise take the place of these! Do the people need place to pray, and calls to hear His word? Then it is no time for smoothing pillars or carving pulpits; let us have enough first of walls and roofs. Do the people need teaching from house to house, and bread from day to day? Then they are deacons and ministers we want, not architects. I insist on this, I plead for this; but let us examine ourselves, and see if this be indeed the reason for our backwardness in the lesser work. The question is not between God's house and His poor: it is not between God's house and His Gospel. It is between God's house and ours. Have we no tesselated colours on our floors? no frescoed fancies on our roofs? no niched statuary in our corridors? no gilded furniture in our chambers? no costly stones in our cabinets? Has even the tithe of these been offered? They are, or they ought to be, the signs that enough has been devoted to the great purposes of human stewardship, and that there remains to us what we can spend in luxury; but there is a greater and prouder luxury than this selfish one—that of bringing a portion of such things as these into sacred service, and presenting them for a memorial that our pleasure as well as our toil has been hallowed by the remembrance of Him who gave both the strength and the reward. And until this

[1] Lamps 27 f

has been done, I do not see how such possessions can be retained in happiness. I do not understand the feeling which would arch our own gates and pave our own thresholds, and leave the church with its narrow door and footworn sill . . .[2]

Imitation of nature

It will be thought that I have somewhat rashly limited the elements of architectural beauty to imitative forms. I do not mean to assert that every happy arrangement of line is directly suggested by a natural object; but that all beautiful lines are adaptations of those which are commonest in the external creation; that, in proportion to the richness of their association, the resemblance to natural work, as a type and help, must be more closely attempted, and more clearly seen; and that beyond a certain point, and that a very low one, man cannot advance in the invention of beauty, without directly imitating natural form. Thus, in the Doric temple the triglyph and cornice are unimitative; or imitative only of artificial cuttings of wood. No one would call these members beautiful. Their influence over us is in their severity and simplicity. The fluting of the column, which I doubt not was the Greek symbol of the bark of the tree, was imitative in its origin, and feebly resembled many canaliculated organic structures. Beauty is instantly felt in it, but of a low order. The decoration proper was sought in the true forms of organic life, and those chiefly human. Again: the Doric capital was unimitative; but all the beauty it had was dependent on the precision of its ovolo, a natural curve of the most frequent occurrence. The Ionic capital (to my mind, as an architectural invention, exceedingly base,) nevertheless depended for all the beauty that it had on its adoption of a spiral line, perhaps the commonest of all that characterise the inferior orders of animal organism and habitation. Farther progress could not be made without a direct imitation of the acanthus leaf.

[2] Lamps 37 f

Again: the Romanesque arch is beautiful as an abstract line. Its type is always before us in that of the apparent vault of heaven, and horizon of the earth. The cylindrical pillar is always beautiful, for God has so moulded the stem of every tree that is pleasant to the eyes. The pointed arch is beautiful; it is the termination of every leaf that shakes in summer wind, and its most fortunate associations are directly borrowed from the trefoiled grass of the field, or from the stars of its flowers. Farther than this, man's invention could not reach without frank imitation. His next step was to gather the flowers themselves, and wreathe them in his capitals.[3]

Honesty in materials and structure

Architectural Deceits are broadly to be considered under three heads:—

1st. The suggestion of a mode of structure or support, other than the true one; as in pendants of late Gothic roofs.

2nd. The painting of surfaces to represent some other material than that of which they actually consist (as in the marbling of wood), or the deceptive representation of sculptured ornament upon them.

3rd. The use of cast or machine-made ornaments of any kind.

Now, it may be broadly stated, that architecture will be noble exactly in the degree in which all these false expedients are avoided. Nevertheless, there are certain degrees of them, which, owing to their frequent usage, or to other causes, have so far lost the nature of deceit as to be admissible; as, for instance, gilding, which is in architecture no deceit, because it is therein not understood for gold; while in jewellery it is a deceit, because it is so understood, and therefore altogether to be reprehended. So that there arise, in the application of the strict rules of right, many exceptions and niceties of conscience; which let us as briefly as possible examine.

1st. Structural Deceits. I have limited these to the de-

[3] Lamps 139 f

termined and purposed suggestion of a mode of support other than the true one. The architect is not *bound* to exhibit structure; nor are we to complain of him for concealing it, any more than we should regret that the outer surfaces of the human frame conceal much of its anatomy; nevertheless, that building will generally be the noblest, which to an intelligent eye discovers the great secrets of its structure, as an animal form does, although from a careless observer they may be concealed. In the vaulting of a Gothic roof it is no deceit to throw the strength into the ribs of it, and make the intermediate vault a mere shell. Such a structure would be presumed by an intelligent observer, the first time he saw such a roof; and the beauty of its traceries would be enhanced to him if they confessed and followed the lines of its main strength. If, however, the intermediate shell were made of wood instead of stone, and whitewashed to look like the rest,—this would, of course, be direct deceit, and altogether unpardonable.

There is, however, a certain deception necessarily occurring in Gothic architecture, which relates, not to the points, but to the manner, of support. The resemblance in its shafts and ribs to the external relations of stems and branches, which has been the ground of so much foolish speculation, necessarily induces in the mind of the spectator a sense or belief of a correspondent internal structure; that is to say, of a fibrous and continuous strength from the root into the limbs, and an elasticity communicated *upwards*, sufficient for the support of the ramified portions. The idea of the real conditions, of a great weight of ceiling thrown upon certain narrow, jointed lines, which have a tendency partly to be crushed, and partly to separate and be pushed outwards, is with difficulty received; and the more so when the pillars would be, if unassisted, too slight for the weight, and are supported by external flying buttresses, as in the apse of Beauvais, and other such achievements of the bolder Gothic. Now, there is a nice question of conscience in this, which we shall hardly settle but by considering that, when the mind is informed beyond the possibility of mistake as to the true nature of things, the affecting it with a contrary impression, however distinct, is no dishonesty, but, on the contrary, a legitimate appeal to the imagination. For instance, the greater part of the happiness which we have in contemplating clouds, results from the impression of their having massive, luminous, warm, and mountain-like surfaces; and our delight in the sky frequently depends upon our considering it as a blue vault. But, if we choose, we may know the contrary, in both instances; and easily ascertain the cloud to be a damp fog, or a drift of snow-flakes; and the sky to be a lightless abyss. There is, therefore, no dishonesty, while there is much delight, in the irresistibly contrary impression. In the same way, so long as we see the stones and joints, and are not deceived as to the points of support in any piece of architecture, we may rather praise than regret the dexterous artifices which compel us to feel as if there were fibre in its shafts and life in its branches. Nor is even the concealment of the support of the external buttress reprehensible, so long as the pillars are not sensibly inadequate to their duty. For the weight of a roof is a circumstance of which the spectator generally has no idea, and the provisions for it, consequently, circumstances whose necessity or adaptation he could not understand. It is no deceit, therefore, when the weight to be borne is necessarily unknown, to conceal also the means of bearing it, leaving only to be perceived so much of the support as is indeed adequate to the weight supposed. For the shafts do, indeed, bear as much as they are ever imagined to bear, and the system of added support is no more, as a matter of conscience, to be exhibited, than, in the human or any other form, mechanical provisions for those functions which are themselves unperceived.

With deceptive concealments of structure are to be classed, though still more blameable, deceptive assumptions of it,—the introduction of members which should have, or profess to have, a duty, and have none. The most flagrant instance of this barbarism that I remember, (though it prevails partially in all the spires of the Netherlands,) is the lantern of St. Ouen at Rouen, where the pierced buttress, having an ogee curve, looks about as much calculated to bear a thrust as a switch of willow; and the pinnacles, huge and richly decorated, have evidently no work to do whatsoever, but stand round the central tower, like four idle servants, as they are—heraldic supporters, that central tower being merely a hollow crown, which needs no more buttressing than a basket does. In fact, I do not know any thing more strange or unwise than the praise lavished upon this lantern; it is one of the basest pieces of Gothic in Europe; its flamboyant traceries being of the last and most degraded forms: and its entire plan and decoration resembling, and deserving little more credit than, the burnt sugar ornaments of elaborate confectionery. There are hardly any of the magnificent and serene methods of construction in the early Gothic, which have not, in the course of time, been gradually thinned and pared away into these skeletons, which sometimes indeed, when their lines truly follow the structure of the original masses, have an interest like that of the fibrous framework of leaves from which the substance has been dissolved, but which are usually distorted as well as emaciated, and remain but the sickly phantoms and mockeries of things that were . . .[4]

2nd. Surface Deceits. These may be generally defined as the inducing the supposition of some form of material which does not actually exist; as commonly in the painting of wood to represent marble, or in the painting of ornaments in deceptive relief, etc. But we must be careful to observe, that the evil of them consists always in definitely attempted *deception,* and that it is a matter of some nicety to mark the point where deception begins or ends.

Touching the false representation of material, the question is infinitely more simple, and the law more sweeping; all such imitations are utterly base and inadmissible. It is melancholy to think of the time and expense lost in marbling the shop fronts of London alone, and of the waste of our resources in absolute vanities, in things about which no mortal cares, by which no eye is ever arrested, unless painfully, and which do not add one whit to comfort, or cleanliness, or even to that great object of commercial art—conspicuousness. But in architecture of a higher rank, how

[4] Lamps 60–65, omit.

much more is it to be condemned! I have made it a rule
in the present work not to blame specifically; but I may,
perhaps, be permitted, while I express my sincere admiration of the very noble entrance and general architecture of
the British Museum, to express also my regret that the
noble granite foundation of the staircase should be mocked
at its landing by an imitation, the more blameable because
tolerably successful.[5] The only effect of it is to cast a sus-
picion upon the true stones below, and upon every bit of
granite afterwards encountered. But even this, however
derogatory to the noble architecture around it, is less painful than the want of feeling with which, in our cheap modern churches, we suffer the wall decorator to erect about
the altar frameworks and pediments daubed with mottled
colour, and to dye in the same fashion such skeletons or
caricatures of columns as may emerge above the pews: this
is not merely bad taste; it is no unimportant or excusable
error which brings even these shadows of vanity and falsehood into the house of prayer. The first condition which
just feeling requires in church furniture is, that it should
be simple and unaffected, not fictitious nor tawdry. It may
not be in our power to make it beautiful, but let it at least
be pure; and if we cannot permit much to the architect,
do not let us permit anything to the upholsterer; if we keep
to solid stone and solid wood, whitewashed, if we like, for
cleanliness' sake, (for whitewash has so often been used
as the dress of noble things that it has thence received a
kind of nobility itself,) it must be a bad design indeed,
which is grossly offensive. I recollect no instance of a want
of sacred character, or of any marked and painful ugliness,
in the simplest or the most awkwardly built village church,
where stone and wood were roughly and nakedly used, and
the windows latticed with white glass. But the smoothly
stuccoed walls, the flat roofs with ventilator ornaments, the
barred windows with jaundiced borders and dead ground
square panes, the gilded or bronzed wood, the painted iron,
the wretched upholstery of curtains and cushions, and pew

[5] (The reference is to the imitation granite blocks on which
rested Egyptian lions.) Lamps 63–76, omit.

heads, and altar railings, and Birmingham metal candle-sticks, and, above all, the green and yellow sickness of the false marble—disguises all, observe; falsehoods all—who are they who like these things? who defend them? who do them? I have never spoken to any one who *did* like them, though to many who thought them matters of no consequence.[6]

The last form of fallacy which it will be remembered we had to deprecate, was the substitution of cast or machine work for that of the hand, generally expressible as Operative Deceit.

There are two reasons, both weighty, against this practice: one, that all cast and machine work is bad, as work; the other, that it is dishonest. Of its badness I shall speak in another place, that being evidently no efficient reason against its use when other cannot be had. Its dishonesty, however, which, to my mind, is of the grossest kind, is, I think, a sufficient reason to determine absolute and unconditional rejection of it.[7]

Massing

Of composition and invention much has been written, it seems to me vainly, for men cannot be taught to compose or to invent; of these, the highest elements of Power in architecture, I do not, therefore, speak; nor, here, of that peculiar restraint in the imitation of natural forms, which constitutes the dignity of even the most luxuriant work of the great periods. [T]he relative majesty of buildings depends more on the weight and vigour of their masses, than on any other attribute of their design: mass of everything, of bulk, of light, of darkness, of colour, not mere sum of any of these, but breadth of them; not broken light, nor scattered darkness, nor divided weight, but solid stone, broad sunshine, starless shade.[8]

While, therefore, it is not to be supposed that mere size will ennoble a mean design, yet every increase of magni-

[6] Lamps 76 f
[7] Lamps 81. See here later section "Iron and Glass."
[8] Lamps 134

tude will bestow upon it a certain degree of nobleness: so that it is well to determine at first, whether the building is to be markedly beautiful, or markedly sublime; and if the latter, not to be withheld by respect to smaller parts from reaching largeness of scale; provided only, that it be evidently in the architect's power to reach at least that degree of magnitude which is the lowest at which sublimity begins, rudely definable as that which will make a living figure look less than life beside it. It is the misfortune of most of our modern buildings that we would fain have an universal excellence in them; and so part of the funds must go in painting, part in gilding, part in fitting up, part in painted windows, part in small steeples, part in ornaments here and there; and neither the windows, nor the steeple, nor the ornaments, are worth their materials. For there is a crust about the impressible part of men's minds, which must be pierced through before they can be touched to the quick; and though we may prick at it and scratch it in a thousand separate places, we might as well have let it alone if we do not come through somewhere with a deep thrust: and if we can give such a thrust anywhere, there is no need of another; it need not be even so "wide as a church door," so that it be *enough.* And mere weight will do this; it is a clumsy way of doing it, but an effectual one, too; and the apathy which cannot be pierced through by a small steeple, nor shone through by a small window, can be broken through in a moment by the mere weight of a great wall. Let, therefore, the architect who has not large resources, choose his point of attack first, and, if he chooses size, let him abandon decoration; for, unless they are concentrated, and numerous enough to make their concentration conspicuous, all his ornaments together will not be worth one huge stone. And the choice must be a decided one, without compromise. It must be no question whether his capitals would not look better with a little carving—let him leave them huge as blocks; or whether his arches should not have richer architraves—let him throw them a foot higher, if he can; a yard more across the nave will be worth more to him than a tesselated pavement; and another fathom of outer wall, than an army of pinnacles. The limitation of size must be only in the uses of the building, or in the ground at his disposal.

It has often been observed that a building, in order to show its magnitude, must be seen all at once;—it would, perhaps, be better to say, must be bounded as much as possible by continuous lines, and that its extreme points should be seen all at once; or we may state, in simpler terms still, that it must have one visible bounding line from top to bottom, and from end to end. This bounding line from top to bottom may either be inclined inwards, and the mass therefore, pyramidical; or vertical, and the mass form one grand cliff; or inclined outwards, as in the advancing fronts of old houses, and, in a sort, in the Greek temple, and in all buildings with heavy cornices or heads. Now, in all these cases, if the bounding line be violently broken; if the cornice project, or the upper portion of the pyramid recede, too violently, majesty will be lost; not because the building cannot be seen all at once,—for in the case of a heavy cornice no part of it is necessarily concealed —but because the continuity of its terminal line is broken, and the *length of that line,* therefore, cannot be estimated.

What is needful in the setting forth of magnitude in height, is right also in the marking it in area—let it be gathered well together. It is especially to be noted with respect to the Palazzo Vecchio and other mighty buildings of its order, how mistakenly it has been stated that dimension, in order to become impressive, should be expanded either in height or length, but not equally: whereas, rather it will be found that those buildings seem on the whole the vastest which have been gathered up into a mighty square, and which look as if they had been measured by the angel's rod, "the length, and the breadth, and the height of it are equal;"[9] and herein something is to be taken notice of, which I believe not to be sufficiently, if at all, considered among our architects.

Of the many broad divisions under which architecture may be considered, none appear to me more significant than that into buildings, whose interest is in their walls,

[9] (Revelation xxi: 16). Lamps 104–08, omit.

and those whose interest is in the lines dividing their walls. In the Greek temple the wall is as nothing; the entire interest is in the detached columns and the frieze they bear; in French Flamboyant, and in our detestable Perpendicular, the object is to get rid of the wall surface, and keep the eye altogether on tracery of line: in Romanesque work and Egyptian, the wall is a confessed and honoured member, and the light is often allowed to fall on large areas of it, variously decorated. Now, both these principles are admitted by Nature, the one in her woods and thickets, the other in her plains, and cliffs, and waters; but the latter is pre-eminently the principle of power, and, in some sense, of beauty also. For, whatever infinity of fair form there may be in the maze of the forest, there is a fairer, as I think, in the surface of the quiet lake; and I hardly know that association of shaft or tracery, for which I would exchange the warm sleep of sunshine on some smooth, broad, human-like front of marble. Nevertheless, if breadth is to be beautiful, its substance must in some sort be beautiful; and we must not hastily condemn the exclusive resting of the northern architects in divided lines, until at least we have remembered the difference between a blank surface of Caen stone, and one mixed from Genoa and Carrara, of serpentine with snow: but as regards abstract power and awfulness, there is no question; without breadth of surface it is in vain to seek them, and it matters little, so that the surface be wide, bold, and unbroken, whether it be of brick or of jasper; the light of heaven upon it, and the weight of earth in it, are all we need: for it is singular how forgetful the mind may become both of material and workmanship, if only it have space enough over which to range, and to remind it, however feebly, of the joy that it has in contemplating the flatness and sweep of great plains and broad seas. And it is a noble thing for men to do this with their cut stone or moulded clay, and to make the face of a wall look infinite, and its edge against the sky like an horizon: or even if less than this be reached, it is still delightful to mark the play of passing light on its broad surface, and to see by how many artifices and gradations of tinting and shadow, time and storm will set their wild signatures upon it; and how in the rising or declining of the day the unbroken twilight rests long and luridly on its high lineless forehead, and fades away untraceably down its tiers of confused and countless stone.

This, then, being, as I think, one of the peculiar elements of sublime architecture, it may be easily seen how necessarily consequent upon the love of it will be the choice of a form approaching to the square for the main outline.

For, in whatever direction the building is contracted, in that direction the eye will be drawn to its terminal lines; and the sense of surface will only be at its fullest when those lines are removed, in every direction, as far as possible. Thus the square and circle are pre-eminently the areas of power among those bounded by purely straight or curved lines; and these, with their relative solids, the cube and sphere, and relative solids of progression, (as in the investigation of the laws of proportion I shall call those masses which are generated by the progression of an area of given form along a line in a given direction,) the square and cylindrical column, are the elements of utmost power in all architectural arrangements. On the other hand, grace and perfect proportion require an elongation in some one direction: and a sense of power may be communicated to this form of magnitude by a continuous series of any marked features, such as the eye may be unable to number; while yet we feel, from their boldness, decision, and simplicity, that it is indeed their multitude which has embarrassed us, not any confusion or indistinctness of form. This expedient of continued series forms the sublimity of arcades and aisles, of all ranges of columns, and, on a smaller scale, of those Greek mouldings, of which, repeated as they now are in all the meanest and most familiar forms of our furniture, it is impossible altogether to weary. Now, it is evident that the architect has choice of two types of form, each properly associated with its own kind of interest or decoration: the square, or greatest area, to be chosen especially when the *surface* is to be the subject of thought; and the elongated area, when the *divisions* of the surface are to be subjects of thought. Both these orders of form, as I think nearly every other source of power and beauty,

are marvellously united in that building which I fear to
weary the reader by bringing forward too frequently, as a
model of all perfection—the Doge's palace at Venice: its
general arrangement, a hollow square; its principal façade,
an oblong, elongated to the eye by a range of thirty-four
small arches, and thirty-five columns, while it is separated
by a richly canopied window in the centre, into two massive divisions, whose height and length are nearly as four
to five; the arcades which give it length being confined to
the lower storeys, and the upper, between its broad windows, left a mighty surface of smooth marble, chequered
with blocks of alternate rose-colour and white. It would be
impossible, I believe, to invent a more magnificent arrangement of all that is in building most dignified and most fair.

So then, that masonry will be generally the most magnificent which, without the use of materials systematically
small or large, accommodates itself, naturally and frankly,
to the conditions and structure of its work, and displays
alike its power of dealing with the vastest masses, and of
accomplishing its purpose with the smallest, sometimes
heaping rock upon rock with Titanic commandment, and
anon binding the dusty remnants and edgy splinters into
springing vaults and swelling domes. And if the nobility of
this confessed and natural masonry were more commonly
felt, we should not lose the dignity of it by smoothing surfaces and fitting joints. The sums which we waste in chiselling and polishing stones which would have been better
left as they came from the quarry, would often raise a
building a storey higher.

Now, it does not seem to me sufficiently recollected, that
a wall surface is to an architect simply what a white canvas
is to a painter, with this only difference, that the wall has
already a sublimity in its height, substance, and other characters already considered, on which it is more dangerous
to break than to touch with shade the canvas surface. And,
for my own part, I think a smooth, broad, freshly laid surface of gesso a fairer thing than most pictures I see painted
on it; much more, a noble surface of stone than most architectural features which it is caused to assume. But how-

ever this may be, the canvas and wall are supposed to be given, and it is our craft to divide them.[10]

Light

. . . I do not believe that ever any building was truly great, unless it had mighty masses, vigorous and deep, of shadow mingled with its surface. And among the first habits that a young architect should learn, is that of thinking in shadow, not looking at a design in its miserable liny skeleton; but conceiving it as it will be when the dawn lights it, and the dusk leaves it; when its stones will be hot, and its crannies cool; when the lizards will bask on the one, and the birds build in the other. Let him design with the sense of cold and heat upon him; let him cut out the shadows, as men dig wells in unwatered plains; and lead along the lights, as a founder does his hot metal; let him keep the full command of both, and see that he knows how they fall, and where they fade. His paper lines and proportions are of no value: all that he has to do must be done by spaces of light and darkness; and his business is to see that the one is broad and bold enough not to be swallowed up by twilight, and the other deep enough not to be dried like a shallow pool by a noon-day sun.

Painters are in the habit of speaking loosely of masses of light and shade, meaning thereby any large spaces of either. Nevertheless, it is convenient sometimes to restrict the term "mass" to the portions to which proper form belongs, and to call the field on which such forms are traced, interval. Thus, in foliage with projecting boughs or stems, we have masses of light, with intervals of shade; and, in light skies with dark clouds upon them, masses of shade, with intervals of light.

This distinction is, in architecture, still more necessary; for there are two marked styles dependent upon it: one in which the forms are drawn with light, upon darkness, as in Greek sculpture and pillars; the other in which they are drawn with darkness upon light, as in early Gothic folia-

[10] Lamps 108–15, omit.

tion. Now, it is not in the designer's power determinately
to vary degrees and places of darkness, but it is altogether
in his power to vary in determined directions his degrees
of light. Hence the use of the dark mass characterises, generally, a trenchant style of design, in which the darks and
lights are both flat, and terminated by sharp edges; while
the use of the light mass is in the same way associated
with a softened and full manner of design, in which the
darks are much warmed by reflected lights, and the lights
are rounded and melt into them. The term applied by Milton to Doric bas-relief—"bossy," is, as is generally the case
with Milton's epithets, the most comprehensive and expressive of this manner, which the English language contains;
while the term which specifically describes the chief member of early Gothic decoration, feuille, foil or leaf, is equally
significative of a flat space of shade.[11]

[11] (The reference is to Milton's *Paradise Lost*, i, 716.) Lamps
117–19, omit.

2

"THE NATURE OF GOTHIC"[12]

I believe, then, that the characteristic or moral elements of Gothic are the following, placed in the order of their importance:

1. Savageness.
2. Changefulness.
3. Naturalism.
4. Grotesqueness.
5. Rigidity.
6. Redundance.

These characters are here expressed as belonging to the building; as belonging to the builder, they would be expressed thus:—1. Savageness or Rudeness. 2. Love of Change. 3. Love of Nature. 4. Disturbed Imagination. 5. Obstinacy. 6. Generosity. And I repeat, that the withdrawal of any one, or any two, will not at once destroy the Gothic character of a building, but the removal of a majority of them will. I shall proceed to examine them in their order.

(1.) SAVAGENESS. I am not sure when the word "Gothic" was first generically applied to the architecture of the North; but I presume that, whatever the date of its original usage, it was intended to imply reproach, and express the barbaric character of the nations among whom that archi-

[12] This section is an abridgment of the famous portion of *The Stones of Venice*, volume II, 1853. To preserve the unity of the condensation, I have not supplied any subheadings. The footnotes (until the next section when the usual procedure will be reinstated) will not cite the pages of the Library Edition since all excerpts have been kept in their original order, SV II, 184–250.

tecture arose. It is true, greatly and deeply true, that the architecture of the North is rude and wild; but it is not true, that, for this reason, we are to condemn it, or despise. Far otherwise: I believe it is in this very character that it deserves our profoundest reverence.

If, however, the savageness of Gothic architecture, merely as an expression of its origin among Northern nations, may be considered, in some sort, a noble character, it possesses a higher nobility still, when considered as an index, not of climate, but of religious principle.

In the 13th and 14th paragraphs of Chapter XXI. of the first volume of this work, it was noticed that the systems of architectural ornament, properly so called, might be divided into three:—1. Servile ornament, in which the execution or power of the inferior workman is entirely subjected to the intellect of the higher;—2. Constitutional ornament, in which the executive inferior power is, to a certain point, emancipated and independent, having a will of its own, yet confessing its inferiority and rendering obedience to higher powers;—and 3. Revolutionary ornament, in which no executive inferiority is admitted at all. I must here explain the nature of these divisions at somewhat greater length.

Of Servile ornament, the principal schools are the Greek, Ninevite, and Egyptian; but their servility is of different kinds. The Greek master-workman was far advanced in knowledge and power above the Assyrian or Egyptian. Neither he nor those for whom he worked could endure the appearance of imperfection in anything; and, therefore, what ornament he appointed to be done by those beneath him was composed of mere geometrical forms,—balls, ridges, and perfectly symmetrical foliage,—which could be executed with absolute precision by line and rule, and were as perfect in their way, when completed, as his own figure sculpture.

But the modern English mind has this much in common with that of the Greek, that it intensely desires, in all things, the utmost completion or perfection compatible with their nature. This is a noble character in the abstract, but becomes ignoble when it causes us to forget the relative dignities of that nature itself, and to prefer the perfectness of the lower nature to the imperfection of the higher; not considering that as, judged by such a rule, all the brute animals would be preferable to man, because more perfect in their functions and kind, and yet are always held inferior to him, so also in the works of man, those which are more perfect in their kind are always inferior to those which are, in their nature, liable to more faults and shortcomings. For the finer the nature, the more flaws it will show through the clearness of it; and it is a law of this universe, that the best things shall be seldomest seen in their best form. The wild grass grows well and strongly, one year with another; but the wheat is, according to the greater nobleness of its nature, liable to the bitterer blight.

Now, in the make and nature of every man, however rude or simple, whom we employ in manual labour, there are some powers for better things; some tardy imagination, torpid capacity of emotion, tottering steps of thought, there are, even at the worst; and in most cases it is all our own fault that they *are* tardy or torpid. But they cannot be strengthened, unless we are content to take them in their feebleness, and unless we prize and honour them in their imperfection above the best and most perfect manual skill. And this is what we have to do with all our labourers; to look for the *thoughtful* part of them, and get that out of them, whatever we lose for it, whatever faults and errors we are obliged to take with it. For the best that is in them cannot manifest itself, but in company with much error. Understand this clearly: You can teach a man to draw a straight line, and to cut one; to strike a curved line, and to carve it; and to copy and carve any number of given lines or forms, with admirable speed and perfect precision; and you find his work perfect of its kind: but if you ask him to think about any of those forms, to consider if he cannot find any better in his own head, he stops; his execution becomes hesitating; he thinks, and ten to one he thinks wrong; ten to one he makes a mistake in the first touch he gives to his work as a thinking being. But you have made a man of him for all that. He was only a machine before, an animated tool.

And observe, you are put to stern choice in this matter. You must either make a tool of the creature, or a man of him. You cannot make both. Men were not intended to work with the accuracy of tools, to be precise and perfect in all their actions. If you will have that precision out of them, and make their fingers measure degrees like cog-wheels, and their arms strike curves like compasses, you must unhumanize them. All the energy of their spirits must be given to make cogs and compasses of themselves. All their attention and strength must go to the accomplishment of the mean act. The eye of the soul must be bent upon the finger-point, and the soul's force must fill all the invisible nerves that guide it, ten hours a day, that it may not err from its steely precision, and so soul and sight be worn away, and the whole human being be lost at last—a heap of sawdust, so far as its intellectual work in this world is concerned: saved only by its Heart, which cannot go into the form of cogs and compasses, but expands, after the ten hours are over, into fireside humanity. On the other hand, if you will make a man of the working creature, you cannot make a tool. Let him but begin to imagine, to think, to try to do anything worth doing; and the engine-turned precision is lost at once. Out come all his roughness, all his dulness, all his incapability; shame upon shame, failure upon failure, pause after pause: but out comes the whole majesty of him also; and we know the height of it only when we see the clouds settling upon him. And, whether the clouds be bright or dark, there will be transfiguration behind and within them.

And now, reader, look round this English room of yours, about which you have been proud so often, because the work of it was so good and strong, and the ornaments of it so finished. Examine again all those accurate mouldings, and perfect polishings, and unerring adjustments of the seasoned wood and tempered steel. Many a time you have exulted over them, and thought how great England was, because her slightest work was done so thoroughly. Alas! if read rightly, these perfectnesses are signs of a slavery in our England a thousand times more bitter and more degrading than that of the scourged African, or helot Greek.

And, on the other hand, go forth again to gaze upon the old cathedral front, where you have smiled so often at the fantastic ignorance of the old sculptors: examine once more those ugly goblins, and formless monsters, and stern statues, anatomiless[13] and rigid; but do not mock at them, for they are signs of the life and liberty of every workman who struck the stone; a freedom of thought, and rank in scale of being, such as no laws, no charters, no charities can secure; but which it must be the first aim of all Europe at this day to regain for her children.

Let me not be thought to speak wildly or extravagantly. It is verily this degradation of the operative into a machine, which, more than any other evil of the times, is leading the mass of the nations everywhere into vain, incoherent, destructive struggling for a freedom of which they cannot explain the nature to themselves. Their universal outcry against wealth, and against nobility, is not forced from them either by the pressure of famine, or the sting of mortified pride. These do much, and have done much in all ages; but the foundations of society were never yet shaken as they are at this day. It is not that men are ill fed, but that they have no pleasure in the work by which they make their bread, and therefore look to wealth as the only means of pleasure. It is not that men are pained by the scorn of the upper classes, but they cannot endure their own; for they feel that the kind of labour to which they are condemned is verily a degrading one, and makes them less than men.

We have much studied and much perfected, of late, the great civilized invention of the division of labour; only we give it a false name. It is not, truly speaking, the labour that is divided; but the men:—Divided into mere segments of men—broken into small fragments and crumbs of life; so that all the little piece of intelligence that is left in a man is not enough to make a pin, or a nail, but exhausts itself in making the point of a pin or the head of a nail. Now it is a good and desirable thing, truly, to make many pins in a day; but if we could only see with what crystal sand

[13] A word coined by Ruskin.

their points were polished,—sand of human soul, much to be magnified before it can be discerned for what it is—we should think there might be some loss in it also. And the great cry that rises from all our manufacturing cities, louder than their furnace blast, is all in very deed for this,—that we manufacture everything there except men; we blanch cotton, and strengthen steel, and refine sugar, and shape pottery; but to brighten, to strengthen, to refine, or to form a single living spirit, never enters into our estimate of advantages. And all the evil to which that cry is urging our myriads can be met only in one way: not by teaching nor preaching, for to teach them is but to show them their misery, and to preach to them, if we do nothing more than preach, is to mock at it. It can be met only by a right understanding, on the part of all classes, of what kinds of labour are good for men, raising them, and making them happy; by a determined sacrifice of such convenience, or beauty, or cheapness as is to be got only by the degradation of the workman; and by equally determined demand for the products and results of healthy and ennobling labour.

And how, it will be asked, are these products to be recognized, and this demand to be regulated? Easily: by the observance of three broad and simple rules:

1. Never encourage the manufacture of any article not absolutely necessary, in the production of which *Invention* has no share.

2. Never demand an exact finish for its own sake, but only for some practical or noble end.

3. Never encourage imitation or copying of any kind, except for the sake of preserving records of great works.

The second of these principles is the only one which directly rises out of the consideration of our immediate subject; but I shall briefly explain the meaning and extent of the first also, reserving the enforcement of the third for another place.

1. Never encourage the manufacture of anything not necessary, in the production of which invention has no share.

For instance. Glass beads are utterly unnecessary, and

there is no design or thought employed in their manufacture. They are formed by first drawing out the glass into rods; these rods are chopped up into fragments of the size of beads by the human hand, and the fragments are then rounded in the furnace. The men who chop up the rods sit at their work all day, their hands vibrating with a perpetual and exquisitely timed palsy, and the beads dropping beneath their vibration like hail. Neither they, nor the men who draw out the rods or fuse the fragments, have the smallest occasion for the use of any single human faculty; and every young lady, therefore, who buys glass beads is engaged in the slave-trade, and in a much more cruel one than that which we have so long been endeavouring to put down.

But glass cups and vessels may become the subjects of exquisite invention; and if in buying these we pay for the invention, that is to say, for the beautiful form, or colour, or engraving, and not for mere finish of execution, we are doing good to humanity.

Our modern glass is exquisitely clear in its substance, true in its form, accurate in its cutting. We are proud of this. We ought to be ashamed of it. The old Venice glass was muddy, inaccurate in all its forms, and clumsily cut, if at all. And the old Venetian was justly proud of it. For there is this difference between the English and Venetian workman, that the former thinks only of accurately matching his patterns, and getting his curves perfectly true and his edges perfectly sharp, and becomes a mere machine for rounding curves and sharpening edges; while the old Venetian cared not a whit whether his edges were sharp or not, but he invented a new design for every glass that he made, and never moulded a handle or a lip without a new fancy in it. And therefore, though some Venetian glass is ugly and clumsy enough when made by clumsy and uninventive workmen, other Venetian glass is so lovely in its forms that no price is too great for it; and we never see the same form in it twice. Now you cannot have the finish and the varied form too. If the workman is thinking about his edges, he cannot be thinking of his design; if of his design, he cannot think of his edges. Choose whether you will pay for the lovely form or the perfect finish, and choose at the same moment whether you will make the worker a man or a grindstone.

[W]e want one man to be always thinking, and another to be always working, and we call one a gentleman, and the other an operative; whereas the workman ought often to be thinking, and the thinker often to be working, and both should be gentlemen, in the best sense. As it is, we make both ungentle, the one envying, the other despising, his brother; and the mass of society is made up of morbid thinkers, and miserable workers. Now it is only by labour that thought can be made healthy, and only by thought that labour can be made happy, and the two cannot be separated with impunity. It would be well if all of us were good handicraftsmen in some kind, and the dishonour of manual labour done away with altogether; so that though there should still be a trenchant distinction of race between nobles and commoners, there should not, among the latter, be a trenchant distinction of employment, as between idle and working men, or between men of liberal and illiberal professions.

But, accurately speaking, no good work whatever can be perfect, and *the demand for perfection is always a sign of a misunderstanding of the ends of art.* [I]mperfection is in some sort essential to all that we know of life. It is the sign of life in a mortal body, that is to say, of a state of progress and change. Nothing that lives is, or can be, rigidly perfect; part of it is decaying, part nascent. The foxglove blossom,—a third part bud, a third part past, a third part in full bloom,—is a type of the life of this world. And in all things that live there are certain irregularities and deficiencies which are not only signs of life, but sources of beauty. No human face is exactly the same in its lines on each side, no leaf perfect in its lobes, no branch in its symmetry. All admit irregularity as they imply change; and to banish imperfection is to destroy expression, to check exertion, to paralyze vitality. All things are literally better, lovelier, and more beloved for the imperfections which have been divinely appointed, that the law of human life may be Effort, and the law of human judgment, Mercy.

Accept this then for a universal law, that neither architecture nor any other noble work of man can be good unless it be imperfect; and let us be prepared for the otherwise strange fact, which we shall discern clearly as we approach the period of the Renaissance, that the first cause of the fall of the arts of Europe was a relentless requirement of perfection, incapable alike either of being silenced by veneration for greatness, or softened into forgiveness of simplicity.

Thus far then of the Rudeness or Savageness, which is the first mental element of Gothic architecture. It is an element in many other healthy architectures also, as the Byzantine and Romanesque; but true Gothic cannot exist without it.

The second mental element above named was CHANGE-FULNESS, or Variety.

I have already enforced the allowing independent operation to the inferior workman, simply as a duty *to him,* and as ennobling the architecture by rendering it more Christian. We have now to consider what reward we obtain for the performance of this duty, namely, the perpetual variety of every feature of the building.

Wherever the workman is utterly enslaved, the parts of the building must of course be absolutely like each other; for the perfection of his execution can only be reached by exercising him in doing one thing, and giving him nothing else to do.

Let us then understand at once that change or variety is as much a necessity to the human heart and brain in buildings as in books; that there is no merit, though there is some occasional use, in monotony; and that we must no more expect to derive either pleasure or profit from an architecture whose ornaments are of one pattern, and whose pillars are of one proportion, than we should out of a universe in which the clouds were all of one shape, and the trees all of one size.

And this we confess in deeds, though not in words. All the pleasure which the people of the nineteenth century take in art, is in pictures, sculpture, minor objects of virtù, or mediæval architecture, which we enjoy under the term picturesque: no pleasure is taken anywhere in modern buildings, and we find all men of true feeling delighting to escape out of modern cities into natural scenery: hence, as I shall hereafter show, that peculiar love of landscape, which is characteristic of the age.

The third constituent element of the Gothic mind was stated to be NATURALISM; that is to say, the love of natural objects for their own sake, and the effort to represent them frankly, unconstrained by artistical laws.

We are to remember, in the first place, that the arrangement of colours and lines is an art analogous to the composition of music, and entirely independent of the representation of facts. Good colouring does not necessarily convey the image of anything but itself. It consists in certain proportions and arrangements of rays of light, but not in likenesses to anything. A few touches of certain greys and purples laid by a master's hand on white paper will be good colouring; as more touches are added beside them, we may find out that they were intended to represent a dove's neck, and we may praise, as the drawing advances, the perfect imitation of the dove's neck. But the good colouring does not consist in that imitation, but in the abstract qualities and relations of the grey and purple.

In like manner, as soon as a great sculptor begins to shape his work out of the block, we shall see that its lines are nobly arranged, and of noble character. We may not have the slightest idea for what the forms are intended, whether they are of man or beast, of vegetation or drapery. Their likeness to anything does not affect their nobleness. They are magnificent forms, and that is all we need care to know of them, in order to say whether the workman is a good or bad sculptor.

Now the noblest art is an exact unison of the abstract value, with the imitative power, of forms and colours. It is the noblest composition, used to express the noblest facts. But the human mind cannot in general unite the two perfections: it either pursues the fact to the neglect of the composition, or pursues the composition to the neglect of the fact.

I say first, that the Gothic builders were of that central

class which unites fact with design; but that the part of the work which was more especially their own was the truthfulness. Their power of artistical invention or arrangement was not greater than that of Romanesque and Byzantine workmen: by those workmen they were taught the principles, and from them received their models, of design; but to the ornamental feeling and rich fancy of the Byzantine the Gothic builder added a love of *fact* which is never found in the South. Both Greek and Roman used conventional foliage in their ornament, passing into something that was not foliage at all, knotting itself into strange cup-like buds or clusters, and growing out of lifeless rods instead of stems; the Gothic sculptor received these types, at first, as things that ought to be, just as we have a second time received them; but he could not rest in them. He saw there was no veracity in them, no knowledge, no vitality. Do what he would, he could not help liking the true leaves better; and cautiously, a little at a time, he put more of nature into his work, until at last it was all true, retaining, nevertheless, every valuable character of the original well-disciplined and designed arrangement.

In that careful distinction of species, and richness of delicate and undisturbed organization, which characterize the Gothic design, there is the history of rural and thoughtful life, influenced by habitual tenderness, and devoted to subtle inquiry; and every discriminating and delicate touch of the chisel, as it rounds the petal or guides the branch, is a prophecy of the development of the entire body of the natural sciences, beginning with that of medicine, of the recovery of literature, and the establishment of the most necessary principles of domestic wisdom and national peace.

The Gothic architecture arose in massy and mountainous strength, axe-hewn, and iron-bound, block heaved upon block by the monk's enthusiasm and the soldier's force; and cramped and stanchioned into such weight of grisly wall, as might bury the anchoret in darkness, and beat back the utmost storm of battle, suffering but by the same narrow crosslet the passing of the sunbeam, or of the arrow. Gradually, as that monkish enthusiasm became more thought-

ful, and as the sound of war became more and more inter-
mittent beyond the gates of the convent or the keep, the
stony pillar grew slender and the vaulted roof grew light,
till they had wreathed themselves into the semblance of
the summer woods at their fairest, and of the dead field-
flowers, long trodden down in blood, sweet monumental
statues were set to bloom for ever, beneath the porch of
the temple, or the canopy of the tomb.

The fourth essential element of the Gothic mind was
above stated to be the sense of the GROTESQUE; but I shall
defer the endeavour to define this most curious and subtle
character until we have occasion to examine one of the divisions of the Renaissance schools, which was morbidly influenced by it (Vol. III. Chap. III.). It is the less necessary
to insist upon it here, because every reader familiar with
Gothic architecture must understand what I mean, and
will, I believe, have no hesitation in admitting, that the
tendency to delight in fantastic and ludicrous, as well as
in sublime, images, is a universal instinct of the Gothic
imagination.

The fifth element above named was RIGIDITY; and this
character I must endeavour carefully to define, for neither
the word I have used, nor any other that I can think of,
will express it accurately. For I mean, not merely stable,
but *active* rigidity; the peculiar energy which gives tension
to movement, and stiffness to resistance, which makes the
fiercest lightning forked rather than curved, and the stout-
est oak-branch angular rather than bending, and is as much
seen in the quivering of the lance as in the glittering of
the icicle.

I have before had occasion to note some manifestations
of this energy or fixedness; but it must be still more at-
tentively considered here, as it shows itself throughout the
whole structure and decoration of Gothic work. Egyptian
and Greek buildings stand, for the most part, by their own
weight and mass, one stone passively incumbent on another; but in the Gothic vaults and traceries there is a stiffness analogous to that of the bones of a limb, or fibres of
a tree; an elastic tension and communication of force from

part to part, and also a studious expression of this through-out every visible line of the building.

Strength of will, independence of character, resoluteness of purpose, impatience of undue control, and that general tendency to set the individual reason against authority, and the individual deed against destiny, which, in the Northern tribes, has opposed itself throughout all ages, to the languid submission, in the Southern, of thought to tradition, and purpose to fatality, are all more or less traceable in the rigid lines, vigorous and various masses, and daringly pro-jecting and independent structure of the Northern Gothic ornament: while the opposite feelings are in like manner legible in the graceful and softly guided waves and wreathed bands, in which Southern decoration is constantly disposed; in its tendency to lose its independence, and fuse itself into the surface of the masses upon which it is traced; and in the expression seen so often, in the arrangement of those masses themselves, of an abandonment of their strength to an inevitable necessity, or a listless repose.

There is virtue in the measure, and error in the excess, of both these characters of mind, and in both of the styles which they have created; the best architecture, and the best temper, are those which unite them both; and this fifth impulse of the Gothic heart is therefore that which needs most caution in its indulgence. It is more definitely Gothic than any other, but the best Gothic building is not that which is *most* Gothic: it can hardly be too frank in its confession of rudeness, hardly too rich in its changefulness, hardly too faithful in its naturalism; but it may go too far in its rigidity, and, like the great Puritan spirit in its ex-treme, lose itself either in frivolity of division, or perversity of purpose. It actually did so in its later times; but it is gladdening to remember that in its utmost nobleness, the very temper which has been thought most adverse to it, the Protestant spirit of self-dependence and inquiry, was expressed in its every line. Faith and aspiration there were, in every Christian ecclesiastical building, from the first cen-tury to the fifteenth; but the moral habits to which Eng-land in this age owes the kind of greatness that she has, —the habits of philosophical investigation, of accurate thought, of domestic seclusion and independence, of stern self-reliance and sincere upright searching into religious truth,—were only traceable in the features which were the distinctive creation of the Gothic schools, in the veined foliage, and thorny fretwork, and shadowy niche, and buttressed pier, and fearless height of subtle pinnacle and crested tower, sent like an "unperplexed question up to Heaven."[14]

Last, because the least essential, of the constituent elements of this noble school, was placed that of REDUNDANCE,—the uncalculating bestowal of the wealth of its labour. There is, indeed, much Gothic, and that of the best period, in which this element is hardly traceable, and which depends for its effect almost exclusively on loveliness of simple design and grace of uninvolved proportion; still, in the most characteristic buildings, a certain portion of their effect depends upon accumulation of ornament; and many of those which have most influence on the minds of men, have attained it by means of this attribute alone. And although, by careful study of the school, it is possible to arrive at a condition of taste which shall be better contented by a few perfect lines than by a whole façade covered with fretwork, the building which only satisfies such a taste is not to be considered the best. For the very first requirement of Gothic architecture being, as we saw above, that it shall both admit the aid, and appeal to the admiration, of the rudest as well as the most refined minds, the richness of the work is, paradoxical as the statement may appear, a part of its humility. No architecture is so haughty as that which is simple; which refuses to address the eye, except in a few clear and forceful lines; which implies, in offering so little to our regards, that all it has offered is perfect; and disdains, either by the complexity or the attractiveness of its features, to embarrass our investigation, or betray us into delight. That humility, which is the very life of the Gothic school, is shown not only in the imperfection, but in the accumulation, of ornament. The inferior

[14] Elizabeth Barrett Browning, *Casa Guidi Windows*, 1851.

rank of the workman is often shown as much in the richness, as the roughness, of his work; and if the co-operation
of every hand, and the sympathy of every heart, are to be
received, we must be content to allow the redundance
which disguises the failure of the feeble, and wins the regard of the inattentive. There are, however, far nobler interests mingling, in the Gothic heart, with the rude love
of decorative accumulation: a magnificent enthusiasm,
which feels as if it never could do enough to reach the
fulness of its ideal; an unselfishness of sacrifice, which
would rather cast fruitless labour before the altar than
stand idle in the market;[15] and, finally, a profound sympathy with the fulness and wealth of the material universe,
rising out of that Naturalism whose operation we have already endeavoured to define.

We have now, I believe, obtained a view approaching
to completeness of the various moral or imaginative elements which composed the inner spirit of Gothic architecture. We have, in the second place, to define its outward
form.

Now, as the Gothic spirit is made up of several elements,
some of which may, in particular examples, be wanting, so
the Gothic form is made up of minor conditions of form,
some of which may, in particular examples, be imperfectly
developed.

We cannot say, therefore, that a building is either Gothic
or not Gothic in form, any more than we can in spirit. We
can only say that it is more or less Gothic, in proportion
to the number of Gothic forms which it unites.

For the fact is, that all good Gothic is nothing more than
the development, in various ways, and on every conceivable scale, of the group formed by the *pointed arch for the
bearing line* below, and *the gable for the protecting line*
above; and from the huge, grey, shaly slope of the cathedral roof, with its elastic pointed vaults beneath, to the
slight crown-like points that enrich the smallest niche of its
doorway, one law and one expression will be found in all.
The modes of support and of decoration are infinitely vari-

15 Matthew xx: 3.

ous, but the real character of the building, in all good Gothic, depends upon the single lines of the gable over the pointed arch, endlessly rearranged or repeated.[16]

[16] SV II, 184–250, omit. (entire section 2 here)

3

TRECENTO ARCHITECTURE

[Y]ou will find that the European art of 1200 includes
all the most developed and characteristic conditions of the
style in the north which you have probably been accustomed to think of as NORMAN, and which you may always
most conveniently call so; and the most developed conditions of the style in the south, which, formed out of effete
Greek, Persian, and Roman tradition, you may, in like manner, most conveniently express by the familiar word BY-
ZANTINE. Whatever you call them, they are in origin adverse in temper, and remain so up to the year 1200. Then
an influence appears, seemingly that of one man, Nicholas
the Pisan (our first MASTER, observe), and a new spirit
adopts what is best in each, and gives to what it adopts a
new energy of its own; namely, this conscientious and didactic power which is the speciality of its progressive existence. And just as the new-born and natural art of Athens
collects and reanimates Pelasgian and Egyptian tradition,
purifying their worship, and perfecting their work, into the
living heathen faith of the world, so this newborn and
natural art of Florence collects and animates the Norman
and Byzantine tradition, and forms out of the perfected
worship and work of both, the honest Christian faith, and
vital craftsmanship, of the world.

Get this first summary, therefore, well into your minds.
The word "Norman" I use roughly for North-savage;—
roughly, but advisedly. I mean Lombard, Scandinavian,
Frankish; everything north-savage that you can think of,
except Saxon. (I have a reason for that exception; never
mind it just now.)

All north-savage I call NORMAN, all south-savage I call

BYZANTINE; this latter including dead native Greek primarily—then dead foreign Greek, in Rome;—then Arabian —Persian—Phœnician—Indian—all you can think of, in art of hot countries, up to this year 1200, I rank under the one term Byzantine. Now all this cold art—Norman, and all this hot art—Byzantine, is virtually dead, till 1200. It has no conscience, no didactic power; it is devoid of both, in the sense that dreams are.

Then in the thirteenth century, men wake as if they heard an alarum through the whole vault of heaven, and true human life begins again, and the cradle of this life is the Val d'Arno. There the northern and southern nations meet; there they lay down their enmities; there they are first baptized unto John's baptism for the remission of sins; there is born, and thence exiled,—thought faithless for breaking the font of baptism to save a child from drowning, in his "bel San Giovanni,"[17]—the greatest of Christian poets; he who had pity even for the lost.

Now, therefore, my whole history of *Christian* architecture and painting begins with this Baptistery of Florence, and with its associated Cathedral. Arnolfo brought the one into the form in which you now see it; he laid the foundation of the other, and that to purpose, and he is therefore the CAPTAIN of our first school. For this Florentine Baptistery is the great one of the world. Here is the centre of Christian knowledge and power.

And it is one piece of large *engraving*. White substance, cut into, and filled with black, and dark green. No more perfect work was afterwards done; and I wish you to grasp the idea of this building clearly and irrevocably,—first, in order (as I told you in a previous lecture) to quit yourselves thoroughly of the idea that ornament should be decorated construction; and, secondly, as the noblest type of the intaglio ornamentation, which developed itself into all minor application of black and white to engraving. That it should do so first at Florence, was the natural sequence, and the just reward, of the ancient skill of Etruria in chased metal-work.[18]

[17] (Dante's name for the Baptistery.) AFlor 341–43
[18] AFlor 343 f

Virtually, you will find that the schools of structural architecture are those which use cement to bind their materials together, and in which, therefore, balance of *weight* becomes a continual and inevitable question. But the schools of sculptural architecture are those in which stones are fitted without cement,—in which, therefore, the question of *fitting* or adjustment is continual and inevitable; but the sustainable weight practically unlimited.

And this example from Lucca is of a very important class indeed. It is from above the east entrance gate of Lucca, which bears the cross above it, as the doors of a Christian city should. Such a city is, or ought to be, a place of peace, as much as any monastery.

This custom of placing the cross above the gate is Byzantine-Christian . . . The mosaic of this cross is so exquisitely fitted that no injury has been received by it to this day from wind or weather. And the horizontal dressed stones are laid so daintily that not an edge of them has stirred; and, both to draw your attention to their beautiful fitting, and as a substitute for cement, the architect cuts his uppermost block so as to dovetail into the course below.

Dovetail, I say deliberately. This is stone carpentry, in which the carpenter despises glue. I don't say he won't use glue, and glue of the best, but he feels it to be a nasty thing, and that it spoils his wood or marble. None, at least, he determines shall be seen outside, and his laying of stones shall be so solid and so adjusted that, take all the cement away, his wall shall yet stand.

Stonehenge, the Parthenon, the walls of the Kings, this gate of Lucca, this window of Orvieto, and this tomb at Verona,[19] are all built on the Cyclopean principle. They will stand without cement, and no cement shall be seen outside. Mr. Burgess [Ruskin's assistant] and I actually tried the experiment on this tomb. Mr. Burgess modelled every stone of it in clay, put them together, and it stood.

Now there are two most notable characteristics about this Cyclopean architecture to which I beg your close attention.

[19] (The Castelbarco Tomb.) Val 98–101, omit.

The first: that as the laying of stones is so beautiful, their joints become a subject of admiration, and great part of the architectural ornamentation is in the beauty of lines of separation, drawn as finely as possible. Thus the separating lines of the bricks at Siena, of this gate at Lucca, of the vault at Verona, of this window at Orvieto, and of the contemporary refectory at Furness Abbey, are a main source of the pleasure you have in the building. Nay, they are not merely engravers' lines, but, in finest practice, they are mathematical lines—length without breadth.[20]

[20] Val 101

4

VENETIAN GOTHIC

We have seen that the wrecks of the Byzantine palaces consisted merely of upper and lower arcades surrounding cortiles; the disposition of the interiors being now entirely changed, and their original condition untraceable. The entrances to these early buildings are, for the most part, merely large circular arches, the central features of their continuous arcades: they do not present us with definitely separated windows and doors.

But a great change takes place in the Gothic period. These long arcades break, as it were, into pieces, and coagulate into central and lateral windows, and small arched doors, pierced in great surfaces of brick wall. The sea story of a Byzantine palace consists of seven, nine, or more arches in a continuous line; but the sea story of a Gothic palace consists of a door and one or two windows on each side, as in a modern house. The first story of a Byzantine palace consists of, perhaps, eighteen or twenty arches, reaching from one side of the house to the other; the first story of a Gothic palace consists of a window of four or five lights in the centre, and one or two single windows on each side. The germ, however, of the Gothic arrangement is already found in the Byzantine, where, as we have seen, the arcades, though continuous, are always composed of a central mass and two wings of smaller arches. The central group becomes the door or the middle light of the Gothic palace, and the wings break into its lateral windows.

But the most essential difference in the entire arrangement, is the loss of the unity of conception which regulated Byzantine composition. How subtle the sense of gradation

which disposed the magnitudes of the early palaces we
have seen already, but I have not hitherto noticed that the
Byzantine work was centralised in its ornamentation as
much as in its proportions. Not only were the lateral capitals and archivolts kept comparatively plain, while the
central ones were sculptured, but the midmost piece of
sculpture, whatever it might be,—capital, inlaid circle, or
architrave,—was always made superior to the rest. In the
Fondaco de' Turchi, for instance, the midmost capital of
the upper arcade is the key to the whole group, larger and
more studied than all the rest; and the lateral ones are so
disposed as to answer each other on the opposite sides,
thus, A being put for the central one,

F E B C A C B E F,

a sudden break of the system being admitted in one
unique capital at the extremity of the series.

Such being the principal differences in the general conception of the Byzantine and Gothic palaces, the particulars in the treatment of the latter are easily stated. The
marble facings are gradually removed from the walls; and
the bare brick either stands forth confessed boldly, contrasted with the marble shafts and archivolts of the windows, or it is covered with stucco painted in fresco, of
which more hereafter. The Ducal Palace, as in all other
respects, is an exact expression of the middle point in the
change. It still retains marble facing; but instead of being
disposed in slabs as in the Byzantine times, it is applied
in solid bricks or blocks of marble, 11½ inches long, by 6
inches high.

The stories of the Gothic palaces are divided by string-
courses, considerably bolder in projection than those of the
Byzantines, and more highly decorated; and while the
angles of the Byzantine palaces are quite sharp and pure,
those of the Gothic palaces are wrought into a chamfer,
filled by small twisted shafts which have capitals under the
cornice of each story.

These capitals are little observed in the general effect,
but the shafts are of essential importance in giving an aspect of firmness to the angle; a point of peculiar necessity
in Venice, where, owing to the various convolutions of the

canals, the angles of the palaces are not only frequent, but often necessarily *acute*, every inch of ground being valuable. In other cities, the appearance as well as the assurance of stability can always be secured by the use of massy stones, as in the fortress palaces of Florence; but it must have been always desirable at Venice to build as lightly as possible, in consequence of the comparative insecurity of the foundations. The early palaces were, as we have seen, perfect models of grace and lightness, and the Gothic, which followed, though much more massive in the style of its details, never admitted more weight into its structure than was absolutely necessary for its strength. Hence, every Gothic palace has the appearance of enclosing as many rooms, and attaining as much strength, as is possible, with a minimum quantity of brick and stone. The traceries of the windows, which in Northern Gothic only support the *glass,* at Venice support the *building;* and thus the greater ponderousness of the *traceries* is only an indication of the greater lightness of the *structure.* Hence, when the Renaissance architects give their opinions as to the stability of the Ducal Palace when injured by fire one of them, Christofore Sorte, says, that he thinks it by no means laudable that the "Serenissimo Dominio" of the Venetian senate "should live in a palace built in the air."[21]

. . . I must be content to lay the succession of the architectural styles plainly before the reader, and leave the collateral questions to the investigation of others; merely noting this one assured fact, that *the root of all that is greatest in Christian art is struck in the thirteenth century;* that the temper of that century is the life-blood of all manly work thenceforward in Europe . . .

Such, then, is the simple fact at Venice, that from the beginning of the thirteenth century there is found a singular increase of simplicity in all architectural ornamentation; the rich Byzantine capitals giving place to a pure and

[21] (Ruskin note: " 'Dice, che non lauda per alcun modo di metter questo Serenissimo Dominio in tanto pericolo d' habitar un palazzo fabricato in aria.'—*Pareri di XV. Architetti, con illustrazioni dell' Abbate Giuseppe Cadorin* [Venice, 1838], p. 104.") SV II, 275–79, omit.

severe type, . . . and the rich sculptures vanishing from the walls, nothing but the marble facing remaining. One of the most interesting examples of this transitional state is a palace at San Severo, just behind the Casa Zorzi. This latter is a Renaissance building, utterly worthless in every respect, but known to the Venetian Ciceroni; and by inquiring for it, and passing a little beyond it down the Fondamenta San Severo, the traveller will see, on the other side of the canal, a palace which the Ciceroni never notice, but which is unique in Venice for the magnificence of the veined purple alabasters with which it has been decorated, and for the manly simplicity of the foliage of its capitals. Except in these, it has no sculpture whatever, and its effect is dependent entirely on colour. Disks of green serpentine are inlaid on the field of purple alabaster; and the pillars are alternately of red marble with white capitals, and of white marble with red capitals.[22]

The Ducal Palace

The palaces built between the final cessation of the Byzantine style, about 1300, and the date of the Ducal Palace (1320–1350), are all completely distinct in character, so distinct that I at first intended the account of them to form a separate section of this volume; and there is literally *no* transitional form between them and the perfection of the Ducal Palace. Every Gothic building in Venice which resembles the latter is a copy of it. I do not mean that there was no Gothic in Venice before the Ducal Palace, but that the mode of its application to domestic architecture had not been determined. The real root of the Ducal Palace is the apse of the Church of the Frari. The traceries of that apse, though earlier and ruder in workmanship, are nearly the same in mouldings, and precisely the same in treatment (especially in the placing of the lions' heads), as those of the great Ducal Arcade; and the originality of thought in the architect of the Ducal Palace consists in his having adapted those traceries, in a more

[22] SV II, 306–09, omit.

highly developed and finished form, to civil uses. In the apse
of the church they form narrow and tall window lights,
somewhat more massive than those of Northern Gothic,
but similar in application: the thing to be done was to
adapt these traceries to the forms of domestic building
necessitated by national usage. The early palaces consisted,
as we have seen, of arcades sustaining walls faced with
marble, rather broad and long than elevated. This form
was kept for the Ducal Palace; but instead of round arches
from shaft to shaft, the Frari traceries were substituted,
with two essential modifications. Besides being enor-
mously increased in scale and thickness, that they might
better bear the superincumbent weight, the quatrefoil,
which in the Frari windows is above the arch, was in the
Ducal Palace put between the arches; the main reason for
this alteration being that the bearing power of the arches,
which was now to be trusted with the weight of a wall
forty feet high, was thus thrown *between* the quatrefoils,
instead of under them, and thereby applied at far better
advantage. And, in the second place, the joints of the
masonry were changed. In the Frari (as often also in St.
John and Paul's), the tracery is formed of two simple cross
bars or slabs of stone, pierced into the requisite forms, and
separated by a horizontal joint, just on a level with the
lowest cusp of the quatrefoils. But at the Ducal Palace
the horizontal joint is in the centre of the quatrefoils, and
two others are introduced beneath it at right angles to the
run of the mouldings . . .[23]

Colouring of the wall

Hence arose the universal and admirable system of the
diapered or chequered backgrounds of early ornamental
art. They are completely developed in the thirteenth century, and extend through the whole of the fourteenth,
gradually yielding to landscape and other pictorial backgrounds, as the designers lost perception of the purpose
of their art, and of the value of colour. The chromatic dec-

[23] SV II, 272 f

oration of the Gothic palaces of Venice was of course
founded on these two great principles, which prevailed
constantly wherever the true chivalric and Gothic spirit possessed any influence. The windows, with their intermediate
spaces of marble, were considered as the objects to be relieved, and variously quartered with vigorous colour. The
whole space of the brick wall was considered as a background; it was covered with stucco, and painted in fresco,
with diaper patterns.

The walls were generally covered with chequers of very
warm colour, a russet inclining to scarlet more or less relieved with white, black, and grey; as still seen in the only
example which, having been executed in marble, has been
perfectly preserved, the front of the Ducal Palace. This,
however, owing to the nature of its materials, was a
peculiarly simple example; the ground is white, crossed
with double bars of pale red, and in the centre of each
chequer there is a cross, alternately black with a red centre and red with a black centre where the arms cross. In
painted work the grounds would be, of course, as varied
and complicated as those of manuscripts; but I only know
of one example left, on the Casa Sagredo, where, on some
fragments of stucco, a very early chequer background is
traceable, composed of crimson quatrefoils interlaced, with
cherubims stretching their wings filling the intervals.[24]

It ought to be especially noticed, that, in all chequered
patterns employed in the coloured designs of these noble
periods, the greatest care is taken to mark that they are
grounds of design rather than designs themselves. Modern
architects, in such minor imitations as they are beginning
to attempt, endeavour to dispose the parts of the patterns
so as to occupy certain symmetrical positions with respect
to the parts of the architecture. A Gothic builder never
does this: he cuts his ground into pieces of the shape he
requires with utter remorselessness, and places his win-

[24] (Ruskin note added in 1881: "All now whitewashed by
'Progresso.' Progressive Italy performs always two fresco opera-
tions in due order. First, blind whitewash, to show that she can
do something in Italy. Then soot, in imitation of England.")
SV III, 26–28, omit.

dows or doors upon it with no regard whatever to the lines in which they cut the pattern: and, in illuminations of manuscripts, the chequer itself is constantly changed in the most subtle and arbitrary way, wherever there is the least chance of its regularity attracting the eye, and making it of importance. So *intentional* is this, that a diaper pattern is often set obliquely to the vertical lines of the designs, for fear it should appear in any way connected with them.

On these russet or crimson backgrounds the entire space of the series of windows was relieved, for the most part, as a subdued white field of alabaster; and on this delicate and veined white were set the circular disks of purple and green. The arms of the family were of course blazoned in their own proper colours, but I think generally on a pure azure ground; the blue colour is still left behind the shields in the Casa Priuli and one or two more of the palaces which are unrestored, and the blue ground was used also to relieve the sculptures of religious subjects. Finally, all the mouldings, capitals, cornices, cusps, and traceries, were either entirely gilded or profusely touched with gold.

The whole front of a Gothic palace in Venice may, therefore, *be simply described as a field of subdued russet, quartered with broad sculptured masses of white and gold; these latter being relieved by smaller inlaid fragments of blue, purple, and deep green.*[25]

[25] SV III, 28 f

5

ST. MARK'S

[Between] the pillars at the end of the "Bocca di Piazza" . . . there opens a great light, and, in the midst of it, as we advance slowly, the vast tower of St. Mark seems to lift itself visibly forth from the level field of chequered stones; and, on each side, the countless arches prolong themselves into ranged symmetry, as if the rugged and irregular houses that pressed together above us in the dark alley had been struck back into sudden obedience and lovely order, and all their rude casements and broken walls had been transformed into arches charged with goodly sculpture, and fluted shafts of delicate stone.

And well may they fall back, for beyond those troops of ordered arches there rises a vision out of the earth, and all the great square seems to have opened from it in a kind of awe, that we may see it far away;—a multitude of pillars and white domes, clustered into a long low pyramid of coloured light; a treasure-heap, it seems, partly of gold, and partly of opal and mother-of-pearl, hollowed beneath into five great vaulted porches, ceiled with fair mosaic, and beset with sculpture of alabaster, clear as amber and delicate as ivory,—sculpture fantastic and involved, of palm leaves and lilies, and grapes and pomegranates, and birds clinging and fluttering among the branches, all twined together into an endless network of buds and plumes; and in the midst of it, the solemn forms of angels, sceptred, and robed to the feet, and leaning to each other across the gates, their figures indistinct among the gleaming of the golden ground through the leaves beside them, interrupted and dim, like the morning light as it faded back among the branches of Eden, when first its gates were angel-guarded long ago. And round the walls of the porches there are set pillars of variegated stones, jasper and porphyry, and deep-green serpentine spotted with flakes of snow, and marbles, that half refuse and half yield to the sunshine, Cleopatra-like, "their bluest veins to kiss"[26]—the shadow, as it steals back from them, revealing line after line of azure undulation, as a receding tide leaves the waved sand; their capitals rich with interwoven tracery, rooted knots of herbage, and drifting leaves of acanthus and vine, and mystical signs, all beginning and ending in the Cross; and above them, in the broad archivolts, a continuous chain of language and of life—angels, and the signs of heaven, and the labours of men, each in its appointed season upon the earth; and above these, another range of glittering pinnacles, mixed with white archers edged with scarlet flowers,—a confusion of delight, amidst which the breasts of the Greek horses are seen blazing in their breadth of golden strength, and the St. Mark's lion, lifted on a blue field covered with stars, until at last, as if in ecstasy, the crests of the arches break into a marble foam, and toss themselves far into the blue sky in flashes and wreaths of sculptured spray, as if the breakers on the Lido shore had been frost-bound before they fell, and the sea-nymphs had inlaid them with coral and amethyst.[27]

Through the heavy door whose bronze network closes the place of his rest, let us enter the church itself. It is lost in still deeper twilight, to which the eye must be accustomed for some moments before the form of the building can be traced; and then there opens before us a vast cave, hewn out into the form of a Cross, and divided into shadowy aisles by many pillars. Round the domes of its roof the light enters only through narrow apertures like large stars; and here and there a ray or two from some far-away casement wanders into the darkness, and casts a narrow phosphoric stream upon the waves of marble that heave and fall in a thousand colours along the floor. What else there is of light is from torches, or silver lamps, burning

[26] (*Antony and Cleopatra,* ii, sc. 5.) SV II, 82 f
[27] SV II, 83

ceaselessly in the recesses of the chapels; the roof sheeted
with gold, and the polished walls covered with alabaster,
give back at every curve and angle some feeble gleaming
to the flames; and the glories round the heads of the sculptured saints flash out upon us as we pass them, and sink
again into the gloom.[28]

"Incrustation"

Now the first broad characteristic of the building, and
the root nearly of every other important peculiarity in it,
is its confessed *incrustation*. It is the purest example in
Italy of the great school of architecture in which the ruling
principle is the incrustation of brick with more precious
materials; and it is necessary, before we proceed to
criticise any one of its arrangements, that the reader
should carefully consider the principles which are likely
to have influenced, or might legitimately influence the
architects of such a school, as distinguished from those
whose designs are to be executed in massive materials.

First, consider the natural circumstances which give rise
to such a style. Suppose a nation of builders, placed far
from any quarries of available stone, and having precarious
access to the mainland where they exist; compelled therefore either to build entirely with brick, or to import whatever stone they use from great distances, in ships of small
tonnage, and, for the most part, dependent for speed on
the oar rather than the sail. The labour and cost of carriage
are just as great, whether they import common or precious
stone, and therefore the natural tendency would always be
to make each shipload as valuable as possible. But in
proportion to the preciousness of the stone, is the limitation
of its possible supply; limitation not determined merely by
cost, but by the physical conditions of the material, for of
many marbles, pieces above a certain size are not to be
had for money. There would also be a tendency in such
circumstances to import as much stone as possible ready
sculptured, in order to save weight; and therefore, if the

[28] SV II, 88

traffic of their merchants led them to places where there were ruins of ancient edifices, to ship the available fragments of them home. Out of this supply of marble, partly composed of pieces of so precious a quality that only a few tons of them could be on any terms obtained, and partly of shafts, capitals, and other portions of foreign buildings, the island architect has to fashion, as best he may, the anatomy of his edifice. It is at his choice either to lodge his few blocks of precious marble here and there among his masses of brick, and to cut out of the sculptured fragments such new forms as may be necessary for the observance of fixed proportions in the new building; or else to cut the coloured stones into thin pieces, of extent sufficient to face the whole surface of the walls, and to adopt a method of construction irregular enough to admit the insertion of fragmentary sculptures; rather with a view of displaying their intrinsic beauty, than of setting them to any regular service in the support of the building.

An architect who cared only to display his own skill, and had no respect for the works of others, would assuredly have chosen the latter alternative, and would have sawn the old marbles into fragments in order to prevent all interference with his own designs. But an architect who cared for the preservation of noble work, whether his own or others', and more regarded the beauty of his building than his own fame, would have done what those old builders of St. Mark's did for us, and saved every relic with which he was entrusted.

In the fifth chapter of the *Seven Lamps*, § 14, the reader will find the opinion of a modern architect of some reputation, Mr. Woods, that the chief thing remarkable in this church "is its extreme ugliness;" and he will find this opinion associated with another, namely, that the works of the Caracci are far preferable to those of the Venetian painters. The second statement of feeling reveals to us one of the principal causes of the first; namely, that Mr. Woods had not any perception of colour, or delight in it. The perception of colour is a gift just as definitely granted to one person, and denied to another, as an ear for music; and the very first requisite for true judgment of St. Mark's, is the perfection of that colour-faculty which few people ever set themselves seriously to find out whether they possess or not. For it is on its value as a piece of perfect and unchangeable colouring, that the claims of this edifice to our respect are finally rested . . .

If, therefore, the reader does not care for colour, I must protest against his endeavour to form any judgment whatever of this church of St. Mark's. But, if he both cares for and loves it, let him remember that the school of incrusted architecture is *the only one in which perfect and permanent chromatic decoration is possible;* and let him look upon every piece of jasper and alabaster given to the architect as a cake of very hard colour, of which a certain portion is to be ground down or cut off, to paint the walls with. Once understand this thoroughly, and accept the condition that the body and availing strength of the edifice are to be in brick, and that this under muscular power of brickwork is to be clothed with the defence of the brightness of the marble, as the body of an animal is protected and adorned by its scales or its skin, and all the consequent fitnesses and laws of the structure will be easily discernible . . .

As the body of the structure is confessedly of inferior, and comparatively incoherent materials, it would be absurd to attempt in it any expression of the higher refinements of construction. It will be enough that by its mass we are assured of its sufficiency and strength; and there is the less reason for endeavouring to diminish the extent of its surface by delicacy of adjustment, because on the breadth of that surface we are to depend for the better display of the colour, which is to be the chief source of our pleasure in the building. The main body of the work, therefore, will be composed of solid walls and massive piers; and whatever expression of finer structural science we may require, will be thrown either into subordinate portions of it, or entirely directed to the support of the external mail, where in arches or vaults it might otherwise appear dangerously independent of the material within.[29]

[29] SV II, 93–100, omit.

6

VENETIAN RENAISSANCE

Now, from the beginning of the fourteenth century, when painting and architecture were thus united, two processes of change went on simultaneously to the beginning of the seventeenth. The merely decorative chequerings on the walls yielded gradually to more elaborate paintings of figure-subject; first small and quaint, and then enlarging into enormous pictures filled by figures generally colossal. As these paintings became of greater merit and importance, the architecture with which they were associated was less studied; and at last a style was introduced in which the framework of the building was little more interesting than that of a Manchester factory, but the whole space of its walls was covered with the most precious fresco paintings. Such edifices are of course no longer to be considered as forming an architectural school; they were merely large preparations of artist's panels; and Titian, Giorgione, and Veronese, no more conferred merit on the later architecture of Venice, as such, by painting on its façades, than Landseer or Watts could confer merit on that of London by first white-washing and then painting its brick streets from one end to the other.

Contemporarily with this change in the relative values of the colour decoration and the stonework, one equally important was taking place in the opposite direction, but of course in another group of buildings. For in proportion as the architect felt himself thrust aside or forgotten in one edifice, he endeavoured to make himself principal in another; and, in retaliation for the painter's entire usurpation of certain fields of design, succeeded in excluding him totally from those in which his own influence was predominant. Or, more accurately speaking, the architects began to be too proud to receive assistance from the colourists; and these latter sought for ground which the architect had abandoned, for the unrestrained display of their own skill. And thus, while one series of edifices is continually becoming feebler in design and richer in superimposed paintings, another, that of which we have so often spoken as the earliest or Byzantine Renaissance, fragment by fragment rejects the pictorial decoration; supplies its place first with marbles, and then, as the latter are felt by the architect, daily increasing in arrogance and deepening in coldness, to be too bright for his dignity, he casts even these aside one by one: and when the last porphyry circle has vanished from the façade, we find two palaces standing side by side, one built, so far as mere masonry goes, with consummate care and skill, but without the slightest vestige of colour in any part of it; the other utterly without any claim to interest in its architecural form, but covered from top to bottom with paintings by Veronese. At this period, then, we bid farewell to colour, leaving the painters to their own peculiar field; and only regretting that they waste their noblest work on walls, from which in a couple of centuries, if not before, the greater part of their labour must be effaced. On the other hand, the architecture whose decline we are tracing, has now assumed an entirely new condition, that of the Central or True Renaissance, whose nature we are to examine in the next chapter.

But before leaving these last palaces over which the Byzantine influence extended itself, there is one more lesson to be learned from them of much importance to us. Though in many respects debased in style, they are consummate in workmanship, and unstained in honour; there is no imperfection in them, and no dishonesty. That there is absolutely *no* imperfection, is indeed . . . a proof of their being wanting in the highest qualities of architecture; but, as lessons in masonry, they have their value, and may well be studied for the excellence they display in methods of levelling stones, for the precision of their inlaying, and other such qualities, which in them are indeed too principal, yet very instructive in their particular way.

For instance, in the inlaid design of the dove with the olive branch, from the Casa Trevisan, it is impossible for anything to go beyond the precision with which the olive leaves are cut out of the white marble; and, in some wreaths of laurel below, the rippled edge of each leaf is as finely and easily drawn, as if by a delicate pencil. No Florentine table is more exquisitely finished than the façade of this entire palace; and as ideals of an executive perfection, which, though we must not turn aside from our main path to reach it, may yet with much advantage be kept in our sight and memory, these palaces are most notable amidst the architecture of Europe. The Rio Façade of the Ducal Palace, though very sparing in colour, is yet, as an example of finished masonry in a vast building, one of the finest things, not only in Venice, but in the world.[30]

Of all the Renaissance works I have ever seen, I should give the palm to [the Rio Façade] for general beauty; nor is it chief among Renaissance works only,—there is hardly a more impressive scene in Venice or in the world than the reach of narrow canal, between the Bridge of Sighs and the Canonica, which laps like an inlet of a lake against the dark and delicate stones of the gigantic wall, that lifts its sculptured precipice so far into the broad light and blue sky. Its majesty, indeed, depends chiefly on this, that it *is* a wall: not a group of regularly designed parts, but one mighty wall, variously pierced and panelled, and its divisions are so irregular, so small and so multitudinous in proportion to its mass, that it is utterly impossible to contemplate it as divided, and very nearly impossible either to analyse or describe the method of its division. The eye is led from one part to another, or rather receives all at once; and it requires considerable effort to fix the mind on any separate part of it, or find the key to anything like an intelligible symmetry among the perpetual varieties of its composition. At last, however, one begins to perceive that it is in reality divided into four stories, each with entabla-

[30] SV III, 29–32

tures, but grouped two and two; the second and fourth
having bold projecting bracket cornices; while the water
story and third story have only richly moulded cornices
without brackets, but the cornice course of the third story
is bolder than that of the first, and the bracket cornice of
the fourth—the true roof cornice—is still more markedly
bolder than the bracket cornice of the second, so that the
energy or value of the respective cornices is to the eye in
alternating proportion, approximating to some such ratio
as this—$5 : 7 :: 6 : 9$.[31]

The demand for perfection

Against this degraded Gothic, then, came up the Renaissance armies; and their first assault was in the requirement of universal perfection. For the first time since the
destruction of Rome, the world had seen, in the work of
the greatest artists of the fifteenth century,—in the painting
of Ghirlandajo, Masaccio, Francia, Perugino, Pinturicchio,
and Bellini; in the sculpture of Mino da Fiesole, of
Ghiberti, and Verrocchio,—a perfection of execution and
fulness of knowledge which cast all previous art into the
shade, and which, being in the work of those men united
with all that was great in that of former days, did indeed
justify the utmost enthusiasm with which their efforts
were, or could be, regarded. But when this perfection had
once been exhibited in anything, it was required in everything; the world could no longer be satisfied with less exquisite execution, or less disciplined knowledge. The first
thing that it demanded in all work was, that it should be
done in a consummate and learned way; and men altogether forgot that it was possible to consummate what
was contemptible, and to know what was useless. Imperatively requiring dexterity of touch, they gradually forgot to look for tenderness of feeling; imperatively requiring accuracy of knowledge, they gradually forgot to ask
for originality of thought. The thought and the feeling
which they despised departed from them, and they were

[31] Later Ruskin ms. notes, inserted by editors, SV III, 32 f

left to felicitate themselves on their small science and their neat fingering. This is the history of the first attack of the Renaissance upon the Gothic schools, and of its rapid results; more fatal and immediate in architecture than in any other art, because there the demand for perfection was less reasonable, and less consistent with the capabilities of the workman; being utterly opposed to that rudeness or savageness on which, as we saw above, the nobility of the elder schools in great part depends. But, inasmuch as the innovations were founded on some of the most beautiful examples of art, and headed by some of the greatest men that the world ever saw, and as the Gothic with which they interfered was corrupt and valueless, the first appearance of the Renaissance feeling had the appearance of a healthy movement. A new energy replaced whatever weariness or dulness had affected the Gothic mind; an exquisite taste and refinement, aided by extended knowledge, furnished the first models of the new school; and over the whole of Italy a style arose, generally now known as cinque-cento, which in sculpture and painting, as I just stated, produced the noblest masters whom the world ever saw, headed by Michael Angelo, Raphael, and Leonardo; but which failed of doing the same in architecture, because, as we have seen above, perfection is therein not possible, and failed more totally than it would otherwise have done, because the classical enthusiasm had destroyed the best types of architectural form.

I hope enough has been advanced, in the chapter on the Nature of Gothic, to show the reader that perfection is *not* to be had from the general workman, but at the cost of everything,—of his whole life, thought, and energy. And Renaissance Europe thought this a small price to pay for manipulative perfection. Men like Verrocchio and Ghiberti were not to be had every day, nor in every place; and to require from the common workman execution or knowledge like theirs, was to require him to become their copyist. Their strength was great enough to enable them to join science with invention, method with emotion, finish with fire; but in them the invention and the fire were first, while Europe saw in them only the method and the finish. This was new to the minds of men, and they pursued it to the neglect of everything else. "This," they cried, "we must have in all our work henceforward:" and they were obeyed. The lower workman secured method and finish, and lost, in exchange for them, his soul.

This, then, the reader must always keep in mind when he is examining for himself any examples of cinque-cento work. When it has been done by a truly great man, whose life and strength could not be oppressed, and who turned to good account the whole science of his day, nothing is more exquisite. I do not believe, for instance, that there is a more glorious work of sculpture existing in the world than that equestrian statue of Bartolomeo Colleone, by Verrocchio, of which, I hope, before these pages are printed, there will be a cast in England. But when the cinque-cento work has been done by those meaner men, who, in the Gothic times, though in a rough way, would yet have found some means of speaking out what was in their hearts, it is utterly inanimate,—a base and helpless copy of more accomplished models; or, if not this, a mere accumulation of technical skill, in gaining which the work-man had surrendered all other powers that were in him.

There is, therefore, of course, an infinite gradation in the art of the period, from the Sistine Chapel down to modern upholstery; but, for the most part, since in architecture the workman *must* be of an inferior order, it will be found that this cinque-cento painting and higher religious sculpture is noble, while the cinque-cento architecture, with its subordinate sculpture, is universally bad; sometimes, however, assuming forms in which the consummate refinement almost atones for the loss of force.[32]

The Casa Grimani

Of all the buildings in Venice, later in date than the final additions to the Ducal Palace, the noblest is, beyond all question, that which, having been condemned by its proprietor, not many years ago, to be pulled down and

[32] SV III, 14–19, omit.

sold for the value of its materials, was rescued by the Austrian Government, and appropriated—the Government officers having no other use for it—to the business of the Post-Office; though still known to the gondolier by its ancient name, the Casa Grimani.[33] It is composed of three stories of the Corinthian order, at once simple, delicate, and sublime; but on so colossal a scale, that the three-storied palaces on its right and left only reach to the cornice which marks the level of its first floor. Yet it is not at first perceived to be so vast; and it is only when some expedient is employed to hide it from the eye, that by the sudden dwarfing of the whole reach of the Grand Canal, which it commands, we become aware that it is to the majesty of the Casa Grimani that the Rialto itself, and the whole group of neighbouring buildings, owe the greater part of their impressiveness. Nor is the finish of its details less notable than the grandeur of their scale. There is not an erring line, nor a mistaken proportion, throughout its noble front; and the exceeding fineness of the chiselling gives an appearance of lightness to the vast blocks of stone out of whose perfect union that front is composed. The decoration is sparing, but delicate: the first story only simpler than the rest, in that it has pilasters instead of shafts, but all with Corinthian capitals, rich in leafage, and fluted delicately; the rest of the walls flat and smooth, and their mouldings sharp and shallow, so that the bold shafts look like crystals of beryl running through a rock of quartz.

This palace is the principal type at Venice, and one of the best in Europe, of the central architecture of the Renaissance schools; that carefully studied and perfectly executed architecture to which those schools owe their principal claims to our respect, and which became the model of most of the important works subsequently produced by civilised nations. I have called it the Roman Renaissance, because it is founded, both in its principles of superimposition, and in the style of its ornament, upon the architecture of classic Rome at its best period. The revival of

[33] (Built in the mid-sixteenth century by Sanmichele.) SV III, 43

Latin literature both led to its adoption and directed its form; and the most important example of it which exists is the modern Roman basilica of St. Peter's. It had, at its Renaissance or new birth, no resemblance either to Greek, Gothic, or Byzantine forms, except in retaining the use of the round arch, vault, and dome; in the treatment of all details, it was exclusively Latin; the last links of connexion with mediæval tradition having been broken by its builders in their enthusiasm for classical art, and the forms of true Greek or Athenian architecture being still unknown to them. The study of these noble Greek forms has induced various modifications of the Renaissance in our own times; but the conditions which are found most applicable to the uses of modern life are still Roman, and the entire style may most fitly be expressed by the term "Roman Renaissance."

It is this style, in its purity and fullest form,—represented by such buildings as the Casa Grimani at Venice (built by San Micheli), the Town Hall at Vicenza (by Palladio), St. Peter's at Rome (by Michael Angelo), St. Paul's and Whitehall in London (by Wren and Inigo Jones),—which is the true antagonist of the Gothic school. The intermediate, or corrupt conditions of it, though multiplied over Europe, are no longer admired by architects, or made the subjects of their study; but the finished work of this central school is still, in most cases, the model set before the student of the nineteenth century, as opposed to those Gothic, Romanesque, or Byzantine forms which have long been considered barbarous, and are so still by most of the leading men of the day.

It will not be necessary for me to enter at length into any examination of its external form. It uses, whether for its roofs of aperture or roofs proper, the low gable or circular arch: but it differs from Romanesque work in attaching great importance to the horizontal lintel or architrave *above* the arch; transferring the energy of the principal shafts to the supporting of this horizontal beam, and thus rendering the arch a subordinate, if not altogether a superfluous, feature.[34]

[34] SV III, 43–46, omit.

San Giorgio Maggiore

A building which owes its interesting effect chiefly to its isolated position, being seen over a great space of lagoon. The traveller should especially notice in its façade the manner in which the central Renaissance architects (of whose style this church is a renowned example) endeavoured to fit the laws they had established to the requirements of their age. Churches were required with aisles and clerestories, that is to say, with a high central nave and lower wings; and the question was, how to face this form with pillars of one proportion. The noble Romanesque architects built story above story, as at Pisa and Lucca; but the base Palladian architects dared not do this. They must needs retain some image of the Greek temple, but the Greek temple was all of one height, a low gable roof being borne on ranges of equal pillars. So the Palladian builders raised first a Greek temple with pilasters for shafts; and, *through the middle of its roof, or horizontal beam,* that is to say, of the cornice which externally represented this beam, they lifted another temple on pedestals, adding these barbarous appendages to the shafts, which otherwise would not have been high enough; fragments of the divided cornice or tie-beam being left between the shafts, and the great door of the church thrust in between the pedestals. It is impossible to conceive a design more gross, more barbarous, more childish in conception, more servile in plagiarism, more insipid in result, more contemptible under every point of rational regard.

Observe, also, that when Palladio had got his pediment at the top of the church, he did not know what to do with it: he had no idea of decorating it except by a round hole in the middle. (The traveller should compare, both in construction and decoration, the Church of the Redentore with this of San Giorgio.) Now, a dark penetration is often a most precious assistance to a building dependent upon colour for its effect; for a cavity is the only means in the architect's power of obtaining certain and vigorous shadow; and for this purpose, a circular penetration, surrounded by a deep russet marble moulding, is beautifully used in the centre of the white field on the side of the Portico of St. Mark's. But Palladio had given up colour, and pierced his pediment with a circular cavity, merely because he had not wit enough to fill it with sculpture. The interior of the church is like a large assembly room, and would have been undeserving of a moment's attention, but that it contains some most precious pictures . . .[35]

[35] SV III, 381 f

7

GOTHIC ARCHITECTURE IN THE NORTH

Read carefully, if you have time, the articles "Pierre" and "Meneau" in M. Viollet le Duc's [*Dictionnaire Raisonné de l'Architecture*, Paris, 1858], and you will know everything that is of importance in the changes dependent on the mere qualities of *matter*. I must, however, try to set in your view also the relative acting qualities of *mind*.

You will find that M. Viollet le Duc traces all the forms of Gothic tracery to the geometrical and practically serviceable development of the stone "chassis," chasing, or frame, for the glass. For instance, he attributes the use of the cusp or "redent," in its more complex forms, to the necessity, or convenience, of diminishing the space of glass which the tracery grasps; and he attributes the reductions of the mouldings in the tracery bar, under portions of one section, to the greater facility thus obtained by the architect in directing his workmen. The plan of a window once given, and the moulding-section,—all is said, thinks M. Viollet le Duc. Very convenient indeed, for modern architects who have commission on the cost. But certainly not necessary, and perhaps even *in*convenient, to Niccola Pisano, who is himself his workman, and cuts his own traceries, with his apron loaded with dust.

Again, the *re*dent—the "tooth within tooth" of a French tracery—may be necessary, to bite its glass. But the cusp, cuspis, spiny or spearlike point of a thirteenth-century illumination is not in the least necessary to transfix the parchment. Yet do you suppose that the structural convenience of the redent entirely effaces from the mind of the designer the æsthetic characters which he seeks in the cusp? If you could for an instant imagine this, you would be undeceived by a glance either at the early redents of Amiens, fringing hollow vaults, or the late redents of Rouen, acting as crockets on the *outer* edges of pediments.

Again: if you think of the tracery in its *bars,* you call the cusp a redent; but if you think of it in the *openings,* you call the apertures of it foils. Do you suppose that the thirteenth century builder thought only of the strength of the bars of his enclosure, and never of the beauty of the form he enclosed? You will find in my chapter on the Aperture, in the *Stones of Venice* [I], full development of the æsthetic laws relating to both these forms, while you may see, in Professor Willis's *Architecture of the Middle Ages* [Cambridge, 1835], a beautiful analysis of the development of tracery from the juxtaposition of aperture; and in the article "Meneau," just quoted of M. Viollet le Duc, an equally beautiful analysis of its development from the masonry of the chassis. You may at first think that Professor Willis's analysis is inconsistent with M. Viollet le Duc's. But they are no more inconsistent than the accounts of the growth of a human being would be, if given by two anatomists, of whom one had examined only the skeleton, and the other only the respiratory system; and who, therefore, supposed—the first, that the animal had been made only to leap, and the other only to sing. I don't mean that either of the writers I name is absolutely thus narrow in his own views, but that, so far as inconsistency appears to exist between them, it is of that partial kind only.

We must, to press our simile a little farther, examine the growth of the animal as if it had been made neither to leap, nor to sing, but only to think. We must observe the transitional states of its nerve power; that is to say, in our window tracery we must consider not merely how its ribs are built (or how it *stands*), nor merely how its openings are shaped (or how it *breathes*); but also what its openings are made to light, or its shafts to receive, of picture or image. As the limbs of the building, it may be much; as the lungs of the building, more. As the *eyes* of the building, what?[36]

[36] Val 94–96, omit.

Line replaces mass in late Gothic

The change [in late Gothic] of which I speak, is expressible in few words; but one more important, more radically influential, could not be. It was the substitution of the *line* for the *mass,* as the element of decoration.

We have seen the mode in which the openings or penetration of the window expanded, until what were, at first, awkward forms of intermediate stone, became delicate lines of tracery; and I have been careful in pointing out the peculiar attention bestowed on the proportion and decoration of the mouldings of the window at Rouen, as compared with earlier mouldings, because that beauty and care are singularly significant. They mark that the traceries had *caught the eye* of the architect. Up to that time, up to the very last instant in which the reduction and thinning of the intervening stone was consummated, his eye had been on the openings only, on the stars of light. He did not care about the stone; a rude border of moulding was all he needed, it was the penetrating shape which he was watching. But when that shape had received its last possible expansion, and when the stone-work became an arrangement of graceful and parallel lines, that arrangement, like some form in a picture, unseen and accidentally developed, struck suddenly, inevitably, on the sight. It had literally not been seen before. It flashed out in an instant, as an independent form. It became a feature of the work. The architect took it under his care, thought over it, and distributed its members as we see.

Now, the great pause was at the moment when the space and the dividing stone-work were both equally considered. It did not last fifty years. The forms of the tracery were seized with a childish delight in the novel source of beauty; and the intervening space was cast aside, as an element of decoration, for ever. I have confined myself, in following this change, to the window, as the feature in which it is clearest. But the transition is the same in every member of architecture . . .

The reader will observe that, up to the last expansion

of the penetrations, the stone-work was necessarily considered, as it actually is, *stiff*, and unyielding. It was so, also, during the pause of which I have spoken, when the forms of the tracery were still severe and pure; delicate indeed, but perfectly firm.

At the close of the period of pause, the first sign of serious change was like a low breeze, passing through the emaciated tracery, and making it tremble. It began to undulate like the threads of a cobweb lifted by the wind. It lost its essence as a structure of stone. Reduced to the slenderness of threads, it began to be considered as possessing also their flexibility. The architect was pleased with this his new fancy, and set himself to carry it out; and in a little time, the bars of tracery were caused to appear to the eye as if they had been woven together like a net. This was a change which sacrificed a great principle of truth; it sacrificed the expression of the qualities of the material; and, however delightful its results in their first developments, it was ultimately ruinous.[37]

It would be too painful a task to follow further the caricatures of form and eccentricities of treatment, which grew out of this single abuse—the flattened arch, the shrunken pillar, the lifeless ornament, the liny moulding, the distorted and extravagant foliation, until the time came when, over these wrecks and remnants, deprived of all unity and principle, rose the foul torrent of the Renaissance, and swept them all away.

So fell the great dynasty of mediæval architecture. It was because it had lost its own strength, and disobeyed its own laws—because its order, and consistency, and organisation, had been broken through—that it could oppose no resistance to the rush of overwhelming innovation.[38]

St. Vulfran of Abbeville

I don't mean that you may not by close search find here and there a fragment of good Gothic later than St. Vulfran of Abbeville, but I do mean that there is no other impor-

[37] Lamps 90–92, omit.
[38] Lamps 97 f

tant building, nor even an unimportant one of beauty, belonging to the true Gothic school, and of later date than
this. Roughly, it belongs to the last quarter of the fifteenth
century,—1475 to 1500—and the Gothic of Flanders was
hopelessly corrupt fifty years before that, the Gothic of
Italy had given way to classicalism a hundred years before,
and the Gothic spirit of England, though not yet dead,
was fastened down and helpless under stern geometrical
construction, and frigid law of vertical line, so that it is
walled up like a condemned nun, and you cannot see it
die. But here, in France, it passes away in your sight;
driven from all other scenes of its ancient power, it came
to this narrow valley of the Somme, and passed away.[39]

So we proceed to read this bit of work [St. Vulfran] as
well as we can. Well—first there are its more physical and
material qualities. What is it made of—built of? That's the
first thing to ask of all building. Egyptian building is essentially of porphyry,—Greek of marble,—St. Mark's at
Venice of glass and alabaster,—and this is—built of chalk,
common chalk—chalk with the flints in it left in, and stick-
ing out here and there. Well, that's the first point to think
about. All flamboyant architecture is essentially chalk architecture,—it is built of some light, soft, greasy stone,
which you can cut like cheese, which you can drive a
furrow into with your chisel an inch deep, as a ploughman furrows his field. Well, of course, with this sort of
stuff the workman goes instinctively in for deep cutting;
he *can* cut deep,—and he does cut deep;—and he can cut
fast, and he does cut fast;—and he can cut fantastically,—
and he goes in for fancy. What is more, the white surface
itself has no preciousness in it, but it becomes piquant
when opposed with black shadow, and this flamboyant
chiselling is therefore exactly, compared to a fine sculpture, what a Prout sketch is to a painting:—black and
white,—against gentle and true colour.

Now what this Abbeville work is typically, all late northern work is broadly:—black and white sketching against
perfect form; and what there is of good and bad in that

[39] Flamb 245

method is all mingled in it. On the one hand there is not a
greater distinction between vital sculpture for building, and
dead sculpture, than that a true workman paints with his
chisel,—does not carve the form of a thing, but cuts the
effect of its form. In the great statue of Voltaire at the
[Théâtre Français]—a miracle of such work—the light in
the eye is obtained by a projecting piece of marble. All
Donatello's work—all Mino of Fiesole's—all the loveliest
Italian cinque-cento—is literally chisel-painting; and it is
continually apt to run into too much trick and under-
cutting. I can't go into that, now—it begins with the use
of the drill in Byzantium capitals. But the issue of it is that
you have at last too much superficial effect,—too much
trickery,—not enough knowledge of real form. But then
you have a knowledge of effect which is quite consummate, and I know nothing in the whole range of art in
which the touch is so exquisitely measured to its distance
as in this flamboyant. Not one accent is ever lost,—it looks
equally fine all over; but at forty feet above the eye you
find it is actually so coarse that you cannot believe it is
the work you saw from below.

But broadly;—here is the final corruption:—that it becomes a design of lace in white, on a black ground; not
a true or intelligent rendering of organic form.[40]

"Excess of ingenuity"

Now the next point of decline is not physical at all; it
is wholly a mental matter—excess, namely, of ingenuity in
construction. There is always a steady increase in this particular kind of skill in every school of building, from its
birth to its fall. It builds more and more ingeniously every
day, and at last expires in small mathematical conceits.

The first idea of construction is the simplest possible;
two stones set on end, and another set on the top. That
is Stonehenge construction,—it is Egyptian construction,—
it is Greek construction. Not ingenious,—but very secure, if
your stone is good. And with that simplest of construc-

[40] Flamb 250–52

tions are connected, without any exception, all the best schools of sculpture; for there is no great sculpturesque school even of advanced Gothic, after the horizontal lintel has quite vanished into the vault. Well, next to this horizontal stone, come two stones, giving a gable;—then the arch, and then endless systems of narrower shafts and higher arches, until the mind of the builder is mainly occupied in finding new ways of making his work stand, and look as if it couldn't stand. Now there is nothing more delightful in their own way than these subtle contrivances of later Gothic, through which Strassburg tower stands up five hundred feet transparent as a cloud,—and Salisbury spire springs like the foam jet over a hollow wave,—foundationless.

But, exactly in proportion as the builder's mind is occupied with these mechanical conditions, it is necessarily unoccupied by thoughts connected with human passion or historical event.

Mathematics are delightful and absorbing, but they are not pathetic; good mason's work, or good engineer's, is intensely satisfactory to the person doing it, and leaves him no time for sentiment, or for what it is now the somewhat vulgar fashion to call sentimentality. And in exactly measured and inevitable degree, as architecture is more ingenious, it is less passionate.

When humanity and history were the main things in the architect's mind, his broad surfaces were everything to him, and his limiting lines unimportant. But when construction became principal with him, and story subordinate, —the shaft and the arch rib became everything, and the wall nothing,—until it was found that, in fact, a building might be constructed by nothing but ribs, a mere osseous thorax of a building, instead of a living body. And the critical moment,—the turn of fate,—the fastening of a disease that might be conquered, into disease that was mortal to Gothic architecture,—was what I long ago defined in the *Stones of Venice,* as the substitution of the line for the mass as the element of decoration. For early work had walls covered with sculpture, and windows divided by pillars. Late work has its walls covered with lace, and its windows spun across with cobwebs. And this is not a mere increase in subtlety, or excess in quantity. It is total and fatal change in principle. Look here,—here's a picture,—and here's a frame. Early architecture decorated with this;—late architecture decorates with that. Literally,—and to the fullest extent,—this is true. In early work, you have a tablet covered with sculpture, and a decorated moulding round it; —that is all right; but in late work, you have no sculpture, —but are to enjoy the moulding.

Interlace and melancholy

But now observe, secondly: it is interwoven Architecture. Not merely linear,—but flexibly linear, twisted and wreathed so as to make the stone look ductile. Herein is its great distinction from the English perpendicular; and it is an entirely essential distinction. And to an architect it would necessarily appear that in this it was inferior to the English school,—and that pretending to make stone look not like stone, and defying many of the laws of mechanical structure, it had forfeited all title to be ranked with the rigid legitimacy of buildings. And that is in the main, true; this system of interweaving is an abandonment of the principle, which is, that every material should have its qualities insisted on, not disguised; and that all ornament is wrong which contradicts or conceals the laws of stable masonry. But it is necessary that the true root and cause of this character should be understood, before we can judge it justly.

You are doubtless all aware that from the earliest times, a system of interwoven ornament has been peculiarly characteristic of northern design, reaching greatest intensity of fancy in the Irish manuscripts represented by the Book of Kells,—and universal in Scandinavia and among the Norman race. But you may not have considered,—that, disguised by other and more subtle qualities, the same instinct is manifest in the living art of the whole world. This delight in the embroidery, intricacy of involution,—the labyrinthine wanderings of a clue, continually lost, continually recovered, belongs—though in a more chastised and delicate phase—as much to Indian, to Arabian, to Egyptian, and to Byzantine work, as to that of Norway and Ireland;—nay, it existed just as strongly in the Greek mind in its best times; only as all other powers and instincts of art were theirs besides, the Greeks never narrowed their ingenuity into mere looping and knotting of lines, and they brought out their delight in involution, only in subordination to truth of human and animal form. What is with a Byzantine nothing but basket work, is with the Greek a confusion of limbs of the horses as they turn in a chariot race; and what with a Norman would have been only a running troop of hunted beasts, or creeping thicket of twisted branches, is with the Greek a procession of youths and maidens. But in all living art this love of involved and recurrent line exists,—and exists essentially—it exists just as much in music as in sculpture, and the continually lost and recovered threads and streams of melody in a perfect fugue, correspond precisely in their sweet science of bewildering succession, to the loveliest traceries over the gold of an early missal, or to the fantasies of the stone work . . .

But in the Northern Gothic, and especially in this flamboyant school, there was another and a quite nobler influence at work; there *was* this licentiousness; but with it there was a strange fear and melancholy, which had descended unbroken from the gloom of Scandinavian religion, —which was associated always with the labour, the darkness, and the hardships of the North, and which in its resistance to the increasing luxury of the time, took now a feverish and frantic tendency towards the contemplation of death,—clinging to this as its only rebuke and safety, tempted by luxury on one side, and tormented by remorse upon the other,—and most of all by the great baseness of illiterate Christianity in the fear of a physical hell—mingled with indignation against the vices of the priests,—which brought a bitter mockery and low grotesque into the art that had once breathed in affectionate faith and childish obedience. So that you have the pensiveness of Albert Dürer's Melencholia, and the majesty of his Knight walking with Death,—and the fantasy and fever of his Apoca-

lypse,—and the luxury of his wanton and floating Fortune,
—and the insatiable intensity of redundant minuteness, and
as it were an avarice of nothing in his pebbles and leaves;
and you have the mixed mockery and despair of Holbein's
Dance of Death,—and a thousand such others,—and all the
powers and instincts of which these were the sign, thrilling
and contending in the breasts of men, and forcing themselves into every line of the last forms of the shrines of
their expiring religion. So that the very threads of the now
thin and nervous stone work catch the ague of mixed
wantonness and terror, and—weak with unwholesome and
ominous fire—flamboyant with a fatal glow—tremble in their
ascent as if they were seen through troubled and heated
air, over a desert horizon;—and lose themselves at last in
the likeness,—no more as the ancient marbles, of the snows
of Olympus,—but of the fires of condemnation.[41]

[41] Flamb 254–61, omit.

8

THE URBAN-INDUSTRIAL WORLD

I cannot express the amazed awe, the crushed humility, with which I sometimes watch a locomotive take its breath at a railway station, and think what work there is in its bars and wheels, and what manner of men they must be who dig brown iron-stone out of the ground, and forge it into THAT! What assemblage of accurate and mighty faculties in them; more than fleshly power over melting crag and coiling fire, fettered, and finessed at last into the precision of watchmaking; Titanian hammer-strokes beating, out of lava, these glittering cylinders and timely-respondent valves, and fine ribbed rods, which touch each other as a serpent writhes, in noiseless gliding, and omnipotence of grasp; infinitely complex anatomy of active steel, compared with which the skeleton of a living creature would seem, to a careless observer, clumsy and vile—a mere morbid secretion and phosphatous prop of flesh! What would the men who thought out this—who beat it out, who touched it into its polished calm of power, who set it to its appointed task, and triumphantly saw it fulfil this task to the utmost of their will—feel or think about this weak hand of mine, timidly leading a little stain of water-colour, which I cannot manage, into an imperfect shadow of something else—mere failure in every motion, and endless disappointment; what, I repeat, would these Iron-dominant Genii think of me? and what ought I to think of them?

But as I reach this point of reverence, the unreasonable thing is sure to give a shriek as of a thousand unanimous vultures, which leaves me shuddering in real physical pain for some half minute following; and assures me, during slow recovery, that a people which can endure such fluting and piping among them is not likely soon to have its modest ear pleased by aught of oaten stop, or pastoral song.[42] Perhaps I am then led on into meditation respecting the spiritual nature of the Tenth Muse, who invented this gracious instrument, and guides its modulation by stokers' fingers; meditation, also, as to the influence of her invention amidst the other parts of the Parnassian melody of English education. Then it cannot but occur to me to inquire how far this modern "pneuma," Steam, may be connected with other pneumatic powers talked of in that old religious literature, of which we fight so fiercely to keep the letters bright, and the working valves, so to speak, in good order (while we let the steam of it all carefully off into the cold condenser), what connection, I say, this modern "spiritus," in its valve-directed inspiration, has with that more ancient spiritus, or warm breath, which people used to think they might be "born of." Whether, in fine, there be any such thing as an entirely human Art, with spiritual motive power, and signal as of human voice, distinct inherently from this mechanical Art, with its mechanical motive force, and signal of vulture voice. For after all, this shrieking thing, whatever the fine make of it may be, can but pull, or push, and do oxen's work in an impetuous manner.[43]

The railroad station

Another of the strange and evil tendencies of the present day is to the decoration of the railroad station. Now, if there be any place in the world in which people are deprived of that portion of temper and discretion which is necessary to the contemplation of beauty, it is there. It is the very temple of discomfort, and the only charity that the builder can extend to us is to show us, plainly as may be, how soonest to escape from it. The whole system of railroad travelling is addressed to people who, being in a hurry, are therefore, for the time being, miserable. No one

[42] (Collins, *Ode to Evening*.) Cestus 60–62
[43] Cestus 62

would travel in that manner who could help it—who had time to go leisurely over hills and between hedges, instead of through tunnels and between banks: at least, those who would, have no sense of beauty so acute as that we need consult it at the station. The railroad is in all its relations a matter of earnest business, to be got through as soon as possible. It transmutes a man from a traveller into a living parcel. For the time he has parted with the nobler characteristics of his humanity for the sake of a planetary power of locomotion. Do not ask him to admire anything. You might as well ask the wind. Carry him safely, dismiss him soon: he will thank you for nothing else. All attempts to please him in any other way are mere mockery, and insults to the things by which you endeavour to do so. There never was more flagrant nor impertinent folly than the smallest portion of ornament in anything concerned with railroads or near them. Keep them out of the way, take them through the ugliest country you can find, confess them the miserable things they are, and spend nothing upon them but for safety and speed. Give large salaries to efficient servants, large prices to good manufacturers, large wages to able workmen; let the iron be tough, and the brickwork solid, and the carriages strong. The time is perhaps not distant when these first necessities may not be easily met: and to increase expense in any other direction is madness. Better bury gold in the embankments, than put it in ornaments on the stations. Will a single traveller be willing to pay an increased fare on the South Western, because the columns of the terminus are covered with patterns from Nineveh?—he will only care less for the Ninevite ivories in the British Museum: or on the North Western, because there are old English-looking spandrels to the roof of the station at Crewe?—he will only have less pleasure in their prototypes at Crewe House. Railroad architecture has, or would have, a dignity of its own if it were only left to its work. You would not put rings on the fingers of a smith at his anvil.[44]

[44] Lamps 159 f

The city

I had occasion only the other day to wait for half-an-hour at the bottom of Ludgate Hill. Standing as much out of the way as I could, under the shadow of the railroad bridge, I watched the faces, all eager, many anxious, and some intensely gloomy, of the hurried passers-by; and listened to the ceaseless crashing, whistling, and thundering sounds which mingled with the murmur of their steps and voices. And in the midst of the continuous roar, which differed only from that of the wildest sea in storm by its complexity and its discordance, I was wondering, if the sum of what all these people were doing, or trying to do, in the course of the day, could be made manifest, what it would come to.

The sum of it would be, I suppose, that they had all contrived to live through the day in that exceedingly unpleasant manner, and that nothing serious had occurred to prevent them from passing the following day likewise. Nay, I knew also that what appeared in their way of life painful to me, might be agreeable to them; and it chanced, indeed, a little while afterwards, that an active and prosperous man of business, speaking to one of my friends of the disappointment he had felt in a visit to Italy, remarked, especially, that he was not able to endure more than three days at Venice, because there was no noise there.[45]

[E]very day puts new machinery at your disposal, and increases, with your capital, the vastness of your undertakings. The changes in the state of this country are now so rapid, that it would be wholly absurd to endeavour to lay down laws of art education for it under its present aspect and circumstances; and therefore I must necessarily ask, how much of it do you seriously intend within the next fifty years to be coal-pit, brick-field, or quarry? For the sake of distinctness of conclusion, I will suppose your success absolute: that from shore to shore the whole of the island is to be set as thick with chimneys as the masts

[45] ENest 163

stand in the docks of Liverpool: that there shall be no meadows in it; no trees; no gardens; only a little corn grown upon the housetops, reaped and threshed by steam: that you do not leave even room for roads, but travel either over the roofs of your mills, on viaducts; or under their floors, in tunnels: that, the smoke having rendered the light of the sun unserviceable, you work always by the light of your own gas: that no acre of English ground shall be without its shaft and its engine; and therefore, no spot of English ground left, on which it shall be possible to stand, without a definite and calculable chance of being blown off it, at any moment, into small pieces.

Under these circumstances, (if this is to be the future of England,) no designing or any other development of beautiful art will be possible. Do not vex your minds, nor waste your money with any thought or effort in the matter. Beautiful art can only be produced by people who have beautiful things about them, and leisure to look at them; and unless you provide some elements of beauty for your workmen to be surrounded by, you will find that no elements of beauty can be invented by them.

I was struck forcibly by the bearing of this great fact upon our modern efforts at ornamentation in an afternoon walk, last week, in the suburbs of one of our large manufacturing towns.

Just outside the town I came upon an old English cottage . . . [B]efore its gate, the stream which had gladdened it now soaking slowly by, black as ebony and thick with curdling scum; the bank above it trodden into unctuous, sooty slime: far in front of it, between it and the old hills, the furnaces of the city foaming forth perpetual plague of sulphurous darkness; the volumes of their storm clouds coiling low over a waste of grassless fields, fenced from each other, not by hedges, but by slabs of square stone, like gravestones, riveted together with iron.

That was your scene for the designer's contemplation in his afternoon walk at Rochdale. Now fancy what was the scene which presented itself, in his afternoon walk, to a designer of the Gothic school of Pisa—Nino Pisano, or any of his men.

On each side of a bright river he saw rise a line of brighter palaces, arched and pillared, and inlaid with deep red porphyry, and with serpentine; along the quays before their gates were riding troops of knights, noble in face and form, dazzling in crest and shield; horse and man one labyrinth of quaint colour and gleaming light—the purple, and silver, and scarlet fringes flowing over the strong limbs and clashing mail, like sea-waves over rocks at sunset. Opening on each side from the river were gardens, courts, and cloisters; long successions of white pillars among wreaths of vine; leaping of fountains through buds of pomegranate and orange . . .

No revival of the past

What think you of that for a school of design?

I do not bring this contrast before you as a ground of hopelessness in our task; neither do I look for any possible renovation of the Republic of Pisa, at Bradford, in the nineteenth century; but I put it before you in order that you may be aware precisely of the kind of difficulty you have to meet, and may then consider with yourselves how far you can meet it. To men surrounded by the depressing and monotonous circumstances of English manufacturing life, depend upon it, design is simply impossible.

I repeat, that I do not ask you nor wish you to build a new Pisa for them. We don't want either the life or the decorations of the thirteenth century back again; and the circumstances with which you must surround your workmen are those simply of happy modern English life, because the designs you have now to ask for from your workmen are such as will make modern English life beautiful. All that gorgeousness of the Middle Ages, beautiful as it sounds in description, noble as in many respects it was in reality, had, nevertheless, for foundation and for end, nothing but the pride of life—the pride of the so-called superior classes; a pride which supported itself by violence and robbery, and led in the end to the destruction both of the arts themselves and the States in which they flourished.

The great lesson of history is, that all the fine arts hitherto—having been supported by the selfish power of the noblesse, and never having extended their range to the comfort or the relief of the mass of the people—the arts, I say, thus practised, and thus matured, have only accelerated the ruin of the States they adorned; and at the moment when, in any kingdom, you point to the triumphs of its greatest artists, you point also to the determined hour of the kingdom's decline. The names of great painters are like passing bells: in the name of Velasquez, you hear sounded the fall of Spain; in the name of Titian, that of Venice; in the name of Leonardo, that of Milan; in the name of Raphael, that of Rome.[46]

We are forced, for the sake of accumulating our power and knowledge, to live in cities: but such advantage as we have in association with each other is in great part counterbalanced by our loss of fellowship with Nature. We cannot all have our gardens now, nor our pleasant fields to meditate in at eventide. Then the function of our architecture is, as far as may be, to replace these; to tell us about Nature; to possess us with memories of her quietness; to be solemn and full of tenderness, like her, and rich in portraitures of her; full of delicate imagery of the flowers we can no more gather, and of the living creatures now far away from us in their own solitude. If ever you felt or found this in a London street,—if ever it furnished you with one serious thought, or one ray of true and gentle pleasure, —if there is in your heart a true delight in its grim railings and dark casements, and wasteful finery of shops, and feeble coxcombry of club-houses,—it is well: promote the building of more like them. But if they never taught you anything, and never made you happier as you passed beneath them, do not think they have any mysterious goodness nor occult sublimity. Have done with the wretched affectation, the futile barbarism, of pretending to enjoy; for, as surely as you know that the meadow grass, meshed with fairy rings, is better than the wood pavement, cut into hexagons; and as surely as you know the fresh winds and sunshine of the upland are better than the choke-damp

[46] TwoP 337–42, omit.

of the vault, or the gas-light of the ball-room, you may
know, as I told you that you should, that the good architecture, which has life, and truth, and joy in it, is better
than the bad architecture, which has death, dishonesty,
and vexation of heart in it, from the beginning to the end
of time.[47]

Art and manufacture

Art may be healthily associated with manufacture, and
probably in future will always be so; but the student must
be strenuously warned against supposing that they can
ever be one and the same thing, that art can ever be followed on the principles of manufacture. Each must be followed separately; the one must influence the other, but
each must be kept distinctly separate from the other.

It would be well if all students would keep clearly in
their mind the real distinction between those words which
we use so often, "Manufacture," "Art," and "Fine Art."
MANUFACTURE is, according to the etymology and right
use of the word, "the making of anything by hands,"—
directly or indirectly, with or without the help of instruments or machines. Anything proceeding from the hand of
man is manufacture; but it must have proceeded from his
hand only, acting mechanically, and uninfluenced at the
moment by direct intelligence.

Then, secondly, ART is the operation of the hand and
the intelligence of man together: there is an art of making
machinery; there is an art of building ships; an art of making carriages; and so on. All these, properly called Arts,
but not Fine Arts, are pursuits in which the hand of man
and his head go together, working at the same instant.

Then FINE ART is that in which the hand, the head,
and the *heart* of man go together.

Recollect this triple group; it will help you to solve
many difficult problems. And remember that though the
hand must be at the bottom of everything, it must also go
to the top of everything; for Fine Art must be produced

[47] SV I, 411 f

by the hand of man in a much greater and clearer sense than Manufacture is. Fine Art must always be produced by the subtlest of all machines, which is the human hand. No machine yet contrived, or hereafter contrivable, will ever equal the fine machinery of the human fingers.[48]

[48] TwoP 294 f

9

IRON AND GLASS

Perhaps the most fruitful sources of these kinds of corruption which we have to guard against in recent times, is one which, nevertheless, comes in a "questionable shape,"[49] and of which it is not easy to determine the proper laws and limits; I mean the use of iron. The definition of the art of architecture, given in the first Chapter, is independent of its materials. Nevertheless, that art having been, up to the beginning of the present century, practised for the most part in clay, stone, or wood, it has resulted that the sense of proportion and the laws of structure have been based, the one altogether, the other in great part, on the necessities consequent on the employment of those materials; and that the entire or principal employment of metallic framework would, therefore, be generally felt as a departure from the first principles of the art. Abstractedly there appears no reason why iron should not be used as well as wood; and the time is probably near when a new system of architectural laws will be developed, adapted entirely to metallic construction. But I believe that the tendency of all present[50] sympathy and association is to limit the idea of architecture to non-metallic work; and that not without reason. For architecture being in its perfection the earliest, as in its elements it is necessarily the first, of arts, will always precede, in any barbarous nation, the possession of the science necessary either for the ob-

[49] (*Hamlet*, i, sc. 4.) Lamps 66
[50] (Ruskin note added in 1880: " 'Present,' i.e. of the day [1848] in which I wrote, as opposed to the ferruginous temper which I saw rapidly developing itself, and which, since that day, has changed our merry England into the Man in the Iron Mask.") Lamps 66

taining or the management of iron. Its first existence and
its earliest laws must, therefore, depend upon the use of
materials accessible in quantity, and on the surface of the
earth; that is to say, clay, wood, or stone: and as I think
it cannot but be generally felt that one of the chief dignities of architecture is its historical use, and since the latter is partly dependent on consistency of style, it will be
felt right to retain as far as may be, even in periods of
more advanced science, the materials and principles of
earlier ages.

But whether this be granted me or not, the fact is, that
every idea respecting size, proportion, decoration, or construction, on which we are at present in the habit of acting
or judging, depends on presupposition of such materials:
and as I both feel myself unable to escape the influence of
these prejudices, and believe that my readers will be
equally so, it may be perhaps permitted to me to assume
that true architecture does not admit iron as a constructive
material, and that such works as the cast-iron central spire
of Rouen Cathedral, or the iron roofs and pillars of our
railway stations, and of some of our churches, are not
architecture at all. Yet it is evident that metals may, and
sometimes must, enter into the construction to a certain
extent, as nails in wooden architecture, and therefore, as
legitimately, rivets and solderings in stone; neither can we
well deny to the Gothic architect the power of supporting
statues, pinnacles, or traceries by iron bars; and if we
grant this, I do not see how we can help allowing Brunelleschi his iron chain around the dome of Florence, or the
builders of Salisbury their elaborate iron binding of the
central tower. If, however, we would not fall into the old
sophistry of the grains of corn and the heap, we must find
a rule which may enable us to stop somewhere. This rule
is, I think, that metals may be used as a *cement*, but not as
a *support*. For as cements of other kinds are often so strong
that the stones may easier be broken than separated, and
the wall becomes a solid mass, without for that reason losing the character of architecture, there is no reason why,
when a nation has obtained the knowledge and practice of
iron work, metal rods or rivets should not be used in the

place of cement, and establish the same or a greater
strength and adherence, without in any wise inducing departure from the types and system of architecture before
established; nor does it make any difference, except as to
sightliness, whether the metal bands or rods so employed
be in the body of the wall or on its exterior, or set as stays
and cross-bands . . .[51]

In a lately built house, No. 86, in Oxford Street, three
huge stone pillars in the second story are carried apparently
by the edges of three sheets of plate glass in the first. I
hardly know anything to match the painfulness of this and
some other of our shop structures, in which the ironwork
is concealed; nor even when it is apparent, can the eye
ever feel satisfied of their security, when built, as at present, with fifty or sixty feet of wall above a rod of iron not
the width of this page [i.e., seven inches].[52]

The Crystal Palace

Before I altogether leave the question of the influence of
labour on architectural effect, the reader may expect from
me a word or two respecting the subject which is every year becoming of greater interest—the applicability,
namely, of glass and iron to architecture in general, as in
some sort exemplified by the Crystal Palace.

It is thought by many that we shall forthwith have great
part of our architecture in glass and iron, and that new
forms of beauty will result from the studied employment
of these materials. It may be told in few words how far this
is possible; how far eternally impossible.

There are two means of delight in all productions of
art—colour and form.

The most vivid conditions of colour attainable by human
art are those of works in glass and enamel, but not the most
perfect. The best and noblest colouring possible to art is
that attained by the touch of the human hand on an
opaque surface, upon which it can command any tint re-

[51] Lamps 66–68
[52] (By 1904 the house number was changed to 134.) SV I,
242

quired, without subjection to alteration by fire or other mechanical means. No colour is so noble as the colour of a good painting on canvas or gesso. This kind of colour being, however, impossible, for the most part, in architecture, the next best is the scientific disposition of the natural colours of stones, which are far nobler than any abstract hues producible by human art.

The delight which we receive from glass painting is one altogether inferior, and in which we should degrade ourselves by over indulgence. Nevertheless, it is possible that we may raise some palaces like Aladdin's with coloured glass for jewels, which shall be new in the annals of human splendour, and good in their places; but not if they superseded nobler lustre.

Now, colour is producible either on opaque or in transparent bodies: but form is only expressible, in its perfection, on opaque bodies, without lustre. This law is imperative, universal, irrevocable. No perfect or refined form can be expressed except in opaque and lustreless matter. You cannot see the form of a jewel, nor, in any perfection, even of a cameo or bronze. You cannot perfectly see the form of a humming-bird, on account of its burnishing; but you can see the form of a swan perfectly. No noble work in form can ever, therefore, be produced in transparent or lustrous glass or enamel. All noble architecture depends for its majesty on its form: therefore you can never have any noble architecture in transparent or lustrous glass or enamel. Iron is, however, opaque; and both it and opaque enamel may, perhaps, be rendered quite lustreless; and, therefore, fit to receive noble form.

Let this be thoroughly done, and both the iron and enamel made fine in paste or grain, and you may have an architecture as noble as cast or struck architecture ever can be: as noble, therefore, as coins can be, or common cast bronzes, and such other multiplicable things;—eternally separated from all good and great things by a gulph which not all the tubular bridges nor engineering of ten thousand nineteenth centuries cast into one great bronze-foreheaded century, will ever overpass one inch of. All art which is worth its room in this world, all art which is not a piece of blundering refuse, occupying the foot or two of earth which, if unencumbered by it, would have grown corn or violets, or some better thing, is *art which proceeds from an individual mind, working through instruments which assist, but do not supersede, the muscular action of the human hand, upon the materials which most tenderly receive, and most securely retain, the impressions of such human labour.*

And the value of every work of art is exactly in the ratio of the quantity of humanity which has been put into it, and legibly expressed upon it for ever:—

First, of thought and moral purpose;

Secondly, of technical skill;

Thirdly, of bodily industry.

The quantity of bodily industry which that Crystal Palace expresses is very great. So far it is good. The quantity of thought it expresses is, I suppose, a single and very admirable thought of Sir Joseph Paxton's, probably not a bit brighter than thousands of thoughts which pass through his active and intelligent brain every hour—that it might be possible to build a greenhouse larger than ever greenhouse was built before. This thought, and some very ordinary algebra, are as much as all that glass can represent of human intellect. "But one poor halfpennyworth of bread to all this intolerable deal of sack." Alas!

"The earth hath bubbles as the water hath:
And this is of them."[53]

A new style in iron and glass?

Perhaps the first idea which a young architect is apt to be allured by, as a head-problem in these experimental days, is its being incumbent upon him to invent a "new style" worthy of modern civilization in general, and of England in particular; a style worthy of our engines and telegraphs; as expansive as steam, and as sparkling as electricity. When our desired style is invented, will not the best

[53] (*Henry IV*, Pt. 1, ii, sc. 4, and *Macbeth*, i, sc. 3.) Appendix SV I, 455 f

we can all do be simply—to build in it?—and cannot you
now do that in styles that are known? Observe, I grant, for
the sake of your argument, what perhaps many of you
know that I would not grant otherwise—that a new style
can be invented. I grant you not only this, but that it shall
be wholly different from any that was ever practised before. We will suppose that capitals are to be at the bottom
of pillars instead of the top; and that buttresses shall be on
the tops of pinnacles instead of at the bottom; that you
roof your apertures with stones which shall neither be
arched nor horizontal; and that you compose your decoration of lines which shall neither be crooked nor straight.
The furnace and the forge shall be at your service: you
shall draw out your plates of glass and beat out your bars
of iron till you have encompassed us all,—if your style is of
the practical kind,—with endless perspective of black skeleton and blinding square,—or if your style is to be of the
ideal kind,—you shall wreathe your streets with ductile
leafage, and roof them with variegated crystal—you shall
put, if you will, all London under one blazing dome of
many colours that shall light the clouds round it with its
flashing, as far as to the sea. And still, I ask you, What
after this? Do you suppose those imaginations of yours
will ever lie down there asleep beneath the shade of your
iron leafage, or within the coloured light of your enchanted
dome? Not so. Those souls, and fancies, and ambitions of
yours, are wholly infinite; and, whatever may be done by
others, you will still want to do something for yourselves;
if you cannot rest content with Palladio, neither will you
with Paxton: all the metal and glass that ever were melted
have not so much weight in them as will clog the wings of
one human spirit's aspiration.

If you will think over this quietly by yourselves, and
can get the noise out of your ears of the perpetual, empty,
idle, incomparably idiotic talk about the necessity of some
novelty in architecture, you will soon see that the very
essence of a Style, properly so called, is that it should be
practised *for ages,* and applied to all purposes; and that
so long as any given style is in practice, all that is left for
individual imagination to accomplish must be within the

scope of that style, not in the invention of a new one. If there are any here, therefore, who hope to obtain celebrity by the invention of some strange way of building which must convince all Europe into its adoption, to them, for the moment, I must not be understood to address myself, but only to those who would be content with that degree of celebrity which an artist may enjoy who works in the manner of his forefathers;—which the builder of Salisbury Cathedral might enjoy in England, though he did not invent Gothic; and which Titian might enjoy at Venice, though he did not invent oil painting. Addressing myself then to those humbler, but wiser, or rather, only wise students who are content to avail themselves of some system of building already understood, let us consider together what room for the exercise of the imagination may be left to us under such conditions. And, first, I suppose it will be said, or thought, that the architect's principal field for exercise of his invention must be in the disposition of lines, mouldings, and masses, in agreeable proportions. Indeed, if you adopt some styles of architecture, you cannot exercise invention in any other way. And I admit that it requires genius and special gift to do this rightly. Not by rule, nor by study, can the gift of graceful proportionate design be obtained; only by the intuition of genius can so much as a single tier of façade be beautifully arranged; and the man has just cause for pride, as far as our gifts can ever be a cause for pride, who finds himself able, in a design of his own, to rival even the simplest arrangement of parts in one by Sanmicheli, Inigo Jones, or Christopher Wren.[54]

The nature of iron

So again, iron is eminently a ductile and tenacious substance—tenacious above all things, ductile more than most. When you want tenacity, therefore, and involved form, take iron. It is eminently made for that. It is the material given to the sculptor as the companion of marble, with a message, as plain as it can well be spoken, from the lips of

[54] TwoP 348–50, omit.

the earth-mother, "Here's for you to cut, and here's for you to hammer. Shape this, and twist that. What is solid and simple, carve out; what is thin and entangled, beat out. I give you all kinds of forms to be delighted in; fluttering leaves as well as fair bodies; twisted branches as well as open brows. The leaf and the branch you may beat and drag into their imagery: the body and brow you shall reverently touch into their imagery. And if you choose rightly and work rightly, what you do shall be safe afterwards. Your slender leaves shall not break off in my tenacious iron, though they may be rusted a little with an iron autumn. Your broad surfaces shall not be unsmoothed in my pure crystalline marble—no decay shall touch them. But if you carve in the marble what will break with a touch, or mould in the metal what a stain of rust or verdigris will spoil, it is your fault—not mine."[55]

The little town of Bellinzona, for instance, on the south of the Alps, and that of Sion on the north, have both of them complete schools of ironwork in their balconies and vineyard gates. That of Bellinzona is the best, though not very old—I suppose most of it of the seventeenth century; still it is very quaint and beautiful. Here, for example, are two balconies, from two different houses: one has been a cardinal's, and the hat is the principal ornament of the balcony, its tassels being wrought with delightful delicacy and freedom; and catching the eye clearly even among the mass of rich wreathed leaves. These tassels and strings are precisely the kind of subject fit for ironwork—noble in ironwork, they would have been entirely ignoble in marble, on the grounds above stated. The real plant of oleander standing in the window enriches the whole group of lines very happily.

The other balcony, from a very ordinary-looking house in the same street, is much more interesting in its details. The plan of the group is exceedingly simple: it is all enclosed in a pointed arch, the large mass of the tulip forming the apex; a six-foiled star on each side; then a jagged star; then a five-foiled star; then an unjagged star or rose;

[55] TwoP 387

finally a small bud, so as to establish relation and cadence through the whole group. The profile is very free and fine, and the upper bar of the balcony exceedingly beautiful in effect;—none the less so on account of the marvellously simple means employed. A thin strip of iron is bent over a square rod; out of the edge of this strip are cut a series of triangular openings—widest at top, leaving projecting teeth of iron; then each of these projecting pieces gets a little sharp tap with the hammer in front, which breaks its edge inwards, tearing it a little open at the same time, and the thing is done.

[O]nly let me leave with you this one distinct assertion —that the quaint beauty and character of many natural objects, such as intricate branches, grass, foliage (especially thorny branches and prickly foliage), as well as that of many animals, plumed, spined, or bristled, is sculpturally expressible in iron only, and in iron would be majestic and impressive in the highest degree; and that every piece of metal work you use might be, rightly treated, not only a superb decoration, but a most valuable abstract of portions of natural forms, holding in dignity precisely the same relation to the painted representation of plants that a statue does to the painted form of man. It is difficult to give you an idea of the grace and interest which the simplest objects possess when their forms are thus abstracted from among the surrounding of rich circumstance which in nature disturbs the feebleness of our attention.[56]

[56] TwoP 392–95, omit.

10

ECLECTICISM: THE NINETEENTH
CENTURY AND THE PAST

[The Gothic window] is the best and strongest building,
as it is the most beautiful. I am not now speaking of the
particular form of Venetian Gothic, but of the general
strength of the pointed arch as opposed to that of the level
lintel of the square window; and I plead for the introduction of the Gothic form into our domestic architecture, not
merely because it is lovely, but because it is the only form
of faithful, strong, enduring, and honourable building, in
such materials as come daily to our hands. By increase of
scale and cost, it is possible to build, in any style, what will
last for ages; but only in the Gothic is it possible to give
security and dignity to work wrought with imperfect means
and materials. And I trust that there will come a time
when the English people may see the folly of building
basely and insecurely. There is hardly a week passes without some catastrophe brought about by the base principles
of modern building: some vaultless floor that drops the
staggering crowd through the jagged rents of its rotten
timbers; some baseless bridge that is washed away by the
first wave of a summer flood . . .

Neither can the objection, so often raised against the
pointed arch, that it will not admit the convenient adjustment of modern sashes and glass, hold for an instant. There
is not the smallest necessity, because the arch is pointed,
that the aperture should be so. The work of the arch is to
sustain the building above; when this is once done securely, the pointed head of it may be filled in any way
we choose. In the best cathedral doors it is always filled
by a shield of solid stone; in many early windows of the
best Gothic it is filled in the same manner, the introduced

slab of stone becoming a field for rich decoration; and
there is not the smallest reason why lancet windows, used
in bold groups, with each pointed arch filled by a sculptured tympanum, should not allow as much light to enter,
and in as convenient a way, as the most luxuriously glazed
square windows of our brick houses. Give the groups of associated lights bold gabled canopies; charge the gables
with sculpture and colour; and instead of the base and
almost useless Greek portico, letting the rain and wind enter it at will, build the steeply vaulted and completely
sheltered Gothic porch; and on all these fields for rich
decoration let the common workman carve what he pleases,
to the best of his power, and we may have a school of
domestic architecture in the nineteenth century, which will
make our children grateful to us, and proud of us, till the
thirtieth.[57]

The failure of revivalism

No book of mine has had so much influence on contemporary art as the *Stones of Venice;* but this influence
has been possessed only by the third part of it, the remaining two-thirds having been resolutely ignored by the British
public. And as a physician would, in most cases, rather
hear that his patient had thrown all his medicine out of
the window, than that he had sent word to his apothecary
to leave out two of its three ingredients, so I would rather,
for my own part, that no architects had ever condescended
to adopt one of the views suggested in this book, than
that any should have made the partial use of it which has
mottled our manufactory chimneys with black and red
brick, dignified our banks and drapers' shops with Venetian
tracery, and pinched our parish churches into dark and
slippery arrangements for the advertisement of cheap coloured glass and pantiles.[58]

Now there is a correspondence . . . between the technical and expressional parts of architecture;—not a true or
entire correspondence, so that when the expression is best,

[57] SV II, 312–15, omit.
[58] Preface of 1874, SV I, 11

the building must be also best; but so much of correspondence as that good building is necessary to good expression,
comes before it, and is to be primarily looked for: and the
more, because the manner of building is capable of being
determinately estimated and classed; but the expressional
character not so: we can at once determine the true value
of technical qualities, we can only approximate to the value
of expressional qualities: and besides this, the looking for
the technical qualities first will enable us to cast a large
quantity of rubbish aside at once, and so to narrow the
difficult field of inquiry into expression: we shall get rid of
Chinese pagodas and Indian temples, and Renaissance Pal-
ladianisms, and Alhambra stucco and filigree, in one great
rubbish heap; and shall not need to trouble ourselves about
their expression, or anything else concerning them. Then
taking the buildings which have been rightly put together,
and which show common sense in their structure, we may
look for their farther and higher excellencies; but on those
which are absurd in their first steps we need waste no
time.[59]

All classicality, all middle-aged patent-reviving, is utterly
vain and absurd; if we are now to do anything great, good,
awful, religious, it must be got out of our own little island,
and out of these very times, railroads and all; if a British
painter, I say this in earnest seriousness, cannot make historical characters out of the British House of Peers, he
cannot paint history; and if he cannot make a Madonna
of a British girl of the nineteenth century, he cannot paint
one at all.[60]

The failure of 'taste'

Meanwhile, the art of sculpture, less capable of ministering to mere amusement, was more or less reserved for
the affectations of taste; and the study of the classical
statues introduced various ideas on the subjects of "purity,"
"chastity," and "dignity," such as it was possible for people

[59] Appendix SV I, 450
[60] MP I, 231

to entertain who were themselves impure, luxurious, and ridiculous. It is a matter of extreme difficulty to explain the exact character of this modern sculpturesque ideal; but its relation to the true ideal may be best understood by considering it as in exact parallelism with the relation of the word "taste" to the word "love." Wherever the word "taste" is used with respect to matters of art, it indicates either that the thing spoken of belongs to some inferior class of objects, or that the person speaking has a false conception of its nature. For, consider the exact sense in which a work of art is said to be "in good or bad taste." It does not mean that it is true or false; that it is beautiful or ugly: but that it does or does not comply either with the laws of choice, which are enforced by certain modes of life, or the habits of mind produced by a particular sort of education. It does not mean merely fashionable, that is, complying with a momentary caprice of the upper classes; but it means agreeing with the habitual sense which the most refined education, common to those upper classes at the period, gives to their whole mind. Now, therefore, so far as that education does indeed tend to make the senses delicate, and the perceptions accurate, and thus enables people to be pleased with quiet instead of gaudy colour, and with graceful instead of coarse form; and, by long acquaintance with the best things, to discern quickly what is fine from what is common;—so far, acquired taste is an honourable faculty, and it is true praise of anything to say it is "in good taste." But so far as this higher education has a tendency to narrow the sympathies and harden the heart, diminishing the interest of all beautiful things by familiarity, until even what is best can hardly please, and what is brightest hardly entertain;—so far as it fosters pride, and leads men to found the pleasure they take in anything, not on the worthiness of the thing, but on the degree in which it indicates some greatness of their own (as people build marble porticoes, and inlay marble floors, not so much because they like the colours of marble, or find it pleasant to the foot, as because such porches and floors are costly, and separated in all human eyes from plain entrances of stone and timber);—so far as it leads people to prefer gracefulness of dress, manner, and aspect, to value of substance and heart, liking a well *said* thing better than a true thing, and a well-trained manner better than a sincere one, and a delicately formed face better than a good-natured one, and in all other ways and things setting custom and semblance above everlasting truth;—so far, finally, as it induces a sense of inherent distinction between class and class, and causes everything to be more or less despised which has no social rank, so that the affection, pleasure, and grief of a clown are looked upon as of no interest compared with the affection and grief of a well-bred man;—just so far, in all these several ways, the feeling induced by what is called a "liberal education" is utterly adverse to the understanding of noble art; and the name which is given to the feeling,—Taste, Goût, Gusto,—in all languages indicates the baseness of it, for it implies that art gives only a kind of pleasure analogous to that derived from eating by the palate.

Modern education, not in art only, but in all other things referable to the same standard, has invariably given taste in this bad sense; it has given fastidiousness of choice without judgment, superciliousness of manner without dignity, refinement of habit without purity, grace of expression without sincerity, and desire of loveliness without love; and the modern "ideal" of high art is a curious mingling of the gracefulness and reserve of the drawing-room with a certain measure of classical sensuality. Of this last element, and the singular artifices by which vice succeeds in combining it with what appears to be pure and severe, it would take us long to reason fully: I would rather leave the reader to follow out for himself the consideration of the influence, in this direction, of statues, bronzes, and paintings, as at present employed by the upper circles of London, and (especially) Paris; and this is not so much in the works which are really fine, as in the multiplied coarse copies of them; taking the widest range, from Dannaeker's Ariadne [of 1813, in Frankfort] down to the amorous shepherd and shepherdess in china on the drawing-room timepiece, rigidly questioning, in each case, how far the charm of the art does indeed depend on some appeal to the inferior passions.[61]

The sin of restoration

Neither by the public, nor by those who have the care of public monuments, is the true meaning of the word *restoration* understood. It means the most total destruction which a building can suffer: a destruction out of which no remnants can be gathered: a destruction accompanied with false description of the thing destroyed. Do not let us deceive ourselves in this important matter; it is *impossible,* as impossible as to raise the dead, to restore anything that has ever been great or beautiful in architecture. That which I have above insisted upon as the life of the whole, that spirit which is given only by the hand and eye of the workman, can never be recalled. Another spirit may be given by another time, and it is then a new building; but the spirit of the dead workman cannot be summoned up, and commanded to direct other hands, and other thoughts. And as for direct and simple copying, it is palpably impossible. What copying can there be of surfaces that have been worn half an inch down? The whole finish of the work was in the half inch that is gone; if you attempt to restore that finish, you do it conjecturally; if you copy what is left, granting fidelity to be possible, (and what care, or watchfulness, or cost can secure it,) how is the new work better than the old? There was yet in the old *some* life, some mysterious suggestion of what it had been, and of what it had lost; some sweetness in the gentle lines which rain and sun had wrought. There can be none in the brute hardness of the new carving.

Do not let us talk then of restoration. The thing is a Lie from beginning to end. You may make a model of a building as you may of a corpse, and your model may have the shell of the old walls within it as your cast might have the skeleton, with what advantage I neither see nor care: but the old building is destroyed, and that more totally and

[61] MP III, 94–96

mercilessly than if it had sunk into a heap of dust, or melted into a mass of clay: more has been gleaned out of desolated Nineveh than ever will be out of re-built Milan.

Take proper care of your monuments, and you will not need to restore them. A few sheets of lead put in time upon a roof, a few dead leaves and sticks swept in time out of a water-course, will save both roof and walls from ruin. Watch an old building with an anxious care; guard it as best you may, and at *any* cost, from every influence of dilapidation. Count its stones as you would jewels of a crown; set watches about it as if at the gates of a besieged city; bind it together with iron where it loosens; stay it with timber where it declines; do not care about the unsightliness of the aid: better a crutch than a lost limb; and do this tenderly, and reverently, and continually, and many a generation will still be born and pass away beneath its shadow. Its evil day must come at last; but let it come declaredly and openly, and let no dishonouring and false substitute deprive it of the funeral offices of memory.[62]

The "sweeping sacrifice of precedent"

The feebleness of childhood is full of promise and of interest,—the struggle of imperfect knowledge full of energy and continuity,—but to see impotence and rigidity settling upon the form of the developed man; to see the types which once had the die of thought struck fresh upon them, worn flat by over use; to see the shell of the living creature in its adult form, when its colours are faded, and its inhabitant perished,—this is a sight more humiliating, more melancholy, than the vanishing of all knowledge, and the return to confessed and helpless infancy.

Nay, it is to be wished that such return were always possible. There would be hope if we could change palsy into puerility; but I know not how far we *can* become children again, and renew our lost life. The stirring which has taken place in our architectural aims and interests within these few years is thought by many to be full of

[62] Lamps 242–45, omit.

promise: I trust it is, but it has a sickly look to me. I cannot tell whether it be indeed a springing of seed or a shaking among bones; and I do not think the time will be lost
which I ask the reader to spend in the inquiry, how far all
that we have hitherto ascertained or conjectured to be best
in principle, may be formally practised without the spirit
or the vitality which alone could give it influence, value,
or delightfulness.

Now, in the first place—and this is rather an important
point—it is no sign of deadness in a present art that it borrows or imitates, but only if it borrows without paying interest, or if it imitates without choice. The art of a great
nation, which is developed without any acquaintance with
nobler examples than its own early efforts furnish, exhibits
always the most consistent and comprehensible growth,
and perhaps is regarded usually as peculiarly venerable in
its self-origination. But there is something to my mind more
majestic yet in the life of an architecture like that of the
Lombards, rude and infantine in itself, and surrounded by
fragments of a nobler art of which it is quick in admiration
and ready in imitation, and yet so strong in its own new
instincts that it re-constructs and re-arranges every fragment that it copies or borrows into harmony with its own
thoughts,—a harmony at first disjointed and awkward, but
completed in the end, and fused into perfect organisation;
all the borrowed elements being subordinated to its own
primal, unchanged life.

It will be asked, How is imitation to be rendered healthy
and vital? Unhappily, while it is easy to enumerate the
signs of life, it is impossible to define or to communicate
life; and while every intelligent writer on Art has insisted
on the difference between the copying found in an advancing or recedent period, none have been able to communicate, in the slightest degree, the force of vitality to the
copyist over whom they might have influence. Yet it is at
least interesting, if not profitable, to note that two very
distinguishing characters of vital imitation are, its Frankness and its Audacity: its Frankness is especially singular;
there is never any effort to conceal the degree of the sources
of its borrowing. Raffaelle carries off a whole figure from

Masaccio, or borrows an entire composition from Perugino, with as much tranquillity and simplicity of innocence as a young Spartan pickpocket; and the architect of a Romanesque basilica gathered his columns and capitals where he could find them, as an ant picks up sticks. There is at least a presumption, when we find this frank acceptance, that there is a sense within the mind of power capable of transforming and renewing whatever it adopts; and too conscious, too exalted, to fear the accusation of plagiarism,—too certain that it can prove, and has proved, its independence, to be afraid of expressing its homage to what it admires in the most open and indubitable way; and the necessary consequence of this sense of power is the other sign I have named—the Audacity of treatment when it finds treatment necessary, the unhesitating and sweeping sacrifice of precedent where precedent becomes inconvenient.[63]

[63] Lamps 194–96, omit.

PART III

SCULPTURE AND ORNAMENT

1

SCULPTURE: THE "LIFE-SHAPING" ART

And now . . . we can sketch out the subject before us in a clear light. We have a structural art, divine and human, of which the investigation comes under the general term Anatomy; whether the junctions or joints be in mountains, or in branches of trees, or in buildings, or in bones of animals. We have next a musical art, falling into two distinct divisions—one using colours, the other masses, for its elements of composition; lastly, we have an imitative art, concerned with the representation of the outward appearances of things. And, for many reasons, I think it best to begin with imitative Sculpture; that being defined as *the art which, by the musical disposition of masses, imitates anything of which the imitation is justly pleasant to us; and does so in accordance with structural laws having due reference to the materials employed.*

Beginning with the simple conception of sculpture as the art of fiction in solid substance, we are now to consider what its subject should be. What—having the gift of imagery—should we by preference endeavour to image? A question which is, indeed, subordinate to the deeper one —why we should wish to image anything at all.

Some years ago, having been always desirous that the education of women should begin in learning how to cook, I got leave, one day, for a little girl of eleven years old to exchange, much to her satisfaction, her schoolroom for the kitchen. But as ill-fortune would have it, there was some pastry toward, and she was left unadvisedly in command of some delicately rolled paste; whereof she made no pies, but an unlimited quantity of cats and mice.

Now you may read the works of the gravest critics of

art from end to end; but you will find, at last, they can give you no other true account of the spirit of sculpture than that it is an irresistible human instinct for the making of cats and mice, and other imitable living creatures, in such permanent form that one may play with the images at leisure. Play with them, or love them, or fear them, or worship them. The cat may become the goddess Pasht, and the mouse, in the hand of a sculptured king, enforce his enduring words "ἐς ἐμέ τις ὀρέων εὐσεβὴς ἔστω";[1] but the great mimetic instinct underlies all such purpose; and is zoo-plastic,—life-shaping,—alike in the reverent and the impious.[2]

We have seen that sculpture is to be a true representation of true internal form. Much more is it to be a representation of true internal emotion. You must carve only what you yourself see as you see it; but, much more, you must carve only what you yourself feel, as you feel it. You may no more endeavour to feel through other men's souls, than to see with other men's eyes. Whereas generally now, in Europe and America, every man's energy is bent upon acquiring some false emotion, not his own, but belonging to the past, or to other persons, because he has been taught that such and such a result of it will be fine. Every attempted sentiment in relation to art is hypocritical; our notions of sublimity, of grace, or pious serenity, are all second-hand: and we are practically incapable of designing so much as a bell-handle or a door-knocker, without borrowing the first notion of it from those who are gone—where we shall not wake them with our knocking. I would we could.[3]

[1] (Herodotus, ii, 141: "And at the present time this king [Sethos] stands in the temple of Hephaestus in stone, holding upon his hand a mouse, and by letters inscribed he says these words, 'Let him who looks upon me be reverent.'") ArP 218–21, omit.
[2] ArP 221
[3] ArP 292

The breakfast plate as sculpture

I have here in my hand one of the simplest possible examples of the union of the graphic and constructive powers,—one of my breakfast plates. Since all the finely architectural arts, we said, began in the shaping of the cup and the platter, we will begin, ourselves, with the platter.

Why has it been made round? For two structural reasons: first, that the greatest holding surface may be gathered into the smallest space; and secondly, that in being pushed past other things on the table, it may come into least contact with them.

Next, why has it a rim? For two other structural reasons: first, that it is convenient to put salt or mustard upon; but secondly, and chiefly, that the plate may be easily laid hold of. The rim is the simplest form of continuous handle.

Farther, to keep it from soiling the cloth, it will be wise to put this ridge beneath, round the bottom; for as the rim is the simplest possible form of continuous handle, so this is the simplest form of continuous leg.

Thus far our art has been strictly utilitarian, having respect to conditions of collision, of carriage, and of support. But now, on the surface of our piece of pottery, here are various bands and spots of colour which are presumably set there to make it pleasanter to the eye. Six of the spots, seen closely, you discover are intended to represent flowers. These then have as distinctly a graphic purpose as the other properties of the plate have an architectural one, and the first critical question we have to ask about them is, whether they are like roses or not. I will anticipate what I have to say in subsequent Lectures so far as to assure you that, if they are to be like roses at all, the liker they can be, the better. In any case, however, that graphic power must have been subordinate to their effect as pink spots, while the band of green-blue round the plate's edge, and the spots of gold, pretend to no graphic power at all, but are meaningless spaces of colour or metal. Still less have they any mechanical office: they add nowise to the serviceableness of the plate; and their agreeableness, if they possess any, depends, therefore, neither on any imitative, nor any structural, character; but on some inherent pleasantness in themselves, either of mere colours to the eye, (as of taste to the tongue,) or in the placing of those colours in relations which obey some mental principle of order, or physical principle of harmony.

These abstract relations and inherent pleasantnesses, whether in space, number, or time, and whether of colours or sounds, form what we may properly term the musical or harmonic element in every art; and the study of them is an entirely separate science. It is the branch of art-philosophy to which the word "æsthetics" should be strictly limited, being the inquiry into the nature of things that in themselves are pleasant to the human senses or instincts, though they represent nothing, and serve for nothing, their only service *being* their pleasantness. Thus it is the province of æsthetics to tell you, (if you did not know it before,) that the taste and colour of a peach are pleasant, and to ascertain, if it be ascertainable, (and you have any curiosity to know,) why they are so.

Returning now to the very elementary form in which the appeal to our æsthetic virtue is made in our breakfast plate, you notice that there are two distinct kinds of pleasantness attempted. One by hues of colour; the other by proportions of space. I have called these the musical elements of the arts relating to sight; and there are indeed two complete sciences, one of the combinations of colour, and the other of the combinations of line and form, which might each of them separately engage us in as intricate study as that of the science of music.

"The simplest primary form"

The second musical science which belongs peculiarly to sculpture, (and to painting, so far as it represents form,) consists in the disposition of beautiful masses. That is to say, beautiful surfaces limited by beautiful lines.

The exact science of sculpture is that of the relations

between outline and the solid form it limits; and it does not matter whether that relation be indicated by drawing or carving, so long as the expression of solid form is the mental purpose; it is the science always of the beauty of relation in three dimensions. To take the simplest possible line of continuous limit—the circle: the flat disc enclosed by it may indeed be made an element of decoration, though a very meagre one; but its relative mass, the ball, being gradated in three dimensions, is always delightful. Here is at once the simplest, and, in mere patient mechanism, the most skilful, piece of sculpture I can possibly show you,—a piece of the purest rock-crystal, chiselled, (I believe, by mere toil of hand,) into a perfect sphere. Imitating nothing, constructing nothing; sculpture for sculpture's sake of purest natural substance into simplest primary form.

But, farther, let the ball have motion; then the form it generates will be that of a cylinder. You have, perhaps, thought that pure early English architecture depended for its charm on visibility of construction. It depends for its charm altogether on the abstract harmony of groups of cylinders, arbitrarily bent into mouldings, and arbitrarily associated as shafts, having no *real* relation to construction whatsoever . . .

And the two points I have been pressing upon you are conclusively exhibited here, namely,—(1) that sculpture is essentially the production of a pleasant bossiness or roundness of surface; (2) that the pleasantness of that bossy condition to the eye is irrespective of imitation on one side, and of structure on the other.

And you will be surprised to find, when you try the experiment, how much the eye must instinctively judge in this manner. Take the front of San Zenone [Verona], for instance. You will find it impossible, without a lens, to distinguish in the bronze gates, and in great part of the wall, anything that their bosses represent. You cannot tell whether the sculpture is of men, animals, or trees; only you feel it to be composed of pleasant projecting masses; you acknowledge that both gates and wall are, somehow, delightfully roughened; and only afterwards, by slow degrees, can you make out what this roughness means; nay, though here I magnify one of the bronze plates of the gate to a scale, which gives you the same advantage as if you saw it quite close, in the reality,—you may still be obliged to me for the information that *this* boss represents the Madonna asleep in her little bed; and this smaller boss, the Infant Christ in His; and this at the top, a cloud with an angel coming out of it; and these jagged bosses, two of the Three Kings, with their crowns on, looking up to the star, (which is intelligible enough, I admit); but what this straggling, three-legged boss beneath signifies, I suppose neither you nor I can tell, unless it be the shepherd's dog, who has come suddenly upon the Kings with their crowns on, and is greatly startled at them.

Farther, and much more definitely, the pleasantness of the surface decoration is independent of structure; that is to say, of any architectural requirement of stability. The greater part of the sculpture here is exclusively ornamentation of a flat wall, or of door-panelling; only a small portion of the church front is thus treated, and the sculpture has no more to do with the form of the building than a piece of lace veil would have, suspended beside its gates on a festal day: the proportions of shaft and arch might be altered in a hundred different ways without diminishing their stability; and the pillars would stand more safely on the ground than on the backs of these carved animals.

I wish you especially to notice these points, because the false theory that ornamentation should be merely decorated structure is so pretty and plausible, that it is likely to take away your attention from the far more important abstract conditions of design. Structure should never be contradicted, and in the best buildings it is pleasantly exhibited and enforced . . .[4]

Expressive qualities

All noble draperies, either in painting or sculpture (colour and texture being at present out of our consideration), have, so far as they are anything more than necessities,

[4] ArP 205–17, omit.

one of two great functions: they are the exponents of motion and of gravitation. They are the most valuable means of expressing past as well as present motion in the figure, and they are almost the only means of indicating to the eye the force of gravity which resists such motion. The Greeks used drapery in sculpture for the most part as an ugly necessity, but availed themselves of it gladly in all representation of action, exaggerating the arrangements of it which express lightness in the material, and follow gesture in the person. The Christian Sculptors, caring little for the body, or disliking it, and depending exclusively on the countenance, received drapery at first contentedly as a veil, but soon perceived a capacity of expression in it which the Greek had not seen or had despised. The principal element of this expression was the entire removal of agitation from what was so pre-eminently capable of being agitated. It fell from their human forms plumb down, sweeping the ground heavily, and concealing the feet; while the Greek drapery was often blown away from the thigh. The thick and coarse stuffs of the monkish dresses, so absolutely opposed to the thin and gauzy web of antique material, suggested simplicity of division as well as weight of fall. There was no crushing nor subdividing them. And thus the drapery gradually came to represent the spirit of repose as it before had of motion, repose saintly and severe. The wind had no power upon the garment, as the passion none upon the soul; and the motion of the figure only bent into a softer line the stillness of the falling veil, followed by it like a slow cloud by drooping rain: only in links of lighter undulation it followed the dances of the angels.

Thus treated, drapery is indeed noble; but it is as an exponent of other and higher things. As that of gravitation, it has especial majesty, being literally the only means we have of fully representing this mysterious natural force of earth (for falling water is less passive and less defined in its lines). So, again, in sails it is beautiful because it receives the forms of solid curved surface, and expresses the force of another invisible element. But drapery trusted to its own merits, and given for its own sake,—drapery like that of Carlo Dolci and the Caraccis,—is always base.[5]

I am not sure whether it is frequently enough observed that sculpture is not the mere cutting of the *form* of any thing in stone; it is the cutting of the *effect* of it. Very often the true form, in the marble, would not be in the least like itself. The sculptor must paint with his chisel: half his touches are not to realize, but to put power into, the form: they are touches of light and shadow; and raise a ridge, or sink a hollow, not to represent an actual ridge or hollow, but to get a line of light, or a spot of darkness. In a coarse way, this kind of execution is very marked in old French woodwork; the irises of the eyes of its chimeric monsters being cut boldly into holes, which, variously placed, and always dark, give all kinds of strange and startling expressions, averted and askance, to the fantastic countenances. Perhaps the highest examples of this kind of sculpture-painting are the works of Mino da Fiesole; their best effects being reached by strange angular, and seemingly rude, touches of the chisel. The lips of one of the children on the tombs in the church of the Badia, appear only half finished when they are seen close; yet the expression is farther carried, and more ineffable, than in any piece of marble I have ever seen, especially considering its delicacy, and the softness of the child-features. In a sterner kind, that of the statues [by Michelangelo] in the sacristy of St. Lorenzo equals it, and there again by incompletion.[6]

Materials

There is, first, work in baked clay, which contracts, as it dries, and is very easily frangible. Then you must put no work into it requiring niceness in dimension, nor any so elaborate that it would be a great loss if it were broken; but as the clay yields at once to the hand, and the sculptor can do anything with it he likes, it is a material for him to

[5] Lamps 150 f
[6] Lamps 215

sketch with and play with,—to record his fancies in, before
they escape him,—and to express roughly, for people who
can enjoy such sketches, what he has not time to complete
in marble. The clay, being ductile, lends itself to all softness of line; being easily frangible, it would be ridiculous
to give it sharp edges, so that a blunt and massive rendering of graceful gesture will be its natural function: but as
it can be pinched, or pulled, or thrust in a moment into
projection which it would take hours of chiselling to get in
stone, it will also properly be used for all fantastic and
grotesque form, not involving sharp edges. Therefore,
what is true of chalk and charcoal, for painters, is equally
true of clay, for sculptors; they are all most precious materials for true masters, but tempt the false ones into fatal
license; and to judge rightly of terra-cotta work is a far
higher reach of skill in sculpture-criticism than to distinguish the merits of a finished statue.

We have, secondly, work in bronze, iron, gold, and
other metals; in which the laws of structure are still more
definite.

All kinds of twisted and wreathen work on every scale
become delightful when wrought in ductile or tenacious
metal; but metal which is to be *hammered* into form
separates itself into two great divisions—solid, and flat.

A. In solid metal-work, *i.e.*, metal cast thick enough to
resist bending, whether it be hollow or not, violent and
various projection may be admitted, which would be offensive in marble; but no sharp edges, because it is difficult
to produce them with the hammer. But since the per-
manence of the material justifies exquisiteness of workmanship, whatever delicate ornamentation can be wrought
with rounded surfaces may be advisedly introduced; and
since the colour of bronze or any other metal is not so
pleasantly representative of flesh as that of marble, a wise
sculptor will depend less on flesh contour, and more on
picturesque accessories, which, though they would be vulgar if attempted in stone, are rightly entertaining in
bronze or silver. Verrocchio's statue of Colleone at Venice,
Cellini's Perseus at Florence, and Ghiberti's gates at Florence, are models of bronze treatment.

B. When metal is beaten thin, it becomes what is technically called "plate," (the *flattened* thing,) and may be treated advisably in two ways: one, by beating it out into bosses, the other by cutting it into strips and ramifications. The vast schools of goldsmiths' work and of iron decoration, founded on these two principles, have had the most powerful influences over general taste in all ages and countries. One of the simplest and most interesting elementary examples of the treatment of flat metal by cutting is the common branched iron bar, used to close small apertures in countries possessing any good primitive style of ironwork, formed by alternate cuts on its sides, and the bending down of the severed portions. The ordinary domestic window balcony of Verona is formed by mere ribands of iron, bent into curves as studiously refined as those of a Greek vase, and decorated merely by their own terminations in spiral volutes.

All cast work in metal, unfinished by hand, is inadmissible in any school of living art, since it cannot possess the perfection of form due to a permanent substance; and the continual sight of it is destructive of the faculty of taste: but metal stamped with precision, as in coins, is to sculpture what engraving is to painting.

Thirdly. Stone-sculpture divides itself into three schools: one in very hard material; one in very soft; and one in that of centrally useful consistence.

A. The virtue of work in hard material is the expression of form in shallow relief, or in broad contours: deep cutting in hard material is inadmissible; and the art, at once pompous and trivial, of gem engraving, has been in the last degree destructive of the honour and service of sculpture.

B. The virtue of work in soft material is deep cutting, with studiously graceful disposition of the masses of light and shade. The greater number of flamboyant churches of France are cut out of an adhesive chalk; and the fantasy of their latest decoration was, in great part, induced by the facility of obtaining contrast of black space, undercut, with white tracery easily left in sweeping and interwoven rods—the lavish use of wood in domestic architecture materially increasing the habit of delight in branched complexity of line.

[c.] To-day, I shall limit myself to the illustration of elementary sculptural structure in the best material,—that is to say, in crystalline marble, neither soft enough to encourage the caprice of the workman, nor hard enough to resist his will.

By the true "Providence" of Nature, the rock which is thus submissive has been in some places stained with the fairest colours, and in others blanched into the fairest absence of colour that can be found to give harmony to inlaying, or dignity to form. The possession by the Greeks of their [white Parian marble] was indeed the first circumstance regulating the development of their art; it enabled them at once to express their passion for light by executing the faces, hands, and feet of their dark wooden statues in white marble, so that what we look upon only with pleasure for fineness of texture was to them an imitation of the luminous body of the deity shining from behind its dark robes . . . In like manner, the existence of quarries of peach-coloured marble within twelve miles of Verona, and of white marble and green serpentine between Pisa and Genoa, defined the manner both of sculpture and architecture for all the Gothic buildings of Italy. No subtlety of education could have formed a high school of art without these materials.

If [in marble] we carve the subject with real delicacy, the cast shadow of the incision will interfere with its outline, so that, for representation of beautiful things you must clear away the ground about it, at all events for a little distance. This, I repeat, is the primal construction of good bas-relief, implying, first, perfect protection to its surface from any transverse blow, and a geometrically limited space to be occupied by the design, into which it shall pleasantly . . . contract itself: implying, secondly, a determined depth of projection, which it shall rarely reach, and never exceed: and implying, finally, the production of the whole piece with the least possible labour of chisel and loss of stone.[7]

[7] ArP 309–17, omit.

2

ORNAMENT

In the progress of national as well as of individual mind, the first attempts at imitation are always abstract and incomplete. Greater completion marks the progress of art, absolute completion usually its decline; whence absolute completion of imitative form is often supposed to be in itself wrong. But it is not wrong always, only dangerous. Let us endeavour briefly to ascertain wherein its danger consists, and wherein its dignity.

I have said that all art is abstract in its beginnings; that is to say, it expresses only a small number of the qualities of the thing represented. Curved and complex lines are represented by straight and simple ones; interior markings of forms are few, and much is symbolical and conventional. There is a resemblance between the work of a great nation, in this phase, and the work of childhood and ignorance, which, in the mind of a careless observer, might attach something like ridicule to it. The form of a tree on the Ninevite sculptures is much like that which, some twenty years ago, was familiar upon samplers; and the types of the face and figure in early Italian art are susceptible of easy caricature. On the signs which separate the infancy of magnificent manhood from every other, I do not pause to insist (they consist entirely in the choice of the symbol and of the features abstracted); but I pass to the next stage of art, a condition of strength in which the abstraction which was begun in incapability is continued in free will. This is the case, however, in pure sculpture and painting, as well as in architecture; and we have nothing to do but with that greater severity of manner which fits either to be associated with the more realist art. I believe it properly consists only in a due expression of their subordination, an expression varying according to their place and office. The question is first to be clearly determined whether the architecture is a frame for the sculpture, or the sculpture an ornament of the architecture. If the latter, then the first office of that sculpture is not to represent the things it imitates, but to gather out of them those arrangements of form which shall be pleasing to the eye in their intended places. So soon as agreeable lines and points of shade have been added to the mouldings which were meagre, or to the lights which were unrelieved, the architectural work of the imitation is accomplished; and how far it shall be wrought towards completeness or not, will depend upon its place, and upon other various circumstances.

[F]or the moment the architect allows himself to dwell on the imitated portions, there is a chance of his losing sight of the duty of his ornament, of its business as a part of the composition, and sacrificing its points of shade and effect to the delight of delicate carving. And then he is lost. His architecture has become a mere framework for the setting of delicate sculpture, which had better be all taken down and put into cabinets. It is well, therefore, that the young architect should be taught to think of imitative ornament as of the extreme of grace in language; not to be regarded at first, not to be obtained at the cost of purpose, meaning, force or conciseness, yet, indeed, a perfection—the least of all perfections, and yet the crowning one of all—one which by itself, and regarded in itself, is an architectural coxcombry, but is yet the sign of the most highly-trained mind and power when it is associated with others. It is a safe manner, as I think, to design all things at first in severe abstraction, and to be prepared, if need were, to carry them out in that form; then to mark the parts where high finish would be admissible, to complete these always with stern reference to their general effect, and then connect them by a graduated scale of abstraction with the rest. And there is one safeguard against danger in this process on which I would finally insist. Never imitate anything but natural forms, and those

the noblest, in the completed parts. The degradation of
the cinque-cento manner of decoration was not owing to
its naturalism, to its faithfulness of imitation, but to its
imitation of ugly, *i.e.* unnatural things. So long as it restrained itself to sculpture of animals and flowers, it remained noble.[8]

"Natural resemblance"

The first so-called ornament, then, which I would attack is that Greek fret . . .[9] which is exactly a case in
point. It so happens that in crystals of bismuth, formed
by the unagitated cooling of the melted metal, there occurs a natural resemblance of it almost perfect. But crystals of bismuth not only are of unusual occurrence in
every-day life, but their form is, as far as I know, unique
among minerals . . . On this ground, then, I allege that
ornament to be ugly; or, in the literal sense of the word,
monstrous; different from anything which it is the nature
of man to admire: and I think an uncarved fillet or plinth
infinitely preferable to one covered with this vile con-
catenation of straight lines: unless indeed it be employed
as a foil to a true ornament, which it may, perhaps, sometimes with advantage; or excessively small, as it occurs on
coins, the harshness of its arrangement being less perceived.

Often in association with this horrible design we find, in
Greek works, one which is as beautiful as this is painful—
that egg and dart moulding, whose perfection, in its place
and way, has never been surpassed. And why is this? Simply because the form of which it is chiefly composed is
one not only familiar to us in the soft housing of the bird's
nest, but happens to be that of nearly every pebble that
rolls and murmurs under the surf of the sea, on all its
endless shore. And that with a peculiar accuracy; for the
mass which bears the light in this moulding is *not* in good

[8] Lamps 170–75, omit.
[9] (This early view later changed; see below under "Greek
Sculpture and Ornament.") Lamps 143

Greek work, as in the frieze of the Erechtheum, merely
of the shape of an egg. It is *flattened* on the upper surface,
with a delicacy and keen sense of variety in the curve
which it is impossible too highly to praise, attaining exactly that flattened, imperfect oval, which, in nine cases out
of ten, will be the form of the pebble lifted at random
from the rolled beach. Leave out this flatness, and the
moulding is vulgar instantly. It is singular also that the
insertion of this rounded form in the hollowed recess has
a *painted* type in the plumage of the Argus pheasant, the
eyes of whose feathers are so shaded as exactly to represent an oval form placed in a hollow.

It will evidently follow, upon our application of this test
of natural resemblance, that we shall at once conclude
that all perfectly beautiful forms must be composed of
curves; since there is hardly any common natural form in
which it is possible to discover a straight line. Nevertheless, Architecture, having necessarily to deal with straight
lines essential to its purposes in many instances and to the
expression of its power in others, must frequently be content with that measure of beauty which is consistent with
such primal forms; and we may presume that utmost
measure of beauty to have been attained when the arrangements of such lines are consistent with the most frequent natural groupings of them we can discover, although, to find right lines in nature at all, we may be
compelled to do violence to her finished work, break
through the sculptured and coloured surfaces of her crags,
and examine the processes of their crystallisation.

I have just convicted the Greek fret of ugliness, because
it has no precedent to allege for its arrangement except
an artificial form of a rare metal. Let us bring into court
an ornament of the Lombard architects, as exclusively
composed of right lines as the other, only, observe, with
the noble element of shadow added. This ornament, taken
from the front of the Cathedral of Pisa, is universal
throughout the Lombard churches of Pisa, Lucca, Pistoja,
and Florence; and it will be a grave stain upon them if it
cannot be defended. Its first apology for itself, made in
a hurry, sounds marvellously like the Greek one, and highly

dubious. It says that its terminal contour is the very image of a carefully prepared artificial crystal of common salt. Salt being, however, a substance considerably more familiar to us than bismuth, the chances are somewhat in favour of the accused Lombard ornament already. But it has more to say for itself, and more to the purpose; namely, that its main outline is one not only of natural crystallisation, but among the very first and commonest of crystalline forms, being the primal condition of the occurrence of the oxides of iron, copper, and tin, of the sulphurets of iron and lead, of fluor spar, etc.; and that those projecting forms in its surface represent the conditions of structure which effect the change into another relative and equally common crystalline form, the cube. This is quite enough. We may rest assured it is as good a combination of such simple right lines as can be put together, and gracefully fitted for every place in which such lines are necessary.[10]

What is the place for ornament? Consider first that the characters of natural objects which the architect can represent are few and abstract. The greater part of those delights by which Nature recommends herself to man at all times, cannot be conveyed by him into his imitative work. He cannot make his grass green and cool and good to rest upon, which in nature is its chief use to man; nor can he make his flowers tender and full of colour and of scent, which in nature are their chief powers of giving joy. Those qualities which alone he can secure are certain severe characters of form, such as men only see in nature on deliberate examination, and by the full and set appliance of sight and thought: a man must lie down on the bank of grass on his breast and set himself to watch and penetrate the intertwining of it, before he finds that which is good to be gathered by the architect. So then while Nature is at all times pleasant to us, and while the sight and sense of her work may mingle happily with all our thoughts, and labours, and times of existence, that image of her which the architect carries away represents what we can only perceive in her by direct intellectual exertion,

[10] Lamps 143–46, omit.

and demands from us, wherever it appears, an intellectual exertion of a similar kind in order to understand it and feel it. It is the written or sealed impression of a thing sought out, it is the shaped result of inquiry and bodily expression of thought.[11]

Suitability of detail

Visibility . . . we must remember, depends, not only on situation, but on distance; and there is no way in which work is more painfully and unwisely lost than in its over delicacy on parts distant from the eye. Here, again, the principle of honesty must govern our treatment: we must not work any kind of ornament which is, perhaps, to cover the whole building (or at least to occur on all parts of it) delicately where it is near the eye, and rudely where it is removed from it. That is trickery and dishonesty. Consider, first, what kinds of ornaments will tell in the distance and what near, and so distribute them, keeping such as by their nature are delicate, down near the eye, and throwing the bold and rough kinds of work to the top; and if there be any kind which is to be both near and far off, take care that it be as boldly and rudely wrought where it is well seen as where it is distant, so that the spectator may know exactly what it is, and what it is worth. Thus chequered patterns, and in general such ornaments as common workmen can execute, may extend over the whole building; but bas-reliefs, and fine niches and capitals, should be kept down; and the common sense of this will always give a building dignity, even though there be some abruptness or awkwardness in the resulting arrangements.

I do not know anything more painful or pitiful than the kind of ivory carving with which the Certosa of Pavia, and part of the Colleone sepulchral chapel at Bergamo, and other such buildings are incrusted, of which it is not possible so much as to think without exhaustion; and a heavy sense of the misery it would be, to be forced to look at it all. And this is not from the quantity of it, nor because it

[11] Lamps 155

is bad work—much of it is inventive and able; but because
it looks as if it were only fit to be put in inlaid cabinets and
velveted caskets, and as if it could not bear one drifting
shower or gnawing frost. We are afraid for it, anxious
about it, and tormented by it; and we feel that a massy
shaft and a bold shadow would be worth it all. Nevertheless, even in cases like these, much depends on the accomplishment of the great ends of decoration. If the ornament
does its duty—if it *is* ornament, and its points of shade
and light tell in the general effect, we shall not be offended
by finding that the sculptor in his fulness of fancy has
chosen to give much more than these mere points of light,
and has composed them of groups of figures. But if the
ornament does not answer its purpose, if it have no distant,
no truly decorative power; if, generally seen, it be a mere
incrustation and meaningless roughness, we shall only be
chagrined by finding when we look close, that the incrustation has cost years of labour, and has millions of figures
and histories in it; and would be the better of being seen
through a Stanhope lens. Hence the greatness of the northern Gothic as contrasted with the latest Italian. It reaches
nearly the same extreme of detail; but it never loses sight
of its architectural purpose, never fails in its decorative
power; not a leaflet in it but speaks, and speaks far off too;
and so long as this be the case, there is no limit to the
luxuriance in which such work may legitimately and nobly
be bestowed.[12]

Temple vs. market

Hence then a general law, of singular importance in
the present day, a law of simple common sense,—not to
decorate things belonging to purposes of active and occupied life. Wherever you can rest, there decorate; where
rest is forbidden, so is beauty. You must not mix ornament with business, any more than you may mix play.
Work first, and then rest. Work first, and then gaze, but
do not use golden ploughshares, nor bind ledgers in en-

[12] Lamps 47–52, omit.

amel. Do not thrash with sculptured flails: nor put bas-reliefs on millstones. What! it will be asked, are we in the habit of doing so? Even so; always and everywhere. The most familiar position of Greek mouldings is in these days on shop fronts. There is not a tradesman's sign nor shelf nor counter in all the streets of all our cities, which has not upon it ornaments which were invented to adorn temples and beautify kings' palaces. There is not the smallest advantage in them where they are. Absolutely valueless—utterly without the power of giving pleasure, they only satiate the eye, and vulgarise their own forms. Many of these are in themselves thoroughly good copies of fine things, which things themselves we shall never, in consequence, enjoy any more. Many a pretty beading and graceful bracket there is in wood or stucco above our grocers' and cheesemongers' and hosiers' shops: how is it that the tradesmen cannot understand that custom is to be had only by selling good tea and cheese and cloth, and that people come to them for their honesty, and their readiness, and their right wares, and not because they have Greek cornices over their windows, or their names in large gilt letters on their house fronts? How pleasurable it would be to have the power of going through the streets of London, pulling down those brackets and friezes and large names, restoring to the tradesmen the capital they had spent in architecture, and putting them on honest and equal terms . . .[13]

'Decorative' art

Observe, then, first—the only essential distinction be-tween Decorative and other art is the being fitted for a fixed place; and in that place, related, either in subor-dination or in command, to the effect of other pieces of art. And all the greatest art which the world has produced is thus fitted for a place, and subordinated to a purpose. There is no existing highest-order art but is decorative. The best sculpture yet produced has been the decoration

[13] Lamps 156–58

of a temple front—the best painting, the decoration of a room. Raphael's best doing is merely the wall-colouring of a suite of apartments in the Vatican, and his cartoons were made for tapestries. Correggio's best doing is the decoration of two small church cupolas at Parma; Michael Angelo's, of a ceiling in the Pope's private chapel; Tintoret's, of a ceiling and side wall belonging to a charitable society at Venice; while Titian and Veronese threw out their noblest thoughts, not even on the inside, but on the outside of the common brick and plaster walls of Venice.

Get rid, then, at once of any idea of Decorative art being a degraded or a separate kind of art. Its nature or essence is simply its being fitted for a definite place; and, in that place, forming part of a great and harmonious whole, in companionship with other art; and so far from this being a degradation to it—so far from Decorative art being inferior to other art because it is fixed to a spot—on the whole it may be considered as rather a piece of degradation that it should be portable. Portable art—independent of all place—is for the most part ignoble art. Your little Dutch landscape, which you put over your sideboard to-day, and between the windows to-morrow, is a far more contemptible piece of work than the extents of field and forest with which Benozzo has made green and beautiful the once melancholy arcade of the Campo Santo at Pisa; and the wild boar of silver which you use for a seal, or lock into a velvet case, is little likely to be so noble a beast as the bronze boar who foams forth the fountain from under his tusks in the marketplace of Florence. It is, indeed, possible that the portable picture or image may be first-rate of its kind, but it is not first-rate because it is portable; nor are Titian's frescoes less than first-rate because they are fixed; nay, very frequently the highest compliment you can pay to a cabinet picture is to say—"It is as grand as a fresco."

Keeping, then, this fact fixed in our minds,—that all art *may* be decorative, and that the greatest art yet produced has been decorative,—we may proceed to distinguish the orders and dignities of Decorative art, thus:—

I. The first order of it is that which is meant for places

where it cannot be disturbed or injured, and where it can be perfectly seen; and then the main parts of it should be, and have always been made, by the great masters, as perfect, and as full of nature as possible.

You will every day hear it absurdly said that room decoration should be by flat patterns—by dead colours—by conventional monotonies, and I know not what. Now, just be assured of this—nobody ever yet used conventional art to decorate with, when he could do anything better, and knew that what he did would be safe. Nay, a great painter will always give you the natural art, safe or not. Correggio gets a commission to paint a room on the ground floor of a palace at Parma [the "Camera di San Paolo"]: any of our people—bred on our fine modern principles—would have covered it with a diaper, or with stripes or flourishes, or mosaic patterns. Not so Correggio: he paints a thick trellis of vine-leaves, with oval openings, and lovely children leaping through them into the room; and lovely children, depend upon it, are rather more desirable decorations than diaper, if you can do them—but they are not quite so easily done. In like manner Tintoret has to paint the whole end of the Council Hall at Venice. An orthodox decorator would have set himself to make the wall look like a wall—Tintoret thinks it would be rather better, if he can manage it, to make it look a little like Paradise;— stretches his canvas right over the wall, and his clouds right over his canvas; brings the light through his clouds —all blue and clear—zodiac beyond zodiac; rolls away the vaporous flood from under the feet of saints, leaving them at last in infinitudes of light—unorthodox in the last degree, but, on the whole, pleasant.

And so in all other cases whatever, the greatest decorative art is wholly unconventional—downright, pure, good painting and sculpture, but always fitted for its place; and subordinated to the purpose it has to serve in that place.

II. But if art is to be placed where it is liable to injury— to wear and tear; or to alteration of its form; as, for instance, on domestic utensils and armour, and weapons, and dress; in which either the ornament will be worn out by the usage of the thing, or will be cast into altered shape

by the play of its folds; then it is wrong to put beautiful
and perfect art to such uses, and you want forms of inferior art, such as will be by their simplicity less liable to
injury: or, by reason of their complexity and continuousness, may show to advantage, however distorted by the
folds they are cast into.

And thus arise the various forms of inferior decorative
art, respecting which the general law is, that the lower the
place and office of the thing, the less of natural or perfect
form you should have in it; a zigzag or a chequer is thus
a better, because a more consistent, ornament for a cup or
platter than a landscape or portrait is . . .[14]

Colour

I do not feel able to speak with any confidence respecting the touching of *sculpture* with colour. I would only
note one point, that sculpture is the representation of an
idea, while architecture is itself a real thing. The idea may,
as I think, be left colourless, and coloured by the beholder's mind: but a reality ought to have reality in all its
attributes: its colour should be as fixed as its form. I cannot, therefore, consider architecture as in anywise perfect
without colour. Farther, as I have above noticed, I think
the colours of architecture should be those of natural
stones; partly because more durable, but also because
more perfect and graceful.

First, then, I think that in making this reference we are
to consider our building as a kind of organised creature;
in colouring which we must look to the single and separately organised creatures of Nature, not to her landscape
combinations. Our building, if it is well composed, is one
thing, and is to be coloured as Nature would colour one
thing—a shell, a flower, or an animal; not as she colours
groups of things.

And the first broad conclusion we shall deduce from observance of natural colour in such cases will be, that it
never follows form, but is arranged on an entirely sepa-

[14] TwoP 320–23

rate system. What mysterious connection there may be between the shape of the spots on an animal's skin and its anatomical system, I do not know, nor even if such a connection has in anywise been traced: but to the eye the systems are entirely separate, and in many cases that of colour is accidentally variable. The stripes of a zebra do not follow the lines of its body or limbs, still less the spots of a leopard.

I hold this, then, for the first great principle of architectural colour. Let it be visibly independent of form. Never paint a column with vertical lines, but always cross it. Never give separate mouldings separate colours (I know this is heresy, but I never shrink from any conclusions, however contrary to human authority, to which I am led by observance of natural principles); and in sculptured ornaments do not paint the leaves or figures (I cannot help the Elgin frieze) of one colour and their ground of another, but vary both the ground and the figures with the same harmony. [I]n general the best place for colour is on broad surfaces, not on the points of interest in form. An animal is mottled on its breast and back, rarely on its paws or about its eyes; so put your variegation boldly on the flat wall and broad shaft, but be shy of it in the capital and moulding; in all cases it is a safe rule to simplify colour when form is rich, and *vice versâ;* and I think it would be well in general to carve all capitals and graceful ornaments in white marble, and so leave them.

Independence then being first secured, what kind of limiting outlines shall we adopt for the system of colour itself?

I am quite sure that any person familiar with natural objects will never be surprised at any appearance of care or finish in them. That is the condition of the Universe. But there is cause both for surprise and inquiry whenever we see anything like carelessness or incompletion: that is not a common condition; it must be one appointed for some singular purpose. I believe that such surprise will be forcibly felt by any one who, after studying carefully the lines of some variegated organic form, will set himself to copy with similar diligence those of its colours. The boundaries of the forms he will assuredly, whatever the object, have found drawn with a delicacy and precision which no human hand can follow. Those of its colours he will find in many cases, though governed always by a certain rude symmetry, yet irregular, blotched, imperfect, liable to all kinds of accidents and awkwardnesses.

Experience teaches us the same thing. Infinite nonsense has been written about the union of perfect colour with perfect form. They never will, never can be united. Colour, to be perfect, *must* have a soft outline or a simple one: . . . and you will never produce a good painted window with good figure-drawing in it. You will lose perfection of colour as you give perfection of line. Try to put in order and form the colours of a piece of opal.

I conclude, then, that all arrangements of colour, for its own sake, in graceful forms, are barbarous; and that, to paint a colour pattern with the lovely lines of a Greek leaf moulding, is an utterly savage procedure. I cannot find anything in natural colour like this: it is not in the bond. I find it in all natural form—never in natural colour. If, then, our architectural colour is to be beautiful as its form was, by being imitative, we are limited to these conditions—to simple masses of it, to zones, as in the rainbow and the zebra; cloudings and flamings, as in marble shells and plumage, or spots of various shapes and dimensions. All these conditions are susceptible of various degrees of sharpness and delicacy, and of complication in arrangement. The zone may become a delicate line, and arrange itself in chequers and zig-zags. The flaming may be more or less defined, as on a tulip leaf, and may at last be represented by a triangle of colour, and arrange itself in stars or other shapes; the spot may be also graduated into a stain or defined into a square or circle.

Curved outlines, especially if refined, deaden the colour, and confuse the mind. Even in figure painting the greatest colourists have either melted their outline away, as often Correggio and Rubens; or purposely made their masses of ungainly shape, as Titian; or placed their brightest hues in costume, where they could get quaint patterns, as Veronese, and especially Angelico, with whom, however, the absolute virtue of colour is secondary to grace of line. Hence, he never uses the blended hues of Correggio, like those on the wing of the little Cupid, in the "Venus and Mercury" [National Gallery, London], but always the severest type—the peacock plume. Any of these men would have looked with infinite disgust upon the leafage and scroll-work which forms the ground of colour in our modern painted windows, and yet all whom I have named were much infected with the love of renaissance designs. We must also allow for the freedom of the painter's subject, and looseness of his associated lines; a pattern being severe in a picture, which is over luxurious upon a building. I believe, therefore, that it is impossible to be over quaint or angular in architectural colouring; and thus many dispositions which I have had occasion to reprobate in form, are, in colour, the best that can be invented.

Rules for ornamentation

Restraining ourselves, therefore, to the use of such simple patterns, so far forth as our colour is subordinate either to architectural structure, or sculptural form, we have yet one more manner of ornamentation to add to our general means of effect,—monochrom design, the intermediate condition between colouring and carving. The relations of the entire system of architectural decoration may then be thus expressed:

1. Organic form dominant. True, independent sculpture, and alto-relievo: rich capitals, and mouldings; to be elaborate in completion of form, not abstract, and either to be left in pure white marble, or most cautiously touched with colour in points and borders only, in a system *not* concurrent with their forms.
2. Organic form sub-dominant. Basso-relievo or intaglio. To be more abstract in proportion to the reduction of depth; to be also more rigid and simple in contour; to be touched with colour more boldly and in an increased degree, exactly in proportion to the reduced depth and fulness of form, but still in a system non-concurrent with their forms.

3. Organic form abstracted to outline. Monochrom design, still farther reduced to simplicity of contour, and therefore admitting for the first time the colour to be concurrent with its outline; that is to say, as its name imports, the entire figure to be detached in one colour from a ground of another.

4. Organic forms entirely lost. Geometrical patterns or variable cloudings in the most vivid colour.

On the opposite side of this scale, ascending from the colour pattern, I would place the various forms of painting which may be associated with architecture: primarily, and as most fit for such purpose, the mosaic, highly abstract in treatment, and introducing brilliant colour in masses; the Madonna of Torcello being, as I think, the noblest type of the manner, and the Baptistery of Parma the richest: next, the purely decorative fresco, like that of the Arena Chapel; finally, the fresco becoming principal, as in the Vatican and Sistine. But I cannot, with any safety, follow the principles of abstraction in this pictorial ornament; since the noblest examples of it appear to me to owe their architectural applicability to their archaic manner; and I think that the abstraction and admirable simplicity which render them fit media of the most splendid colouring, cannot be recovered by a voluntary condescension. The Byzantines themselves would not, I think, if they could have drawn the figure better, have used it for a colour decoration; and that use, as peculiar to a condition of childhood, however noble and full of promise, cannot be included among those modes of adornment which are now legitimate or even possible. There is a difficulty in the management of the painted window for the same reason, which has not yet been met, and we must conquer that first, before we can venture to consider the wall as a painted window on a large scale. Pictorial subject, without such abstraction, becomes necessarily principal, or, at all events, ceases to be the architect's concern; its plan must be left to the painter after the completion of the building, as in the works of Veronese and Giorgione on the palaces of Venice.[15]

[15] Lamps 176–85, omit.

3

GREEK SCULPTURE AND ORNAMENT

[O]n one side Greek art is the root of all simplicity; and, on the other, of all complexity.

On one side, I say, it is the root of all simplicity. If you were for some prolonged period to study Greek sculpture exclusively in the Elgin Room of the British Museum, and were then suddenly transported to the Hôtel de Cluny, or any other museum of Gothic and barbarian workmanship, you would imagine the Greeks were the masters of all that was grand, simple, wise, and tenderly human, opposed to the pettiness of the toys of the rest of mankind.

On one side of their work they are so. From all vain and mean decoration—all weak and monstrous error, the Greeks rescue the forms of man and beast, and sculpture them in the nakedness of their true flesh, and with the fire of their living soul. Distinctively from other races, as I have now, perhaps to your weariness, told you, this is the work of the Greek, to give health to what was diseased, and chastisement to what was untrue. So far as this is found in any other school, hereafter, it belongs to them by inheritance from the Greeks, or invests them with the brotherhood of the Greek. And this is the deep meaning of the myth of Dædalus as the giver of motion to statues. The literal change from the binding together of the feet to their separation, and the other modifications of action which took place, either in progressive skill, or often, as the mere consequence of the transition from wood to stone, (a figure carved out of one wooden log must have necessarily its feet near each other, and hands at its sides,) these literal changes are as nothing, in the Greek fable, compared to the bestowing of apparent life. The figures of monstrous gods on Indian temples have their legs separate enough; but they are infinitely more dead than the rude figures at Branchidæ [British Museum] sitting with their hands on their knees. And, briefly, the work of Dædalus is the giving of deceptive life, as that of Prometheus the giving of real life . . .

In this aspect of it, then, I say it is the simplest and nakedest of lovely veracities. But it has another aspect, or rather another pole, for the opposition is diametric. As the simplest, so also it is the most complex of human art. Thus, when the luxurious city is opposed to the simple and healthful one, in the second book of Plato's *Polity,* you find that, next to perfumes, pretty ladies, and dice, you must have in it "ποικιλία," which observe, both in that place and again in the third book, is the separate art of joiners' work, or inlaying; but the idea of exquisitely divided variegation or division, both in sight and sound— the "ravishing division to the lute," as in Pindar's "ποικίλοι ὕμνοι"—runs through the compass of all Greek art-description; and if, instead of studying that art among marbles, you were to look at it only on vases of a fine time, your impression of it would be, instead of breadth and simplicity, one of universal spottiness and chequeredness, "ἐν ἀγγέων ἔρκεσιν παμποικίλοις;" and of the artist's delighting in nothing so much as in crossed or starred or spotted things . . .[16]

The Greeks have been thus the origin, not only of all broad, mighty, and calm conception, but of all that is divided, delicate, and tremulous; "variable as the shade, by the light quivering aspen made."[17] To them, as first leaders of ornamental design, belongs, of right, the praise of glistenings in gold, piercings in ivory, stainings in purple, burnishings in dark blue steel; of the fantasy of the Arabian roof,—quartering of the Christian shield,—rubric and arabesque of Christian scripture; in fine, all enlargement, and all diminution of adorning thought, from the

[16] (The words in quotation marks in this paragraph successively: *Republic,* ii, 373 A; *Henry IV,* Pt. 1, iii, sc. 1; *Nemea,* v, 76, and *Nemea,* x, 66.) ArP 347–50, omit.

[17] (Scott, *Marmion,* vi, 30.) ArP 350

temple to the toy, and from the mountainous pillars of Agrigentum to the last fineness of fretwork in the Pisan Chapel of the Thorn.

And in their doing all this, they stand as masters of human order and justice, subduing the animal nature, guided by the spiritual one.[18]

Three periods of Greek sculpture

Then the ninth, eighth, and seventh centuries are the period of archaic Greek art, steadily progressive wherever it existed. The sixth, fifth, and fourth are the period of Central Greek art; the fifth, or central, century producing the finest. That is easily recollected by the battle of Marathon. And the third, second, and first centuries are the period of steady decline.

It is generally impossible to date with precision art of the archaic period—often difficult to date even that of the central three hundred years. I will not weary you with futile minor divisions of time; here are three coins roughly, but decisively, characteristic of the three ages. The first is an early coin of Tarentum. The city was founded, as you know, by the Spartan Phalanthus late in the eighth century. I believe the head is meant for that of Apollo Archegetes; it may however be Taras, the son of Poseidon; it is no matter to us at present whom it is meant for, but the fact that we cannot know, is itself of the greatest import. We cannot say, with any certainty, unless by discovery of some collateral evidence, whether this head is intended for that of a god, or demigod, or a mortal warrior. Ought not that to disturb some of your thoughts respecting Greek idealism? Farther, if by investigation we discover that the head is meant for that of Phalanthus, we shall know nothing of the character of Phalanthus from the face; for there is no portraiture at this early time.

The second coin is of Ænus in Macedonia; probably of the fifth or early fourth century, and entirely characteristic of the central period. This we know to represent

[18] ArP 350 f

the face of a god—Hermes. The third coin is a king's, not a
city's. I will not tell you, at this moment, what king's; but
only that it is a late coin of the third period, and that it
is as distinct in purpose as the coin of Tarentum is obscure.
We know of this coin, that it represents no god nor demigod, but a mere mortal; and we know precisely, from the
portrait, what that mortal's face was like.

A glance at the three coins, as they are set side by side,
will now show you the main differences in the three great
Greek styles. The archaic coin is sharp and hard; every
line decisive and numbered, set unhesitatingly in its place;
nothing is wrong, though everything incomplete, and, to
us who have seen finer art, ugly. The central coin is as
decisive and clear in arrangement of masses, but its contours are completely rounded and finished. There is no
character in its execution so prominent that you can give
an epithet to the style. It is not hard, it is not soft, it is not
delicate, it is not coarse, it is not grotesque, it is not beautiful; and I am convinced, unless you had been told that
this is fine central Greek art, you would have seen nothing at all in it to interest you. Do not let yourselves be
anywise forced into admiring it; there is, indeed, nothing
more here than an approximately true rendering of a
healthy youthful face, without the slightest attempt to give
an expression of activity, cunning, nobility, or any other
attribute of the Mercurial mind. Extreme simplicity, un-
pretending vigour of work, which claims no admiration
either for minuteness or dexterity, and suggests no idea of
effort at all; refusal of extraneous ornament, and perfectly
arranged disposition of counted masses in a sequent order, whether in the beads, or the ringlets of hair; this is
all you have to be pleased with; neither will you ever
find, in the best Greek Art, more. You might at first suppose that the chain of beads round the cap was an extraneous ornament; but I have little doubt that it is as
definitely the proper fillet for the head of Hermes, as the
olive for Zeus, or corn for Triptolemus. The cap or petasus
cannot have expanded edges; there is no room for them
on the coin; these must be understood, therefore; but the
nature of the cloud-petasus is explained by edging it with

beads, representing either dew or hail. The shield of
Athena often bears white pellets for hail, in like manner.

The third coin will, I think, at once strike you by what
we moderns should call its "vigour of character." You
may observe also that the features are finished with great
care and subtlety, but at the cost of simplicity and breadth.
But the *essential* difference between it and the central
art, is its disorder in design—you see the locks of hair
cannot be counted any longer—they are entirely dishevelled
and irregular. Now the individual character may, or may
not, be a sign of decline; but the licentiousness, the casting
loose of the masses in the design, is an infallible one.

What I want you to observe is, that though the master
of the great time does not attempt portraiture, he *does* attempt animation. And as far as his means will admit, he
succeeds in making the face—you might almost think—
vulgarly animated; as like a real face, literally, "as it can
stare." Yes: and its sculptor meant it to be so; and that was
what Phidias meant his Jupiter to be, if he could manage
it. Not, indeed, to be taken for Zeus himself; and yet, to
be as like a living Zeus as art could make it.[19]

Qualities of Greek sculpture

If you look from some distance at these two engravings
of Greek coins, you will find the relief on each of them
simplifies itself into a pearl-like portion of a sphere, with
exquisitely gradated light on its surface. When you look
at them nearer, you will see that each smaller portion into
which they are divided—cheek, or brow, or leaf, or tress
of hair—resolves itself also into a rounded or undulated
surface, pleasant by gradation of light. Every several surface is delightful in itself, as a shell, or a tuft of rounded
moss, or the bossy masses of distant forest would be. That
these intricately modulated masses present some resemblance to a girl's face, such as the Syracusans imagined
that of the water-goddess Arethusa, is entirely a secondary matter; the primary condition is that the masses shall

[19] ArP 278–82, omit.

be beautifully rounded, and disposed with due discretion and order.

It is difficult for you, at first, to feel this order and beauty of surface, apart from the imitation. But you can see there is a pretty disposition of, and relation between, the projections of a fir-cone, though the studded spiral imitates nothing. Order exactly the same in kind, only much more complex; and an abstract beauty of surface rendered definite by increase and decline of light—(for every curve of surface has its own luminous law, and the light and shade on a parabolic solid differs, specifically, from that on an elliptical or spherical one)—it is the essential business of the sculptor to obtain; as it is the essential business of a painter to get good colour, whether he imitates anything or not. At a distance from the picture, or carving, where the things represented become absolutely unintelligible, we must yet be able to say, at a glance, "That is good painting, or good carving."[20]

The projection of the heads of the four horses [Parthenon frieze], one behind the other, is certainly not more, altogether, than three-quarters of an inch from the flat ground, and the one in front does not in reality project more than the one behind it, yet . . . you see the sculptor has got them to appear to recede in due order, and by the soft rounding of the flesh surfaces, and modulation of the veins, he has taken away all look of flatness from the necks. He has drawn the eyes and nostrils with dark incision, careful as the finest touches of a painter's pencil: and then, at last, when he comes to the manes, he has let fly hand and chisel with their full force; and where a base workman, (above all, if he had modelled the thing in clay first,) would have lost himself in laborious imitation of hair, the Greek has struck the tresses out with angular incisions, deep driven, every one in appointed place and deliberate curve, yet flowing so free under his noble hand that you cannot alter, without harm, the bending of any single ridge, nor contract, nor extend, a point of them.[21]

[20] ArP 214 f
[21] ArP 327

[I]n the management of the sculptures of the Parthenon, shadow is frequently employed as a dark field on which the forms are drawn. This is visibly the case in the metopes, and must have been nearly as much so in the pediment. But the use of that shadow is entirely to show the confines of the figures; and it is to *their lines*, and not to the shapes of the shadows behind them, that the art and the eye are addressed. The figures themselves are conceived, as much as possible, in full light, aided by bright reflections; they are drawn exactly as, on vases, white figures on a dark ground; and the sculptors have dispensed with, or even struggled to avoid, all shadows which were not absolutely necessary to the explaining of the form. On the contrary, in Gothic sculpture, the shadow becomes itself a subject of thought. It is considered as a dark colour, to be arranged in certain agreeable masses; the figures are very frequently made even subordinate to the placing of its divisions: and their costume is enriched at the expense of the forms underneath, in order to increase the complexity and variety of the points of shade.

One of the chief distinctions between the dramatic and picturesque schools of sculpture is found in the treatment of the hair. By the artists of the time of Pericles it was considered as an excrescence, indicated by few and rude lines, and subordinated, in every particular, to the principality of the features and person. How completely this was an artistical, not a national idea, it is unnecessary to prove. We need but remember the employment of the Lacedæmonians, reported by the Persian spy on the evening before the battle of Thermopylæ,[22] or glance at any Homeric description of ideal form, to see how purely *sculpturesque* was the law which reduced the markings of the hair, lest, under the necessary disadvantages of material, they should interfere with the distinctness of the personal forms. On the contrary, in later sculpture [i.e., Roman], the hair receives almost the principal care of the workman; and, while the features and limbs are clumsily

[22] (Herodotus, vii, 208, a reference to the Lacedæmonians arranging their hair on the eve of peril.) Lamps 238 f, omit.

and bluntly executed, the hair is curled and twisted, cut into bold and shadowy projections, and arranged in masses elaborately ornamental: there is true sublimity in the lines and the chiaroscuro of these masses, but it is, as regards the creature represented, parasitical and therefore picturesque.[23]

The Greek labyrinth

Mother-naked sits Theseus: and around about him [on the Parthenon], not much more veiled, ride his Athenians, in Pan-Athenaic procession, honouring their Queen-Goddess. Admired, beyond all other marble shapes in the world . . .

All the more strange then, all the more instructive, as the disembodied Cincinnatus of the Roman, so this disembodied Theseus of the Ionian; though certainly Mr. Stuart Mill could not consider him, even in that ponderous block of marble imagery, a "utility fixed and embodied in a material object." Not even a disembodied utility—not even a ghost—if he never lived. An idea only; yet one that has ruled all minds of men to this hour, from the hour of its first being born, a dream, into this practical and solid world.

Ruled, and still rules, in a thousand ways, which you know no more than the paths by which the winds have come that blow in your face. But you never pass a day without being brought, somehow, under the power of Theseus.

You cannot pass a china-shop, for instance, nor an upholsterer's, without seeing, on some mug or plate, or curtain, or chair, the pattern known as the "Greek fret," simple or complex. Well, that Greek fret, ugly in itself, has yet definite and noble service in decorative work, as black has among colours; much more, has it a significance, very precious, though very solemn, when you can read it.

There is so much in it, indeed, that I don't well know where to begin. Perhaps it will be best to go back to our

[23] Lamps 239 f

cathedral door at Lucca, where we have been already. For as, after examining the sculpture on the bell, with the help of the sympathetic ringer, I was going in to look at the golden lamp, my eyes fell on a slightly traced piece of sculpture and legend on the southern wall of the porch, . . . which is in English:—

> "This is the labyrinth which the Cretan Dedalus built,
> Out of which nobody could get who was inside,
> Except Theseus; nor could he have done it, unless he had been helped with a thread by Adriane, all for love."

Upon which you are to note, first, that the grave announcement, "This is the labyrinth which the Cretan Dedalus built," may possibly be made interesting even to some of your children, if reduced from mediæval sublimity, into your more popular legend—"This is the house that Jack built." The cow with the crumpled horn will then remind them of the creature who, in the midst of this labyrinth, lived as a spider in the centre of his web; and the "maiden all forlorn" may stand for Ariadne, or Adriane, . . . while the gradual involution of the ballad, and necessity of clear-mindedness as well as clear utterance on the part of its singer, is a pretty vocal imitation of the deepening labyrinth. Theseus, being a pious hero, and the first Athenian knight who cut his hair short in front, may not inaptly be represented by the priest all shaven and shorn; the cock that crew in the morn is the proper Athenian symbol of a pugnacious mind; and the malt that lay in the house fortunately indicates the connection of Theseus and the Athenian power with the mysteries of Eleusis, where corn first, it is said, grew in Greece.

Lastly, in our nursery rhyme, observe that the name of Jack, the builder, stands excellently for Dædalus, retaining the idea of him down to the phrase, "Jack-of-all-Trades." Of this Greek builder you will find some account at the end of my *Aratra Pentelici:* to-day I can only tell you he is distinctively the power of finest human, as opposed to Divine, workmanship or craftsmanship. Whatever good there is, and whatever evil, in the labour of the hands,

separated from that of the soul, is exemplified by his history and performance. In the deepest sense, he was to
the Greeks, Jack of all trades, yet Master of none; the real
Master of every trade being always a God. His own special
work or craft was inlaying or dovetailing, and especially
of black in white.

And this house which he built was his finest piece of
involution, or cunning workmanship; and the memory of
it is kept by the Greeks for ever afterwards, in that running border of theirs, involved in and repeating itself,
called the Greek fret, of which you will at once recognize
the character in these two pictures of the labyrinth of
Dædalus itself, on the coins of the place where it was
built, Cnossus, in the island of Crete; and which you see
surrounding the head of Theseus, himself, on a coin of the
same city.

Of course frets and returning lines were used in ornamentation when there were no labyrinths—probably long
before labyrinths. A symbol is scarcely ever invented just
when it is needed. Some already recognized and accepted
form or thing becomes symbolic at a particular time.
Horses had tails, and the moon quarters, long before there
were Turks; but the horse-tail and crescent are not less
definitely symbolic to the Ottoman. So, the early forms of
ornament are nearly alike, among all nations of any capacity for design: they put meaning into them afterwards, if
they ever come themselves to *have* any meaning. Vibrate
but the point of a tool against an unbaked vase, as it revolves, set on the wheel,—you have a wavy or zigzag line.
The vase revolves once; the ends of the wavy line do not
exactly tally when they meet; you get over the blunder by
turning one into a head, the other into a tail,—and have a
symbol of eternity—if, first, which is wholly needful, you
have an *idea* of eternity!

Again, the free sweep of a pen at the finish of a large
letter has a tendency to throw itself into a spiral. There
is no particular intelligence, or spiritual emotion, in the
production of this line. A worm draws it with his coil, a
fern with its bud, and a periwinkle with his shell. Yet,
completed in the Ionic capital, and arrested in the bend-

ing point of the acanthus leaf in the Corinthian one, it has become the primal element of beautiful architecture and ornament in all the ages; and is eloquent with endless symbolism, representing the power of the winds and waves in Athenian work, and of the old serpent, which is the Devil, and Satan, in Gothic work: or, indeed, often enough, of both, the Devil being held prince of the power of the air—as in the story of Job, and the lovely story of Buonconte of Montefeltro, in Dante . . .[24]

[24] Fors 1872, 397–405, omit.

4

BYZANTINE SCULPTURE AND ORNAMENT

Go round therefore to the side [of St. Mark's] farthest
from the sea, where, in the first broad arch, you will see a
panel . . . set horizontally; the sculpture of which represents twelve sheep—six on one side, six on the other, of a
throne: on which throne is set a cross; and on the top of
the cross a circle; and in the circle, a little caprioling
creature.

And outside of all, are two palm trees, one on each
side; and under each palm tree, two baskets of dates; and
over the twelve sheep, is written in delicate Greek letters
"The holy Apostles"; and over the little caprioling creature, "The Lamb."

Take your glass and study the carving of this bas-relief
intently. It is full of sweet care, subtlety, tenderness of
touch, and mind; and fine cadence and change of line in
the little bowing heads and bending leaves. Decorative in
the extreme; a kind of stone-stitching or sampler-work,
done with the innocence of a girl's heart, and in a like unlearned fulness. Here is a Christian man, bringing order
and loveliness into the mere furrows of stone. Not by any
means as learned as a butcher, in the joints of lambs; nor
as a grocer, in baskets of dates; nor as a gardener, in en-
dogenous plants: but an artist to the heart's core; and no
less true a lover of Christ and His word. Helpless, with his
childish art, to carve Christ, he carves a cross, and caprioling little thing in a ring at the top of it. You may try—
you—to carve Christ, if you can. Helpless to conceive the
Twelve Apostles, these nevertheless are sacred letters for
the bearers of the Gospel of Peace.

Of such men Venice learned to touch the stone;—to become a Lapicida, and furrower of the marble as well as the sea.[25]

I gave you the bas-relief of the twelve sheep and little caprioling lamb for a general type of all Byzantine art, to fix in your mind at once, respecting it, that its intense first character is symbolism. The thing represented means more than itself,—is a sign, or letter, more than an image.

And this is true, not of Byzantine art only, but of all Greek art, pur sang. Let us leave, to-day, the narrow and degrading word "Byzantine." There is but one Greek school, from Homer's day down to the Doge Selvo's; and these St. Mark's mosaics are as truly wrought in the power of Dædalus, with the Greek constructive instinct, and in the power of Athena, with the Greek religious soul, as ever chest of Cypselus or shaft of Erechtheum. And therefore, whatever is represented here, be it flower or rock, animal or man, means more than it is in itself. Not sheep, these twelve innocent woolly things,—but the twelve voices of the gospel of heaven;—not palm-trees, these shafts of shooting stem and beaded fruit,—but the living grace of God in the heart, springing up in joy at Christ's coming;—not a king, merely, this crowned creature in his sworded state, —but the justice of God in His eternal Law;—not a queen, nor a maid only, this Madonna in her purple shade,—but the love of God poured forth, in the wonderfulness that passes the love of woman. *She* may forget—yet will I not forget thee.[26]

And in this function of his art, remember, it does not matter to the Greek how far his image be *perfect* or not. That it should be *understood* is enough,—if it can be beautiful also, well; but its function is not beauty, but instruction. You cannot have purer examples of Greek art than the drawings on any good vase of the Marathonian time. Black figures on a red ground,—a few white scratches through them, marking the joints of their armour or the folds of their robes,—white circles for eyes,—pointed pyramids for beards,—you don't suppose that in these the

[25] Rest 1877, 241–43, omit.
[26] (Isaiah xlix: 15.) Rest 1879, 280 f

Greek workman thought he had given the likeness of
gods? Yet here, to his imagination, were Athena, Poseidon,
and Herakles,—and all the powers that guarded his land,
and cleansed his soul, and led him in the way everlasting.[27]

Byzantine light and shadow

[T]he Greek workman cared for shadow only as a dark
field wherefrom his light figure or design might be intelli-
gibly detached: his attention was concentrated on the one
aim at readableness and clearness of accent; and all
composition, all harmony, nay, the very vitality and energy
of separate groups were, when necessary, sacrificed to
plain speaking. Nor was there any predilection for one
kind of form rather than another. Rounded forms were, in
the columns and principal decorative members, adopted,
not for their own sake, but as characteristic of the things
represented. They were beautifully rounded, because the
Greek habitually did well what he had to do, not because
he loved roundness more than squareness; severely recti-
linear forms were associated with the curved ones in the
cornice and triglyph, and the mass of the pillar was divided
by a fluting, which, in distant effect, destroyed much of
its breadth. What power of light these primal arrangements left, was diminished in successive refinements and
additions of ornament; and continued to diminish through
Roman work, until the confirmation of the circular arch
as a decorative feature. Its lovely and simple line taught
the eye to ask for a similar boundary of solid form; the
dome followed, and necessarily the decorative masses were
thenceforward managed with reference to, and in sympathy with, the chief feature of the building. Hence arose,
among the Byzantine architects, a system of ornament,
entirely restrained within the superficies of curvilinear
masses, on which the light fell with as unbroken gradation
as on a dome or column, while the illumined surface was
nevertheless cut into details of singular and most ingenious intricacy. Something is, of course, to be allowed for
the less dexterity of the workmen; it being easier to cut

[27] (Psalms cxxxix: 24.) Rest 1879, 281

down into a solid block, than to arrange the projecting
portions of leaf on the Greek capital: such leafy capitals
are nevertheless executed by the Byzantines with skill
enough to show that their preference of the massive form
was by no means compulsory, nor can I think it unwise.
On the contrary, while the arrangements of *line* are far
more artful in the Greek capital, the Byzantine light and
shade are as incontestably more grand and masculine,
based on that quality of pure gradation, which nearly all
natural objects possess, and the attainment of which is, in
fact, the first and most palpable purpose in natural arrangements of grand form. The rolling heap of the thunder-
cloud, divided by rents, and multiplied by wreaths, yet
gathering them all into its broad, torrid, and towering
zone, and its midnight darkness opposite; the scarcely less
majestic heave of the mountain side, all torn and traversed
by depth of defile and ridge of rock, yet never losing the
unity of its illumined swell and shadowy decline; and the
head of every mighty tree, rich with tracery of leaf and
bough, yet terminated against the sky by a true line, and
rounded by a green horizon, which, multiplied in the distant forest, makes it look bossy from above; all these mark,
for a great and honoured law, that diffusion of light for
which the Byzantine ornaments were designed; and show
us that those builders had truer sympathy with what God
made majestic, than the self-contemplating and self-con-
tented Greek. I know that they are barbaric in comparison;
but there is a power in their barbarism of sterner tone, a
power not sophistic nor penetrative, but embracing and
mysterious; a power faithful more than thoughtful, which
conceived and felt more than it created; a power that
neither comprehended nor ruled itself, but worked and
wandered as it listed, like mountain streams and winds;
and which could not rest in the expression or seizure of
finite form. It could not bury itself in acanthus leaves. Its
imagery was taken from the shadows of the storms and
hills, and had fellowship with the night and day of the
earth itself.[28]

[28] Lamps 119–21

Mosaic

Now observe, the old Byzantine mosaicist [at St. Mark's] begins his work at enormous disadvantage. It is to be some one hundred and fifty feet above the eye, in a dark cupola; executed not with free touches of the pencil, but with square pieces of glass; not by his own hand, but by various workmen under his superintendence; finally, not with a principal purpose of drawing olive-trees, but mainly as a decoration of the cupola. There is to be an olive-tree beside each apostle, and their stems are to be the chief lines which divide the dome. He therefore at once gives up the irregular twisting of the boughs hither and thither, but he will not give up their fibres. Other trees have irregular and fantastic branches, but the knitted cordage of fibres is the olive's own. Again, were he to draw the leaves of their natural size, they would be so small that their forms would be invisible in the darkness; and were he to draw them so large as that their shape might be seen, they would look like laurel instead of olive. So he arranges them in small clusters of five each, nearly of the shape which the Byzantines give to the petals of the lily, but elongated so as to give the idea of leafage upon a spray; and these clusters,—his object always, be it remembered, being *decoration* not less than *representation*,—he arranges symmetrically on each side of his branches, laying the whole on a dark ground most truly suggestive of the heavy rounded mass of the tree, which, in its turn, is relieved against the gold of the cupola. Lastly, comes the question respecting the fruit. The whole power and honour of the olive is in its fruit; and, unless that be represented, nothing is represented. But if the berries were coloured black or green, they would be totally invisible; if of any other colour, utterly unnatural, and violence would be done to the whole conception. There is but one conceivable means of showing them, namely, to represent them as golden. For the idea of golden fruit of various kinds was already familiar to the mind, as in the apples of the Hesperides, without any violence to the distinctive conception of the fruit itself. So the mosaicist introduced small round golden berries into the dark ground between each leaf, and his work was done. Each bough is connected with a separate line of fibre in the trunk, and the junctions of the arms and stem are indicated, down to the very root of the tree, with a truth in structure which may well put to shame the tree anatomy of modern times.

The white branching figures upon the serpentine band below [in Ruskin's illustration] are two of the clusters of flowers which form the foreground of a mosaic in the atrium. I have printed the whole plate in blue, because that colour approaches more nearly than black to the distant effect of the mosaics, of which the darker portions are generally composed of blue, in greater quantity than any other colour. But the waved background, in this instance, is of various shades of blue and green alternately, with one narrow black band to give it force; the whole being intended to represent the distant effect and colour of deep grass, and the wavy line to *express its bending motion,* just as the same symbol is used to represent the waves of water. Then the two white clusters are representative of the distinctly visible herbage close to the spectator, having buds and flowers of two kinds, springing in one case out of the midst of twisted grass, and in the other out of their own proper leaves; the clusters being kept each so distinctly symmetrical, as to form, when set side by side, an ornamental border of perfect architectural severity; and yet each cluster different from the next, and every flower, and bud, and knot of grass, varied in form and thought. The way the mosaic tesseræ are arranged, so as to give the writhing of the grass blades round the stalks of the flowers, is exceedingly fine.

The three circles below are examples of still more severely conventional forms, adopted, on principle, when the decoration is to be in white and gold, instead of colour; these ornaments being cut in white marble on the outside of the church, and the ground laid in with gold, though necessarily here represented, like the rest of the plate, in blue. And it is exceedingly interesting to see how the noble workman, the moment he is restricted to more conventional materials, retires into more conventional forms, and reduces his various leafage into symmetry, now nearly perfect; yet observe, in the central figure, where the symbolic meaning of the vegetation beside the cross required it to be more distinctly indicated, he has given it life and growth by throwing it into unequal curves on the opposite sides.

I believe the reader will now see, that in these mosaics, which the careless traveller is in the habit of passing by with contempt, there is a depth of feeling and of meaning greater than in most of the best sketches from nature of modern times; and, without entering into any question whether these conventional representations are as good as, under the required limitations, it was possible to render them, they are at all events good enough completely to illustrate that mode of symbolical expression which appeals altogether to thought, and in nowise trusts to realization. And little as, in the present state of our schools, such an assertion is likely to be believed, the fact is that this kind of expression is the *only one allowable in noble art*.

I do not mean that no art is noble but Byzantine mosaic; but that no art is noble which in any wise depends upon direct imitation for its effect upon the mind.[29]

[29] SV III, 209–12, omit.

5

MEDIEVAL SCULPTURE

The West Portals at Chartres

These statues [of the West Portals] have been long, and justly, considered as representative of the highest skill of the twelfth or earliest part of the thirteenth century in France; and they indeed possess a dignity and delicate charm, which are for the most part wanting in later works. It is owing partly to real nobleness of feature, but chiefly to the grace, mingled with severity, of the falling lines of excessively *thin* drapery; as well as to a most studied finish in composition, every part of the ornamentation tenderly harmonizing with the rest. So far as their power over certain tones of religious mind is owing to a palpable degree of non-naturalism in them, I do not praise it—the exaggerated thinness of body and stiffness of attitude are faults; but they are noble faults, and give the statues a strange look of forming part of the very building itself, and sustaining it—not like the Greek caryatid, without effort—nor like the Renaissance caryatid, by painful or impossible effort—but as if all that was silent, and stern, and withdrawn apart, and stiffened in chill of heart against the terror of earth, had passed into a shape of eternal marble; and thus the Ghost had given, to bear up the pillars of the church on earth, all the patient and expectant nature that it needed no more in heaven. This is the transcendental view of the meaning of those sculptures. I do not dwell upon it. What I do lean upon is their purely naturalistic and vital power. They are all portraits—unknown, most of them, I believe,—but palpably and unmistakably portraits, if not taken from the actual person for whom the statue stands, at all events studied from some living person whose features might fairly represent those of the king or saint intended. Several of them I suppose to be authentic; there is one of a queen, who has evidently, while she lived, been notable for her bright black eyes. The sculptor has cut the iris deep into the stone, and her dark eyes are still suggested with her smile.

There is another thing I wish you to notice especially in these statues—the way in which the floral moulding is associated with the vertical lines of the figure. You have thus the utmost complexity and richness of curvature set side by side with the pure and delicate parallel lines, and both the characters gain in interest and beauty; but there is deeper significance in the thing than that of mere effect in composition;—significance not intended on the part of the sculptor, but all the more valuable because unintentional. I mean the close association of the beauty of lower nature in animals and flowers, with the beauty of higher nature in human form. You never get this in Greek work. Greek statues are always isolated; blank fields of stone, or depths of shadow, relieving the form of the statue, as the world of lower nature which they despised retired in darkness from their hearts. Here, the clothed figure seems the type of the Christian spirit—in many respects feebler and more contracted—but purer; clothed in its white robes and crown, and with the riches of all creation at its side.

The next step in the change will be set before you in a moment, merely by comparing this statue from the west front of Chartres with that of the Madonna, from the south transept door of Amiens.

This Madonna, with the sculpture round her, represents the culminating power of Gothic art in the thirteenth century. Sculpture has been gaining continually in the interval; gaining, simply because becoming every day more truthful, more tender, and more suggestive. By the way, the old Douglas motto, "Tender and true," may wisely be taken up again by all of us, for our own, in art no less than in other things. Depend upon it, the first universal characteristic of all great art is Tenderness, as the second is Truth. I find this more and more every day: an infinitude of tenderness is the chief gift and inheritance of all the truly great men. It is sure to involve a relative intensity of disdain towards base things, and an appearance of sternness and arrogance in the eyes of all hard, stupid, and vulgar people—quite terrific to such, if they are capable of terror, and hateful to them, if they are capable of nothing higher than hatred. Dante's is the great type of this class of mind. I say the *first* inheritance is Tenderness —the *second* Truth, because the Tenderness is in the make of the creature, the Truth in his acquired habits and knowledge: besides, the love comes first in dignity as well as in time, and that is always pure and complete: the truth, at best, imperfect.

To come back to our statue. You will observe that the arrangement of this sculpture is exactly the same as at Chartres—severe falling drapery, set off by rich floral ornament at the side; but the statue is now completely animated; it is no longer fixed as an upright pillar, but bends aside out of its niche, and the floral ornament, instead of being a conventional wreath, is of exquisitely arranged hawthorn. The work, however, as a whole, though perfectly characteristic of the advance of the age in style and purpose, is in some subtler qualities inferior to that of Chartres. The individual sculptor, though trained in a more advanced school, has been himself a man of inferior order of mind compared to the one who worked at Chartres. But I have not time to point out to you the subtler characters by which I know this.

This statue, then, marks the culminating point of Gothic art, because, up to this time, the eyes of its designers had been steadily fixed on natural truth—they had been advancing from flower to flower, from form to form, from face to face,—gaining perpetually in knowledge and veracity —therefore, perpetually in power and in grace. But at this point a fatal change came over their aim. From the statue they now began to turn the attention chiefly to the niche of the statue, and from the floral ornament to the mouldings that enclosed the floral ornament. The first result of this was, however, though not the grandest, yet the most finished of northern genius. You have, in the earlier Gothic, less wonderful construction, less careful masonry, far less

expression of harmony of parts in the balance of the building. Earlier work always has more or less of the character
of a good solid wall with irregular holes in it, well carved
wherever there was room. But the last phase of good Gothic
has no room to spare; it rises as high as it can on narrowest
foundation, stands in perfect strength with the least possible substance in its bars; connects niche with niche, and
line with line, in an exquisite harmony, from which no
stone can be removed, and to which you can add not a
pinnacle; and yet introduces in rich, though now more
calculated profusion, the living element of its sculpture:
sculpture in the quatrefoils—sculpture in the brackets—
sculpture in the gargoyles—sculpture in the niches—sculpture in the ridges and hollows of its mouldings,—not a
shadow without meaning, and not a light without life. But
with this very perfection of his work came the unhappy
pride of the builder in what he had done. As long as he
had been merely raising clumsy walls and carving them,
like a child, in waywardness of fancy, his delight was in
the things he thought of as he carved; but when he had
once reached this pitch of constructive science, he began
to think only how cleverly he could put the stones together.
The question was not now with him, What can I represent?
but, How high can I build—how wonderfully can I hang
this arch in air, or weave this tracery across the clouds?
And the catastrophe was instant and irrevocable. Architecture became in France a mere web of waving lines,—
in England a mere grating of perpendicular ones. Redundance was substituted for invention, and geometry for passion; the Gothic art became a mere expression of wanton
expenditure, and vulgar mathematics; and was swept
away, as it then deserved to be swept away, by the severer
pride, and purer learning, of the schools founded on classical traditions.[30]

[30] TwoP 279–83

The Campanile at Florence

The Master's own estimate of the power of these bas-reliefs must have been very high; for instead of making them a part of such encrusted and continuous decoration as the most powerful sculptor of the Pisan school had accustomed the populace to expect, he sets them as gems in a kind of Etruscan chain round the base of his tower, minute in the extreme compared to the extent of its surface; so far above the eye as to secure them absolutely from all chance of injury or wear, but by time and its mud and rain; and entirely unrecommended and unassisted by the slightest external minor imageries of organic form. In all fine northern sculpture of the time, the external courses of foliage, and crockets, and bosses of pinnacle, relieve the simplicity of falling draperies, and disguise or enrich with picturesque shadow the harshness of feature and expression in the figures. But here the Master allows only the severest masonry and mouldings to approach or limit his subject; requires, in concentrated space, undisturbed attention; and trusts, without the slightest link of decoration, to the inner sequence and consistency of thought.[31]

CREATION OF WOMAN. Far, in its essential qualities, the transcendent sculpture of this subject; Ghiberti's is only a dainty elaboration and beautification of it, losing its solemnity and simplicity in a flutter of feminine grace. The older sculptor thinks of the Uses of Womanhood, and of its dangers and sins, before he thinks of its beauty; but, were the arm not lost, the quiet naturalness of this head and breast of Eve, and the bending grace of the submissive rendering of soul and body to perpetual guidance by the hand of Christ—(*grasping* the arm, note, for full support)—would

[31] (Ruskin believed Giotto to be largely responsible for the Campanile sculpture, a role today's historians give to Andrea Pisano.) *The Shepherd's Tower*, preface to a set of 29 reproductions of the Campanile, published in 1881, *Works*, vol. XXIII, 463 f

be felt to be far beyond Ghiberti's in beauty, as in mythic truth.

The line of her body joins with that of the serpent-ivy round the tree trunk above her: a double myth—of her fall, and her support afterwards by her husband's strength. "Thy desire shall be to thy husband."[32] The fruit of the tree—double-set filbert,—telling nevertheless the happy equality.

The leaves in this piece are finished with consummate poetical care and precision. Above Adam, laurel (a virtuous woman is a crown to her husband); the filbert for the two together; the fig, for fruitful household joy (under thy vine and fig-tree—but vine properly the masculine joy); and the fruit taken by Christ for type of all naturally growing food, in His own hunger.

Examine with lens the ribbing of these leaves, and the insertion on their stem of the three laurel leaves on extreme right: and observe that in all cases the sculptor works the moulding *with* his own part of the design; look how he breaks variously deeper into it, beginning from the foot of Christ, and going up to the left into full depth above the shoulder.

JABAL. If you have looked long enough, and carefully enough, at the three previous sculptures, you cannot but feel that the hand here is utterly changed. The drapery sweeps in broader, softer, but less true folds; the handling is far more delicate; exquisitely sensitive to gradation over broad surfaces—scarcely using an incision of any depth but in outline; studiously reserved in appliance of shadow, as a thing precious and local—look at it above the puppy's head, and under the tent. This is assuredly painter's work, not mere sculptor's. I have no doubt whatever it is by the own hand of the shepherd boy of Fésole.

Take the lens and look at every piece of the work from corner to corner—note especially as a thing which would only have been enjoyed by a painter, and which all great

[32] (Genesis iii: 16.) MorFlor 421 f

painters do intensely enjoy—the *fringe* of the tent, and precise insertion of its point in the angle of the hexagon, prepared for by the archaic masonry indicated in the oblique joint above; architect and painter thinking at once, and *doing* as they thought.

ASTRONOMY. We have a new hand here altogether. The hair and drapery bad; the face expressive, but blunt in cutting; the small upper heads, necessarily little more than blocked out, on the small scale; but not suggestive of grace in completion: the minor detail worked with great mechanical precision, but little feeling; the lion's head, with leaves in its ears, is quite ugly; and by comparing the work of the small cusped arch at the bottom with Giotto's soft handling of the mouldings of his, in [*Jubal*] you may for ever know common mason's work from fine Gothic. The zodiacal signs are quite hard and common in the method of bas-relief, but quaint enough in design: Capricorn, Aquarius, and Pisces, on the broad heavenly belt; Taurus upside down, Gemini, and Cancer, on the small globe.

I think the whole a restoration of the original panel, or else an inferior workman's rendering of Giotto's design, which the next piece is, with less question.[33]

Niccola Pisano

Among the spoils brought by [Pisan] fleets from Greece, is a sarcophagus, with Meleager's hunt on it, wrought "con bellissima maniera," says Vasari.

You may see that sarcophagus—any of you who go to Pisa;—touch it, for it is on a level with your hand; study it, as Niccola studied it, to your mind's content. Within ten yards of it, stand equally accessible pieces of Niccola's own work and of his son's. Within fifty yards of it, stands the Byzantine font of the chapel of St. John. Spend but the good hours of a single day quietly by these three pieces

[33] MorFlor 422–25, omit.

of marble, and you may learn more than in general any
of you bring home from an entire tour in Italy.

The sarcophagus is not, however (with Vasari's pardon), in "bellissima maniera" by any means. But it is in
the classical Greek manner instead of the Byzantine Greek
manner. You have to learn the difference between these.

Now I have explained to you sufficiently, in *Aratra
Pentelici*, what the classical Greek manner is. The manner
and matter of it being easily summed—as those of natural
and unaffected life;—nude life when nudity is right and
pure; not otherwise.

Niccola followed the facts, then. He is the Master of
Naturalism in Italy. And I have drawn for you his lioness
and cubs [from the pulpit at Siena] to fix that in your
minds. And beside it, I put the Lion of St. Mark's, that
you may see exactly the kind of change he made. The
Lion of St. Mark's (all but his wings, which have been
made and fastened on in the fifteenth century) is in the
central Byzantine manner; a fine decorative piece of work,
descending in true genealogy from the Lion of Nemea, and
the crested skin of him that clothes the head of the Hera-
cles of Camarina. It has all the richness of Greek Daedal
work,—nay, it has fire and life beyond much Greek Daedal
work; but in so far as it is non-natural, symbolic, decorative, and not like an actual lion, it would be felt by Niccola
Pisano to be imperfect. And instead of this decorative evangelical preacher of a lion, with staring eyes, and its paw
on a gospel, he carves you a quite brutal and maternal
lioness, with affectionate eyes, and paw set on her cub.

Fix that in your minds, then. Niccola Pisano is the Master of Naturalism in Italy,—therefore elsewhere: of Naturalism, and all that follows. Generally of truth, common-sense,
simplicity, vitality,—and of all these, with consummate
power.

You hear the fame of him as of a sculptor only. It is
right that you should; for every great architect must be a
sculptor, and be renowned, as such, more than by his
building. But Niccola Pisano had even more influence on
Italy as a builder than as a carver.

For Italy, at this moment, wanted builders more than

carvers; and a change was passing through her life, of which external edifice was a necessary sign. I complained of you just now that you never looked at the Byzantine font in the temple of St. John. The sacristan generally will not let you. He takes you to a particular spot on the floor, and sings a musical chord. The chord returns in prolonged echo from the chapel roof, as if the building were all one sonorous marble bell.

Which indeed it is; and travellers are always greatly amused at being allowed to ring this bell; but it never occurs to them to ask how it came to be ringable:—how that tintinnabulate roof differs from the dome of the Pantheon, expands into the dome of Florence, or declines into the whispering gallery of St. Paul's.

When you have had full satisfaction of the tintinnabulate roof, you are led by the sacristan and Murray to Niccola Pisano's pulpit; which, if you have spare time to examine it, you find to have six sides, to be decorated with tablets of sculpture, like the sides of the sarcophagus, and to be sustained on seven pillars, three of which are themselves carried on the backs of as many animals.

All this arrangement had been contrived before Niccola's time, and executed again and again. But behold! between the capitals of the pillars and the sculptured tablets there are interposed five cusped arches, the hollow beneath the pulpit showing dark through their foils. You have seen such cusped arches before, you think?

Yes, gentlemen, *you* have; but the Pisans had *not*. And that intermediate layer of the pulpits means—the change, in a word, for all Europe, from the Parthenon to Amiens Cathedral. For Italy it means the rise of her Gothic dynasty; it means the duomo of Milan instead of the temple of Paestum.

I say the duomo of Milan, only to put the change well before your eyes, because you all know that building so well. The duomo of Milan is of entirely bad and barbarous Gothic, but the passion of pinnacle and fret is in it, visibly to you, more than in other buildings. It will therefore serve to show best what fulness of change this pulpit of Niccola Pisano signifies.

In *it* there is no passion of pinnacle nor of fret. You see the edges of it, instead of being bossed, or knopped, or crocketed, are mouldings of severest line. No vaulting, no clustered shafts, no traceries, no fantasies, no perpendicular flights of aspiration. Steady pillars, each of one polished block; useful capitals, one trefoiled arch between them; your panel above it; thereon your story of the founder of Christianity. The whole standing upon beasts, they being indeed the foundation of us (which Niccola knew far better than Mr. Darwin); Eagle to carry your Gospel message —Dove you think it ought to be? Eagle, says Niccola, and not as symbol of St. John Evangelist only, but behold! with prey between its claws. For the Gospel, it is Niccola's opinion, is not altogether a message that you may do whatever you like, and go straight to heaven. Finally, a slab of marble, cut hollow a little to bear your book; space enough for you to speak from at ease,—and here is your first architecture of Gothic Christianity![34]

Giovanni Pisano

Here is John of Pisa,—here Giotto. They are contemporary for twenty years; but these are the prime of Giotto's life, and the last of John's life: virtually, Giotto is the later workman by full twenty years.

But Giotto always uses severe geometrical mouldings, and disdains all luxuriance of leafage to set off interior sculpture. John of Pisa not only adopts Gothic tracery, but first allows himself enthusiastic use of rampant vegetation;—and here, in the façade of Orvieto, you have not only perfect Gothic in the sentiment of Scripture history, but such luxurious ivy ornamentation as you cannot afterwards match for two hundred years. Nay, you can scarcely match it then—for grace of line, only in the richest flamboyant of France.

Now this fact would set you, if you looked at art from its æsthetic side only, at once to find out what German artists had taught Giovanni Pisano. There *were* Germans

[34] Val 17–23, omit.

teaching him,—some teaching him many things; and the intense conceit of the modern German artist imagines them to have taught him all things.

But he learnt his luxuriance, and Giotto his severity, in another school. The quality in both is Greek, and altogether moral. The grace and the redundance of Giovanni are the first strong manifestation of those characters in the Italian mind which culminate in the Madonnas of Luini and the arabesques of Raphael. The severity of Giotto belongs to him, on the contrary, not only as one of the strongest practical men who ever lived on this solid earth, but as the purest and firmest reformer of the discipline of the Christian Church of whose writings any remains exist.

Of whose writings, I say; and you look up, as doubtful that he has left any. Hieroglyphics, then, let me say instead; or, more accurately still, hierographics. St. Francis, in what he wrote and said, taught much that was false; but Giotto, his true disciple, nothing but what was true. And where *he* uses an arabesque of foliage, depend upon it, it will be to purpose—not redundant. I return for the time to our soft and luxuriant John of Pisa.

Soft, but with no unmanly softness; luxuriant, but with no unmannered luxury. To him you owe, as to their first sire in art, the grace of Ghiberti, the tenderness of Raphael, the awe of Michael Angelo. Second-rate qualities in all the three, but precious in their kind, and learned, as you shall see, essentially from this man. Second-rate he also, but with most notable gifts of this inferior kind. He is the Canova of the thirteenth century; but the Canova of the thirteenth, remember, was necessarily a very different person from the Canova of the eighteenth.

The Canova of the eighteenth century mimicked the Greek grace for the delight of modern revolutionary sensualists. The Canova of the thirteenth century brought living Gothic truth into the living faith of his own time.[35]

[T]he next point you have to look to, after the absolute characters of form, is the mode in which the sculptor has placed his shadows, both to express these, and to force

[35] Val 107 f

the eye to the points of his composition which he wants
looked at. You cannot possibly see a more instructive piece
of work, in these respects, than Giovanni's design of the
Nativity. So far as I yet know Christian art, this is the central type of the treatment of the subject; it has all the intensity and passion of the earliest schools, together with a
grace of repose which even in Ghiberti's beautiful Nativity, founded upon it, has scarcely been increased, but
rather lost in languor. The motive of the design is the frequent one among all the early masters; the Madonna lifts
the covering from the cradle to show the Child to one of
the servants, who starts forward adoring. All the light and
shade is disposed to fix the eye on these main actions. First,
one intense deeply-cut mass of shadow, under the pointed
arch, to throw out the head and lifted hand of the Virgin.
A vulgar sculptor would have cut all black behind the
head; Giovanni begins with full shadow; then subdues it
with drapery absolutely quiet in fall; then lays his fullest
possible light on the head, the hand, and the edge of the
lifted veil.

He has undercut his Madonna's profile, being his main
aim, too delicately for time to spare; happily the deep-cut
brow is left, and the exquisitely refined line above, of the
veil and hair. The rest of the work is uninjured, and the
sharpest edges of light are still secure. You may note how
the passionate action of the servant is given by the deep
shadows under and above her arm, relieving its curves in
all their length, and by the recess of shade under the cheek
and chin, which lifts the face.[36]

[36] Val 173 f

6

RENAISSANCE SCULPTURE

We enter to-day on the study of the group of artists whom I wish you to think of as characteristically mathematic in their temper of work—desirous, that is to say, of correcting the impressions of sense by the appliance of the laws of reason, and the measurement or other sure determination of the facts—so that their minds instead of being in a habitual state of αἴσθησις, or perception, are in a habitual state of μάθησις, or learning and demonstration.

The Mathematic school begins with Niccola Pisano; culminates in Michael Angelo; its central captain is Brunelleschi.

All three men of gigantic power, and of apparently universal faculty; all three sculptors and architects. Michael Angelo, a painter also; all three recognized in their time as absolute masters and lawful authorities—men not merely to be admired, but obeyed.

All these three men, then, had a special power in Italy. Niccola Pisano taught her physical truth and trustworthiness in all things; Brunelleschi the dignity of abstract mathematical law; Michael Angelo the majesty of the human frame. To Niccola you owe the veracity, to Brunelleschi the harmony, and to Michael Angelo the humanity, of mathematic art.

To Brunelleschi, I say, you owe its harmony, he being a man of entirely harmonious, exalted, and refined nature, no less intense than scrupulous, no less strong than patient, and no less daring than subtle. He is the discerner of all that has been recovered, and the founder of all that has been done, in classical architecture justly and honourably so called. Michael Angelo, San Micheli, Sansovino, Palladio,

Inigo Jones, and Wren are all his scholars; to him you, in
reality, owe whatever is good and pure, whatever is delicate and learned, in the architecture of modern Europe.
But above all things you especially owe to him—what perhaps some of my audience may be more grateful to him
for than I am—the three great domes of Florence, Rome,
and London.[37]

Quercia

You have then, I repeat, in this tomb [of Ilaria], a standard of perfect rightness—the most accurately faultless
achievement of that Mathematical school of which the
aim is primarily to be right.[38] [It] is the only piece of
monumental work I know in the world which unites in
perfect and errorless balance the softest mysteries of emotion with the implacable severities of science, and that, if
any of my pupils had time to see only one statue in Italy,
and permitted me to choose for them, out of all her
churches and all her galleries, the one which would teach
them most, I should name to them no ideal statue of God
or Goddess, Saint or Athlete, but this perfect image of the
early dead wife of an Etruscan noble.

Yet observe I do not praise it to you as a supremely
wonderful thing at all, but only as a supremely right one;
nay, the singly quite right one, which you can see in all
Italy. There are many which come near it, many which
in artistic skill equal it; none which, as a standard of art,
judgment, and feeling, matches it. And, for the present at
least, you can perfectly see it. Its canopy, as I said, is gone;
the sarcophagus with its recumbent figure stands as simply
by the transept wall of Lucca Cathedral as a table at the
side of your room, and just at the height of your hand, if
you wished to raise the head on its pillow which will never
move more. Fortunately, again, the wall behind is of dark
brown marble, relieving the white form; and a cross and
circle, cut deep into its stone, before the tomb was placed

[37] SchFlor 211–14, omit.
[38] SchFlor 223

there, sign her resting-place with sweet fortuitous sacredness.[39]

Every decoration that can be parted with he refuses: there is no fringe or embroidery here to be played with in presence of death. All *terror* also he refuses: there is no ghastliness of winding-sheet, no wasting of sickness on the features. All *curiosity* he refuses: there is no fine impressing of the pillow by the head, no subtle crumpling of the wrinkles of the dress about the limbs. Nay, all too attractive extreme of the fairest truth he refuses: a lock of the hair escapes from its fillet and trembles loosely down upon the cheek with a perfect tenderness, and had Ghiberti or Luca della Robbia touched it, it would have been so soft, so finishedly like hair, that the eye might have been caught by it, and the meaner thought intended—how wonderful. Not so with Quercia. A few quiet resolute touches, ineffably subtle and unperceived in their skill, and the lock lies on the cheek indeed, but you do not look at it—only at the face.

Again, he is as much master of all the laws of balance and weight in the human body as Michael Angelo himself. But he does not want you to think of balances or weight. In Michael Angelo's Adonis, or David, or Twilight, or Bound Slave you instantly think how languid the Adonis, how balanced in youthful strength the David, how deep in dream the Twilight, how bowed in toil the Slave; and had Michael Angelo cut this, you would have felt instantly how heavily she lies—how dead. Not so Quercia. He will not let you think of anything secondary for an instant— not of flesh, not of death, and least of all, of him or his knowledge. The young matron lies at rest, like a fallen flower. Her hands are crossed as they fall, not on her breast —that would have been too emotional for Quercia; only so. Any other sculptor would have made them daintily beautiful; not he. They are just natural, even not tapered to the finger-ends a bit, but bluntish, though small and soft; just a simple lady's hands, laid one on the other as easily as if she had but that moment put them so. You don't think of

[39] SchFlor 222 f

saying, "What pretty hands"; still less, "How exquisitely they are cut." But try to draw them, and you will find dimpled Nature herself not more inimitable.

Again, with all this reserve and restraint of power, all is done with such consummate point that, had he disposed the folds of the drapery entirely by natural laws, the statue would have been deceptive, and every fool would have gaped at it for its deception. Quercia will not have it so. I must not have the mob coming here, he thinks, to see how like marble can be to clothes: he arranges the dress over the breast in perfectly natural but close-drawn folds, and thus permits the soft outline of the form beneath, but from the shoulder he draws these terminal folds straight to the feet. They would be only possible if the statue was erect, nor then in this continuousness; no drapery unless under tension could take so unbroken lines, whereas these are not even absolutely straight, but curves of extreme subtlety.[40]

This sculpture is central in every respect; being the last Florentine work in which the proper form of the Etruscan tomb is preserved, and the first in which all right Christian sentiment respecting death is embodied. It is perfectly severe in classical tradition, and perfectly frank in concession to the passions of existing life. It submits to all the laws of the past, and expresses all the hopes of the future.

Now every work of the great Christian schools expresses primarily, conquest over death; conquest not grievous, but absolute and serene; rising with the greatest of them into rapture.

But this, as a *central* work, has all the peace of the Christian Eternity, but only in part its gladness. Young children wreathe round the tomb a garland of abundant flowers, but she herself, Ilaria, yet sleeps; the time is not yet come for her to be awakened out of sleep.

Her image is a simple portrait of her—how much less beautiful than she was in life, we cannot know—but as beautiful as marble can be.

And through and in the marble we may see that the damsel is not dead, but sleepeth: yet as visibly a sleep that

[40] SchFlor 230 f

shall know no ending until the last day break, and the last
shadow flee away; until then, she "shall not return."[41] Her
hands are laid on her breast—not praying—she has no need
to pray now. She wears her dress of every day, clasped at
her throat, girdled at her waist, the hem of it drooping over
her feet. No disturbance of its folds by pain of sickness,
no binding, no shrouding of her sweet form, in death more
than in life. As a soft, low wave of summer sea, her breast
rises; no more: the rippled gathering of its close mantle
droops to the belt, then sweeps to her feet, straight as drifting snow. And at her feet her dog lies watching her; the
mystery of his mortal life joined, by love, to her immortal
one.

Few know, and fewer love, the tomb and its place,—
not shrine, for it stands bare by the cathedral wall: only,
by chance, a cross is cut deep into one of the foundation
stones behind her head. But no goddess statue of the Greek
cities, no nun's image among the cloisters of Apennine, no
fancied light of angel in the homes of heaven, has more
divine rank among the thoughts of men.[42]

Ghiberti

[In the fifteenth century] came the Mathematic school
—Brunelleschi, Quercia, Ghiberti. I have dwelt in my last
lecture only on the perfect truth and justice of emotion in
their purest masters, and on the magnificent energy with
which Brunelleschi restored all the laws of classic architecture and its forms. But neither the truth and tenderness
of Quercia nor the energy of Brunelleschi would at once
have prevailed in all outward form against the school of
Giotto, but for the accomplished grace and infinitely decorative invention of Ghiberti.

Vainly the classic innovators would have striven to reduce the rapture of the Goth, the dream of the Etruscan,
under the rigid law of Athenian Grace. Pallas of the Acrop-
olis would never have reigned in Florence had not Aphro-

[41] (Successively Mark v: 39; Song of Solomon ii: 13, and 2
Samuel xii: 23.) Colours 170 f
[42] Colours 171

dite returned at her side, and Ghiberti forged the gates of
the Baptistery with her cestus round his breast.

And now, before Florence, as before the shepherd of
Ida, the great goddesses stood side by side—Athena and
the Queen of Beauty—and she chose as the shepherd of
Ida chose. She chose delight before instruction; and the
art, which had hitherto been wrought in the Fear of God,
which is the beginning of Wisdom, was wrought, thenceforward, for the lust of the eyes and the pride of life.

That is the chart of her life, but to-day we pause at
her central exquisiteness of wisdom and pleasure in her
Mathematic school—the central deliciousness of its composed and studious symmetries.

"Worthy to be the gates of Paradise," said Michael Angelo. Yes, it may be; but again I ask you not to put too
much faith in the depth of the saying. Paradise it may be,
but what kind of Paradise? The gates shall answer to you
for themselves. Their first tablet is of the great story of
Creation and its fall. I have enlarged it for you. I think you
can all see its grace, and the circle of its lovely symmetry.
It is constructed like a heraldic shield, carried by supporters indeed, but these subordinate and of little moment.
God the Creator of man subordinate. Man the sinner subordinate. The condemning angel at the gates a dragon-fly
rather than an angel. But in the centre, the shield borne
by the rest, the Creation of woman as the queen of all
things, the angels round her changed almost into Loves. It
is the birth of Aphrodite, not of Eve.

"And this I call mathematic art," you ask me, "not æsthetic?" Yes, assuredly. There is no perception here whatsoever, and no feeling.

Do you suppose a man who had true eyes and heart
would have made the omnipotence of man and the victory
of Satan and death over humanity mere heraldic supporters to the apparition of a pretty woman? This is not the
beginning of Creation, but of operatic scenes in it. This
panel of Ghiberti's is the first of our coldly mellifluous
pieties; it is a religious ballet. Coldly mellifluous oratorio,
tickling with studious art the dull ear which is incapable of
pleasure from true sacred song.

The Creation is represented simply by that of man, though trees, clouds, water, and rocks are given as beautiful accessories. The creation of Adam, in the left-hand corner; above the shoulder of the standing figure of Christ the Creator, is a crowd of witnessing angels. In a channel in the foreground runs one of the rivers of Paradise in finely threaded current between the rocks. At the side of it Adam is sleeping on an artificial bank of earth, supported by props in a circle, a quite exquisite piece of perspective in bas-relief. The body of Adam, though thin, seems to me, as far as I know or can feel anatomy, quite insuperable in its qualities of physical form. Mind, I don't profess judgment in this matter, but there is no Greek coin, there is no antique statue whatsoever, on which I can recognize more exquisite rendering of flesh than here. Greek forms are indeed simpler; there is a certain Frenchness and affectation about this, but for masterhood in pure flesh sculpture I can't myself conceive anything to go beyond it.

Then, above him, Eve is raised from his shoulder, not from his side, Ghiberti not caring for the religious tradition in the least. I must beg you to note the fading of faith in this matter.

I would not myself say of this Eve what I have said of the Adam. I think the Venus de' Medici much more beautiful as a female form; nevertheless, this Eve is renowned among sculptors, and I doubt not justly. Of the way in which she is sustained by the angels I do not think we can speak too highly as a mathematical design. Assume that Eve is heavy and must be held up, and you can't do it more beautifully. But a sculptor of the Æsthetic school . . . wouldn't have thought she needed holding up when God was making her.

The circle of witnessing angels above is perfect again in perspective and pretty placing—each is delightfully in its own little stall at the opera; but a sculptor of the Æsthetic school would instantly have thought, "Can those angels at the back all see?" And he would have given up all his symmetries, and never minded the box-keeper's tickets a bit. If Botticelli or Tintoret had drawn that group the cherubs would have been huddling over one another as

close as they could squeeze; in Tintoret's Adoration of the
Magi, indeed, there is one quite naughty angel who pushes
another's head out of the way because he can't see through
it. Well, having got your pretty Eve well made for all
time, what happens in consequence, thinks Ghiberti, really
doesn't much matter. Flattened far back in the left-hand
corner you can just make out the serpent and the apple-
eating.[43]

Michelangelo

Of unimaginative work, Bandinelli and Canova supply
us with characteristic instances of every kind: the Hercules
and Cacus of the former, and its criticism by Cellini, will
occur at once to every one; the disgusting statue ["The
Dead Christ"] now placed so as to conceal Giotto's important tempera picture in Santa Croce is a better instance;
but a still more impressive lesson might be received by
comparing the inanity of Canova's garland grace, and ball-
room sentiment, with the intense truth, tenderness, and
power of men like Mino da Fiesole, whose chisel leaves
many a hard edge, and despises down and dimple, but it
seems to cut light and carve breath, the marble burns beneath it, and becomes transparent with very spirit. Yet
Mino stopped at the human nature; he saw the soul, but
not the ghostly presences about it; it was reserved for
Michael Angelo to pierce deeper yet, and to see the in-
dwelling angels. No man's soul is alone; Laocoon or Tobit,
the serpent has it by the heart or the angel by the hand;
the light or the fear of the Spiritual things that move beside it may be seen on the body; and that bodily form
with Buonarotti, white, solid, distinct, material, though it
be, is invariably felt as the instrument or the habitation of
some infinite, invisible power. The earth of the Sistine
Adam that begins to burn ["Creation of Adam"]; the
woman-embodied burst of Adoration from his sleep ["Creation of Eve"]; the twelve great torrents of the Spirit of
God that pause above us there, urned in their vessels of

[43] SchFlor 242–45, omit.

clay [Sibyls and Prophets]; the waiting in the shadow of futurity of those through whom the Promise and Presence of God went down from the Eve to the Mary, each still and fixed, fixed in his expectation, silent, foreseeing, faithful, seated each on his stony throne, the building stones of the word of God, building on and on, tier by tier, to the Refused one the head of the corner; not only these, not only the troops of terror torn up from the earth by the four-quartered winds of the Judgment, but every fragment and atom of stone that he ever touched became instantly inhabited by what makes the hair stand up and the words be few: the St. Matthew [Accademia, Florence], not yet disengaged from his sepulchre, bound hand and foot by his grave clothes, it is left for us to loose him; the strange spectral wreath of the Florence Pietà, casting its pyramidal, distorted shadow, full of pain and death, among the faint purple light that cross and perish under the obscure dome of Santa Maria del Fiore; the white lassitude of joyous limbs, panther-like, yet passive, fainting with their own delight, that gleam among the Pagan formalisms of the Uffizii, far away, separating themselves in their lustrous lightness as the waves of an Alpine torrent do by their dancing from the dead stones, though the stones be as white as they ["Bacchus"]; and finally, and perhaps more than all, those four ineffable types, not of darkness nor of day—not of morning nor evening, but of the departure and the resurrection, the twilight and the dawn of the souls of men—together with the spectre sitting in the shadow of the niche above them; all these, and all else that I could name of his forming, have borne, and in themselves retain and exercise the same inexplicable power—inexplicable because proceeding from an imaginative perception almost superhuman, which goes whither we cannot follow, and is where we cannot come; throwing naked the final, deepest root of the being of man, whereby he grows out of the invisible, and holds on his God home.[44]

[44] MP II, 279–83

PART IV

PAINTING

1

GREEK PAINTING

The distinctions between schools of art which I have
so often asked you to observe are, you must be aware,
founded only on the excess of certain qualities in one group
of painters over another, or the difference in their tendencies; and not in the absolute possession by one group, and
absence in the rest, of any given skill. But this impossibility
of drawing trenchant lines of parting need never interfere
with the distinctness of our conception of the opponent
principles which balance each other in great minds, or
paralyse each other in weak ones; and I cannot too often
urge you to keep clearly separate in your thoughts the
school which I have called "of Crystal," because its distinctive virtue is seen unaided in the sharp separations
and prismatic harmonies of painted glass, and the other,
the "School of Clay," because its distinctive virtue is seen
in the qualities of any fine work in uncoloured terra-cotta,
and in every drawing which represents them.

You know I sometimes speak of these generally as the
Gothic and Greek schools, sometimes as the colourist and
chiaroscurist. All these oppositions are liable to infinite
qualification and gradation, as between species of animals;
and you must not be troubled, therefore, if sometimes momentary contradictions seem to arise in examining special
points. Nay, the modes of opposition in the greatest men
are inlaid and complex; difficult to explain, though in themselves clear. Thus you know in your study of sculpture we
saw that the essential aim of the Greek art was tranquil
action; the chief aim of Gothic art was passionate rest, a
peace, an eternity of intense sentiment. As I go into detail,
I shall continually therefore have to oppose Gothic pas-

sion, ἔκστασις, to Greek temperance; yet Gothic rigidity,
στάσις, to Greek action and ἐλευθερία. You see how doubly, how intimately, opposed the ideas are; yet how difficult to explain without apparent contradiction.

Now, to-day, I must guard you carefully against a mis-
apprehension of this kind. I have told you that the Greeks
as Greeks made real and material what was before indefinite; they turned the clouds and the lightning of Mount
Ithome into the human flesh and eagle upon the extended
arm of the Messenian Zeus. And yet, being in all things set
upon absolute veracity and realization, they perceive as
they work and think forward that to see in all things truly
is to see in all things dimly and through hiding of cloud
and fire.

So that the schools of Crystal, visionary, passionate, and
fantastic in purpose, are, in method, trenchantly formal
and clear; and the schools of Clay, absolutely realistic,
temperate, and simple in purpose, are, in method, mysterious and soft; sometimes licentious, sometimes terrific,
and always obscure.

Look once more at this Greek dancing-girl [collection
unknown] which is from a terra-cotta, and therefore intensely of the school of Clay; look at her beside this Madonna of Filippo Lippi's [Uffizi]: Greek motion against
Gothic absolute quietness; Greek indifference—dancing
careless—against Gothic passion, the mother's—what word
can I use except phrensy of love; Greek fleshliness against
hungry wasting of the self-forgetful body; Greek softness
of diffused shadow and ductile curve, against Gothic sharpness of crystalline colour and acuteness of angle, and Greek
simplicity and human veracity against Gothic redundance
of irrational vision.[1]

In the earliest Greek drawings of animals, bars of white
are used as one means of detaching the figures from the
ground; ordinarily on the under side of them, marking the
lighter colour of the hair in wild animals. But the placing
of this bar of white, or the direction of the face in deities
of light, (the faces and flesh of women being always repre-

[1] Land 49–51

sented as white,) may become expressive of the direction of the light, when that direction is important. Thus we are enabled at once to read the intention of this Greek symbol of the course of a day . . . At the top[2] you have an archaic representation of Hermes stealing Io from Argus. Argus is here the Night; his grotesque features monstrous; his hair overshadowing his shoulders; Hermes on tiptoe, stealing upon him, and taking the cord which is fastened to the horn of Io out of his hand without his feeling it. Then, underneath, you have the course of an entire day.[3] Apollo first, on the left, dark, entering his chariot, the sun not yet risen. In front of him Artemis, as the moon, ascending before him, playing on her lyre, and looking back to the sun. In the centre, behind the horses, Hermes, as the cumulus cloud at mid-day, wearing his petasus heightened to a cone, and holding a flower in his right hand; indicating the nourishment of the flowers by the rain from the heat cloud. Finally, on the right, Latona, going down as the evening, lighted from the right by the sun, now sunk; and with her feet reverted, signifying the reluctance of the departing day.

Finally, underneath,[4] you have Hermes of the Phidian period, as the floating cumulus cloud, almost shapeless (as you see him at this distance); with the tortoise-shell lyre in his hand, barred with black, and a fleece of white cloud, not level but *oblique,* under his feet. (Compare the "διὰ τῶν κοίλων—πλάγιαι," and the relations of the "αἰγίδος ἡνίοχος 'Αθάνα," with the clouds as the moon's messengers in Aristophanes;[5] and note of Hermes generally, that you never find him flying as a Victory flies, but always, if moving fast at all, *clambering* along, as it were, as a cloud gathers and heaps itself: the Gorgons stretch and stride in

2 (Ruskin derived his illustrations from plates in C. Lenormant's and J. de Witte's classic *Elite des monuments céramographiques,* 4 vols., Paris, 1837 et seq., in this instance, vol. iii, pl. 99.) Lect 149

3 (Lenormant ii, pl. 50.) Lect 150

4 (Lenormant iii, pl. 89.) Lect 150

5 (*Clouds,* 325 and 602.) Lect 151

their flight, half kneeling, for the same reason, running or gliding shapelessly along in this stealthy way.)

These few instances will be enough to show you how we may read in the early art of the Greeks their strong impressions of the power of light. You will find the subject entered into at somewhat greater length in my *Queen of the Air;* and if you will look at the beginning of the 7th book of Plato's *Polity,* and read carefully the passages in the context respecting the sun and intellectual sight, you will see how intimately this physical love of light was connected with their philosophy, in its search, as blind and captive, for better knowledge. I shall not attempt to define for you to-day the more complex but much shallower forms which this love of light, and the philosophy that accompanies it, take in the mediæval mind; only remember that in future, when I briefly speak of the Greek school of art with reference to questions of delineation, I mean the entire range of the schools, from Homer's days to our own, which concern themselves with the representation of light, and the effects it produces on material form—beginning practically for us with these Greek vase paintings, and closing practically for us with Turner's sunset on the *Téméraire* [National Gallery, London]; being throughout a school of captivity and sadness, but of intense power; and which in its technical method of shadow on material form, as well as in its essential temper, is centrally represented to you by Dürer's two great engravings of the "Melencolia" and the "Knight and Death." On the other hand, when I briefly speak to you of the Gothic school, with reference to delineation, I mean the entire and much more extensive range of schools extending from the earliest art in Central Asia and Egypt down to our own day in India and China: —schools which have been content to obtain beautiful harmonies of colour without any representation of light; and which have, many of them, rested in such imperfect expressions of form as could be so obtained; schools usually in some measure childish, or restricted in intellect, and similarly childish or restricted in their philosophies or faiths: but contented in the restriction; and in the more powerful races, capable of advance to nobler development than the Greek schools, though the consummate art of Europe has only been accomplished by the union of both.[6]

[6] Lect 151–54, omit.

2

GIOTTO

The Greeks had painted anything anyhow,—gods black, horses red, lips and cheeks white; and when the Etruscan vase expanded into a Cimabue picture, or a Tafi mosaic, still—except that the Madonna was to have a blue dress, and everything else as much gold on it as could be managed,—there was very little advance in notions of colour. Suddenly, Giotto threw aside all the glitter, and all the conventionalism; and declared that he saw the sky blue, the tablecloth white, and angels, when he dreamed of them, rosy. And he simply founded the schools of colour in Italy—Venetian and all, as I will show you to-morrow morning, if it is fine. And what is more, nobody discovered much about colour after him.

But a deeper result of his resolve to look at things as they were, was his getting so heartily interested in them that he couldn't miss their decisive *moment*. There is a decisive instant in all matters; and if you look languidly, you are sure to miss it. Nature seems always, somehow, trying to make you miss it. "I will see that through," you must say, "without turning my head"; or you won't see the trick of it at all. And the most significant thing in all his work, you will find hereafter, is his choice of moments.[7]

The fusion of North and South

You had then the Norman and Lombard races coming down on this: kings, and hunters—splendid in war—insatiable of action. You had the Greek and Arabian races flow-

ing from the east, bringing with them the law of the City,
and the dream of the Desert.

Cimabue—Etruscan born, gave, we saw, the life of the
Norman to the tradition of the Greek: eager action to holy
contemplation. And what more is left for his favourite
shepherd boy Giotto to do, than this, except to paint with
ever-increasing skill? We fancy he only surpassed Cimabue
—eclipsed by greater brightness.

Not so. The sudden and new applause of Italy would
never have been won by mere increase of the already kin-
dled light. Giotto had wholly another work to do. The
meeting of the Norman race with the Byzantine is not
merely that of action with repose—not merely that of war
with religion,—it is the meeting of *domestic* life with *monastic*, and of practical household sense with unpractical Desert insanity.

I have no other word to use than this last. I use it reverently, meaning a very noble thing; I do not know how far
I ought to say—even a divine thing. Decide that for yourselves. Compare the Northern farmer with St. Francis; the
palm hardened by stubbing Thornaby waste, with the palm
softened by the imagination of the wounds of Christ. To
my own thoughts, both are divine: decide that for yourselves; but assuredly, and without possibility of other
decision, one is, humanly speaking, healthy; the other
*un*healthy; one sane, the other—insane.

To reconcile Drama with Dream, Cimabue's task was
comparatively an easy one. But to reconcile Sense with—
I still use even this following word reverently—Non-sense,
is not so easy; and he who did it first,—no wonder he has
a name in the world.

I must lean, however, still more distinctly on the word
"domestic." For it is not Rationalism and commercial com-
petition—Mr. Stuart Mill's "other career for woman than
that of wife and mother"—which are reconcilable, by
Giotto, or by anybody else, with divine vision. But household wisdom, labour of love, toil upon earth according to
the law of Heaven—*these* are reconcilable, in one code of
glory, with revelation in cave or island, with the endurance

of desolate and loveless days, with the repose of folded
hands that wait Heaven's time.

Domestic and monastic. He was the first of Italians—the
first of Christians—who *equally* knew the virtue of both
lives; and who was able to show it in the sight of men of
all ranks,—from the prince to the shepherd; and of all powers,—from the wisest philosopher to the simplest child.

For, note the way in which the new gift of painting, be-
queathed to him by his great master, strengthened his
hands. Before Cimabue, no beautiful rendering of human
form was possible; and the rude or formal types of the
Lombard and Byzantine, though they would serve in the
tumult of the chase, or as the recognized symbols of creed,
could not represent personal and domestic character. Faces
with goggling eyes and rigid lips might be endured with
ready help of imagination, for gods, angels, saints, or hunters—or for anybody else in scenes of recognized legend;
but would not serve for pleasant portraiture of one's own
self—or of the incidents of gentle, actual life. And even
Cimabue did not venture to leave the sphere of conventionally reverenced dignity. He still painted—though beautifully—only the Madonna, and the St. Joseph, and the
Christ. These he made living,—Florence asked no more:
and "Credette Cimabue nella pintura tener lo campo."

But Giotto came from the field; and saw with his simple
eyes a lowlier worth. And he painted—the Madonna, and
St. Joseph, and the Christ,—yes, by all means, if you choose
to call them so, but essentially,—Mamma, Papa, and the
Baby. And all Italy threw up its cap,—"Ora ha Giotto il
grido."

For he defines, explains, and exalts every sweet incident
of human nature; and makes dear to daily life every mystic
imagination of natures greater than our own. He recon-
ciles, while he intensifies, every virtue of domestic and
monastic thought. He makes the simplest household duties
sacred; and the highest religious passions, serviceable, and
just.[8]

[8] MorFlor 331–33

Bardi Chapel frescoes

Now you must observe that painting a Gothic chapel rightly is just the same thing as painting a Greek vase rightly. The [Bardi] chapel is merely the vase turned upside down, and outside in. The principles of decoration are exactly the same. Your decoration is to be proportioned to the size of your vase; to be together delightful when you look at the cup, or chapel, as a whole; to be various and entertaining when you turn the cup round (you turn *yourself* round in the chapel); and to bend its heads and necks of figures about, as it best can, over the hollows, and ins and outs, so that anyhow, whether too long or too short— possible or impossible—they may be living, and full of grace. This is nothing else than a large, beautiful, coloured Etruscan vase you have got, inverted over your heads like a diving-bell.[9]

[I]f I had been told that a careful early fresco by Titian had been recovered in Santa Croce, I could have believed both report and my own eyes, more quickly than I have been able to admit that ["Before the Sultan"] is indeed by Giotto. It is so great that—had its principles been understood—there was in reality nothing more to be taught of art in Italy; nothing to be invented afterwards, except Dutch effects of light.

That there is no "effect of light" here arrived at, I beg you at once to observe as a most important lesson. The subject is St. Francis challenging the Soldan's Magi,—fire-worshippers—to pass with him through the fire, which is blazing red at his feet. It is so hot that the two Magi on the other side of the throne shield their faces. But it is represented simply as a red mass of writhing forms of flame; and casts no firelight whatever. There is no ruby colour on anybody's nose; there are no black shadows under anybody's chin; there are no Rembrandtesque gradations of gloom, or glitterings of sword-hilt and armour.

That the fire be *luminous* or not, is no matter just now.

[9] MorFlor 341 f, omit.

But that the fire is *hot*, he would have you to know. Now, will you notice what colours he has used in the whole picture? First, the blue background, necessary to unite it with the other three subjects, is reduced to the smallest possible space. St. Francis must be in grey, for that is his dress; also the attendant of one of the Magi is in grey; but so warm, that, if you saw it by itself, you would call it brown. The shadow behind the throne, which Giotto knows he *can* paint, and therefore does, is grey also. The rest of the picture in at least six-sevenths of its area—is either crimson, gold, orange, purple, or white, all as warm as Giotto could paint them; and set off by minute spaces only of intense black,—the Soldan's fillet at the shoulders, his eyes, beard, and the points necessary in the golden pattern behind. And the whole picture is one glow.

A single glance round at the other subjects will convince you of the special character in this; but you will recognize also that the four upper subjects, in which St. Francis's life and zeal are shown, are all in comparatively warm colours, while the two lower ones—of the death, and the visions after it—have been kept as definitely sad and cold.

Necessarily, you might think, being full of monks' dresses. Not so. Was there any need for Giotto to have put the priest at the foot of the dead body, with the black banner stooped over it in the shape of a grave? Might he not, had he chosen, in either fresco, have made the celestial visions brighter? Might not St. Francis have appeared in the centre of a celestial glory to the dreaming Pope, or his soul been seen of the poor monk, rising through more radiant clouds? Look, however, how radiant, in the small space allowed out of the blue, they are in reality. You cannot anywhere see a lovelier piece of Giottesque colour, though here, you have to mourn over the smallness of the piece, and its isolation. For the face of St. Francis himself is repainted, and all the blue sky; but the clouds and four sustaining angels are hardly retouched at all, and their iridescent and exquisitely graceful wings are left with really very tender and delicate care by the restorer of the sky.

All the other great Italian colourists see only the beauty of colour, but Giotto also its brightness. And none of the

others, except Tintoret, understood to the full its symbolic
power; but with those—Giotto and Tintoret—there is always, not only a colour harmony, but a colour secret. It
is not merely to make the picture glow, but to remind
you that St. Francis preaches to a fire-worshipping king,
that Giotto covers the wall with purple and scarlet . . . Of
course certain conventional colours were traditionally employed by all painters; but only Giotto and Tintoret invent
a symbolism of their own for every picture.

[T]he casts of drapery . . . are so simply right, in the
figure of the Soldan, that we do not think of them;—we
see him only, not his dress. But we see dress first, in the
figures of the discomfited Magi. Very fully draped personages these, indeed,—with trains, it appears, four yards long,
and bearers of them.

The one nearest the Soldan has done his devoir as
bravely as he could; would fain go up to the fire, but cannot; is forced to shield his face, though he has not turned
back. Giotto gives him full sweeping breadth of fold; what
dignity he can;—a man faithful to his profession at all
events.

The next one has no such courage. Collapsed altogether,
he has nothing more to say for himself or his creed. Giotto
hangs the cloak upon him, in Ghirlandajo's fashion, as from
a peg, but with ludicrous narrowness of fold. Literally, he
is a "shut-up" Magus—closed like a fan. He turns his head
away, hopelessly. And the last Magus shows nothing but
his back, disappearing through the door.

Lastly, for the Soldan himself. In a modern work, you
would assuredly have had him staring at St. Francis with
his eyebrows up, or frowning thundrously at his Magi,
with them bent as far down as they would go. Neither of
these aspects does he bear, according to Giotto. A perfect
gentleman and king, he looks on his Magi with quiet eyes
of decision; he is much the noblest person in the room—
though an infidel, the true hero of the scene, far more
than St. Francis. It is evidently the Soldan whom Giotto
wants you to think of mainly, in this picture of Christian
missionary work.

He does not altogether take the view of the Heathen

which you would get in an Exeter Hall meeting. Does not
expatiate on their ignorance, their blackness, or their nakedness. Does not at all think of the Florentine Islington and
Pentonville, as inhabited by persons in every respect superior to the kings of the East; nor does he imagine every
other religion but his own to be log-worship. Probably the
people who really worship logs—whether in Persia or Pentonville—will be left to worship logs to their hearts' content,
thinks Giotto. But to those who worship *God*, and who
have obeyed the laws of heaven written in their hearts, and
numbered the stars of it visible to them,—to these, a nearer
star may rise; and a higher God be revealed.

You are to note, therefore, that Giotto's Soldan is the
type of all noblest religion and law, in countries where the
name of Christ has not been preached. There was no doubt
what king or people should be chosen: the country of the
three Magi had already been indicated by the miracle of
Bethlehem; and the religion and morality of Zoroaster were
the purest, and in spirit the oldest, in the heathen world.[10]

Arena Chapel frescoes

In consequence of the intermediate position which Giotto
occupies between the Byzantine and Naturalist schools,
two relations of treatment are to be generally noted in his
work. As compared with the Byzantines, he is a realist,
whose power consists in the introduction of living character and various incidents, modifying the formerly received
Byzantine symbols. So far as he has to do this, he is a
realist of the purest kind, endeavouring always to conceive
events precisely as they were likely to have happened; not
to idealize them into forms artfully impressive to the spectator. But in so far as he was compelled to retain, or did
not wish to reject, the figurative character of the Byzantine symbols, he stands opposed to succeeding realists, in
the quantity of meaning which probably lies hidden in any
composition, as well as in the simplicity with which he
will probably treat it, in order to enforce or guide to this

[10] MorFlor 348–54, omit.

meaning: the figures being often letters of a hieroglyphic, which he will not multiply, lest he should lose in force of suggestion what he gained in dramatic interest.

None of the compositions display more clearly this typical and reflective character than that of the Raising of Lazarus. Later designers dwell on vulgar conditions of wonder or horror, such as they could conceive likely to attend the resuscitation of a corpse; but with Giotto the physical reanimation is the type of a spiritual one, and, though shown to be miraculous, is yet in all its deeper aspects unperturbed, and calm in awfulness. It is also visibly gradual. "His face was bound about with a napkin."[11] The nearest Apostle has withdrawn the covering from the face, and looks for the command which shall restore it from wasted corruption, and sealed blindness, to living power and light.[12]

Of all the compositions in the Arena Chapel I think ["The Virgin Returns to her House"] the most characteristic of the noble time in which it was done. It is not so notable as exhibiting the mind of Giotto, which is perhaps more fully seen in subjects representing varied emotion, as in the simplicity and repose which were peculiar to the compositions of the early fourteenth century. In order to judge of it fairly, it ought first to be compared with any classical composition—with a portion, for instance, of the Elgin frieze—which would instantly make manifest in it a strange seriousness and dignity and slowness of motion, resulting chiefly from the excessive simplicity of all its terminal lines. Observe, for instance, the pure wave from the back of the Virgin's head to the ground; and again, the delicate swelling line along her shoulder and left arm, opposed to the nearly unbroken fall of the drapery of the figure in front. It should then be compared with an Egyptian or Ninevite series of figures, which, by contrast, would bring out its perfect sweetness and grace, as well as its variety of expression: finally, it should be compared with any composition subsequent to the time of Raffaelle, in or-

[11] (John xi: 44.) Padua 1854, 88 f
[12] Padua 1854, 89

der to feel its noble freedom from pictorial artifice and attitude. These three comparisons cannot be made carefully without a sense of profound reverence for the national spirit which could produce a design so majestic, and yet remain content with one so simple.[13]

[13] Padua 1853, 65 f

3

THE BURDEN OF
RENAISSANCE KNOWLEDGE

[W]hen in the thirteenth century, the Nativity was habitually represented by such a symbol [from a Book of Hours, c. 1300, of the Arras district, collection now unknown], there was not the smallest possibility that such a picture could disturb, in the mind of the reader of the New Testament, the simple meaning of the words "wrapped Him in swaddling clothes, and laid Him in a manger." That this manger was typified by a trefoil arch would no more prevent his distinct understanding of the narrative, than the grotesque heads introduced above it would interfere with his firm comprehension of the words "ox" or "ass"; while if there were anything in the action of the principal figures suggestive of real feeling, that suggestion he would accept, together with the general pleasantness of the lines and colours in the decorative letter; but without having his faith in the unrepresented and actual scene obscured for a moment. But it was far otherwise when Francia or Perugino, with exquisite power of representing the human form, and high knowledge of the mysteries of art, devoted all their skill to the delineation of an impossible scene; and painted, for their subjects of the Nativity, a beautiful and queenly lady, her dress embroidered with gold, and with a crown of jewels upon her hair, kneeling, on a floor of inlaid and precious marble, before a crowned child, laid under a portico of Lombardic[14] architecture; with a sweet, verdurous, and vivid landscape in the dis-

[14] (Ruskin note: "Lombardic, i.e. in the style of Pietro and Tullio Lombardo, in the fifteenth century, not *Lombard*.") MP III, 74 f

tance, full of winding rivers, village spires, and baronial towers. It is quite true that the frank absurdity of the thought prevented its being received as a deliberate contradiction of the truths of Scripture; but it is no less certain, that the continual presentment to the mind of this beautiful and fully realized imagery more and more chilled its power of apprehending the real truth; and that when pictures of this description met the eye in every corner of every chapel, it was physically impossible to dwell distinctly upon facts the direct reverse of those represented. The word "Virgin" or "Madonna," instead of calling up the vision of a simple Jewish girl, bearing the calamities of poverty, and the dishonours of inferior station, summoned instantly the idea of a graceful princess, crowned with gems, and surrounded by obsequious ministry of kings and saints. The fallacy which was presented to the imagination was indeed discredited, but also the fact which was *not* presented to the imagination was forgotten; all true grounds of faith were gradually undermined, and the beholder was either enticed into mere luxury of fanciful enjoyment, believing nothing; or left, in his confusion of mind, the prey of vain tales and traditions; while in his best feelings he was unconsciously subject to the power of the fallacious picture, and, with no sense of the real cause of his error, bowed himself, in prayer or adoration, to the lovely lady on her golden throne, when he would never have dreamed of doing so to the Jewish girl in her outcast poverty, or, in her simple household, to the carpenter's wife.

But a shadow of increasing darkness fell upon the human mind as art proceeded to still more perfect realization. These fantasies of the earlier painters, though they darkened faith, never hardened *feeling;* on the contrary, the frankness of their unlikelihood proceeded mainly from the endeavour on the part of the painter to express, not the actual fact, but the enthusiastic state of his own feelings about the fact; he covers the Virgin's dress with gold, not with any idea of representing the Virgin as she ever was, or ever will be seen, but with a burning desire to show what his love and reverence would think fittest for her.

He erects for the stable a Lombardic portico, not because
he supposes the Lombardi to have built stables in Pales-
tine in the days of Tiberius, but to show that the manger
in which Christ was laid is, in his eyes, nobler than the
greatest architecture in the world. He fills his landscape
with church spires and silver streams, not because he supposes that either were in sight at Bethlehem, but to remind the beholder of the peaceful course and succeeding
power of Christianity. And, regarded with due sympathy
and clear understanding of these thoughts of the artist,
such pictures remain most impressive and touching, even
to this day. I shall refer to them in future, in general terms,
as the pictures of the "Angelican Ideal"—Angelico being
the central master of the school.

The loss of feeling

It was far otherwise in the next step of the Realistic
progress. The greater his powers became, the more the
mind of the painter was absorbed in their attainment, and
complacent in their display. The early arts of laying on
bright colours smoothly, of burnishing golden ornaments,
or tracing, leaf by leaf, the outlines of flowers, were not so
difficult as that they should materially occupy the thoughts
of the artist, or furnish foundation for his conceit; he
learned these rudiments of his work without pain, and employed them without pride, his spirit being left free to
express, so far as it was capable of them, the reaches of
higher thought. But when accurate shade, and subtle colour, and perfect anatomy, and complicated perspective,
became necessary to the work, the artist's whole energy
was employed in learning the laws of these, and his whole
pleasure consisted in exhibiting them. His life was devoted,
not to the objects of art, but to the cunning of it; and the
sciences of composition and light and shade were pursued
as if there were abstract good in them;—as if, like astronomy or mathematics, they were ends in themselves, irrespective of anything to be effected by them. And without
perception, on the part of any one, of the abyss to which
all were hastening, a fatal change of aim took place

throughout the whole world of art. In early times *art was employed for the display of religious facts;* now, *religious facts were employed for the display of art.* The transition, though imperceptible, was consummate; it involved the entire destiny of painting. It was passing from the paths of life to the paths of death.

And this change was all the more fatal, because at first veiled by an appearance of greater dignity and sincerity than were possessed by the older art. One of the earliest results of the new knowledge was the putting away the greater part of the *unlikelihoods* and fineries of the ancient pictures, and an apparently closer following of nature and probability. All the fantasy which I have just been blaming as disturbant of the simplicity of faith, was first subdued, —then despised and cast aside. The appearances of nature were more closely followed in everything; and the crowned Queen-Virgin of Perugino sank into a simple Italian mother in Raphael's Madonna of the Chair.

Was not this, then, a healthy change? No. It *would* have been healthy if it had been effected with a pure motive, and the new truths would have been precious if they had been sought for truth's sake. But they were not sought for truth's sake, but for pride's; and truth which is sought for display may be just as harmful as truth which is spoken in malice. The glittering childishness of the old art was rejected, not because it was false, but because it was easy; and, still more, because the painter had no longer any religious passion to express. He could think of the Madonna now very calmly, with no desire to pour out the treasures of earth at her feet, or crown her brows with the golden shafts of heaven. He could think of her as an available subject for the display of transparent shadows, skilful tints, and scientific foreshortenings,—as a fair woman, forming, if well painted, a pleasant piece of furniture for the corner of a boudoir, and best imagined by combination of the beauties of the prettiest contadinas. He could think of her, in her last maternal agony, with academical discrimination; sketch in first her skeleton, invest her, in serene science, with the muscles of misery and the fibres of sorrow; then cast the grace of antique drapery over the nakedness

of her desolation, and fulfil, with studious lustre of tears
and delicately painted pallor, the perfect type of the "Mater
Dolorosa."

[In Raphael's cartoon of the Charge to Peter (Victoria
and Albert Museum), note] first, the bold fallacy—the
putting *all* the Apostles there, a mere lie to serve the Papal
heresy of the Petric supremacy, by putting them all in the
background while Peter receives the charge, and making
them all witnesses to it. Note the handsomely curled hair
and neatly tied sandals of the men who had been out all
night in the sea-mists and on the slimy decks. Note their
convenient dresses for going a-fishing, with trains that lie a
yard along the ground, and goodly fringes,—all made to
match, an apostolic fishing costume. Note how Peter especially (whose chief glory was in his wet coat *girt* about
him, and naked limbs) is enveloped in folds and fringes,
so as to kneel and hold his keys with grace. No fire of
coals at all, nor lonely mountain shore, but a pleasant
Italian landscape, full of villas and churches, and a flock
of sheep to be pointed at; and the whole group of Apostles, not round Christ, as they would have been naturally,
but straggling away in a line, that they may all be shown.

The simple truth is, that the moment we look at the
picture we feel our belief of the whole thing taken away.
There is, visibly, no possibility of that group ever having
existed, in any place, or on any occasion. It is all a mere
mythic absurdity, and faded concoction of fringes, muscular arms, and curly heads of Greek philosophers.

Now, the evil consequences of the acceptance of this
kind of religious idealism for true, were instant and manifold. So far as it was received and trusted in by thoughtful
persons, it only served to chill all the conceptions of
sacred history which they might otherwise have obtained.
Whatever they could have fancied for themselves about
the wild, strange, infinitely stern, infinitely tender, infinitely varied veracities of the life of Christ, was blotted
out by the vapid fineries of Raphael . . .

But although Calvin, and Knox, and Luther, and their
flocks, with all the hardest-headed and truest-hearted faithful left in Christendom, thus spurned away the spurious

art, and all art with it, (not without harm to themselves, such as a man must needs sustain in cutting off a decayed limb,) certain conditions of weaker Christianity suffered the false system to retain influence over them; and to this day, the clear and tasteless poison of the art of Raphael infects with sleep of infidelity the hearts of millions of Christians. It is the first cause of all that pre-eminent *dulness* which characterises what Protestants call sacred art; a dulness not merely baneful in making religion distasteful to the young, but in sickening, as we have seen, all vital belief of religion in the old. A dim sense of impossibility attaches itself always to the graceful emptiness of the representation; we feel instinctively that the painted Christ and painted apostle are not beings that ever did or could exist; and this fatal sense of fair fabulousness, and well-composed impossibility, steals gradually from the picture into the history, until we find ourselves reading St. Mark or St. Luke with the same admiring, but uninterested, incredulity, with which we contemplate Raphael.[15]

"Pride of science"

Knowledge is, at best, the pilgrim's burden or the soldier's panoply, often a weariness to them both; and the Renaissance knowledge is like the Renaissance armour of plate, binding and cramping the human form; while all good knowledge is like the crusader's chain mail, which throws itself into folds with the body, yet it is rarely so forged as that the clasps and rivets do not gall us. All men feel this, though they do not think of it, nor reason out its consequences. They look back to the days of childhood as of greatest happiness, because those were the days of greatest wonder, greatest simplicity, and most vigorous imagination. And the whole difference between a man of genius and other men, it has been said a thousand times, and most truly, is that the first remains in great part a child, seeing with the large eyes of children, in perpetual wonder, not conscious of much knowledge,—conscious, rather,

[15] MP III, 75–84, omit.

of infinite ignorance, and yet infinite power; a fountain of eternal admiration, delight, and creative force within him, meeting the ocean of visible and governable things around him.

The sciences ceased at once to be anything more than different kinds of grammars,—grammar of language, grammar of logic, grammar of ethics, grammar of art; and the tongue, wit, and invention of the human race were supposed to have found their utmost and most divine mission in syntax and syllogism, perspective and five orders.

Of such knowledge as this, nothing but pride could come; and, therefore, I have called the first mental characteristic of the Renaissance schools the "pride" of science. If they had reached any science worthy the name, they might have loved it; but of the paltry knowledge they possessed they could only be proud. There was not anything in it capable of being loved. Anatomy, indeed, then first made a subject of accurate study, is a true science, but not so attractive as to enlist the affections strongly on its side; and therefore, like its meaner sisters, it became merely a ground of pride; and the one main purpose of the Renaissance artists, in all their work, was to show how much they knew.

There were, of course, noble exceptions; but chiefly belonging to the earliest periods of the Renaissance, when its teaching had not yet produced its full effect. Raphael, Leonardo, and Michael Angelo were all trained in the old school; they all had masters who knew the true ends of art, and had reached them; masters nearly as great as they were themselves, but imbued with the old religious and earnest spirit, which their disciples receiving from them, and drinking at the same time deeply from all the fountains of knowledge opened in their day, became the world's wonders. Then the dull wondering world believed that their greatness rose out of their new knowledge, instead of out of that ancient religious root, in which to abide was life, from which to be severed was annihilation. And from that day to this, they have tried to produce Michael Angelos and Leonardos by teaching the barren sciences, and still have mourned and marvelled that no more Michael Angelos came; not perceiving that those great Fathers were only able to receive such nourishment because they were rooted on the rock of all ages, and that our scientific teaching, nowadays, is nothing more nor less than the assiduous watering of trees whose stems are cut through. Nay, I have even granted too much in saying that those great men were able to receive pure nourishment from the sciences; for my own conviction is, and I know it to be shared by most of those who love Raphael truly,—that he painted best when he knew least. Michael Angelo was betrayed, again and again, into such vain and offensive exhibition of his anatomical knowledge as, to this day, renders his higher powers indiscernible by the greater part of men; and Leonardo fretted his life away in engineering, so that there is hardly a picture left to bear his name. But, with respect to all who followed, there can be no question that the science they possessed was utterly harmful; serving merely to draw away the hearts at once from the purposes of art and the power of nature, and to make, out of the canvas and marble, nothing more than materials for the exhibition of petty dexterity and useless knowledge.[16]

[16] SV III, 66–71, omit.

4

ANGELICO

In the sacristy of Sta. Maria Novella [now in San Marco]
is what I think on the whole his most *perfect* work, the
small Annunciation of which I have a study. I have above
noticed the exquisite jewellery of Angelico; it is here carried farther than in any other of his works, the gold deeper,
and the ornaments more detailed and delicate. The glories
are formed of rays indented in the gold deeper and deeper
as they approach the head, so that there is always a vivid
light on some portion of them, playing in the most miraculous way round the head as the spectator moves, and always brightest close to the head and graduated away so
that the effect is absolutely real, and a positive light of the
brightest brilliancy is obtained which throws the purest
pale flesh colour out in dark relief—an advantage possessed
by no other painter. The glories of the angels in the large
Uffizii picture are executed with rays in the same way, but
have also an outer circle of stars. The style of ornament
adopted by Angelico in the dress is also very instructive.
Had he made it perfectly regular and of complicated design, he would have given the dresses the appearance of
having been embroidered, and the weight of the embroidery would have pulled his angels to earth in an instant.
But he has used only rays or dashes of light in clusters,
not joined at the roots (Note this in speaking of functional
unity), and curved lines with dots at the end not particularly graceful, but varied and irregular looking like no
earthly ornament, but simple and childish and therefore
heavenly. The Madonna's dress is blue; the angel's, lilac-
purple. No other work of the painter can be set beside

this for action and expression. The Virgin's face is absolutely luminous with love.[17]

[In the Uffizi there is] a picture very sad and dingy at
first glance, and in great part rubbed quite out. It is nevertheless the most precious Angelico in Florence, and, as far
as I know, in the world. It represents Our Lady enthroned,
with the infant Christ. St. Cosmo and Damian kneel before
the throne. On the Madonna's left hand, St. Dominic, St.
Francis, and St. Peter Martyr; on her right, St. Mark, St.
John the Evangelist, and St. Lawrence—in the guidebook
called St. Stephen, though his name is written on the
nimbus.

The picture has been wrought by Angelico with the most
extreme care I have ever seen him give. He has intended
it to be his masterpiece. And Angelico differs from nearly
all other great painters in this, that he can't be too careful.
The more he endeavours the more he achieves. All his
work prospers in his hands.

St. Lawrence is dressed in the following manner. He
has a rose-coloured tunic studded with golden stars, each
star centred by a turquoise. On his breast is a large square
scroll of gold, with an arabesque of pearls upon it, and his
sleeves are embroidered with silver.

Now I said in the second volume of *Modern Painters*
that Angelico did not paint real jewels but only abstract
ornaments. I was utterly wrong. It is true that in his ordinary work he does a great deal with mere engraving in the
gold in lines and dots, and with spots of colour. But here
we have him doing his best; and every turquoise and pearl
is painted to a point beyond everything else in art. Chinese,
Indian, American, old Spanish, Venetian, German, what
you will,—no gold and pearls were ever designed or done
in the world like these. Van Eyck, Memling, Mantegna,
even Botticelli, are nowhere in comparison.

Now what is the meaning of this? It is the old Etruscan
faculty—Fésole faculty—of jewellery, with Christian passion
in it. Every pearl is painted as if he had sold all that he

[17] From Ruskin's notebook of 1845, inserted by editors, MP
II, 263 f

had to buy it; but what do you think the result will be on St. Lawrence? A very fine St. Lawrence you think perhaps he will be, and nothing else. Yes; in the hands of any other painter that would have been so. In his pearly affluence St. Lawrence would only have reminded you [in the *Arabian Nights*] of the principal dish at the Princess Parizade's dinner—cucumbers stuffed with pearls. With Angelico it is the exact reverse. By the entirely passionate and perfect painting of them the jewels become divine; they become worthy of the saint in their own supreme perfectness; their beauty is so great that it becomes beauty of holiness; and instead of feeling as if they disguised St. Lawrence, you feel as if he could have been dressed no otherwise, nay, had I not told you to look at his breastplate of pearl, you never would have looked at it. Quercia withdraws all ornament from the statue of Ilaria that you may see her face; but Angelico pours out every earthly treasure around his St. Lawrence, and forces you to look only at the face still—the highest visible expression of religious life yet, as far as I know, achieved by man.[18]

[18] SchFlor 261–63

5

BOTTICELLI

Of Delineators, the chief is Botticelli. Taught by a gold-smith, he learnt by goldbeating and engraving, and is him-self a master goldsmith and engraver. Ghirlandajo is a gold-smith selling plated goods; Botticelli's is pure gold tried in the fire, and engraved as Bezaleel and Aholiab engraved.[19] There is no drawing like Botticelli's; but under it is colour and chiaroscuro as subtle as Angelico's and Tintoret's, but subordinate. He draws first with the point of the brush; but, like all masters who begin with the point, he soon gets a wonderful power with the side of it, and we find leaves drawn by Botticelli with a single stroke,—the point of the brush beginning, and the brush opening out as it goes. Angelico entered a convent at twenty, painting and living only for the poor, and called "Beatus." Botticelli lived amidst the concourse of Florence, admiring all earthly beauty, himself untainted by it. He is in one the most learned theologian, the most perfect artist, and the most kind gentleman whom Florence produced. He knows all that Dante knew of theology, and much more; and he is the only unerring, unfearing, and to this day trustworthy and true preacher of the reformed doctrine of the Church of Christ. As an artist he is incomparable. He has the power of Tintoret, with the virtue of Angelico; and he is such a gentleman that he interprets all things with charity in days of grievous guilt, spends himself and all he has in the pas-sionate service of men and of God, and dies in Florence, having given not half but all his goods to the poor—engrav-ing the triumph of the faith of Savonarola.[20]

[19] (Revelation iii: 18.) SchFlor 265 f
[20] SchFlor 266

"Pure mental passion"

The St. Michael of Botticelli [in the Uffizi's "St. Barnabas Altarpiece"] is a simple knight of Florence, standing before the Madonna, and there is no dragon beneath him, and no look of victory in his face. St. Catherine stands opposite him, and in the sweet coronal of holy creatures, you cannot think of her pain any more than of St. Michael's war; you know her by her look, not by her jagged wheel. Her veil falls over it, and St. Michael seems entirely without trophy. Only at last you see that he holds a globe in his hand, the globe of the world, and on its surface the dark seas take the cloudy shape of the dragon. He is the St. Michael of Peace, who stilleth the noise of the crowd and the tumult of the people, who maketh wars to cease in all the world.

The picture in which you will find this St. Michael is one of two in the Academy of Florence, by the greatest of all her masters at his greatest time, and alike in pure manual skill and pure mental passion, they are beyond all other work in Italy. Of manual skill especially nothing unites so much as a crowning of the Madonna [Uffizi] the favourite Florentine subject. She is surrounded by a choir of twelve angels, not dancing, nor flying, but carried literally in a whorl, or vortex, whirlwind of the breath of heaven; their wings lie level, interwoven among the clouds, pale sky of intense light, yet darker than the white clouds they pass through, their arms stretched to each other, their hands clasped—it is as if the morning sky had all been changed into marble, and they into living creatures; they are led in their swift wheel by Gabriel, who is opposite to you, between the Christ and the Madonna; a close rain of golden rays falls from the hand of Christ, He placing the crown on the Virgin's head; and Gabriel is seen through it as a white bird through rain, looking up, seeing the fulfilment of his message. And as I told you that all the delight of Angelico in material things became sacred in its intensity, so the material workmanship of this greater master be-

comes sacred in its completion. Of this falling golden rain
he has burnished every separate ray into enduring perfectness; it is not gilding, but beaten gold, wrought with
the inherited Etruscan skill of a thousand years, and able
to stand for a thousand years to come.

Now observe what he had to do in this way. The main
figures are the size of life. The surrounding choir of angels
—about one-third the size of life—and the Gabriel is diminished by perspective on the farther side, so that his face
is only about two inches wide. Well, across his face, between you and him, fall eight or ten straight bars of this
golden rain like the base of a helmet visor. Right down
across the face, every edge of them as fine and true as a
line of gossamer, but you think the face will be spoiled. It
is as perfect as if no line crossed it; you see it as through a
veil, tender, infinite in rejoicing, lifted in a light of the
spirit brighter than gold.

I never saw such a thing. Fancy what command of his
materials, what unstinted care and time, what knowledge
of all possibilities of change are involved in doing such a
piece of work to stand for four hundred years without one
sparkle failing.[21]

Judith

[In the Uffizi's "Judith and Holofernes," Judith] is returning to the camp of her Israel, followed by her maid
carrying the head of Holofernes. And she walks in one of
Botticelli's light dancing actions, her drapery all on flutter,
and her hand, like Fortitude's, light on the sword-hilt, but
daintily—not nervously, the little finger laid over the cross
of it.

And at the first glance—you will think the figure merely
a piece of fifteenth-century affectation. "Judith, indeed!
—say rather the daughter of Herodias, at her mincingest."

Well, yes—Botticelli *is* affected, in the way that all men
in that century necessarily were. Much euphuism, much
studied grace of manner, much formal assertion of scholar-

[21] SchFlor 273 f

ship, mingling with his force of imagination. And he likes twisting the fingers of hands about, just as Correggio does. But he never does it like Correggio, without cause.

Look at Judith again,—at her face, not her drapery,— and remember that when a man is base at the heart, he blights his virtues into weaknesses; but when he is true at the heart, he sanctifies his weaknesses into virtues. It is a weakness of Botticelli's, this love of dancing motion and waved drapery; but why has he given it full flight here?

Now, as in many other cases of noble history, apocryphal and other, I do not in the least care how far the literal facts are true. The conception of facts, and the idea of Jewish womanhood, are there, grand and real as a marble statue,—possession for all ages. And you will feel, after you have read this piece of history, or epic poetry, with honourable care, that there is somewhat more to be thought of and pictured in Judith, than painters have mostly found it in them to show you: that she is not merely the Jewish Delilah to the Assyrian Samson; but the mightiest, purest, brightest type of high passion in severe womanhood offered to our human memory. Sandro's picture is but slight; but it is true to her, and the only one I know that is; and after writing out these verses [from the Book of Judith], you will see why he gives her that swift, peaceful motion, while you read in her face only sweet solemnity of dreaming thought. "My people delivered, and by my hand; and God has been gracious to His handmaid!" The triumph of Miriam over a fallen host, the fire of exulting mortal life in an immortal hour, the purity and severity of a guardian angel —all are here . . .[22]

Zipporah, "the Etruscan Athena"

To Botticelli, Moses [in the fresco, "The Life of Moses" in the Sistine Chapel] is the Christian knight, as much as the Christian lawgiver. The Florentine Christian is, however, a Greek; and to him quite one of the first conditions of his [Moses'] perfectness was in the being bred by the

[22] MorFlor 335-37, omit.

272 PAINTING

Princess of Egypt, learned in all wisdom, even of the world he had to leave. His Zipporah is simply the Etruscan Athena, becoming queen of a household in Christian humility. Her spear is changed to a reed and becomes then her sceptre, cloven at the top into the outline of Florentine Fleur-de-lys, and in the cleft she fastens her spindle. Her χιτών falls short of the feet, that it may not check her motion, and is lightly embroidered; above, the πέπλος unites with its own character that of the ægis. Where Athena's had the wars of the giants, it is embroidered with mystic letters, golden on blue, but it becomes the αἰγὶς θυσσανόεσσα[23] at its edge, where what are only light tassels in the πέπλος become this waving fringe, typical of sacrificial fire, for you know she is a priest's daughter; but when the peplus falls in Greek statues into its κόλπος, sinus, gulph, or lap, the ægis is here replaced by a goat-skin satchel, in which the maiden holds lightly with her left hand apples, here taking the character of the Etruscan Pomona, and oak for the strength of life. Her hair is precisely that of the Phidian Athena, only unhelmed, and with three leaves of myrtle in its wreaths.[24]

Botticelli, trained in the great Etruscan Classic School, retains in his ideal of the future wife of Moses every essential character of the Etrurian Pallas, regarding her as the Heavenly Wisdom given by inspiration to the Lawgiver for his helpmate; yet changing the attributes of the goddess into such as become a shepherd maiden. To show the perfect correspondence with still earlier tradition, I have sent also [to the exhibition] my woodcut of the Attic Pallas, of the Phidian period, in which every piece of the dress will be found to have its corresponding piece in that of Zipporah.

There is first the sleeved chiton or linen robe, falling to the feet, looped up a little by the shepherdess; then the peplus or covering mantle, very nearly our shawl, but fitting closer; Athena's, crocus coloured, embroidered by herself with the battle against the giants; Zipporah's, also

[23] (*Iliad*, xv, 229, meaning "tasseled.") SchFlor 275 f
[24] SchFlor 276

crocus coloured, almost dark golden, embroidered with
blue and purple, with mystic golden letters on the blue
ground; the fringes of the ægis are, however, transposed
to the peplus; and these being of warm crimson complete
the sacred chord of colour (blue, purple, and scarlet),
Zipporah being a priest's daughter.

The ægis of Pallas becomes for Zipporah a goatskin
satchel, in which she carries apples and oak (for pleasure
and strength); her lance becomes a reed, in which she
carries her wool and spindle; the tresses of her hair are
merely softened from the long black falling tresses of
Athena; a leaf of myrtle replaces the olive. The scarcely
traceable thin muslin veil over her breast represents the
part of the ægis which, in the Pallas, is drawn with dots,
meaning soft dew instead of storm.

The black outlines are very carefully traced, being used
by Botticelli to give distinctness to the painting, which is
about eighteen feet from the ground, and in shade.[25]

[25] "A Note on Botticelli's 'Zipporah,' " catalogue entry for an
exhibition in Brighton of paintings and copies lent by Ruskin
and the Arundel Society, 1876, in *Works*, vol. XXIII, 478 f.

6

MICHELANGELO AND TINTORETTO

(I have printed this Lecture separately, that strangers
visiting the [Oxford] Galleries may be able to use it for
reference to the drawings. But they must observe that its
business is only to point out what is to be blamed in Michael Angelo, and that it assumes the facts of his power
to be generally known.)[26]

In preceding lectures on sculpture I have included references to the art of painting, so far as it proposes to itself
the same object as sculpture (idealization of form); and
I have chosen for the subject of [this] inquiry, the works
of the two masters who accomplished or implied the unity
of these arts. Tintoret entirely conceives his figures as solid
statues: sees them in his mind on every side; detaches each
from the other by imagined air and light; and foreshortens,
interposes, or involves them as if they were pieces of clay
in his hand. On the contrary, Michael Angelo conceives his
sculpture partly as if it were painted; and using (as I told
you formerly) his pen like a chisel, uses also his chisel like
a pencil; is sometimes as picturesque as Rembrandt, and
sometimes as soft as Correggio.

The cycle of art history

The course of Art divides itself hitherto, among all nations of the world that have practised it successfully, into
three great periods.

[26] This section is an abridgment of "The Relation between
Michael Angelo and Tintoret," probably Ruskin's most contro-
versial lecture (June 1871), kept together here since it expresses
so many of Ruskin's views of the Renaissance. All excerpts have
been kept in their original order, MTint 76–104.

The first, that in which their conscience is undeveloped, and their condition of life in many respects savage; but, nevertheless, in harmony with whatever conscience they possess. The most powerful tribes, in this stage of their intellect, usually live by rapine, and under the influence of vivid, but contracted, religious imagination. The early predatory activity of the Normans, and the confused minglings of religious subjects with scenes of hunting, war, and vile grotesque, in their first art, will sufficiently exemplify this state of a people; having, observe, their conscience undeveloped, but keeping their conduct in satisfied harmony with it.

The second stage is that of the formation of conscience by the discovery of the true laws of social order and personal virtue, coupled with sincere effort to live by such laws as they have discovered.

All the Arts advance steadily during this stage of national growth, and are lovely, even in their deficiencies, as the buds of flowers are lovely by their vital force, swift change, and continent beauty.

The third stage is that in which the conscience is entirely formed, and the nation, finding it painful to live in obedience to the precepts it has discovered, looks about to discover, also, a compromise for obedience to them. In this condition of mind its first endeavour is nearly always to make its religion pompous, and please the gods by giving them gifts and entertainments, in which it may piously and pleasurably share itself; so that a magnificent display of the powers of art it has gained by sincerity, takes place for a few years, and is then followed by their extinction, rapid and complete exactly in the degree in which the nation resigns itself to hypocrisy.

The works of Raphael, Michael Angelo, and Tintoret belong to this period of compromise in the career of the greatest nation of the world; and are the most splendid efforts yet made by human creatures to maintain the dignity of states with beautiful colours, and defend the doctrines of theology with anatomical designs.

Farther, and as an universal principle, we have to remember that the Arts express not only the moral temper,

but the scholarship, of their age; and we have thus to study
them under the influence, at the same moment of, it may
be, declining probity, and advancing science.

Now in this the Arts of Northern and Southern Europe
stand exactly opposed. The Northern temper never accepts
the Catholic faith with force such as it reached in Italy.
Our sincerest thirteenth-century sculpture is cold and formal compared with that of the Pisani; nor can any Northern poet be set for an instant beside Dante, as an exponent
of Catholic faith: on the contrary, the Northern temper
accepts the scholarship of the Reformation with absolute
sincerity, while the Italians seek refuge from it in the partly
scientific and completely lascivious enthusiasms of literature and painting, renewed under classical influence. We
therefore, in the north, produce our Shakespeare and Holbein; they their Petrarch and Raphael. And it is nearly
impossible for you to study Shakespeare or Holbein too
much, or Petrarch and Raphael too little.

Do not . . . think that I speak with any purpose of defending one system of theology against another; least of all,
reformed against Catholic theology. There probably never
was a system of religion so destructive to the loveliest arts
and the loveliest virtues of men, as the modern Protestant-
ism, which consists in an assured belief in the Divine forgiveness of all your sins, and the Divine correctness of all
your opinions. But in the first searching and sincere activi-
ties, the doctrines of the Reformation produced the most
instructive art, and the grandest literature, yet given to the
world; while Italy, in her interested resistance to those doctrines, polluted and exhausted the arts she already possessed. Her iridescence of dying statesmanship—her magnificence of hollow piety,—were represented in the arts of
Venice and Florence by two mighty men on either side—
Titian and Tintoret,—Michael Angelo and Raphael. Of the
calm and brave statesmanship, the modest and faithful religion, which had been her strength, I am content to name
one chief representative artist at Venice,—John Bellini.

Bellini and the High Renaissance

Let me now map out for you roughly the chronological relations of these five men.

In . . . forty years all the new effort and deadly catastrophe took place. 1480 to 1520. Now, you have only to fasten to those forty years, the life of Bellini, who represents the best art before them, and of Tintoret, who represents the best art after them. John Bellini precedes the change, meets, and resists it victoriously to his death. Nothing of flaw or failure is ever to be discerned in him. Then Raphael, Michael Angelo, and Titian, together, bring about the deadly change, playing into each other's hands—Michael Angelo being the chief captain in evil; Titian, in natural force.

The art of Bellini is centrally represented by two pictures at Venice: one, the Madonna in the Sacristy of the Frari, with two saints beside her, and two angels at her feet; the second, the Madonna with four Saints, over the second altar of San Zaccaria.

In the first of these, the figures are under life size, and it represents the most perfect kind of picture for rooms; in which, since it is intended to be seen close to the spectator, every right kind of finish possible to the hand may be wisely lavished; yet which is not a miniature, nor in any wise petty, or ignoble.

In the second, the figures are of life size, or a little more, and it represents the class of great pictures in which the boldest execution is used, but all brought to entire completion. These two, having every quality in balance, are as far as my present knowledge extends, and as far as I can trust my judgment, the two best pictures in the world.

It is not possible, of course, always literally to observe the . . . condition, that there shall be quiet action or none; but Bellini's treatment of violence in action you may see exemplified in a notable way in his St. Peter Martyr [National Gallery, London]. The soldier is indeed striking the sword down into his breast; but in the face of the Saint is only resignation, and faintness of death, not pain—that of the executioner is impassive; and, while a painter of the later schools would have covered breast and sword with blood, Bellini allows no stain of it; but pleases himself by the most elaborate and exquisite painting of a soft crimson feather in the executioner's helmet.

The role of Michelangelo

Now the changes brought about by Michael Angelo—and permitted, or persisted in calamitously, by Tintoret—are in the four points these:

1st. Bad workmanship.

The greater part of all that these two men did is hastily and incompletely done; and all that they did on a large scale in colour is in the best qualities of it perished.

2nd. Violence of transitional action.

The figures flying,—falling,—striking,—or biting. Scenes of Judgment,—battle,—martyrdom,—massacre; anything that is in the acme of instantaneous interest and violent gesture. They cannot any more trust their public to care for anything but that.

3rd. Physical instead of mental interest. The body, and its anatomy, made the entire subject of interest: the face, shadowed, as in the Duke [Julian], unfinished, as in the Twilight, or entirely foreshortened, backshortened, and despised, among labyrinths of limbs, and mountains of sides and shoulders.

4th. Evil chosen rather than good. On the face itself, instead of joy or virtue, at the best, sadness, probably pride, often sensuality, and always, by preference, vice or agony as the subject of thought. In the Last Judgment of Michael Angelo, and the Last Judgment of Tintoret, it is the wrath of the Dies Iræ, not its justice, in which they delight; and their only passionate thought of the coming of Christ in the clouds, is that all kindreds of the earth shall wail because of Him.

Those are the four great changes wrought by Michael Angelo. I repeat them:

Ill work for good.

Tumult for Peace.

The Flesh of Man for his Spirit.

And the Curse of God for His blessing.

Hitherto, I have massed, necessarily, but most unjustly, Michael Angelo and Tintoret together, because of their common relation to the art of others. I shall now proceed to distinguish the qualities of their own. And first as to the general temper of the two men.

Nearly every existing work by Michael Angelo is an attempt to execute something beyond his power, coupled with a fevered desire that his power may be acknowledged. He is always matching himself either against the Greeks whom he cannot rival, or against rivals whom he cannot forget. He is proud, yet not proud enough to be at peace; melancholy, yet not deeply enough to be raised above petty pain; and strong beyond all his companion workmen, yet never strong enough to command his temper, or limit his aims.

Tintoret, on the contrary, works in the consciousness of supreme strength, which cannot be wounded by neglect, and is only to be thwarted by time and space. He knows precisely all that art can accomplish under given conditions; determines absolutely how much of what can be done he will himself for the moment choose to do; and fulfils his purpose with as much ease as if, through his human body, were working the great forces of nature. Not that he is ever satisfied with what he has done, as vulgar and feeble artists are satisfied. He falls short of his ideal, more than any other man; but not more than is necessary; and is content to fall short of it to that degree, as he is content that his figures, however well painted, do not move nor speak. He is also entirely unconcerned respecting the satisfaction of the public. He neither cares to display his strength to them, nor convey his ideas to them; when he finishes his work, it is because he is in the humour to do so; and the sketch which a meaner painter would have left incomplete to show how cleverly it was begun, Tintoret simply leaves because he has done as much of it as he likes.

Both Raphael and Michael Angelo are thus, in the most vital of all points, separate from the great Venetian. They are always in dramatic attitudes, and always appealing to the public for praise. They are the leading athletes in the gymnasium of the arts, and the crowd of the circus cannot take its eyes away from them; while the Venetian walks or rests with the simplicity of a wild animal; is scarcely noticed in his occasionally swifter motion; when he springs, it is to please himself; and so calmly, that no one thinks of estimating the distance covered.

The heritage of Greece

I pass to . . . the priority of flesh to spirit, and of the body to the face.

In this alone, of the four innovations, Michael Angelo and Tintoret have the Greeks with them;—in this, alone, have they any right to be called classical. The Greeks gave them no excuse for bad workmanship; none for temporary passion; none for the preference of pain. Only in the honour done to the body may be alleged for them the authority of the ancients.

You remember, I hope, how often in my preceding lectures I had to insist on the fact that Greek sculpture was essentially ἀπρόσωπος;—independent, not only of the expression, but even of the beauty of the face. Nay, independent of its being so much as seen. The greater number of the finest pieces of it which remain for us to judge by, have had the heads broken away;—we do not seriously miss them either from the Three Fates, the Ilissus, or the Torso of the Vatican. The face of the Theseus is so far destroyed by time that you can form little conception of its former aspect. But it is otherwise in Christian sculpture. Strike the head off even the rudest statue in the porch of Chartres and you will greatly miss it—the harm would be still worse to Donatello's St. George:—and if you take the heads from a statue of Mino, or a painting of Angelico— very little but drapery will be left;—drapery made redundant in quantity and rigid in fold, that it may conceal the forms, and give a proud or ascetic reserve to the actions, of the bodily frame. Bellini and his school, indeed, rejected at once the false theory, and the easy mannerism, of such religious design; and painted the body without fear or reserve, as, in its subordination, honourable and lovely. But the inner heart and fire of it are by them always first thought of, and no action is given to it merely to show its beauty. Whereas the great culminating masters, and chiefly of these, Tintoret, Correggio, and Michael Angelo, delight in the body for its own sake, and cast it into every conceivable attitude, often in violation of all natural probability, that they may exhibit the action of its skeleton, and the contours of its flesh. The movement of a hand with Cima or Bellini expresses mental emotion only; but the clustering and twining of the fingers of Correggio's St. Catherine [Parma Gallery] is enjoyed by the painter just in the same way as he would enjoy the twining of the branches of a graceful plant, and he compels them into intricacies which have little or no relation to St. Catherine's mind. In the two drawings of Correggio it is the rounding of limbs and softness of foot resting on cloud which are principally thought of in the form of the Madonna; and the countenance of St. John is foreshortened into a section, that full prominence may be given to the muscles of his arms and breast.

So in Tintoret's drawing of the Graces [Palazzo Ducale], he has entirely neglected the individual character of the Goddesses, and been content to indicate it merely by attributes of dice or flower, so only that he may sufficiently display varieties of contour in thigh and shoulder.

Again. The Greeks, Correggio, and Tintoret, learn the body from the living body, and delight in its breath, colour, and motion.

Raphael and Michael Angelo learned it essentially from the corpse, and had no delight in it whatever, but great pride in showing that they knew all its mechanism; they therefore sacrifice its colours, and insist on its muscles, and surrender the breath and fire of it, for what is—not merely carnal,—but osseous, knowing that for one person who can recognize the loveliness of a look, or the purity of a colour, there are a hundred who can calculate the length of a bone.

"Love of sensation"

In the . . . last place, as Tintoret does not sacrifice, except as he is forced by the exigences of display, the face
for the body, so also he does not sacrifice happiness for
pain. The chief reason why we all know the "Last Judgment" of Michael Angelo, and not the "Paradise" of Tintoret, is the same love of sensation which makes us read
the *Inferno* of Dante, and not his *Paradise;* and the choice,
believe me, is our fault, not his; some farther evil influence is due to the fact that Michael Angelo has invested
all his figures with picturesque and palpable elements of
effect, while Tintoret has only made them lovely in themselves and has been content that they should deserve, not
demand, your attention.

You are accustomed to think the figures of Michael Angelo sublime—because they are dark, and colossal, and involved, and mysterious—because, in a word, they look
sometimes like shadows, and sometimes like mountains, and
sometimes like spectres, but never like human beings. Believe me, yet once more, in what I told you long since—
man can invent nothing nobler than humanity.

Now, though in nearly all his greater pictures, Tintoret
is entirely carried away by his sympathy with Michael
Angelo, and conquers him in his own field;—outflies him
in motion, outnumbers him in multitude, outwits him in
fancy, and outflames him in rage,—he can be just as gentle
as he is strong: and that Paradise, though it is the largest
picture in the world, without any question, is also the
thoughtfullest, and most precious.

The Thoughtfullest!—it would be saying but little, as far
as Michael Angelo is concerned. For consider of it yourselves. You have heard, from your youth up (and all educated persons have heard for three centuries), of this Last
Judgment of his, as the most sublime picture in existence.

In every vain and proud designer who has since lived,
that dark carnality of Michael Angelo's has fostered inso-
lent science, and fleshly imagination. Daubers and block-
heads think themselves painters, and are received by the

public as such, if they know how to foreshorten bones and decipher entrails; and men with capacity of art either shrink away (the best of them always do) into petty felicities and innocencies of genre painting—landscapes, cattle, family breakfasts, village schoolings, and the like; or else, if they have the full sensuous art-faculty that would have made true painters of them, being taught, from their youth up, to look for and learn the body instead of the spirit, have learned it, and taught it to such purpose, that at this hour, when I speak to you, the rooms of the Royal Academy of England, receiving also what of best can be sent there by the masters of France, contain *not one* picture honourable to the arts of their age; and contain many which are shameful in their record of its manners.[27]

[27] MTint 76–104, omit. (entire section 6 here)

7

VENETIAN PAINTING

The Venetians began, I repeat, with asceticism; always, however, delighting in more massive and deep colour than other religious painters. They are especially fond of saints who have been cardinals, because of their red hats, and they sunburn all their hermits into splendid russet brown.

They differed from the Pisans in having no Maremma between them and the sea; from the Romans in continually quarrelling with the Pope; and from the Florentines in having no gardens.

They had another kind of garden, deep furrowed, with blossom in white wreaths—fruitless. Perpetual May therein, and singing of wild, nestless birds. And they had no Maremma to separate them from this garden of theirs. The destiny of Pisa was changed, in all probability, by the ten miles of marsh-land and poisonous air between it and the beach. The Genoese energy was feverish; too much heat reflected from their torrid Apennine. But the Venetian had his free horizon, his salt breeze, and sandy Lido-shore; sloped far and flat,—ridged sometimes under the Tramontane winds with half a mile's breadth of rollers;—sea and sand shrivelled up together in one yellow careering field of fall and roar.

They were, also, we said, always quarrelling with the Pope. Their religious liberty came, like their bodily health, from that wave training; for it is one notable effect of a life passed on ship-board to destroy weak beliefs in appointed forms of religion. A sailor may be grossly superstitious, but his superstitions will be connected with amulets and omens, not cast in systems. He must accustom himself, if he prays at all, to pray anywhere and anyhow.

Candlesticks and incense not being portable into the main-top, he perceives those decorations to be, on the whole, inessential to a maintop mass. Sails must be set and cables bent, be it never so strict a saint's day, and it is found that no harm comes of it. Absolution on a lee-shore must be had of the breakers, it appears, if at all, and they give it plenary and brief, without listening to confession.

Whereupon our religious opinions become vague, but our religious confidences strong; and the end of it all is that we perceive the Pope to be on the other side of the Apennines, and able, indeed, to sell indulgences, but not winds, for any money. Whereas, God and the sea are with us, and we must even trust them both, and take what they shall send.

The vigilance of seamen

Then, farther. This ocean-work is wholly adverse to any morbid conditions of sentiment. Reverie, above all things, is forbidden by Scylla and Charybdis. By the dogs and the depths, no dreaming! The first thing required of us is presence of mind. Neither love, nor poetry, nor piety, must ever so take up our thoughts as to make us slow or unready. In sweet Val d'Arno it is permissible enough to dream among the orange blossoms, and forget the day in twilight of ilex. But along the avenues of the Adrian waves there can be no careless walking. Vigilance, night and day, required of us, besides learning of many practical lessons in severe and humble dexterities. It is enough for the Florentine to know how to use his sword and to ride. We Venetians, also, must be able to use our swords, and on ground which is none of the steadiest; but, besides, we must be able to do nearly everything that hands can turn to—rudders, and yards, and cables, all needing workmanly handling and workmanly knowledge, from captain as well as from men. To drive a nail, lash a spar, reef a sail—rude work this for noble hands; but to be done sometimes, and done well on pain of death. All which not only takes mean pride out of us, and puts nobler pride of power in its stead;

but it tends partly to soothe, partly to chasten, partly to employ and direct, the hot Italian temper, and make us every way greater, calmer, and happier.

Moreover, it tends to induce in us great respect for the whole human body; for its limbs, as much as for its tongue or its wit. Policy and eloquence are well; and, indeed, we Venetians can be politic enough, and can speak melodiously when we choose; but to put the helm up at the right moment is the beginning of all cunning—and for that we need arm and eye;—not tongue. And with this respect for the body as such, comes also the sailor's preference of massive beauty in bodily form. The landsmen, among their roses and orange-blossoms, and chequered shadows of twisted vine, may well please themselves with pale faces, and finely drawn eyebrows, and fantastic braiding of hair. But from the sweeping glory of the sea we learn to love another kind of beauty; broad-breasted, level-browed, like the horizon; —thighed and shouldered like the billows; footed like their stealing foam;—bathed in cloud of golden hair like their sunsets.

The Venetian possessed, and cared for, neither fields nor pastures. Being delivered, to his loss, from all the wholesome labours of tillage, he was also shut out from the sweet wonders and charities of the earth, and from the pleasant natural history of the year. As in the classical landscape, nearly all rural labour is banished from the Titianesque: there is one bold etching of a landscape, with grand ploughing in the foreground, but this is only a caprice; the customary Venetian background is without sign of laborious rural life. We find, indeed, often a shepherd with his flock, sometimes a woman spinning, but no division of fields, no growing crops, nor nestling villages. In the numerous drawings and woodcuts variously connected with or representative of Venetian work, a watermill is a frequent object, a river constant, generally the sea. But the prevailing idea in all the great pictures I have seen is that of mountainous land with wild but graceful forest, and rolling or horizontal clouds. The mountains are dark blue; the clouds glowing or soft gray, always massive; the light, deep, clear, melancholy; the foliage, neither intricate nor graceful, but compact and sweeping (with undulated trunks), dividing much into horizontal flakes, like the clouds; the ground rocky and broken somewhat monotonously, but richly green with wild herbage; here and there a flower, by preference white or blue, rarely yellow, still more rarely red.

It was stated that this heroic landscape of theirs was peopled by spiritual beings of the highest order. And in this rested the dominion of the Venetians over all later schools. They were the *last believing* school of Italy. Although, as I said above, always quarrelling with the Pope, there is all the more evidence of an earnest faith in their religion. People who trusted the Madonna less, flattered the Pope more. But down to Tintoret's time, the Roman Catholic religion was still real and sincere at Venice; and though faith in it was compatible with much which to us appears criminal or absurd, the religion itself was entirely sincere.

Throughout the rest of Italy, piety had become abstract, and opposed theoretically to worldly life; hence the Florentine and Umbrian painters generally separated their saints from living men. They delighted in imagining scenes of spiritual perfectness;—Paradises, and companies of the redeemed at the judgment;—glorified meetings of martyrs;—madonnas surrounded by circles of angels. If, which was rare, definite portraitures of living men were introduced, these real characters formed a kind of chorus or attendant company, taking no part in the action. At Venice all this was reversed, and so boldly as at first to shock, with its seeming irreverence, a spectator accustomed to the formalities and abstractions of the so-called sacred schools. The madonnas are no more seated apart on their thrones, the saints no more breathe celestial air. They are on our own plain ground—nay, here in our houses with us. All kind of worldly business going on in their presence, fearlessly; our own friends and respected acquaintances, with all their mortal faults, and in their mortal flesh, looking at them face to face unalarmed: nay, our dearest children playing with their pet dogs at Christ's very feet.

I once myself thought this irreverent. How foolishly! As if children whom He loved *could* play anywhere else.[28]

[28] MP V, 279–90, omit.

8

CARPACCIO

I have brought you a little sketch to-day from the foreground of a Venetian picture, in which there is a bit that
will show you this precision of method. It is the head of
a parrot with a little flower in his beak from a picture of
Carpaccio's, one of his series of the Life of St. George
["Baptising the Princess and her Father," Scuola di S.
Giorgio]. I could not get the curves of the leaves, and they
are patched and spoiled; but the parrot's head, however
badly done, is put down with no more touches than the
Venetian gave it, and it will show you exactly his method.
First, a thin, warm ground had been laid over the whole
canvas, which Carpaccio wanted as an undercurrent
through all the colour, just as there is an undercurrent
of grey in the Loire drawings. Then on this he strikes his
parrot in vermilion, almost flat colour; rounding a little
only with a glaze of lake; but attending mainly to get the
character of the bird by the pure outline of its form, as if
it were cut out of a piece of ruby glass.

Then he comes to the beak of it. The brown ground
beneath is left, for the most part; one touch of black is
put for the hollow; two delicate lines of dark grey define
the outer curve; and one little quivering touch of white
draws the inner edge of the mandible. There are just four
touches—fine as the finest penmanship—to do that beak;
and yet you will find that in the peculiar parroquettish
mumbling and nibbling action of it, and all the character
in which this nibbling beak differs from the tearing beak
of the eagle, it is impossible to go farther or be more pre-

cise. And this is only an incident, remember, in a large picture.[29]

"The Dream of St. Ursula"

In the year 1869, just before leaving Venice, I had been carefully looking at a picture by Victor Carpaccio, representing the dream of a young princess ["The Dream of St. Ursula," Accademia]. Carpaccio has taken much pains to explain to us, as far as he can, the kind of life she leads, by completely painting her little bedroom in the light of dawn, so that you can see everything in it. It is lighted by two doubly-arched windows, the arches being painted crimson round their edges, and the capitals of the shafts that bear them, gilded. They are filled at the top with small round panes of glass; but beneath, are open to the blue morning sky, with a low lattice across them: and in the one at the back of the room are set two beautiful white Greek vases with a plant in each; one having rich dark and pointed green leaves, the other crimson flowers, but not of any species known to me, each at the end of a branch like a spray of heath.

These flower-pots stand on a shelf which runs all round the room, and beneath the window, at about the height of the elbow, and serves to put things on anywhere: beneath it, down to the floor, the walls are covered with green cloth; but above, are bare and white. The second window is nearly opposite the bed, and in front of it is the princess's reading-table, some two feet and a half square, covered by a red cloth with a white border and dainty fringe; and beside it her seat, not at all like a reading-chair in Oxford, but a very small three-legged stool like a music-stool, covered with crimson cloth. On the table are a book set up at a slope fittest for reading, and an hourglass. Under the shelf, near the table, so as to be easily reached by the outstretched arm, is a press full of books. The door of this has been left open, and the books, I am grieved to say, are rather in disorder, having been pulled about before the princess went to bed, and one left standing on its side.

[29] Land 53 f

Opposite this window, on the white wall, is a small shrine or picture (I can't see which, for it is in sharp retiring perspective) with a lamp before it, and a silver vessel hung from the lamp, looking like one for holding incense.

The bed is a broad four-poster, the posts being beautifully wrought golden or gilded rods, variously wreathed and branched, carrying a canopy of warm red. The princess's shield is at the head of it, and the feet are raised entirely above the floor of the room, on a dais which projects at the lower end so as to form a seat, on which the child has laid her crown. Her little blue slippers lie at the side of the bed,—her white dog beside them. The coverlid is scarlet, the white sheet folded half-way back over it; the young girl lies straight, bending neither at waist nor knee, the sheet rising and falling over her in a narrow unbroken wave, like the shape of the coverlid of the last sleep, when the turf scarcely rises. She is some seventeen or eighteen years old, her head is turned towards us on the pillow, the cheek resting on her hand, as if she were thinking, yet utterly calm in sleep, and almost colourless. Her hair is tied with a narrow riband, and divided into two wreaths, which encircle her head like a double crown. The white nightgown hides the arm raised on the pillow, down to the wrist.

At the door of the room an angel enters (the little dog, though lying awake, vigilant, takes no notice). He is a very small angel, his head just rises a little above the shelf round the room, and would only reach as high as the princess's chin, if she were standing up. He has soft grey wings, lustreless; and his dress, of subdued blue, has violet sleeves, open above the elbow, and showing white sleeves below. He comes in without haste, his body, like a mortal one, casting shadow from the light through the door behind, his face perfectly quiet; a palm-branch in his right hand —a scroll in his left.

So dreams the princess, with blessed eyes, that need no earthly dawn. It is very pretty of Carpaccio to make her dream out the angel's dress so particularly, and notice the slashed sleeves; and to dream so little an angel—very nearly a doll angel,—bringing her the branch of palm, and mes-

sage. But the lovely characteristic of all is the evident delight of her continual life. Royal power over herself, and
happiness in her flowers, her books, her sleeping, and waking, her prayers, her dreams, her earth, her heaven.

American tourists

After I had spent my morning over this picture, I had
to go to Verona by the afternoon train. In the carriage
with me were two American girls with their father and
mother, people of the class which has lately made so much
money, suddenly, and does not know what to do with it:
and these two girls, of about fifteen and eighteen, had
evidently been indulged in everything (since they had had
the means) which western civilization could imagine. And
here they were, specimens of the utmost which the money
and invention of the nineteenth century could produce in
maidenhood,—children of its most progressive race,—enjoying the full advantages of political liberty, of enlightened
philosophical education, of cheap pilfered literature, and of
luxury at any cost.

But the two American girls were neither princesses, nor
seers, nor dreamers. By infinite self-indulgence, they had
reduced themselves simply to two pieces of white putty
that could feel pain. The flies and the dust stuck to them
as to clay, and they perceived, between Venice and Verona,
nothing but the flies and the dust. They pulled down the
blinds the moment they entered the carriage, and then
sprawled, and writhed, and tossed among the cushions of
it, in vain contest, during the whole fifty miles, with every
miserable sensation of bodily affliction that could make
time intolerable. Only one sentence was exchanged, in the
fifty miles, on the subject of things outside the carriage
(the Alps being once visible from a station where they had
drawn up the blinds).

"Don't those snow-caps make you cool?"

"No—I wish they did."

And so they went their way, with sealed eyes and tormented limbs, their numbered miles of pain.

There are the two states for you, in clearest opposition;

Blessed, and Accursed. The happy industry, and eyes full
of sacred imagination of things that are not . . . and the
tortured indolence, and infidel eyes, blind even to the things
that are.[30]

The Angel of Death

Carpaccio begins his story with what the myth calls a
dream. But he wishes to tell you that it was no dream,—
but a vision;—that a real angel came, and was seen by
Ursula's soul, when her mortal eyes were closed.

"The Angel of the Lord," says the legend. What!—thinks
Carpaccio;—to this little maid of fifteen, the angel that
came to Moses and Joshua? Not so, but her own guardian
angel.

Guardian, and to tell her that God will guide her heart
to-morrow, and put His own answer on her lips, concerning her marriage. Shall not such angel be crowned with
light, and strew her chamber with lilies?

There is no glory round his head; there is no gold on
his robes; they are of subdued purple and grey. His wings
are colourless—his face calm, but sorrowful,—wholly in
shade. In his right hand he bears the martyr's palm; in
his left, the fillet borne by the Greek angels of victory,
and, together with it, gathers up, knotted in his hand, the
folds of shroud with which the Etrurians veil the tomb.[31]

I could not see this symbol at the height at which the
picture hung from the ground, when I described it in 1872.
The folds of the drapery in the *hand* are all but invisible,
even when the picture is seen close; and so neutral in their
grey-green colour that they pass imperceptibly into violet,
as the faint green of evening sky fades into its purple. But
the folds are continued under the wrist in the alternate
waves which the reader may see on the Etruscan tomb in
the first room of the British Museum, with a sculpturesque
severity which I could not then understand, and could only
account for by supposing that Carpaccio had meant the

[30] Fors 1872, 342–47, omit.
[31] Fors 1876, 744

Princess to "dream out the angel's dress so particularly"! I mistook the fillet of victory also for a scroll; and could not make out the flowers in the window. They are pinks, the favourite ones in Italian windows to this day, and having a particular relation to St. Ursula in the way they rend their calyx; and I believe also in their peculiar relation to the grasses . . . St. Ursula is not meant, herself, to recognize the angel. He enters under the door over which she has put her little statue of Venus; and through that door the room is filled with light, so that it will not seem to her strange that his own form, as he enters, should be in shade; and she cannot see his dark wings. On the tassel of her pillow (Etrurian also) is written "Infantia"; and above her head, the carving of the bed ends in a spiral flame, typical of the finally ascending Spirit. She lies on her bier, in the last picture but one, exactly as here on her bed; only the coverlid is there changed from scarlet to pale violet.[32]

He comes to her, "in the clear light of morning"; the Angel of Death.

You see it is written in the legend that she had shut close the doors of her chamber.

They have opened as the angel enters,—not one only, but all in the room,—all in the house. He enters by one at the foot of her bed; but beyond it is another—open into the passage; out of that another into some luminous hall or street. All the window-shutters are wide open; they are made dark that you may notice them,—nay, all the press doors are open! No treasure bars shall hold, where *this* angel enters.

Carpaccio has been intent to mark that he comes in the light of dawn. The blue-green sky glows between the dark leaves of the olive and dianthus in the open window. But its light is low compared to that which enters *behind* the angel, falling full on Ursula's face, in divine rest.

In the last picture but one, of this story, he has painted her lying in the rest which the angel came to bring: and in the last, is her rising in the eternal Morning.[33]

[32] Fors 1876, 744 f, Ruskin note attached to the preceding paragraph.
[33] Fors 1876, 745 f

9

TITIAN

The finest Titian in the [Louvre, "The Entombment," is] glowing, simple, broad and grand. It is to be opposed to "The Flagellation," in which the shades are brown instead of grey, the outlines strong brown lines, the draperies broken up by folds, the light very round and vivid, and foiled by deep shades; the flesh forms the highest lights, and the draperies are subdued.

In "The Entombment" every one of these conditions is reversed. Even the palest flesh is solemn, and dark, in juxtaposition with bright golden white drapery. All the masses broad and flat, the shades grey, the outlines chaste and severe. May be taken as an example of the highest dignity of impression, wrought out by mere grandeur of colour and composition, for the head of Christ is entirely sacrificed, being put in the deepest possible shade, against clear sky, and it is disagreeable in itself. The head of the St. John and St. Joseph are however grand conceptions, and the foliage of the landscape graceful in the extreme. It is curious that in this broadest of all broad pictures there should be one of the most delicate transitions of colour I remember. It begins with St. John's robe—crimson, in shade intensely dark; then same in light. Then St. Joseph's face nearly purely crimson, carried off by the juxtaposition of the robe. Then his neck, paler; then his arm, paler still, which joins robe of Magdalen, which is *warmed* near it by a few reflected lights, but in its palest part, joins and unites with the corpse-cold hand of the Madonna.

The colour throughout amounts to little more than exquisite staining. The bright draperies and the chequers upon them exquisitely delicate, and finished and full of

hue, appear the result of the same operation as the dark
retiring ground; incorporated with it, and showing no edge
in many places. The most palpable piece of painting is the
white drapery under the Christ which is visibly superimposed, and has a raised edge.[34]

Titian's religion

I have, in other places, entered enough into the examination of the great religious mind of Tintoret; supposing then,
that he was distinguished from Titian chiefly by this character. But in this I was mistaken;—the religion of Titian is
like that of Shakspere—occult behind his magnificent
equity. It is not possible, however, within the limits of this
work, to give any just account of the mind of Titian: nor
shall I attempt it; but will only explain some of those more
strange and apparently inconsistent attributes of it, which
might otherwise prevent the reader from getting clue to its
real tone. The first of these is its occasional coarseness in
choice of type of feature.

In the second volume [of *Modern Painters*] I had to
speak of Titian's Magdalen, in the Pitti Palace, as treated
basely, and that in strong terms, "the disgusting Magdalen
of the Pitti." Truly she is so, as compared with the received types of the Magdalen. A stout, red-faced woman,
dull, and coarse of feature, with much of the animal in
even her expression of repentance—her eyes strained, and
inflamed with weeping. I ought, however, to have remembered another picture of the Magdalen by Titian (Mr.
Rogers's, now in the National Gallery), in which she is
just as refined, as in the Pitti Palace she is gross; and had
I done so, I should have seen Titian's meaning. It had
been the fashion before his time to make the Magdalen
always young and beautiful; her, if no one else, even the
rudest painters flattered; her repentance was not thought
perfect unless she had lustrous hair and lovely lips. Titian
first dared to doubt the romantic fable, and reject the

[34] From Ruskin's notebook of 1844, inserted by editors, LAP

452

narrowness of sentimental faith. He saw that it was possible for plain women to love no less vividly than beautiful ones; and for stout persons to repent, as well as those more delicately made. It seemed to him that the Magdalen would have received her pardon not the less quickly because her wit was none of the readiest; and would not have been regarded with less compassion by her Master because her eyes were swollen, or her dress disordered. It is just because he has set himself sternly to enforce this lesson that the picture is so painful: the only instance, so far as I remember, of Titian's painting a woman markedly and entirely belonging to the lowest class.

It may perhaps appear more difficult to account for the alternation of Titian's great religious pictures with others devoted wholly to the expression of sensual qualities, or to exulting and bright representation of heathen deities.

The Venetian mind, we have said, and Titian's especially, as the central type of it, was wholly realist, universal, and manly. In this breadth and realism, the painter saw that sensual passion in man was, not only a fact, but a Divine fact; the human creature, though the highest of the animals, was, nevertheless, a perfect animal, and his happiness, health, and nobleness, depended on the due power of every animal passion, as well as the cultivation of every spiritual tendency.

He thought that every feeling of the mind and heart, as well as every form of the body, deserved painting. Also to a painter's true and highly trained instinct, the human body is the loveliest of all objects. I do not stay to trace the reasons why, at Venice, the female body could be found in more perfect beauty than the male; but so it was, and it becomes the principal subject, therefore, both with Giorgione and Titian. They painted it fearlessly, with all right and natural qualities; never, however, representing it as exercising any overpowering attractive influence on man; but only on the Faun or Satyr.

Yet they did this so majestically that I am perfectly certain no untouched Venetian picture ever yet excited one base thought (otherwise than in base persons anything may do so); while in the greatest studies of the female body by the Venetians, all other characters are overborne by majesty, and the form becomes as pure as that of a Greek statue.[35]

[35] MP V, 295–97

10

TINTORETTO

[A]s the painter of Space [Tintoret] stands altogether alone among dead masters; being the first who introduced the slightness and confusion of touch which are expressive of the effects of luminous objects seen through large spaces of air, and the principles of aerial colour which have been since carried out in other fields by Turner. I conceive him to be the most powerful painter whom the world has seen, and that he was prevented from being also the most perfect, partly by untoward circumstances in his position and education, partly by the very fulness and impetuosity of his own mind, partly by the want of religious feeling and its accompanying perception of beauty; for his noble treatment of religious subjects, of which I shall give several examples in the third part, appears to be the result only of that grasp which a great and well-toned intellect necessarily takes of any subject submitted to it, and is wanting in the signs of the more withdrawn and sacred sympathies.[36]

Now, I wish the reader particularly to observe throughout all these works [in the Scuolo di San Rocco] of Tintoret, the distinction of the Imaginative Verity from falsehood on the one hand, and from realism on the other. The power of every picture depends on the penetration of the imagination into the TRUE nature of the thing represented, and on the utter scorn of the imagination for all shackles and fetters of mere external fact that stand in the way of its suggestiveness. In the Baptism it cuts away the trunks of trees as if they were so much cloud or vapour, that it may exhibit to the thought the completed sequency of the scene; in the Massacre it covers the marble floor with visionary

[36] MP I, 182

light, that it may strike terror into the spectator without
condescending to butchery; it defies the bare fact, but
creates in him the fearful feeling; in the Crucifixion it an-
nihilates locality, and brings the palm leaves to Calvary,
so only that it may bear the mind to the Mount of Olives;
as in the Entombment [Parma] it brings the manger to
Jerusalem, that it may take the heart to Bethlehem; and
all this it does in the daring consciousness of its higher
and spiritual verity, and in the entire knowledge of the
fact and substance of all that it touches. The imaginary
boat of the demon angel expands the rush of the visible
river into the descent of irresistible condemnation; but to
make that rush and roar felt by the eye and heard by the
ear, the rending of the pine branches above the cataract is
taken directly from nature; it is an abstract of Alpine storm.
Hence, while we are always placed face to face with whatever is to be told, there is in and beyond its reality a voice
supernatural; and that which is doubtful in the vision has
strength, sinew, and assuredness, built up in it by fact.[37]

MOSES STRIKING THE ROCK [Scuola di San Rocco]. We
now come to the series of pictures upon which the painter
concentrated the strength he had reserved for the upper
room; and in some sort wisely, for, though it is not pleasant
to examine pictures on a ceiling, they are at least distinctly visible without straining the eyes against the light.
They are carefully conceived, and thoroughly well painted
in proportion to their distance from the eye. This careful-
ness of thought is apparent at a glance: the "Moses Striking
the Rock" embraces the whole of the seventeenth chapter
of Exodus, and even something more, for it is not from
that chapter, but from parallel passages, that we gather
the facts of the impatience of Moses and the wrath of God
at the waters of Meribah; both which facts are shown by
the leaping of the stream out of the rock half-a-dozen ways
at once, forming a great arch over the head of Moses, and
by the partial veiling of the countenance of the Supreme
Being. This latter is the most painful part of the whole
picture, at least as it is seen from below; and I believe that

[37] MP II, 278

in some repairs of the roof this head must have been destroyed and repainted. It is one of Tintoret's usual fine thoughts that the lower part of the figure is veiled, not merely by clouds, but in a kind of watery sphere, showing the Deity coming to the Israelites at that particular moment as the Lord of the Rivers and of the Fountain of the Waters. The whole figure, as well as that of Moses, and the greater number of those in the foreground, is at once dark and warm, black and red being the prevailing colours, while the distance is bright gold touched with blue, and seems to open into the picture like a break of blue sky after rain. How exquisite is this expression, by mere colour, of the main force of the fact represented! that is to say, joy and refreshment after sorrow and scorching heat. But, when we examine of what this distance consists, we shall find still more cause for admiration. The blue in it is not the blue of sky, it is obtained by blue stripes upon white tents glowing in the sunshine; and in front of these tents is seen that great battle with Amalek of which the account is given in the remainder of the chapter, and for which the Israelites received strength in the streams which ran out of the rock in Horeb. Considered merely as a picture, the opposition of cool light to warm shadow is one of the most remarkable pieces of colour in the Scuola, and the great mass of foliage which waves over the rocks on the left appears to have been elaborated with his highest power and his most sublime invention. But this noble passage is much injured, and now hardly visible.

PLAGUE OF SERPENTS. The figures in the distance are remarkably important in this picture, Moses himself being among them; in fact, the whole scene is filled chiefly with middle-size figures, in order to increase the impression of space. It is interesting to observe the difference in the treatment of this subject by the three great painters, Michael Angelo, Rubens, and Tintoret. The first two, equal to the latter in energy, had less love of liberty: they were fond of binding their compositions into knots, Tintoret of scattering his far and wide; they all alike preserve the unity of composition, but the unity in the first two is obtained by binding, and that of the last by springing from one source; and, together with this feeling, comes his love of space, which makes him less regard the rounding and form of objects themselves than their relations of light and shade and distance. Therefore Rubens and Michael Angelo made the fiery serpents huge boa-constrictors and knotted the sufferers together with them. Tintoret does not like to be so bound; so he makes the serpents little flying and fluttering monsters, like lampreys with wings; and the children of Israel, instead of being thrown into convulsed and writhing groups, are scattered, fainting in the fields, far away in the distance.[38]

[38] SV III, 419–21

11

VERONESE

Veronese . . . chooses to represent the great relations of
visible things to each other, to the heaven above, and to
the earth beneath them. He holds it more important to
show how a figure stands relieved from delicate air, or
marble wall; how as a red, or purple, or white figure, it
separates itself, in clear discernibility, from things not red,
nor purple, nor white; how infinite daylight shines round
it; how innumerable veils of faint shadow invest it; how
its blackness and darkness are, in the excess of their nature,
just as limited and local as its intensity of light; all this, I
say, he feels to be more important than showing merely
the exact *measure* of the spark of sunshine that gleams on
a dagger-hilt, or glows on a jewel. All this, moreover, he
feels to be harmonious,—capable of being joined in one
great system of spacious truth. And with inevitable watchfulness, inestimable subtlety, he unites all this in tenderest
balance, noting in each hair's-breadth of colour, not merely
what its rightness or wrongness is in itself, but what its relation is to every other on his canvas; restraining, for truth's
sake, his exhaustless energy, reining back, for truth's sake,
his fiery strength; veiling, before truth, the vanity of brightness; penetrating, for truth, the discouragement of gloom;
ruling his restless invention with a rod of iron; pardoning
no error, no thoughtlessness, no forgetfulness; and subduing
all his powers, impulses, and imaginations, to the arbitra-
ment of a merciless justice, and the obedience of an in-
corruptible verity.[39]

Meantime, note further of Veronese, as we saw that the
black outlines were much left, so the painting ["The Feast

[39] MP III, 59 f

in the House of Simon," Louvre] seems extremely thin; being on the floor, I saw the picture divinely, out of its frame. At the bottom, the canvass where the frame had gone over it, appeared covered with a very thin film of gesso, and over this a rich, somewhat dark brown was scratched very rudely in small touches, not like the hand of a master, unless done so on purpose. Nevertheless, all the greys of the architecture, and blues of sky, appeared to me to be painted over this brown, and to have its dark gleaming through them continually, and giving depth. The greys themselves were the most pearly and lovely possible, and, to my amazement, of pure colour blended as finely as Turner's own—how, on such a scale, heaven knows; but there were pure blues, and gold and rose colour, and the under brown—all most ætherial and amalgamating, and melting into the opalescent grey which made me write in my small notebook, when I first sat down before this architecture, that it had properties which in nature were "almost peculiar to snow." The touching of the high lights is not so confused as Turner's, more like scene-painting—fitter for background—as less studied, quite as *white* but more commonplace in stroke. The strong darks, throughout the pictures, are dreadfully chilled, only a patch here and there showing their original intensity. The vermilions are just as raw and bad as in Cuyp.

Observe also that nothing is thought by Veronese beneath his notice, or beneath his pains. It is impossible to fix any general rule as to what is grand or not, in his hands: Sir Joshua Reynolds' rule of "it is drapery and nothing more," is set at utter defiance: indeed I am beginning to think it ought to be. The sitting figure on the extreme left, next the column in a brown tambour, has a dress up to his neck, of green and warm buff in vertical stripes, very broad; the buff has a narrow pink *satin* bar in the centre, and this, where the dress is wrinkled at the neck, is touched with excessive care and delight, the points of its lustre flashing like sparks of fire. So in the picture of the "Supper at Emmaus," with the two little girls, the figure of the matron on the left has a drapery of blue satin, with touches of gold (by-the-bye, look at this again: an example of disunity—yet beautiful in *colour*, though it would be wretched in form) which is studied as carefully as a bit of Chalon—but in such a manly and magnificent way. The damask white and gold of the two children marvellous also—the pattern so thoroughly drawn without stiffness, so also in the tablecloth of the Magdalen—every bit of its pierced border painted thoroughly.

It struck me, on Saturday, that Veronese and such other men were afraid to give colour to their architecture, lest it should become too important and too solid, but felt that they might give it to their draperies, and yet keep them subordinate, by the various superimpositions of the colours. The negro boy so often mentioned, has assuredly been painted over two plates, and the crease of the table-cloth at the edge of the table, and yet the *final* white of the table-cloth is *most certainly* painted up to it, and stops at it (as also it does, and this is especially remarkable, at the plates of fruit on the other side, the outline of the flat cherries being sharply given by the circum-dragged white): and the head is most marvellously brought out; there has (I am not *quite* sure of any of these assertions respecting method, except in the particular spots described, which may be sometimes exceptional) first been a black ground, part of the figures on the other side of table; on this a yellow wine-glass has been painted, leaving at one side, as it was struck on, the outline of the negro's most marked features in the black ground. Over this left space, the complexion and such drawing as is required, are given by one coat of the peculiar negro brown of Veronese, which is, of course, struck on and modelled as a light, leaving just an edge of the original black ground between it and the glass yellow, which touched with a vivid brown about the lips serves for an outline.[40]

[40] From Ruskin's notebook of 1849, inserted by editors, LAP 464–66, omit.

12

LANDSCAPE

Landscape painting is the thoughtful and passionate representation of the physical conditions appointed for human existence.[41]

Only *natural phenomena in their direct relation to humanity*—these are to be your subjects in landscape. Rocks and water and air may no more be painted for their own sakes, than the armour carved without the warrior.

But, secondly. I said landscape is to be a *passionate representation* of these things. It must be done, that is to say, with strength and depth of soul. This is indeed to some extent merely the particular application of a principle that has no exception. If you are without strong passions, you cannot be a painter at all. The laying of paint by an insensitive person, whatever it endeavours to represent, is not painting, but daubing or plastering; and that, observe, irrespective of the boldness or minuteness of the work. An insensitive person will daub with a camel's-hair brush and ultramarine; and a passionate one will paint with mortar and a trowel.

But far more than common passion is necessary to paint landscape. The physical conditions there are so numerous, and the spiritual ones so occult, that you are sure to be overpowered by the materialism, unless your sentiment is strong.

For one thing, the passion is necessary for the mere quantity of design. In good art, whether painting or sculpture, I have again and again told you every touch is necessary and beautifully intended. Now it falls within the compass of ordinary application to place rightly all the folds

[41] Land 12

of drapery or gleams of light on a chain, or ornaments in a pattern; but when it comes to placing every leaf in a tree, the painter gets tired. Here, for instance, is a little bit of Sandro Botticelli background [from the "Primavera"]; I have purposefully sketched it in the slightest way, that you might see how the entire value of it depends on thoughtful placing. There is no texture aimed at, no completion, scarcely any variety of light and shade; but by mere care in the placing the thing is beautiful.

But though the virtue of all painting (and similarly of sculpture and every other art) is in passion, I must not have you begin by working passionately. The discipline of youth, in all its work, is in cooling and curbing itself, as the discipline of age is in warming and urging itself; you know the Bacchic chorus of old men in Plato's *Laws*.[42]

The schools of landscape

We may arrange nearly all existing landscape under the following heads:—

I. HEROIC.—Representing an imaginary world, inhabited by men not perhaps perfectly civilized, but noble, and usually subjected to severe trials, and by spiritual powers of the highest order. It is frequently without architecture; never without figure-action, or emotion. Its principal master is Titian.

II. CLASSICAL.—Representing an imaginary world, inhabited by perfectly civilized men, and by spiritual powers of an inferior order.

It generally assumes this condition of things to have existed among the Greek and Roman nations. It contains usually architecture of an elevated character, and always incidents of figure-action, or emotion. Its principal master is Nicolo Poussin.

III. PASTORAL.—Representing peasant life and its daily work, or such scenery as may naturally be suggestive of it, consisting usually of simple landscape, in part subjected to agriculture, with figures, cattle, and domestic buildings.

[42] Land 17–19, omit.

No supernatural being is ever visibly present. It does not in ordinary cases admit architecture of an elevated character nor exciting incident. Its principal master is Cuyp.

IV. CONTEMPLATIVE.—Directed principally to the observance of the powers of Nature, and record of the historical associations connected with landscape, illustrated by, or contrasted with, existing states of human life. No supernatural being is visibly present. It admits every variety of subject, and requires, in general, figure incident, but not of an exciting character. It was not developed completely until recent times. Its principal master is Turner.

These are the four true orders of landscape, not of course distinctly separated from each other in all cases, but very distinctly in typical examples. Two spurious forms require separate note.

(A) PICTURESQUE.—This is indeed rather the degradation (or sometimes the undeveloped state) of the contemplative, than a distinct class; but it may be considered generally as including pictures meant to display the skill of the artist, and his powers of composition; or to give agreeable forms and colours, irrespective of sentiment. It will include much modern art, with the street views and church interiors of the Dutch, and the works of Canaletto, Guardi, Tempesta, and the like.

(B) HYBRID.—Landscape in which the painter endeavours to unite the irreconcilable sentiment of two or more of the above-named classes. Its principal masters are Berghem and Wouvermans.[43]

The presence of death

The art which, since the writings of Rio and Lord Lindsay,[44] is specially known as "Christian," erred by pride in its denial of the animal nature of man;—and, in connection with all monkish and fanatical forms of religion, by looking always to another world instead of this. It wasted

[43] MP V, 254 f

[44] (*De la Poésie Chrétienne*, Paris, 1835, and *Sketches of the History of Christian Art*, London, 1847.) MP V, 264

its strength in visions, and was therefore swept away, notwithstanding all its good and glory, by the strong truth of the naturalist art of the sixteenth century. But that naturalist art erred on the other side; denied at last the spiritual nature of man, and perished in corruption.

A contemplative reaction is taking place in modern times, out of which it may be hoped a new spiritual art may be developed. The first school of landscape, named, in the foregoing chapter, the Heroic, is that of the noble naturalists. The second (Classical), and third (Pastoral), belong to the time of sensual decline. The fourth (Contemplative) is that of modern revival.

But why, the reader will ask, is no place given in this scheme to the "Christian" or spiritual art which preceded the naturalists? Because all landscape belonging to that art is subordinate, and in one essential principle false. It is subordinate, because intended only to exalt the conception of saintly or Divine presence:—rather therefore to be considered as a landscape decoration or type, than an effort to paint nature. If I included it in my list of schools, I should have to go still farther back, and include with it the conventional and illustrative landscape of the Greeks and Egyptians.

But also it cannot constitute a real school, because its first assumption is false, namely, that the natural world can be represented without the element of death.

The real schools of landscape are primarily distinguished from the preceding unreal ones by their introduction of this element. They are not at first in any sort the worthier for it. But they are more true, and capable, therefore, in the issue, of becoming worthier.[45]

Now, as far as I have watched the main powers of human mind, they have risen first from the resolution to see fearlessly, pitifully, and to its very worst, what these deep colours mean, wheresoever they fall; not by any means to pass on the other side, looking pleasantly up to the sky, but to stoop to the horror, and let the sky, for the present, take care of its own clouds. However this may be in moral

[45] MP V, 264 f

matters, with which I have nothing here to do, in my own field of inquiry the fact is so; and all great and beautiful work has come of first gazing without shrinking into the darkness. If, having done so, the human spirit can, by its courage and faith, conquer the evil, it rises into conceptions of victorious and consummated beauty. It is then the spirit of the highest Greek and Venetian Art. If unable to conquer the evil, but remaining in strong though melancholy war with it, not rising into supreme beauty, it is the spirit of the best northern art, typically represented by that of Holbein and Dürer. If, itself conquered by the evil, infected by the dragon breath of it, and at last brought into captivity, so as to take delight in evil for ever, it becomes the spirit of the dark, but still powerful sensualistic art, represented typically by that of Salvator.[46]

[46] MP V, 271

13

MEDIEVAL LANDSCAPE

Hence a degree of personal beauty, both male and female, was attained in the Middle Ages, with which classical periods could show nothing for a moment comparable; and this beauty was set forth by the most perfect splendour, united with grace, in dress, which the human race have hitherto invented. The strength of their art-genius was directed in great part to this object; and their best workmen and most brilliant fanciers were employed in wreathing the mail or embroidering the robe. The exquisite arts of enamelling and chasing metal enabled them to make the armour as radiant and delicate as the plumage of a tropical bird; and the most various and vivid imaginations were displayed in the alternations of colour, and fiery freaks of form, on shield and crest: so that of all the beautiful things which the eyes of men could fall upon, in the world about them, the most beautiful must have been a young knight riding out in morning sunshine, and in faithful hope.

Now, the effect of this superb presence of human beauty on men in general was, exactly as it had been in Greek times, first to turn their thoughts and glances in great part away from all other beauty but that, and to make the grass of the field take to them always more or less the aspect of a carpet to dance upon, a lawn to tilt upon, or a serviceable crop of hay; and, secondly, in what attention they paid to this lower nature, to make them dwell exclusively on what was graceful, symmetrical, and bright in colour. All that was rugged, rough, dark, wild, unterminated, they rejected at once, as the domain of "salvage men"[47] and monstrous giants: all that they admired was tender, bright,

---

[47] (In the old sense of "savage.") MP III, 256 f, omit.

balanced, enclosed, symmetrical—only symmetrical in the
noble and free sense: for what we moderns call "symmetry," or "balance," differs as much from mediæval symmetry as the poise of a grocer's scales, or the balance of
an Egyptian mummy with its hands tied to its sides, does
from the balance of a knight on his horse, striking with
the battle-axe, at the gallop; the mummy's balance looking
wonderfully perfect, and yet sure to be one-sided if you
weigh the dust of it,—the knight's balance swaying and
changing like the wind, and yet as true and accurate as
the laws of life.

And this love of symmetry was still further enhanced by
the peculiar duties required of art at the time; for, in order
to fit a flower or leaf for inlaying in armour, or showing
clearly in glass, it was absolutely necessary to take away
its complexity, and reduce it to the condition of a disciplined and orderly pattern; and this the more, because, for
all military purposes, the device, whatever it was, had to
be distinctly intelligible at extreme distance. That it should
be a good imitation of nature, when seen near, was of no
moment; but it was of highest moment that when first the
knight's banner flashed in the sun at the turn of the mountain road, or rose, torn and bloody, through the drift of
the battle dust, it should still be discernible what the bearing was.

Farther, it was necessary to the brilliant harmony of
colour, and clear setting forth of everything, that all confusing shadows, all dim and doubtful lines should be rejected: hence at once an utter denial of natural appearances by the great body of workmen; and a calm rest in a
practice of representation which would make either boar
or lion blue, scarlet, or golden, according to the device of
the knight, or the need of such and such a colour in that
place of the pattern; and which wholly denied that any
substance ever cast a shadow, or was affected by any kind
of obscurity.

All this was in its way, and for its end, absolutely right,
admirable, and delightful; and those who despise it, laugh
at it, or derive no pleasure from it, are utterly ignorant of

the highest principles of art, and are mere tyros and beginners in the practice of colour. But, admirable though it might be, one necessary result of it was a farther withdrawal of the observation of men from the refined and subtle beauty of nature; so that the workman who first was led to think *lightly* of natural beauty, as being subservient to human, was next led to think *inaccurately* of natural beauty, because he had continually to alter and simplify it for his practical purposes.

"Medieval feeling towards nature"

Now, assembling all these different sources of the peculiar mediæval feeling towards nature in one view, we have:

1st. Love of the garden instead of love of the farm, leading to a sentimental contemplation of nature, instead of a practical and agricultural one.

2nd. Loss of sense of actual Divine presence, leading to fancies of fallacious animation, in herbs, flowers, clouds, etc.

3rd. Perpetual, and more or less undisturbed, companionship with wild nature.

4th. Apprehension of demoniacal and angelic presence among mountains, leading to a reverent dread of them.

5th. Principalness of delight in human beauty, leading to comparative contempt of natural objects.

6th. Consequent love of order, light, intelligibility, and symmetry, leading to dislike of the wildness, darkness, and mystery of nature.

7th. Inaccuracy of observance of nature, induced by the habitual practice of change on its forms.

From these mingled elements, we should necessarily expect to find resulting, as the characteristic of mediæval landscape art, compared with Greek, a far higher sentiment about it, and affection for it, more or less subdued by still greater respect for the loveliness of man, and therefore subordinated entirely to human interests; mingled with curious traces of terror, piety, or superstition, and cramped by various formalisms,—some wise and necessary, some feeble, and some exhibiting needless ignorance and inaccuracy.

Under these lights, let us examine the facts.

The landscape of the Middle Ages is represented in a central manner by the illuminations of the MSS. of Romances, executed about the middle of the fifteenth century. On one side of these stands the earlier landscape work, more or less treated as simple decoration; on the other, the later landscape work, becoming more or less affected with modern ideas and modes of imitation.

These central fifteenth century landscapes are almost invariably composed of a grove or two tall trees, a winding river, and a castle, or a garden: the peculiar feature of both these last being *trimness;* the artist always dwelling especially on the fences; wreathing the espaliers indeed prettily with sweetbriar, and putting pots of orange-trees on the tops of the walls, but taking great care that there shall be no loose bricks in the one, nor broken stake in the other,—the trouble and ceaseless warfare of the times having rendered security one of the first elements of pleasantness, and making it impossible for any artist to conceive Paradise but as surrounded by a moat, or to distinguish the road to it better than by its narrow wicket gate, and watchful porter.

One of these landscapes is thus described by Macaulay: —"We have an exact square, enclosed by the rivers Pison, Gihon, Hiddekel, and Euphrates, each with a convenient bridge in the centre; rectangular beds of flowers; a long canal neatly bricked and railed in; the tree of knowledge, clipped like one of the limes behind the Tuileries, standing in the centre of the grand alley; the snake turned around it, the man on the right hand, the woman on the left, and the beasts drawn up in an exact circle round them."[48]

All this is perfectly true; and seems in the description very curiously foolish. The only curious folly, however, in the matter is the exquisite *naïveté* of the historian, in sup-

[48] ("Moore's Life of Lord Byron," in Macaulay's *Essays.*) MP III, 257–61, omit.

posing that the quaint landscape indicates in the understanding of the painter so marvellous an inferiority to his own; whereas, it is altogether his own wit that is at fault, in not comprehending that nations, whose youth had been decimated among the sands and serpents of Syria, knew probably nearly as much about Eastern scenery as youths trained in the schools of the modern Royal Academy; and that this curious symmetry was entirely symbolic, only more or less modified by the various instincts which I have traced above. Mr. Macaulay is evidently quite unaware that the serpent with the human head, and body twisted round the tree, was the universally-accepted symbol of the evil angel, from the dawn of art up to Michael Angelo; that the greatest sacred artists invariably place the man on the one side of the tree, the woman on the other, in order to denote the enthroned and balanced dominion about to fall by temptation; that the beasts are ranged (when they *are* so, though this is much more seldom the case,) in a circle round them, expressly to mark that they were then not wild, but obedient, intelligent, and orderly beasts; and that the four rivers are trenched and enclosed on the four sides, to mark that the waters which now wander in waste, and destroy in fury, had then for their principal office to "water the garden" of God. The description is, however, sufficiently apposite and interesting as bearing upon what I have noted respecting the eminent *fence*-loving spirit of the mediævals.

Together with this peculiar formality, we find an infinite delight in drawing pleasant flowers, always articulating and outlining them completely; the sky is always blue, having only a few delicate white clouds in it, and in the distance are blue mountains, very far away, if the landscape is to be simply delightful; but brought near, and divided into quaint overhanging rocks, if it is intended to be meditative, or a place of saintly seclusion. But the whole of it always,—flowers, castles, brooks, clouds, and rocks,—subordinate to the human figures in the foreground, and painted for no other end than that of explaining their adventures and occupations.

The advent of imitative landscape

Before the idea of landscape had been thus far developed, the representations of it had been purely typical: the objects which had to be shown in order to explain the scene of the event, being firmly outlined, usually on a pure golden or chequered colour background, not on sky. The change from the golden background (characteristic of the finest thirteenth century work) and the coloured chequer (which in like manner belongs to the finest fourteenth) to the blue sky, gradated to the horizon, takes place early in the fifteenth century, and is the *crisis* of change in the spirit of mediæval art. Strictly speaking, we might divide the art of Christian times into two great masses—Symbolic and Imitative;—the symbolic, reaching from the earliest periods down to the close of the fourteenth century, and the imitative from that close, to the present time; and then the most important circumstance indicative of the culminating point, or turn of tide, would be this of the change from chequered background to sky background.

The moment the sky is introduced (and it is curious how perfectly it is done *at once,* many manuscripts presenting in alternate pages, chequered backgrounds, and deep blue skies exquisitely gradated to the horizon)—the moment, I say, the sky is introduced, the spirit of art becomes for evermore changed, and thenceforward it gradually proposes imitation more and more as an end, until it reaches the Turnerian landscape. This broad division into two schools would therefore be the most true and accurate we could employ, but not the most convenient. For the great mediæval art lies in a cluster about the culminating point, including symbolism on one side, and imitation on the other, and extending like a radiant cloud upon the mountain peak of ages, partly down both sides of it, from the year 1200 to 1500; the brightest part of the cloud leaning a little backwards, and poising itself between 1250 and 1350. And therefore the most convenient arrangement is into Romanesque and barbaric art, up to 1200, mediæval art, 1200 to 1500,—and modern art, from 1500 downwards.

But it is only in the earlier or symbolic mediæval art, reaching up to the close of the fourteenth century, that the peculiar modification of natural forms for decorative purposes is seen in its perfection, with all its beauty, and all its necessary shortcomings; the minds of men being accurately balanced between that honour for the superior human form which they shared with the Greek ages, and the sentimental love of nature which was peculiar to their own. The expression of the two feelings will be found to vary according to the material and place of the art; in painting, the conventional forms are more adopted, in order to obtain definition, and brilliancy of colour, while in sculpture the life of nature is often rendered with a love and faithfulness which put modern art to shame.[49]

[49] MP III, 261–64, omit.

14

CLASSICAL LANDSCAPE

The classical landscape, properly so called, is . . . the representative of perfectly trained and civilized human life, associated with perfect natural scenery and with decorative spiritual powers.

I will expand this definition a little.

(1.) Perfectly civilized human life; that is, life freed from the necessity of humiliating labour, from passions inducing bodily disease, and from abasing misfortune. The personages of the classical landscape, therefore, must be virtuous and amiable; if employed in labour, endowed with strength, such as may make it not oppressive. (Considered as a practical ideal, the classical life necessarily implies slavery, and the command, therefore, of a higher order of men over a lower, occupied in servile work.) Pastoral occupation is allowable as a contrast with city life. War, if undertaken by classical persons, must be a contest for honour, more than for life, not at all for wealth, and free from all fearful or debasing passion. Classical persons must be trained in all the polite arts, and, because their health is to be perfect, chiefly in the open air. Hence, the architecture around them must be of the most finished kind, the rough country and ground being subdued by frequent and happy humanity.

(2.) Such personages and buildings must be associated with natural scenery, uninjured by storms or inclemency of climate (such injury implying interruption of the open-air life); and it must be scenery conducing to pleasure, not to material service; all cornfields, orchards, olive-yards, and such like, being under the management of slaves, and the superior beings having nothing to do with them; but passing their lives under avenues of scented and otherwise delightful trees,—under picturesque rocks, and by clear fountains.

(3.) The spiritual powers in classical scenery must be decorative; ornamental gods, not governing gods; otherwise they could not be subjected to the principles of taste, but would demand reverence. In order, therefore, as far as possible, without taking away their supernatural power, to destroy their dignity, they are made more criminal and capricious than men, and, for the most part, those only are introduced who are the lords of lascivious pleasures. For the appearance of any great god would at once destroy the whole theory of the classical life; therefore, Pan, Bacchus, and the Satyrs, with Venus and the Nymphs, are the principal spiritual powers of the classical landscape.[50]

Claude

[Claude] may be considered as Turner's principal master. Claude's capacities were of the most limited kind; but he had tenderness of perception, and sincerity of purpose, and he affected a revolution in art. This revolution consisted mainly in setting the sun in heaven. Till Claude's time no one had seriously thought of painting the sun but conventionally; that is to say, as a red or yellow star, (often) with a face in it, under which type it was constantly represented in illumination; else it was kept out of the picture, or introduced in fragmentary distances, breaking through clouds with almost definite rays.

Claude took up the new idea seriously, made the sun his subject, and painted the effects of misty shadows cast by his rays over the landscape, and other delicate aerial transitions, as no one had ever done before, and, in some respects, as no one has done in oil colour since.

"But, how, if this were so, could his capacities be of the meanest order?" Because doing *one* thing well, or better than others have done it, does not necessarily imply large capacity. If Claude had been a great man he would not

[50] MP V, 317 f

have been so steadfastly set on painting effects of sun: he would have looked at all nature, and at all art, and would have painted sun effects somewhat worse, and nature universally much better. Such as he was, however, his discovery of the way to make pictures look warm was very delightful to the shallow connoisseurs of the age. Not that they cared for sunshine; but they liked seeing jugglery. They could not feel Titian's noble colour, nor Veronese's noble composition; but they thought it highly amusing to see the sun brought into a picture: and Claude's works were bought and delighted in by vulgar people then, for their real-looking suns, as pictures are now by vulgar people for having real timepieces in their church towers.

I have been obliged to laugh a little—though I hope reverently—at Ghirlandajo's landscapes, which yet we saw had a certain charm of quaintness in them when contrasted with his grand figures; but could any one have believed that Claude, with all the noble landscapes of Titian set before him, and all nature round about him, should yet go back to Ghirlandajo for types of form? Yet such is the case. I said that the Venetian influence came dimly down to Claude: but the old Florentine influence came clearly. The Claudesque landscape is not, as so commonly supposed, an idealized abstract of the nature about Rome. It is an ultimate condition of the Florentine conventional landscape, more or less softened by reference to nature.[51]

[In summary, Claude] had a fine feeling for beauty of form, and considerable tenderness of perception. His aerial effects are unequalled. Their character appears to me to arise rather from a delicacy of bodily constitution in Claude, than from any mental sensibility: such as they are, they give a kind of feminine charm to his work, which partly accounts for its wide influence. To whatever the character may be traced, it renders him incapable of enjoying or painting anything energetic or terrible. Hence the weakness of his conceptions of rough sea.

He had sincerity of purpose. But in common with other landscape painters of his day, neither earnestness, humility,

[51] MP III, 400–05, omit.

nor love, such as would ever cause him to forget himself. That is to say, so far as he felt the truth, he tried to be true; but he never felt it enough to sacrifice supposed propriety or habitual method to it. Very few of his sketches, and none of his pictures, show evidence of interest in other natural phenomena than the quiet afternoon sunshine which would fall methodically into a composition. One would suppose he had never seen scarlet in a morning cloud, nor a storm burst on the Apennines. But he enjoys a quiet misty afternoon in a ruminant sort of way, yet truly; and strives for the likeness of it, therein differing from Salvator, who never attempts to be truthful, but only to be impressive.

His seas are the most beautiful in old art. For he studied tame waves, as he did tame skies, with great sincerity, and some affection; and modelled them with more care not only than any other landscape painter of his day, but even than any of the great men; for they, seeing the perfect painting of sea to be impossible, gave up the attempt, and treated it conventionally. But Claude took so much pains about this, feeling it was one of his *fortes*, that I suppose no one can model a small wave better than he.

He first set the pictorial sun in the pictorial heaven. We will give him the credit of this, with no drawbacks.

He had hardly any knowledge of physical science, and shows a peculiar incapacity of understanding the main point of a matter. Connected with which incapacity is his want of harmony in expression.

Such were the principal qualities of the leading painter of classical landscape, his effeminate softness causing him to dislike all evidences of toil, or distress, or terror, and to delight in the calm formalities which mark the school.

Although he often introduces romantic incidents and mediæval as well as Greek or Roman personages, his landscape is always in the true sense classic—everything being "elegantly" (selectingly or tastefully), not passionately, treated. The absence of indications of rural labour, of hedges, ditches, haystacks, ploughed fields, and the like; the frequent occurrence of ruins of temples, or masses of unruined palaces; and the graceful wildness of growth in his trees, are the principal sources of the "elevated" character which so many persons feel in his scenery.

There is no other sentiment traceable in his work than this weak dislike to entertain the conception of toil or suffering. Ideas of relation, in the true sense, he has none; nor ever makes an effort to conceive an event in its probable circumstances, but fills his foregrounds with decorative figures, using commonest conventionalism to indicate the subject he intends.

The admiration of his works was legitimate, so far as it regarded their sunlight effects and their graceful details. It was base, in so far as it involved irreverence both for the deeper powers of nature, and carelessness as to conception of subject. Large admiration of Claude is wholly impossible in any period of national vigour in art. He may by such tenderness as he possesses, and by the very fact of his banishing painfulness, exercise considerable influence over certain classes of minds; but this influence is almost exclusively hurtful to them.

Nevertheless, on account of such small sterling qualities as they possess, and of their general pleasantness, as well as their importance in the history of art, genuine Claudes must always possess a considerable value, either as drawing-room ornaments or museum relics. They may be ranked with fine pieces of china manufacture, and other agreeable curiosities, of which the price depends on the rarity rather than the merit, yet always on a merit of a certain low kind.[52]

Poussin

I named Claude first, because the forms of scenery he has represented are richer and more general than Poussin's; but Poussin has a far greater power, and his landscapes, though more limited in material, are incomparably nobler than Claude's. It would take considerable time to enter into accurate analysis of Poussin's strong but degraded mind; and bring us no reward, because whatever he has done

[52] MP V, 318–22, omit.

has been done better by Titian. His peculiarities are, without exception, weaknesses, induced in a highly intellectual and inventive mind by being fed on medals, books, and bassi-relievi instead of nature, and by the want of any deep sensibility. His best works are his Bacchanalian revels, always brightly wanton and wild, full of frisk and fire; but they are coarser than Titian's, and infinitely less beautiful. In all minglings of the human and brutal character he leans on the bestial, yet with a sternly Greek severity of treatment. This restraint, peculiarly classical, is much too manifest in him; for, owing to his habit of never letting himself be free, he does nothing as well as it ought to be done, rarely even as well as he can himself do it; and his best beauty is poor, incomplete, and characterless, though refined. The Nymph pressing the honey in the "Nursing of Jupiter," and the Muse leaning against the tree, in the "Inspiration of Poet" (both in the Dulwich Gallery), appear to me examples of about his highest reach in this sphere.

His want of sensibility permits him to paint frightful subjects, without feeling any true horror: his pictures of the Plague, the Death of Polydectes, etc., are thus ghastly in incident, sometimes disgusting, but never impressive. The prominence of the bleeding head in the Triumph of David [Dulwich Gallery] marks the same temper. His battlepieces are cold and feeble; his religious subjects wholly nugatory, they do not excite him enough to develop even his ordinary powers of invention. Neither does he put much power into his landscape when it becomes principal; the best pieces of it occur in fragments behind his figures. Beautiful vegetation, more or less ornamental in character, occurs in nearly all his mythological subjects, but his pure landscape is notable only for its dignified reserve; the great squareness and horizontality of its masses, with lowness of tone, giving it a deeply meditative character. His Deluge might be much depreciated, under this head of ideas of relation, but it is so uncharacteristic of him that I pass it by. Whatever power this lowness of tone, light in the distance, etc., give to his landscape, or to Gaspar's, is in both conventional and artificial.[53]

After looking carefully at three of his important landscapes—the Deluge, the Eden, and the Gideon ["Diogenes throwing away his Bowl"]—and generally at those scattered through the rooms [of the Louvre], I was thoroughly puzzled as to his character, intellectual or moral. In the three landscapes he is cold, artificial, lifeless, feeble, ignorant, conventional, yet always of course a painter; the thing is well painted from beginning to end, and there is always the same quaint power of composition about certain passages. But no words are too strong to reprobate the vileness and meanness of the oak branches and general outline (the foliage being characteristically painted—thorough oak). On the left of the "Gideon" they are as meanly, as they are visibly, *composed,* and the cottage or town architecture in the valley beyond that on the hill looking like La Riccia, and rather grand, is a curious example of the selection exactly of those forms which I should have called the ugliest, both in feeling and line, in the world, all tiled roofs over half-built walls, with windows exactly in the middle; the windows, one straight ruled square of grey, *flat grey paint,* neither varied on edge nor surface, tiles ruled straight, eaves straight—all formalized to a physically impossible degree, as if that could idealize such buildings. Consider this as the very and literal anti-picturesque spirit, without grandeur or quaintness or anything else to recommend it.

The trees and hills and water and sky are all grey, the first greenish, the last bluish, passing down into good, though lifeless and joyless, gold in the left-hand corner of horizon, the best bit on the whole of the picture; the sky is cloudy, the clouds *cirro-cumuli,* neither grand nor mean, not absolutely commonplace, but far less striking or sublime, and very cold in colour; the ground goes down into the water in the usual formal bank, a dull coloured gravel appearing in places, the water not ill painted, reflections rather studied; but *enfin,* a bit of stagnant water, and there an end. The sentiment of the picture, however, has been well intended; for Poussin has taken the most extraordinary pains to paint the pebbles under the water, in the stream of the foreground, and not only so, but, to my delight, a trunk of a tree has fallen across the stream; it goes under the water, whose flow across it is marked by a gleam of white at the edge, and casts its shadow, detached from it, beneath across the *bottom*, none on the surface; the pebbles are all of the usual commonplace ill-grouped ellipse—the water lowers their tone a little, and shows chiefly by white touches at edge. Poussin has evidently made a study for it; but with all, it is quite uninteresting, and has none of the ripple or brightness or murmur of a stream.

A few rooms on, facing this landscape—which throughout may be described as the very type of a painter-like frigidity, the Niobe of landscapes, the dullest, flattest, joylessest formality of propriety in wood and water: the trees and grass afraid to be green, the sky too grand to be blue, the water too polite to be noisy or to move, the moss taken off the tiles, and the beads out of the timbers and the cracks out of the stones, and the whole thing coloured like the world in a fainting fit, as if the man who did it had never seen a brighter colour than a Dutch fog, and had painted an Italian landscape by hearsay; or as if he had never seen, or at any rate never enjoyed, a tint of colour or an energetic form in his life, and had about as much sensation as a tortoise and as much hilarity as a Quaker—opposite this picture, I say, is that one of the Triumph of Flora with a sky as blue as a gentian, and massy white clouds, as pure as snow; and a burning distance, all orange gold, as if all summer and autumn were gathered into one sunset over deep, deep blue hills, carried down by fiery flakes among the figures; the trees filling all the blue sky with stars of blossom, and the figures one bright, unrestrainable riot of pure delight—a Keats-like revel of body and soul of most heavenly creatures—limbs and raiment, thoughts and feelings all astir, one laugh of life and of colour; two blue-winged Cupids dancing as they drag the car, or dragging it rather by their dancing unconsciously; a nymph with dusky yellow dress, and bright brown hair

with a white rose in it, and fair, light limbs—a very au-
tumnal sunbeam, made mortal, dancing first of all; Flora
herself, a sweet throned intense personified gladness; another nymph stooping as she flies along to gather a (celandine?), but all so pure and yet so wildly glad, that one
might think the spring wind had turned a drift of loose
rose leaves into living creatures.

Note especially of the tree above, it has more white blossoms than leaves, and they are like hawthorn blossom exaggerated—much larger than real hawthorn—I think, compared with the figures, they would be about the size of a
wine-glass each flower, and the leaves smaller than flowers.
It is an ideal of spring blossom; compare that which I saw
at Vevay, apple-blossom against blue hills. The celandine
is almost white, best in shade, and may have been meant
for a daisy; if it ever were, it is very coarse and large,
and square petalled. I forgot that the figures which come
against the sunset in this picture increase its heat in a glorious way; they have red dresses, or fragments of dress,
their limbs are burning orange red—half sunshine, half
bronzed flesh; and just between the limbs and (under the
arm?) of one or two fragments of the most intense orange
dress complete sparks of fire, which bring the colour of
the sky down among them. As an example of increase of
warmth of colour by sympathy into one flash, it would be
difficult to match it.[54]

[54] From Ruskin's notebook of 1849, inserted by editors, LAP
469 f

15

LOWLANDS LANDSCAPE

So far as I can hear or read, this is an entirely new and wonderful state of things achieved by the Hollanders. The human being never got wholly quit of the terror of spiritual being before. Persian, Egyptian, Assyrian, Hindoo, Chinese, all kept some dim, appalling record of what they called "gods." Farthest savages had—and still have—their Great Spirit, or, in extremity, their feather-idols, large-eyed; but here in Holland we have at last got utterly done with it all. Our only idol glitters dimly, in tangible shape of a pint pot, and all the incense offered thereto, comes out of a small censer or bowl at the end of a pipe. "Of deities or virtues, angels, principalities, or powers in the name of our ditches, no more. Let us have cattle and market vegetables."

This is the first and essential character of the Holland landscape art. Its second is a worthier one; respect for rural life.

I should attach greater importance to this rural feeling, if there were any true humanity in it, or any feeling for beauty. But there is neither. No incidents of this lower life are painted for the sake of the incidents, but only for the effects of light. You will find that the best Dutch painters do not care about the people, but about the lustres on them. Paul Potter, their best herd and cattle painter, does not care even for sheep, but only for wool; regards not cows, but cowhide. He attains great dexterity in drawing tufts and locks, lingers in the little parallel ravines and furrows of fleece that open across sheep's backs as they turn; is unsurpassed in twisting a horn or pointing a nose; but he cannot paint eyes, nor perceive any condition of an animal's mind, except its desire of grazing. Cuyp can, indeed, paint sunlight, the best that Holland's sun can show; he is a man of large natural gift, and sees broadly, nay, even seriously; finds out—a wonderful thing for men to find out in those days—that there are reflections in water, and that boats require often to be painted upside down. A brewer by trade, he feels the quiet of a summer afternoon, and his work will make you marvellously drowsy. It is good for nothing else that I know of; strong; but unhelpful and unthoughtful. Nothing happens in his pictures, except some indifferent person's asking the way of somebody else, who, by his cast of countenance, seems not likely to know it. For farther entertainment perhaps a red cow and a white one; or puppies at play, not playfully; the man's heart not going even with the puppies. Essentially he sees nothing but the shine on the flaps of their ears.

Observe always, the fault lies not in the thing's being little, or the incident being slight. Titian could have put issues of life and death into the face of a man asking the way; nay, into the back of him, if he had so chosen. Into the causes of which grandeur we must look a little, with respect not only to these puppies, and gray horses, and cattle of Cuyp, but to the hunting pieces of Rubens and Snyders. For closely connected with the Dutch rejection of motives of spiritual interest, is the increasing importance attached by them to animals, seen either in the chase or in agriculture . . .[55]

I am not qualified to judge of the merit of the equestrian statues; but, in painting, I find that no real interest is taken in the horse until Vandyck's time, he and Rubens doing more for it than all previous painters put together. Rubens was a good rider, and rode nearly every day, as I doubt not, Vandyck also. The horse has never, I think, been painted worthily again, since [Vandyck] died.

Lastly, of cattle. The period when the interest of men began to be transferred from the ploughman to his oxen is very distinctly marked by Bassano. In him the descent is

[55] MP V, 331–34, omit.

even greater, being, accurately, from the Madonna to the Manger—one of perhaps his best pictures representing an adoration of shepherds with nothing to adore, they and their herds forming the subject, and the Christ "being supposed" at the side. From that time cattle-pieces become frequent, and gradually form a staple art commodity. Cuyp's are the best; nevertheless, neither by him nor any one else have I ever seen an entirely well-painted cow. All the men who have skill enough to paint cattle nobly, disdain them. The real influence of these Dutch cattle-pieces, in subsequent art, is difficult to trace, and is not worth tracing. They contain a certain healthy appreciation of simple pleasure which I cannot look upon wholly without respect. On the other hand, their cheap tricks of composition degraded the entire technical system of landscape; and their clownish and blunt vulgarities too long blinded us, and continue, so far as in them lies, to blind us yet, to all the true refinement and passion of rural life.[56]

[56] MP V, 340–42, omit.

16

RUBENS

No phenomenon in human mind is more extraordinary than the junction of this cold and worldly temper with great rectitude of principle, and tranquil kindness of heart. Rubens was an honourable and entirely well-intentioned man, earnestly industrious, simple and temperate in habits of life, high-bred, learned and discreet. His affection for his mother was great; his generosity to contemporary artists unfailing. He is a healthy, worthy, kind-hearted, courtly-phrased—Animal—without any clearly perceptible traces of a soul, except when he paints his children. Few descriptions of pictures could be more ludicrous in their pure animalism than those which he gives of his own. "It is a subject," he writes to Sir D. Carleton, "neither sacred nor profane, although taken from Holy Writ, namely, Sarah in the act of scolding Hagar, who, pregnant, is leaving the house in a feminine and graceful manner, assisted by the Patriarch Abram." (What a graceful apology, by the way, instantly follows, for not having finished the picture himself.) "I have engaged, as is my custom, a very skilful man in his pursuit to finish the landscapes, solely to augment the enjoyment of Y. E.!"

Observe, however, Rubens is always entirely honourable in his statements of what is done by himself and what not. He is religious too, after his manner; hears mass every morning, and perpetually uses the phrase "by the grace of God," or some other such, in writing of any business he takes in hand; but the tone of his religion may be determined by one fact.

We saw how Veronese painted himself, and his family, as worshipping the Madonna. Rubens has also painted him-

self and his family in an equally elaborate piece. But they
are not *worshipping* the Madonna. They are *performing*
the Madonna, and her saintly entourage. His favourite wife
"en Madonne"; his youngest boy "as Christ"; his father-
in-law (or father, it matters not which) "as Simeon"; another elderly relation, with a beard, "as St. Jerome"; and
he himself "as St. George."

Rembrandt has also painted (it is, on the whole, his
greatest picture, so far as I have seen) himself and his
wife in a state of ideal happiness. He sits at supper with
his wife on his knee, flourishing a glass of champagne,
with a roast peacock on the table.

The Rubens is in the Church of St. James at Antwerp;
the Rembrandt at Dresden—marvellous pictures, both. No
more precious works by either painter exist. Their hearts,
such as they have, are entirely in them; and the two pictures, not inaptly, represent the Faith and Hope of the
seventeenth century. We have to stoop somewhat lower,
in order to comprehend the pastoral and rustic scenery of
Cuyp and Teniers, which must yet be held as forming one
group with the historical art of Rubens, being connected
with it by Rubens' pastoral landscape. To these, I say, we
must stoop lower; for they are destitute, not of spiritual
character only, but of spiritual thought.

Rubens often gives instructive and magnificent allegory;
Rembrandt, pathetic or powerful fancies, founded on real
scripture reading, and on his interest in the picturesque
character of the Jew. And Vandyck, a graceful dramatic
rendering of received scriptural legends.[57]

But I perceive a tendency among some of the more
thoughtful critics of the day to forget that the business of
a painter is *to paint*, and so altogether to despise those
men, Veronese and Rubens for instance, who were painters,
par excellence, and in whom the expressional qualities are
subordinate. Now it is well, when we have strong moral
or poetical feeling manifested in painting, to mark this as
the best part of the work; but it is not well to consider as
a thing of small account, the painter's language in which

[57] MP V, 329–31, omit.

that feeling is conveyed; for if that language be not good and lovely, the man may indeed be a just moralist or a great poet, but he is not a *painter*, and it was wrong of him to paint. He had much better have put his morality into sermons, and his poetry into verse, than into a language of which he was not master. And this mastery of the language is that of which we should be cognisant by a glance of the eye; and if that be not found, it is wasted time to look farther; the man has mistaken his vocation, and his expression of himself will be cramped by his awkward efforts to do what he was not fit to do. On the other hand, if the man be a painter indeed, and have the gift of colours and lines, what is in him will come from his hand freely and faithfully; and the language itself is so difficult and so vast, that the mere possession of it argues the man is great, and that his works are worth reading. So that I have never yet seen the case in which this true artistical excellence, visible by the eye-glance, was not the index of some true expressional worth in the work. Neither have I ever seen a good expressional work without high artistical merit: and that this is ever denied is only owing to the narrow view which men are apt to take both of expression and of art; a narrowness consequent on their own especial practice and habits of thought. A man long trained to love the monk's visions of Fra Angelico, turns in proud and ineffable disgust from the first work of Rubens which he encounters on his return across the Alps. But is he right in his indignation? He has forgotten, that while Angelico prayed and wept in his olive shade, there was different work doing in the dank fields of Flanders;—wild seas to be banked out; endless canals to be dug, and boundless marshes to be drained; hard ploughing and harrowing of the frosty clay; careful breeding of stout horses and fat cattle; close setting of brick walls against cold winds and snow; much hardening of hands and gross stoutening of bodies in all this; gross jovialities of harvest homes and Christmas feasts which were to be the reward of it; rough affections, and sluggish imaginations; fleshy, substantial, iron-shod humanities, but humanities still; humanities which God had His eye upon, and which won,

perhaps, here and there, as much favour in His sight as
the wasted aspects of the whispering monks of Florence
(Heaven forbid it should not be so, since the most of us
cannot be monks, but must be ploughmen and reapers
still). And are we to suppose there is no nobility in Rubens'
masculine and universal sympathy with all this, and with
his large human rendering of it, Gentleman though he was,
by birth, and feeling, and education, and place; and, when
he chose, lordly in conception also? He had his faults, perhaps great and lamentable faults, though more those of
his time and his country than his own; he has neither
cloister breeding nor boudoir breeding, and is very unfit
to paint either in missals or annuals; but he has an open
sky and wide-world breeding in him, that we may not be
offended with, fit alike for king's court, knight's camp, or
peasant's cottage.[58]

Well, . . . Rubens is not *par excellence* a colourist; nay,
is not even a good colourist. He is a very second-rate and
coarse colourist; and therefore his colour catches the lower
public, and gets talked about. But he is *par excellence* a
splendid draughtsman of the Greek school . . . Farther,
that he never became a great colourist does not mean that
he could not, had he chosen. He was warped from colour
by his lower Greek instincts, by his animal delight in coarse
and violent forms and scenes—in fighting, in hunting, and
in torments of martyrdom and of hell: but he had the
higher gift in him, if the flesh had not subdued it. There
is one part of this picture ["Juno and Argus," then Earl
of Dudley] which he learned how to do at Venice, the
Iris, with the golden hair, in the chariot behind Juno. In
her he has put out his full power, under the teaching of
Veronese and Titian; and he has all the splendid Northern-
Gothic, Reynolds or Gainsborough play of feature with
Venetian colour. Scarcely anything more beautiful than
that head, or more masterly than the composition of it,
with the inlaid pattern of Juno's robe below, exists in the
art of any country. *Si sic omnia!*—but I know nothing else
equal to it throughout the entire works of Rubens.

[58] SV I, 448 f

See, then, how the picture divides itself. In the fleshly baseness, brutality and stupidity of its main conception, is the Dutch part of it; that is Rubens' own. In the noble drawing of the dead body and of the birds you have the Phidias-Greek part of it, brought down to Rubens through Michael Angelo. In the embroidery of Juno's robe you have the Dædalus-Greek part of it, brought down to Rubens through Veronese. In the head of Iris you have the pure Northern-Gothic part of it, brought down to Rubens through Giorgione and Titian.[59]

[59] Land 42 f

17

REYNOLDS

What mental qualities, especially English, you find in
the painted heroes and beauties of Reynolds and Gainsborough, I can only discuss with you hereafter. But what
external and corporeal qualities these masters of our masters love to paint, I must ask you to-day to consider for a
few moments, under Mr. Carlyle's guidance, as well as
mine, and with the analysis of *Sartor Resartus*. Take, as
types of the best work ever laid on British canvas,—types
which I am sure you will without demur accept,—Sir
Joshua's Age of Innocence, and Mrs. Pelham feeding chickens; Gainsborough's Mrs. Graham, divinely doing nothing,
and Blue Boy similarly occupied; and, finally, Reynolds'
Lord Heathfield[60] magnanimously and irrevocably lock-
ing up Gibraltar. Suppose, now, under the instigation of
Mr. Carlyle and *Sartor*, and under the counsel of Zeuxis
and Parrhasius, we had it really in our power to bid Sir
Joshua and Gainsborough paint all these over again, in
the classic manner. Would you really insist on having her
white frock taken off the Age of Innocence; on the Blue
Boy's divesting himself of his blue; on—we may not dream
of anything more classic—Mrs. Graham's taking the feathers out of her hat; and on Lord Heathfield's parting,—I
dare not suggest, with his regimentals, but his orders of
the Bath, or what else?

I own that I cannot, even myself, as I propose the alter-
natives, answer absolutely as a Goth, nor without some

[60] (The five paintings mentioned are, respectively, National
Gallery, London; Earl of Radnor; National Gallery, Scotland;
Huntington Collection, and National Gallery, London.) ArtEng
311 f

wistful leanings towards classic principle. Nevertheless, I feel confident in your general admission that the charm of all these pictures is in great degree dependent on toilette; that the fond and graceful flatteries of each master do in no small measure consist in his management of frillings and trimmings, cuffs and collarettes; and on beautiful fling-ings or fastenings of investiture, which can only here and there be called a *drapery*, but insists on the perfectness of the forms it conceals, and deepens their harmony by its contradiction. And although now and then, when great ladies wish to be painted as sibyls or goddesses, Sir Joshua does his best to bethink himself of Michael Angelo, and Guido, and the Lightnings, and the Auroras, and all the rest of it,—you will, I think, admit that the culminating sweetness and rightness of him are in some little Lady So-and-so, with round hat and strong shoes; and that a final separation from the Greek art which can be proud in a torso without a head, is achieved by the master who paints for you five little girls' heads, without ever a torso! ["Heads of Angels," National Gallery, London][61]

If you truly want to know what good work of painter's hand is, study those two pictures ["The Holy Family" and "The Graces," both National Gallery, London] from side to side, and miss no inch of them (you will hardly, eventu-ally, be inclined to miss one): in some respects there is no execution like it; none so open in the magic. For the work of other great men is hidden in its wonderfulness—you can-not see how it was done. But in Sir Joshua's there is no mystery: it is all amazement. No question but that the touch was so laid; only that it *could* have been so laid, is a marvel for ever. So also there is no painting so majes-tic in sweetness. He is lily-sceptred: his power blossoms, but burdens not. All other men of equal dignity paint more slowly; all others of equal force paint less lightly. Tintoret lays his line like a king marking the boundaries of con-quered lands; but Sir Joshua leaves it as a summer wind its trace on a lake; he could have painted on a silken veil, where it fell free, and not bent it.

[61] ArtEng 312

Such at least is his touch when it is life that he paints: for things lifeless he has a severer hand. If you examine that picture of the *Graces* you will find it reverses all the ordinary ideas of expedient treatment. By other men flesh is firmly painted, but accessories lightly. Sir Joshua paints accessories firmly, flesh lightly;—nay, flesh not at all, but spirit. The wreath of flowers he feels to be material; and gleam by gleam strikes fearlessly the silver and violet leaves out of the darkness. But the three maidens are less substantial than rose petals. No flushed nor frosted tissue that ever faded in night wind is so tender as they; no hue may reach, no line measure, what is in them so gracious and so fair. Let the hand move softly—itself as a spirit; for this is Life, of which it touches the imagery.

Why did not Sir Joshua—or could not—or would not Sir Joshua—paint Madonnas? neither he, nor his great rival-friend Gainsborough? Both of them painters of women, such as since Giorgione and Correggio had not been; both painters of men, such as had not been since Titian. How is it that these English friends can so brightly paint that particular order of humanity which we call "gentlemen and ladies," but neither heroes, nor saints, nor angels?[62]

[T]he two great—the two only painters of their age—happy in a reputation founded as deeply in the heart as in the judgment of mankind, demanded no higher function than that of soothing the domestic affections; and achieved for themselves at last an immortality not the less noble, because in their lifetime they had concerned themselves less to claim it than to bestow.

Yet, while we acknowledge the discretion and simpleheartedness of these men, honouring them for both: and the more when we compare their tranquil powers with the hot egotism and hollow ambition of their inferiors: we have to remember, on the other hand, that the measure they thus set to their aims was, if a just, yet a narrow one; that amiable discretion is not the highest virtue, nor to please the frivolous, the best success. There is probably some strange weakness in the painter, and some fatal error in the

[62] ReyHolb 3–5, omit.

age, when in thinking over the examples of their greatest
work, for some type of culminating loveliness or veracity,
we remember no expression either of religion or heroism,
and instead of reverently naming a Madonna di San Sisto,
can only whisper, modestly, "Mrs. Pelham feeding chickens."

The nature of the fault, so far as it exists in the painters
themselves, may perhaps best be discerned by comparing
them with a man who went not far beyond them in his
general range of effort, but who did all his work in a wholly
different temper—Hans Holbein.

Reynolds and Holbein

The first great difference between them is of course in
completeness of execution. Sir Joshua's and Gainsborough's
work, at its best, is only magnificent sketching; giving indeed, in places, a perfection of result unattainable by other
methods, and possessing always a charm of grace and
power exclusively its own; yet, in its slightness addressing
itself, purposefully, to the casual glance, and common
thought—eager to arrest the passer-by, but careless to de-
tain him; or detaining him, if at all, by an unexplained
enchantment, not by continuance of teaching, or development of idea. But the work of Holbein is true and thorough; accomplished, in the highest as the most literal sense,
with a calm entireness of unaffected resolution, which sacrifices nothing, forgets nothing, and fears nothing.

In the portrait of the Hausmann George Gyzen [Kaiser-
Friedrich, Berlin], every accessory is perfect with a fine
perfection: the carnations in the glass vase by his side—
the ball of gold, chased with blue enamel, suspended on
the wall—the books—the steelyard—the papers on the table,
the seal-ring, with its quartered bearings,—all intensely
there, and there in beauty of which no one could have
dreamed that even flowers or gold were capable, far less
parchment or steel. But every change of shade is felt, every
rich and rubied line of petal followed; every subdued gleam
in the soft blue of the enamel and bending of the gold
touched with a hand whose patience of regard creates

rather than paints. The jewel itself was not so precious as the rays of enduring light which form it, and flash from it, beneath that errorless hand. The man himself, what he was—not more; but to all conceivable proof of sight—in all aspect of life or thought—not less. He sits alone in his accustomed room, his common work laid out before him; he is conscious of no presence, assumes no dignity, bears no sudden or superficial look of care or interest, lives only as he lived—but for ever.

The time occupied in painting this portrait was probably twenty times greater than Sir Joshua ever spent on a single picture, however large. The result is, to the general spectator, less attractive. In some qualities of force and grace it is absolutely inferior. But it is inexhaustible. Every detail of it wins, retains, rewards the attention with a continually increasing sense of wonderfulness. It is also wholly true. So far as it reaches, it contains the absolute facts of colour, form, and character, rendered with an unaccusable faithfulness. There is no question respecting things which it is best worth while to know, or things which it is unnecessary to state, or which might be overlooked with advantage. What of this man and his house were visible to Holbein, are visible to us: we may despise if we will; deny or doubt, we shall not; if we care to know anything concerning them, great or small, so much as may by the eye be known is for ever knowable, reliable, indisputable.

Respecting the advantage, or the contrary, of so great earnestness in drawing a portrait of an uncelebrated person, we raise at present no debate: I only wish the reader to note this quality of earnestness, as entirely separating Holbein from Sir Joshua,—raising him into another sphere of intellect. For here is no question of mere difference in style or in power, none of minuteness or largeness. It is a question of Entireness. Holbein is *complete* in intellect: what he sees, he sees with his whole soul: what he paints, he paints with his whole might. Sir Joshua sees partially, slightly, tenderly—catches the flying lights of things, the momentary glooms: paints also partially, tenderly, never with half his strength; content with uncertain visions, insecure delights; the truth not precious nor significant to him, only pleasing; falsehood also pleasurable, even useful on occasion—must, however, be discreetly touched, just enough to make all men noble, all women lovely: "we do not need this flattery often, most of those we know being such; and it is a pleasant world, and with diligence—for nothing can be done without diligence—every day till four" (says Sir Joshua)—"a painter's is a happy life."[63]

[63] ReyHolb 9–12, omit.

18

BEWICK, AND CONSTABLE

The execution of the plumage in Bewick's birds is the most masterly thing ever yet done in woodcutting; it is worked just as Paul Veronese would have worked in wood, had he taken to it. His vignettes, though too coarse in execution, and vulgar in types of form, to be good copies, show, nevertheless, intellectual power of the highest order; and there are pieces of sentiment in them, either pathetic or satirical, which have never since been equalled in illustrations of this simple kind; the bitter intensity of the feeling being just like that which characterises some of the leading Pre-Raphaelites. Bewick is the Burns of painting.[64]

For example, here is a little tailpiece of Bewick's [from *Aesop's Fables*], to the fable of the Frogs and the Stork. He is, as I told you, as stout a reformer as Holbein, or Botticelli, or Luther, or Savonarola; and, as an impartial reformer, hits right and left, at lower or upper classes, if he sees them wrong. Most frequently, he strikes at vice, without reference to class; but in this vignette he strikes definitely at the degradation of the viler popular mind which is incapable of being governed, because it cannot understand the nobleness of kingship. He has written—better than written, engraved, sure to suffer no slip of type —his legend under the drawing; so that we know his meaning:

"Set them up with a king, indeed!"

There is an audience of seven frogs, listening to a speaker, or croaker, in the middle; and Bewick has set himself to show in all, but especially in the speaker, essential frogginess of mind—the marsh temper. He could not

[64] ED 223

have done it half so well in painting as he has done by
the abstraction of wood-outline. The characteristic of a
manly mind, or body, is to be gentle in temper, and firm
in constitution; the contrary essence of a froggy mind and
body is to be angular in temper, and flabby in constitution.
I have enlarged Bewick's orator-frog for you, and I think
you will feel that he is entirely expressed in those essential
particulars.

This being perfectly good wood-cutting, notice especially its deliberation. No scrawling or scratching, or cross-
hatching, or *"free"* work of any sort. Most deliberate laying
down of solid lines and dots, of which you cannot change
one. The real difficulty of wood engraving is to cut every
one of these black lines or spaces of the exactly right shape,
and not at all to cross-hatch them cleanly.

Next, examine the technical treatment of the pig, above.
I have purposely chosen this as an example of a white
object on dark ground, and the frog as a dark object on
light ground, to explain to you what I mean by saying
that fine engraving regards local colour, but not light and
shade. You see both frog and pig are absolutely without
light and shade. The frog, indeed, casts a shadow; but his
hind leg is as white as his throat. In the pig you don't
even know which way the light falls. But you know at once
that the pig is white, and the frog brown or green.

There are, however, two pieces of chiaroscuro *implied*
in the treatment of the pig. It is assumed that his curly
tail would be light against the background—dark against
his own rump. This little piece of heraldic quartering is
absolutely necessary to solidify him. He would have been
a white ghost of a pig, flat on the background, but for that
alternative tail, and the bits of dark behind the ears. Secondly: Where the shade is necessary to suggest the position of his ribs, it is given with graphic and chosen points
of dark, as few as possible; not for the sake of the shade
at all, but of the skin and bone.

That, then, being the law of refused chiaroscuro, observe further the method of outline. We said that we were
to have thick lines in wood, if possible. Look what thick-

ness of black outline Bewick has left under our pig's chin, and above his nose.

But that is not a line at all, you think?

No;—a modern engraver would have made it one, and prided himself on getting it fine. Bewick leaves it actually thicker than the snout, but puts all his ingenuity of touch to vary the forms, and break the extremities of his white cuts, so that the eye may be refreshed and relieved by new forms at every turn. The group of white touches filling the space between snout and ears might be a wreath of fine-weather clouds, so studiously are they grouped and broken. And nowhere, you see, does a single black line cross another.[65]

Constable

I have already alluded to the simplicity and earnestness of the mind of Constable; to its vigorous rupture with school laws, and to its unfortunate error on the opposite side. Unteachableness seems to have been a main feature of his character, and there is corresponding want of veneration in the way he approaches nature herself. His early education and associations were also against him; they induced in him a morbid preference of subjects of a low order. I have never seen any work of his in which there were any signs of his being able to draw, and hence even the most necessary details are painted by him inefficiently. His works are also eminently wanting both in rest and refinement: and Fuseli's jesting compliment ["I am going to see Constable; bring me mine ombrella."] is too true; for the showery weather, in which the artist delights, misses alike the majesty of storm and the loveliness of calm weather; it is great-coat weather, and nothing more. There is strange want of depth in the mind which has no pleasure in sunbeams but when piercing painfully through clouds, nor in foliage but when shaken by the wind, nor in light itself but when flickering, glistening, restless and feeble. Yet, with all these deductions, his works are to be deeply

[65] AFlor 364–66

respected, as thoroughly original, thoroughly honest, free from affectation, manly in manner, frequently successful in cool colour, and realizing certain motives of English scenery with perhaps as much affection as such scenery, unless when regarded through media of feeling derived from higher sources, is calculated to inspire.[66]

[66] MP I, 191

19

TURNER

Before 1820

Towards the close of the last century, among the various drawings executed, according to the quiet manner of the time, in greyish blue, with brown foregrounds, some began to be noticed as exhibiting rather more than ordinary diligence and delicacy, signed W. Turner.[67] There was nothing, however, in them at all indicative of genius, or even of more than ordinary talent, unless in some of the subjects a large perception of space, and excessive clearness and decision in the arrangement of masses. Gradually and cautiously the blues became mingled with delicate green, and then with gold; the browns in the foreground became first more positive, and then were slightly mingled with other local colours; while the touch, which had at first been heavy and broken, like that of the ordinary drawing masters of the time, grew more and more refined and expressive, until it lost itself in a method of execution often too delicate for the eye to follow, rendering, with a precision before unexampled, both the texture and the form of every object. The style may be considered as perfectly formed about the year 1800, and it remained unchanged for twenty years.

During that period the painter had attempted, and with more or less success had rendered, every order of landscape subject, but always on the same principle, subduing the colours of nature into a harmony of which the keynotes are greyish green and brown; pure blues, and delicate golden yellows being admitted in small quantity as the lowest and highest limits of shade and light: and bright

[67] (Ruskin note: "He did not use his full signature, 'J.M.W.,' until about the year 1800.") PRB 365

PAINTING

local colours in extremely small quantity in figures or other minor accessories.

Pictures executed on such a system are not, properly speaking, works in *colour* at all; they are studies of light and shade, in which both the shade and the distance are rendered in the general hue which best expresses their attributes of coolness and transparency; and the lights and the foreground are executed in that which best expresses their warmth and solidity.

A stone in the foreground might in nature have been cold grey, but it will be drawn nevertheless of a rich brown, because it is in the foreground; a hill in the distance might in nature be purple with heath, or golden with furze; but it will be drawn, nevertheless, of a cool grey, because it is in the distance.

This at least was the general theory,—carried out with great severity in many, both of the drawings and pictures executed by him during the period: in others more or less modified by the cautious introduction of colour, as the painter felt his liberty increasing; for the system was evidently never considered as final, or as anything more than a means of progress: the conventional, easily manageable colour, was visibly adopted, only that his mind might be at perfect liberty to address itself to the acquirement of the first and most necessary knowledge in all art—that of form. But as form, in landscape, implies vast bulk and space, the use of the tints which enabled him best to express them, was actually auxiliary to the mere drawing; and, therefore, not only permissible, but even necessary, while more brilliant or varied tints were never indulged in, except when they might be introduced without the slightest danger of diverting his mind for an instant from his principal object. And, therefore, it will be generally found in the works of this period, that exactly in proportion to the importance and general toil of the composition, is the severity of the tint; and that the play of colour begins to show itself first in slight and small drawings, where he felt that he could easily secure all that he wanted in form.

The system of his colour being thus simplified, he could address all the strength of his mind to the accumulation

of facts of form; his choice of subject, and his methods
of treatment, are therefore as various as his colour is simple; and it is not a little difficult to give the reader who is
unacquainted with his works, an idea either of their infinitude of aims, on the one hand, or of the kind of feeling
which pervades them all, on the other. No subject was too
low or too high for him; we find him one day hard at work
on a cock and hen, with their family of chickens in a farm-
yard; and bringing all the refinement of his execution into
play to express the texture of the plumage; next day he is
drawing the Dragon of Colchis. One hour he is much interested in a gust of wind blowing away an old woman's
cap; the next, he is painting the fifth plague of Egypt.
Every landscape painter before him had acquired distinction by confining his efforts to one class of subject. Hobbima painted oaks; Ruysdael, waterfalls and copses; Cuyp,
river or meadow scenes in quiet afternoons; Salvator and
Poussin, such kind of mountain scenery as people could
conceive, who lived in towns in the seventeenth century.
But I am well persuaded that if all the works of Turner,
up to the year 1820, were divided into classes (as he has
himself divided them in the *Liber Studiorum*), no pre-
ponderance could be assigned to one class over another.[68]

The two Carthages[69] are mere rationalizations of
Claude; one of them excessively bad in colour, the other a
grand thought, and yet one of the kind which does no one
any good, because everything in it is reciprocally sacrificed; the foliage is sacrificed to the architecture, the architecture to the water, the water is neither sea, nor river, nor
lake, nor brook, nor canal, and savours of Regent's Park;
the foreground is uncomfortable ground—let on building
leases.[70]

[68] PRB 365–69, omit.
[69] ("Dido building Carthage," 1815, National Gallery, and
the "Decline of Carthage," 1817, Tate Gallery.) MP I, 241
[70] MP I, 241

After 1820

Had Turner died early, the reputation he would have left, though great and enduring, would have been strangely different from that which ultimately must now attach to his name. He would have been remembered as one of the severest of painters; his iron touch and positive forms would have been continually opposed to the delicacy of Claude and richness of Titian; he would have been spoken of, popularly, as a man who had no eye for colour. Perhaps here and there a watchful critic might have shown this popular idea to be false; but no conception could have been formed by any one of the man's real disposition or capacity.

It was only after the year 1820 that these were determinable, and his peculiar work discerned.

He had begun by faithful declaration of the sorrow there was in the world. It is now permitted him to see also its beauty. He becomes, separately and without rival, the painter of the loveliness and light of the creation.

Of its loveliness: that which may be beloved in it, the tenderest, kindest, most feminine of its aspects. Of its light: light not merely diffused, but interpreted; light seen preeminently in colour.

Claude and Cuyp had painted the sun*shine*, Turner alone, the sun *colour*.

Observe this accurately. Those easily understood effects of afternoon light, gracious and sweet so far as they reach, are produced by the softly warm or yellow rays of the sun falling through mist. They are low in tone, even in nature, and disguise the colours of objects. They are imitable even by persons who have little or no gift of colour, if the tones of the picture are kept low and in true harmony, and the reflected lights warm. But they never could be painted by great colourists. The fact of blue and crimson being effaced by yellow and gray, puts such effect at once out of the notice or thought of a colourist, unless he has some special interest in the motive of it. You might as well ask a musician to compose with only three notes, as Titian to paint without crimson and blue. Accordingly the colourists in general, feeling that no other than this yellow sunshine was imitable, refused it, and painted in twilight, when the colour was full. Therefore, from the imperfect colourists,—from Cuyp, Claude, Both, Wilson, we get deceptive effect of sunshine; never from the Venetians, from Rubens, Reynolds, or Velasquez. From these we get only conventional substitutions for it, Rubens being especially daring in frankness of symbol.[71]

Turner's sense of beauty was perfect; deeper, therefore, far than Byron's; only that of Keats and Tennyson being comparable with it. And Turner's love of truth was as stern and patient as Dante's; so that when over these great capacities come the shadows of despair, the wreck is infinitely sterner and more sorrowful. With no sweet home for his childhood—friendless in youth, loveless in manhood, —and hopeless in death, Turner was what Dante might have been, without the "bello ovile," without Casella, without Beatrice, and without Him who gave them all, and took them all away.

I will trace this state of his mind farther, in a little while. Meantime, I want you to note only the result upon his work;—how, through all the remainder of his life, wherever he looked, he saw ruin.

Ruin, and twilight. What was the distinctive effect of light which he introduced, such as no man had painted before? Brightness, indeed, he gave, as we have seen, because it was true and right; but in this he only perfected what others had attempted. His own favourite light is not Æglé, but Hesperid Æglé. Fading of the last rays of sunset. Faint breathing of the sorrow of night.

And fading of sunset, note also, on ruin. I cannot but wonder that this difference between Turner's work and previous art-conception has not been more observed. None of the great early painters draw ruins, except compulsorily. The shattered buildings introduced by them are shattered artificially, like models. There is no real sense of decay; whereas Turner only momentarily dwells on anything else

[71] MP V, 409–11

than ruin. Take up the Liber Studiorum, and observe how this feeling of decay and humiliation gives solemnity to all its simplest subjects; even to his view of daily labour. There is no exultation in thriving city, or mart, or in happy rural toil, or harvest gathering. Only the grinding at the mill, and patient striving with hard conditions of life. Observe the two disordered and poor farm-yards, cart, and ploughshare, and harrow rotting away: note the pastoral by the brook side, with its neglected stream and haggard trees, and bridge with the broken rail, and decrepit children—fever-struck—one sitting stupidly by the stagnant stream, the other in rags, and with an old man's hat on, and lame, leaning on a stick. Then the "Hedging and Ditching," with its bleak sky and blighted trees—hacked, and bitten, and starved by the clay soil into something between trees and firewood; its meanly-faced, sickly labourers—pollard labourers, like the willow trunk they hew; and the slatternly peasant-woman, with worn cloak and battered bonnet—an English Dryad. Then the water-mill, beyond the fallen steps, overgrown with the thistle: itself a ruin, mud-built at first, now propped on both sides;—the planks torn from its cattle-shed; a feeble beam, splintered at the end, set against the dwelling-house from the ruined pier of the water-course; the old mill-stone—useless for many a day—half-buried in slime, at the bottom of the wall; the listless children, listless dog, and the poor gleaner bringing her single sheaf to be ground.[72]

Colour

He saw also that the finish and specific grandeur of nature had been given, but her fulness, space, and mystery never; and he saw that the great landscape painters had always sunk the lower middle tints of nature in extreme shade, bringing the entire melody of colour as many degrees down as their possible light was inferior to nature's; and that in so doing a gloomy principle had influenced them even in their choice of subject.

[72] MP V, 431–33, omit.

For the conventional colour he substituted a pure straight-forward rendering of fact, as far as was in his power; and that not of such fact as had been before even suggested, but of all that is *most* brilliant, beautiful, and inimitable; he went to the cataract for its iris, to the conflagration for its flames, asked of the sea its intensest azure, of the sky its clearest gold. For the limited space and defined forms of elder landscape he substituted the quantity and the mystery of the vastest scenes of earth; and for the subdued chiaroscuro he substituted first a balanced diminution of opposition throughout the scale, and afterwards, in one or two instances, attempted the reverse of the old principle, taking the lowest portion of the scale truly, and merging the upper part in high light.

To obtain perfectly satisfactory results in colour under the new conditions introduced by Turner would at least have required the exertion of all his energies in that sole direction. But colour has always been only his second object. The effects of space and form, in which he delights, often require the employment of means and method totally at variance with those necessary for the obtaining of pure colour. It is physically impossible, for instance, rightly to draw certain forms of the upper clouds with the brush; nothing will do it but the pallet knife with loaded white after the blue ground is prepared. Now it is impossible that a cloud so drawn, however glazed afterwards, should have the virtue of a thin warm tint of Titian's, showing the canvas throughout. So it happens continually. Add to these difficulties, those of the peculiar subjects attempted, and to these again, all that belong to the altered system of chiaroscuro, and it is evident that we must not be surprised at finding many deficiencies or faults in such works, especially in the earlier of them, nor even suffer ourselves to be withdrawn by the pursuit of what seems censurable from our devotion to what is mighty.

Notwithstanding, in some chosen examples of pictures of this kind (I will name three: Juliet and her Nurse; the Old Téméraire; and the Slave Ship).[73] I do not admit

[73] (Respectively H. P. Whitney, National Gallery, London, and Museum of Fine Arts, Boston.) MP I, 246 f, omit.

that there are at the time of their first appearing on the walls of the Royal Academy, any demonstrably avoidable faults; I do not deny that there may be, nay, that it is likely there are: but there is no living artist in Europe whose judgment might safely be taken on the subject, or who could without arrogance affirm of any part of such a picture, that it was *wrong*. I am perfectly willing to allow, that the lemon yellow is not properly representative of the yellow of the sky, that the loading of the colour is in many places disagreeable, that many of the details are drawn with a kind of imperfection different from what they would have in nature, and that many of the parts fail of imitation, especially to an uneducated eye. But no living authority is of weight enough to prove that the virtues of the picture could have been obtained at a less sacrifice, or that they are not worth the sacrifice . . .[74]

The reader will have observed that I strictly limited the perfection of Turner's works to the time of their first appearing on the walls of the Royal Academy. It bitterly grieves me to have to do this, but the fact is indeed so. No *picture* of Turner's is seen in perfection a month after it is painted. The Walhalla cracked before it had been eight days in the Academy rooms; the vermilions frequently lose lustre long before the Exhibition is over; and when all the colours begin to get hard a year or two after the picture is painted, a painful deadness and opacity come over them, the whites especially becoming lifeless, and many of the warmer passages settling into a hard valueless brown, even if the paint remains perfectly firm, which is far from being always the case. I believe that in some measure these results are unavoidable, the colours being so peculiarly blended and mingled in Turner's present manner, as almost to necessitate their irregular drying; but that they are not necessary to the extent in which they sometimes take place, is proved by the comparative safety of some even of the more brilliant works. Thus the Old Téméraire is nearly safe in colour, and quite firm; while the Juliet and her Nurse is now the ghost of what it was; the Slaver shows no cracks,

[74] MP I, 247 f

though it is chilled in some of the darker passages, while the Walhalla and several of the recent Venices cracked in the Royal Academy. It is true that the damage makes no farther progress after the first year or two, and that even in its altered state the picture is always valuable and records its intention; but how are we enough to regret that so great a painter should not leave a single work by which in succeeding ages he might be entirely estimated? The fact of his using means so imperfect, together with that of his utter neglect of the pictures in his own gallery, are a phenomenon in human mind which appears to me utterly inexplicable; and both are without excuse. If the effects he desires cannot be to their full extent produced except by these treacherous means, one picture only should be painted each year as an exhibition of immediate power, and the rest should be carried out, whatever the expense of labour and time, in safe materials, even at the risk of some deterioration of immediate effect.[75]

Every picture of this great colourist has, in one or two parts of it (keynotes of the whole), points where the system of each individual colour is concentrated by a single stroke, as pure as it can come from the pallet; but throughout the great space and extent of even the most brilliant of his works, there will not be found a raw colour; that is to say, there is no warmth which has not grey in it, and no blue which has not warmth in it; and the tints in which he most excels and distances all other men, the most cherished and inimitable portions of his colour, are, as with all perfect colourists they must be, his greys.

Intimately associated with this toning down and connection of the colours actually used, is his inimitable power of varying and blending them, so as never to give a quarter of an inch of canvas without a change in it, a melody as well as a harmony of one kind or another. Observe, I am not at present speaking of this as artistical or desirable in itself, not as a characteristic of the great colourist, but as the aim of the simple follower of nature. For it is strange to see how marvellously nature varies the most general and

75 MP I, 249, Ruskin note

simple of her tones. Pick up a common flint from the roadside, and count, if you can, its changes and hues of colour.
Every bit of bare ground under your feet has in it a thousand such; the grey pebbles, the warm ochre, the green of
incipient vegetation, the greys and blacks of its reflexes
and shadows, might keep a painter at work for a month,
if he were obliged to follow them touch for touch: how
much more when the same infinity of change is carried
out with vastness of object and space. The extreme of distance may appear at first monotonous; but the least examination will show it to be full of every kind of change;
that its outlines are perpetually melting and appearing
again,—sharp here, vague there,—now lost altogether, now
just hinted and still confused among each other; and so
for ever in a state and necessity of change. Hence, wherever in a painting we have unvaried colour extended even
over a small space, there is falsehood.[76]

[I]t may be noted that Turner's colour is founded more
on Correggio and Bassano than on the central Venetians; it
involves a more tender and constant reference to light and
shade than that of Veronese; and a more sparkling and
gem-like lustre than that of Titian. I dislike using a technical word which has been disgraced by affectation, but there
is no other word to signify what I mean in saying that
Turner's colour has, to the full, Correggio's "morbidezza,"
including also, in due place, conditions of mosaic effect,
like that of the colours in an Indian design, unaccom-
plished by any previous master in painting; and a fantasy
of inventive arrangement corresponding to that of Beet-
hoven in music. In its concurrence with and expression of
texture or construction of surfaces (as their bloom lustre,
or intricacy) it stands unrivalled—no still-life painting by
any other master can stand for an instant beside Turner's,
when his work is of life-size, as in his numerous studies of
birds and their plumage. This "morbidezza" of colour is
associated, precisely as it was in Correggio, with an exquisite sensibility to fineness and intricacy of curvature:

[76] MP I, 292–95, omit.

curvature, as already noticed, . . . being to lines what gradation is to colours.[77]

Effects of light

Words are not accurate enough, nor delicate enough, to express or trace the constant, all-pervading influence of the finer and vaguer shadows throughout his works, that thrilling influence which gives to the light they leave its passion and its power. There is not a stone, not a leaf, not a cloud, over which light is not felt to be actually passing and palpitating before our eyes. There is the motion, the actual wave and radiation of the darted beam: not the dull universal daylight, which falls on the landscape without life, or direction, or speculation, equal on all things and dead on all things; but the breathing, animated, exulting light, which feels, and receives, and rejoices, and acts,— which chooses one thing, and rejects another,—which seeks, and finds, and loses again,—leaping from rock to rock, from leaf to leaf, from wave to wave—glowing, or flashing, or scintillating, according to what it strikes; or, in its holier moods, absorbing and enfolding all things in the deep fulness of its repose, and then again losing itself in bewilderment, and doubt, and dimness,—or perishing and passing away, entangled in drifting mist, or melted into melancholy air, but still,—kindling or declining, sparkling or serene,—it is the living light, which breathes in its deepest, most entranced rest, which sleeps, but never dies.[78]

The following list, of course, does not name the hundredth part of the effects of light given by Turner; it only names those which are distinctly and markedly separate from each other, and representative each of an entire class. Ten or twelve examples, often many more, might be given of each; every one of which would display the effects of the same hour and light, modified by different circumstances of weather, situation, and character of objects subjected to them, and especially by the management of the

[77] MP V, 416, Ruskin note
[78] MP I, 308

sky; but it will be generally sufficient for our purposes to examine thoroughly one good example of each.

The prefixed letters express the direction of the light. F. front light, the sun in the centre, or near the top of the picture; L. lateral light, the sun out of the picture, on the right or left of the spectator; L. F. the light partly lateral, partly fronting the spectator, as when he is looking south, with the sun in the south-west; L. B. light partly lateral, partly behind the spectator, as when he is looking north, with the sun in the south-west.

MORNING

EFFECTS	NAMES OF PICTURES
L. An hour before sunrise in winter. Violent storm, with rain, on the sea. Lighthouses seen through it.	Lowestoft, Suffolk.
F. An hour before sunrise. Serene sky, with light clouds. Dawn in the distance.	Vignette to Voyage of Columbus.
L. Ten minutes before sunrise. Violent storm. Torchlight.	Fowey Harbour.
F. Sunrise. Sun only half above the horizon. Clear sky with light cirri.	Vignette to Human Life.
F. Sun just disengaged from horizon. Misty, with light cirri.	Alps at Daybreak.
F. Sun a quarter of an hour risen. Sky covered with scarlet clouds.	Castle Upnor.
L.F. Serene sky. Sun emerging from a bank of cloud on horizon, a quarter of an hour risen.	Orford, Suffolk.
L.F. Same hour. Light mists in flakes on hill sides. Clear air.	Skiddaw.
L.F. Same hour. Light flying rain-clouds gathering in valleys.	Oakhampton.
L.B. Same hour. A night storm rising off the mountains. Dead calm.	Lake of Geneva.

L. Sun half an hour risen. Cloudless sky.	Beaugency.
L. Same hour. Light mists lying in the valleys.	Kirkby Lonsdale.
F. Same hour. Bright cirri. Sun dimly seen through battle smoke, with conflagration.	Hohenlinden.
L. Sun an hour risen, cloudless and clear.	Buckfastleigh . . .[79]

"Mystery"

Turner, and Turner only, would follow and render on the canvas that mystery of decided line, that distinct, sharp, visible, but unintelligible and inextricable richness, which, examined part by part, is to the eye nothing but confusion and defeat, which, taken as a whole, is all unity, symmetry, and truth.

Nor is this mode of representation true only with respect to distances. Every object, however near the eye, has something about it which you cannot see, and which brings the mystery of distance even into every part and portion of what we suppose ourselves to see most distinctly.

But if there be this mystery and inexhaustible finish merely in the more delicate instances of architectural decoration, how much more in the ceaseless and incomparable decoration of nature. The detail of a single weedy bank laughs the carving of ages to scorn. Every leaf and stalk has a design and tracery upon it; every knot of grass an intricacy of shade which the labour of years could never imitate, and which, if such labour could follow it out even to the last fibres of the leaflets, would yet be falsely represented, for, as in all other cases brought forward, it is not clearly seen, but confusedly and mysteriously. That which is nearness for the bank, is distance for its details; and however near it may be, the greater part of those details are still a beautiful incomprehensibility.

Hence, throughout the picture, the expression of space

[79] MP I, 420 f. In the original, the list of effects here begun continued on through the day.

and size is dependent upon obscurity, united with, or rather resultant from, exceeding fulness. We destroy both space and size, either by the vacancy which affords us no measure of space, or by the distinctness which gives us a false one. The distance of Poussin, having no indication of trees, nor of meadows, nor of character of any kind, may be fifty miles off, or may be five: we cannot tell; we have no measure, and in consequence, no vivid impression. But a middle distance of Hobbima's involves a contradiction in terms; it states a distance by perspective, which it contradicts by distinctness of detail.

A single dusty roll of Turner's brush is more truly expressive of the infinity of foliage, than the niggling of Hobbima could have rendered his canvas, if he had worked on it till doomsday.[80]

Drawing from nature

This example ["Lausanne, from the road to Fribourg," National Gallery, London] is entirely characteristic of his usual drawings from nature, which unite two characters, being *both* commemorative and determinant:—Commemorative, in so far as they note certain facts about the place: determinant, in that they record an impression received from the place there and then, together with the principal arrangement of the composition in which it was afterwards to be recorded. In this mode of sketching, Turner differs from all other men whose work I have studied. He never draws accurately on the spot, with the intention of modifying or composing afterwards from the materials; but instantly modifies as he draws, placing his memoranda where they are to be ultimately used, and taking exactly what he wants, not a fragment or line more.

This sketch has been made in the afternoon. He had been impressed, as he walked up the hill, by the vanishing of the lake in the golden horizon, without end of waters, and by the opposition of the pinnacled castle and cathedral to its level breadth. That must be drawn! and from this

[80] MP I, 336–39, omit.

spot, where all the buildings are set well together. But it lucklessly happens that, though the buildings come just where he wants them in situation, they don't in height. For the castle (the square mass on the right) is in reality higher than the cathedral, and would block out the end of the lake. Down it goes instantly a hundred feet, that we may see the lake over it; without the smallest regard for the military position of Lausanne.

Next: The last low spire on the left is in truth concealed behind the nearer bank, the town running far down the hill (and climbing another hill) in that direction. But the group of spires, without it, would not be rich enough to give a proper impression of Lausanne, as a spiry place. Turner quietly sends to fetch the church from round the corner, places it where he likes, and indicates its distance only by aerial perspective (much greater in the pencil drawing than in the woodcut).

But again: Not only the spire of the lower church, but the peak of the Rochers d'Enfer (that highest in the distance) would in reality be out of sight; it is much farther round to the left. This would never do either; for without it, we should have no idea that Lausanne was opposite the mountains, nor should we have a nice sloping line to lead us into the distance.

With the same unblushing tranquillity of mind in which he had ordered up the church, Turner sends also to fetch the Rochers d'Enfer; and puts *them* also where he chooses, to crown the slope of distant hill, which, as every traveller knows, in its decline to the west, is one of the most notable features of the view from Lausanne.

These modifications, easily traceable in the large features of the design, are carried out with equal audacity and precision in every part of it. Every one of those confused lines on the right indicates something that is really there, only everything is shifted and sorted into the exact places that Turner chose. The group of dark objects near us at the foot of the bank is a cluster of mills, which, when the picture was completed, were to be the blackest things in it, and to throw back the castle, and the golden horizon; while the rounded touches at the bottom, under the castle, indicate a row of trees, which follow a brook coming out of the ravine behind us; and were going to be made very round indeed in the picture (to oppose the spiky and angular masses of castle), and very consecutive, in order to form another conducting line into the distance.

These motives, or motives like them, might perhaps be guessed on looking at the sketch. But no one without going to the spot would understand the meaning of the vertical lines in the left-hand lowest corner.

They are a "memorandum" of the artificial verticalness of a low sandstone cliff, which has been cut down there to give space for a bit of garden belonging to a public-house beneath, from which garden a path leads along the ravine to the Lausanne rifle-ground. The value of these vertical lines in repeating those of the cathedral, is very great; it would be greater still in the completed picture, increasing the sense of looking down from a height, and giving grasp of, and power over, the whole scene.

Throughout the sketch, as in all that Turner made, the observing and combining intellect acts in the same manner. Not a line is lost, nor a moment of time; and though the pencil flies, and the whole thing is literally done as fast as a piece of shorthand writing, it is to the full as purposeful and compressed, so that while there are indeed dashes of the pencil which are unintentional, they are only unintentional as the form of a letter is, in fast writing, not from want of intention, but from the accident of haste.

I know not if the reader can understand,—I myself cannot, though I see it to be demonstrable,—the simultaneous occurrence of idea which produces such a drawing as this: the grasp of the whole, from the laying of the first line, which induces continual modifications of all that is done, out of respect to parts not done yet.[81]

I do not know whether any of you were interested enough in the little note in my catalogue on this view near Blair Athol[82] to look for the scene itself during your sum-

[81] MP V, 241–44
[82] (*Catalogue of Examples*, *Works*, vol. XXI, 88; "Blair Athol" and, next paragraph, "Dunblane" are both from the *Liber Studiorum*.) Land 35

mer rambles. If any did, and found it, I am nearly certain their impression would be only that of an extreme wonder how Turner could have made so little of so beautiful a spot. The projecting rock, when I saw it last in 1857, and I am certain, when Turner saw it, was covered with lichens having as many colours as a painted window. The stream —or rather, powerful and deep Highland river, the Tilt— foamed and eddied magnificently through the narrowed channel; and the wild vegetation in the rock crannies was a finished arabesque of living sculpture . . . Turner has absolutely stripped the rock of its beautiful lichens to bare slate, with one quartz vein running up through it; he has quieted the river into a commonplace stream; he has given, of all the rich vegetation, only one cluster of quite unin- teresting leaves and a clump of birches with ragged trunks. Yet, observe, I have told you of it, he has put into one scene the spirit of Scotland.

Similarly, those of you who in your long vacations have ever stayed near Dunblane will be, I think, disappointed in no small degree by this study of the abbey . . . [Y]ou find Turner representing the lancet window by a few bare oval lines like the hoop of a barrel; and indicating the rest of the structure by a monotonous and thin piece of out- line, of which I was asked by one of yourselves last term, and quite naturally and rightly, how Turner came to draw it so slightly—or, we may even say, so badly.

Dunblane Abbey is a pretty piece of building enough, it is true; but the virtue of the whole scene, and meaning, is not in the masonry of it. There is much better masonry and much more wonderful ruin of it elsewhere; Dunblane Abbey—tower and aisles and all—would go under one of the arches of buildings such as there are in the world.

Now, it is true, there are beautiful lichens at Blair Athol, and good building at Dunblane; but there are lovely lichens all over the cold regions of the world, and there is far more interesting architecture in other countries than in Scotland. The essential character of Scotland is that of a wild and thinly inhabited rocky country, not sublimely mountainous, but beautiful in low rock and light streamlet everywhere; with sweet copsewood and rudely growing

trees. This wild land possesses a subdued and imperfect
school of architecture, and has an infinitely tragic feudal,
pastoral, and civic history. And in the events of that history
a deep tenderness of sentiment is mingled with a cruel and
barren rigidity of habitual character, accurately corresponding to the conditions of climate and earth.

Now I want you especially to notice, with respect to
these things, Turner's introduction of the ugly square tower
high up on the left. Your first instinct would be to exclaim,
"How unlucky that was there at all! Why, at least, could
not Turner have kept it out of sight?" He has quite gratuitously brought it into sight; gratuitously drawn firmly the
three lines of stiff drip-stone which mark its squareness
and blankness. It is precisely that blank vacancy of decoration, and setting of the meagre angles against wind and
war, which he wants to force on your notice, that he may
take you thoroughly out of Italy and Greece, and put
you wholly into a barbarous and frost-hardened land; that
once having its gloom defined he may show you all the
more intensely what pastoral purity and innocence of
life, and loveliness of nature, are underneath the banks and
braes of Doune, and by every brooklet that feeds the Forth
and Clyde.[83]

"The Image of the Sea"

Of one thing I am certain; Turner never drew anything
that could be *seen*, without having seen it. That is to say,
though he would draw Jerusalem from some one else's
sketch, it would be, nevertheless, entirely from his own
experience of ruined walls: and though he would draw
ancient shipping (for an imitation of Vandevelde, or a vignette to the voyage of Columbus) from such data as he
could get about things which he could no more see with
his own eyes, yet when, of his own free will, in the subject
of Ilfracombe [*The Southern Coast*, No. 9] he, in the year
1818, introduces a shipwreck, I am perfectly certain that,
before the year 1818, he had *seen* a shipwreck, and, moreover, one of that horrible kind—a ship dashed to pieces in

[83] Land 35–38, omit.

deep water, at the foot of an inaccessible cliff. Having once seen this, I perceive, also, that the image of it could not be effaced from his mind. It taught him two great facts, which he never afterwards forgot; namely, that both ships and sea were things that broke to pieces. *He never afterwards painted a ship quite in fair order.* There is invariably a feeling about his vessels of strange awe and danger; the sails are in some way loosening, or flapping as if in fear; the swing of the hull, majestic as it may be, seems more at the mercy of the sea than in triumph over it; the ship never looks gay, never proud, only warlike and enduring.

But he had seen more than the death of the ship. He had seen the sea feed her white flames on souls of men; and heard what a storm-gust sounded like, that had taken up with it, in its swirl of a moment, the last breaths of a ship's crew. He never forgot either the sight or the sound. Among the last plates prepared by his own hand for the Liber Studiorum, (all of them, as was likely from his advanced knowledge, finer than any previous pieces of the series, and most of them unfortunately never published, being retained beside him for some last touch—for ever delayed,) perhaps the most important is one of the body of a drowned sailor, dashed against a vertical rock in the jaws of one merciless, immeasurable wave. He hardly ever painted a steep rocky coast without some fragment of a devoured ship, grinding in the blanched teeth of the surges, —just enough left to be a token of utter destruction. Of his two most important paintings of definite shipwreck I shall speak presently.

I said that at this period he first was assured of another fact, namely, that the *Sea* also was a thing that broke to pieces. The sea up to that time had been generally regarded by painters as a liquidly composed, level-seeking consistent thing, with a smooth surface, rising to a water-mark on sides of ships; in which ships were scientifically to be embedded, and wetted, up to said water-mark, and to remain dry above the same. But Turner found during his Southern Coast tour that the sea was *not* this: that it was, on the contrary, a very incalculable and unhorizon-

tal thing, setting its "water-mark" sometimes on the highest
heavens, as well as on sides of ships;—very breakable into
pieces; half of a wave separable from the other half, and
on the instant carriageable miles inland;—not in any wise
limiting itself to a state of apparent liquidity, but now
striking like a steel gauntlet, and now becoming a cloud,
and vanishing, no eye could tell whither; one moment a
flint cave, the next a marble pillar, the next a mere white
fleece thickening the thundery rain. He never forgot those
facts; never afterwards was able to recover the idea of
positive distinction between sea and sky, or sea and land.
Steel gauntlet, black rock, white cloud, and men and masts
gnashed to pieces and disappearing in a few breaths and
splinters among them;—a little blood on the rock angle,
like red sea-weed, sponged away by the next splash of the
foam, and the glistering granite and green water all pure
again in vacant wrath. So stayed by him, for ever, the
Image of the Sea.

One effect of this revelation of the nature of ocean to
him was not a little singular. It seemed that ever afterwards his appreciation of the calmness of water was deep-
ened by what he had witnessed of its frenzy, and a certain
class of entirely tame subjects were treated by him even
with increased affection after he had seen the full manifestation of sublimity. He had always a great regard for
canal boats, and instead of sacrificing these old, and one
would have thought unentertaining, friends to the deities
of Storm, he seems to have returned with a lulling pleasure
from the foam and danger of the beach to the sedgy bank
and stealthy barge of the lowland river. Thenceforward
his work which introduces shipping is divided into two
classes; one embodying the poetry of silence and calmness,
the other of turbulence and wrath. Of intermediate conditions he gives few examples; if he lets the wind down upon
the sea at all, it is nearly always violent, and though the
waves may not be running high, the foam is torn off them
in a way which shows they will soon run higher. On the
other hand, nothing is so perfectly calm as Turner's calmness. To the canal barges of England he soon added other
types of languid motion; the broad-ruddered barques of

the Loire, the drooping sails of Seine, the arcaded barques of the Italian lakes slumbering on expanse of mountain-guarded wave, the dreamy prows of pausing gondolas on lagoons at moon-rise; in each and all commanding an intensity of calm, chiefly because he never admitted an instant's rigidity. The surface of quiet water with other painters becomes FIXED. With Turner it looks as if a fairy's breath would stir it, but the fairy's breath is not there.[84]

"Scarborough"

I said in the course of the introduction, that nothing is so perfectly calm as Turner's calmness; and I know very few better examples of this calmness than the plate before us ["Scarborough," National Gallery, London], uniting, as it does, the glittering of the morning clouds, and trembling of the sea, with an infinitude of peace in both. There are one or two points of interest in the artifices by which the intense effect of calm is produced. Much is owing, in the first place, to the amount of absolute gloom obtained by the local blackness of the boats on the beach; like a piece of the midnight left unbroken by the dawn. But more is owing to the treatment of the distant harbour mouth. In general, throughout nature, Reflection and Repetition are *peaceful* things; that is to say, the image of any object, seen in calm water, gives us an impression of quietness, not merely because we know the water must be quiet in order to be reflective; but because the fact of the repetition of this form is lulling to us in its monotony, and associated more or less with an idea of quiet succession, or reproduction, in events or things throughout nature:—that one day should be like another day, one town the image of another town, or one history the repetition of another history, being more or less results of quietness, while dissimilarity and nonsuccession are also, more or less, results of interference and disquietude. And thus, though an echo actually increases the quantity of sound heard, its repetition of the notes or syllables of sound, gives an idea of calmness

[84] Harb 42–45, omit.

attainable in no other way; hence the feeling of calm given to a landscape by the notes of the cuckoo. Understanding this, observe the anxious *doubling* of every object by a visible echo or shadow throughout this picture. The grandest feature of it is the steep distant cliff; and therefore the dualism is more marked here than elsewhere; the two promontories or cliffs, and two piers below them, being arranged so that the one looks almost like the shadow of the other, cast irregularly on mist. In all probability, the more distant pier would in reality, unless it is very greatly higher than the near one, have been lowered by perspective so as not to continue in the same longitudinal line at the top,—but Turner will not have it so; he reduces them to exactly the same level, so that the one looks like the phantom of the other; and so of the cliffs above.

Then observe, each pier has, just below the head of it, in a vertical line, another important object, one a buoy, and the other a stooping figure. These carry on the double group in the calmest way, obeying the general law of vertical reflection, and throw down two long shadows on the near beach. The intenseness of the parallelism would catch the eye in a moment, but for the lighthouse, which breaks the group and prevents the artifice from being too open. Next come the two heads of boats, with their two bowsprits, and the two masts of the one farthest off, all monotonously double, but for the diagonal mast of the nearer one, which again hides the artifice. Next, put your finger over the white central figure, and follow the minor incidents round the beach; first, under the lighthouse, a stick, with its echo below a little to the right; above, a black stone, and its echo to the right; under the white figure, another stick, with its echo to the left; then a starfish, and a white spot its echo to the left; then a dog, and a basket to double its light; above, a fisherman, and his wife for an echo; above them, two lines of curved shingle; above them, two small black figures; above them, two unfinished ships, and two forked masts; above the forked masts, a house with two gables, and its echo exactly over it in two gables more; next to the right, two fishing-boats with sails down; farther on, two fishing-boats with sails up, each with its little white reflection below; then two larger ships, which, lest his trick should be found out, Turner puts a dim third between; then below, two fat colliers, leaning away from each other, and two thinner colliers, leaning towards each other; and now at last, having doubled everything all round the beach, he gives one strong single stroke to gather all together, places his solitary central white figure, and the Calm is complete.

It is also to be noticed, that not only the definite repetition has a power of expressing serenity, but even the slight sense of *confusion* induced by the continual doubling is useful; it makes us feel not well awake, drowsy, and as if we were out too early, and had to rub our eyes yet a little, before we could make out whether there were really two boats or one.[85]

"The Fighting Téméraire"

The painting of the *"Téméraire"* [1839; National Gallery, London] was received with a general feeling of sympathy. No abusive voice, as far as I remember, was ever raised against it. And the feeling was just; for of all pictures of subjects not visibly involving human pain, this is, I believe, the most pathetic that was ever painted. The utmost pensiveness which can ordinarily be given to a landscape depends on adjuncts of ruin: but no ruin was ever so affecting as this gliding of the vessel to her grave. A ruin cannot be, for whatever memories may be connected with it, and whatever witness it may have borne to the courage or the glory of men, it never seems to have offered itself to their danger, and associated itself with their acts, as a ship of battle can. The mere facts of motion, and obedience to human guidance, double the interest of the vessel: nor less her organized perfectness, giving her the look, and partly the character of a living creature, that may indeed be maimed in limb, or decrepit in frame, but must either live or die, and cannot be added to nor diminished from—heaped up and dragged down—as a building

[85] Harb 73-75

can. And this particular ship, crowned in the Trafalgar hour of trial with chief victory—prevailing over the fatal vessel that had given Nelson death—surely, if ever anything without a soul deserved honour or affection, we owed them here. Those sails that strained so full bent into the battle—that broad bow that struck the surf aside, enlarging silently in steadfast haste, full front to the shot—resistless and without reply—those triple ports whose choirs of flame rang forth in their courses, into the fierce revenging monotone, which, when it died away, left no answering voice to rise any more upon the sea against the strength of England—those sides that were wet with the long runlets of English life-blood, like press-planks at vintage, gleaming goodly crimson down to the cast and clash of the washing foam—those pale masts that stayed themselves up against the war-ruin, shaking out their ensigns through the thunder, till sail and ensign drooped—steep in the death-stilled pause of Andalusian air, burning with its witness-cloud of human souls at rest,—surely, for these some sacred care might have been left in our thoughts—some quiet space amidst the lapse of English waters?

Nay, not so. We have stern keepers to trust her glory to —the fire and the worm. Never more shall sunset lay golden robe on her, nor starlight tremble on the waves that part at her gliding. Perhaps, where the low gate opens to some cottage-garden, the tired traveller may ask, idly, why the moss grows so green on its rugged wood; and even the sailor's child may not answer, nor know, that the night-dew lies deep in the war-rents of the wood of the old *Téméraire*.[86]

"The Slave Ship"

[T]he noblest sea that Turner has ever painted, and, if so, the noblest certainly ever painted by man, is that of the Slave Ship [Museum of Fine Arts, Boston], the chief Academy picture of the Exhibition of 1840. It is a sunset on the Atlantic, after prolonged storm; but the storm is

[86] Bequest 170–72

partially lulled, and the torn and streaming rain-clouds are moving in scarlet lines to lose themselves in the hollow of the night. The whole surface of sea included in the picture is divided into two ridges of enormous swell, not high, nor local, but a low broad heaving of the whole ocean, like the lifting of its bosom by deep-drawn breath after the torture of the storm. Between these two ridges the fire of the sunset falls along the trough of the sea, dyeing it with an awful but glorious light, the intense and lurid splendour which burns like gold, and bathes like blood. Along this fiery path and valley, the tossing waves by which the swell of the sea is restlessly divided, lift themselves in dark, indefinite, fantastic forms, each casting a faint and ghastly shadow behind it along the illumined foam. They do not rise everywhere, but three or four together in wild groups, fitfully and furiously, as the under strength of the swell compels or permits them; leaving between them treacherous spaces of level and whirling water, now lighted with green and lamp-like fire, now flashing back the gold of the declining sun, now fearfully dyed from above with the undistinguishable images of the burning clouds, which fall upon them in flakes of crimson and scarlet, and give to the reckless waves the added motion of their own fiery flying. Purple and blue, the lurid shadows of the hollow breakers are cast upon the mist of night, which gathers cold and low, advancing like the shadow of death upon the guilty[87] ship as it labours amidst the lightning of the sea, its thin masts written upon the sky in lines of blood, girded with condemnation in that fearful hue which signs the sky with horror, and mixes its flaming flood with the sunlight, and, cast far along the desolate heave of the sepulchral waves, incarnadines the multitudinous sea.[88]

"Snowstorm"

In the year 1842 this picture [National Gallery, London] was thus described by Turner in the Academy Cata-

[87] (Ruskin note: "She is a slaver, throwing her slaves overboard. The near sea is encumbered with corpses.") MP I, 571 f
[88] (*Macbeth,* ii, sc. 2.) MP I, 572

logue: "Snowstorm. Steamboat off the harbour mouth making signals, and going by the lead. The author was in this
storm the night the *Ariel* left Harwich."

It was characterized by some of the critics of the day
as a mass of "soapsuds and whitewash." Turner was passing the evening at my father's house on the day this criticism came out: and after dinner, sitting in his arm-chair
by the fire, I heard him muttering low to himself at intervals, "Soapsuds and whitewash!" again, and again, and
again. At last I went to him, asking "why he minded what
they said?" Then he burst out;—"Soapsuds and whitewash!
What would they have? I wonder what they think the sea's
like? I wish they'd been in it."

The following anecdote respecting this picture, and the
conversation with Turner which arose out of the circumstance, were communicated to me by my friend the Rev.
W. Kingsley, of Sidney College, Cambridge. I give simply
the words of his letter: there can be no need of insisting,
in any wise, on the singular value of the record they contain.

"The story I told you about the 'Snowstorm' was this:
—I had taken my mother and a cousin to see Turner's pictures, and, as my mother knows nothing about art, I was
taking her down the gallery to look at the large 'Richmond
Park,' but as we were passing the 'Snowstorm' she stopped
before it, and I could hardly get her to look at any other
picture; and she told me a great deal more about it than
I had any notion of, though I have seen many sea storms.
She had been in such a scene on the coast of Holland during the war. When, some time afterwards, I thanked Turner
for his permission for her to see his pictures, I told him
that he would not guess which had caught my mother's
fancy, and then named the picture; and he then said, 'I
did not paint it to be understood, but I wished to show
what such a scene was like; I got the sailors to lash me
to the mast to observe it; I was lashed for four hours, and
I did not expect to escape, but I felt bound to record it if
I did. But no one had any business to like the picture.'
'But,' said I, 'my mother once went through just such a
scene, and it brought it all back to her.' 'Is your mother

a painter?' 'No.' 'Then she ought to have been thinking of something else.' These were nearly his words; I observed at the time he used 'record' and 'painting,' as the title 'author' had struck me before."

Interesting, however, as this picture is, in marking how far the sense of foaming mystery, and blinding whiteness of surf and salt, now influenced Turner's conception of the sea, rather than the old theories of black clouds relieving terminated edges of waves, the sea is, however, even thus, not quite right: it is not yeasty *enough:* the linear wave-action is still too much dwelt upon, and confused with the true foam.[89]

[89] Bequest 161–63

20

THE PRE-RAPHAELITE ARTISTS

Letters to the Times, *1851*

SIR,—Your usual liberality will, I trust, give a place in your columns to this expression of my regret that the tone of the critique which appeared in the *Times* of Wednesday last on the works of Mr. Millais and Mr. Hunt, now in the Royal Academy, should have been scornful as well as severe.

I regret it, first, because the mere labour bestowed on those works, and their fidelity to a certain order of truth, (labour and fidelity which are altogether indisputable,) ought at once to have placed them above the level of mere contempt; and, secondly, because I believe these young artists to be at a most critical period of their career—at a turning-point, from which they may either sink into nothingness or rise to very real greatness; and I believe also, that whether they choose the upward or the downward path, may in no small degree depend upon the character of the criticism which their works have to sustain. I do not wish in any way to dispute or invalidate the general truth of your critique on the Royal Academy; nor am I surprised at the estimate which the writer formed of the pictures in question when rapidly compared with works of totally different style and aim: nay, when I first saw the chief picture by Millais in the Exhibition of last year ["Christ in the House of his Parents," National Gallery, London], I had nearly come to the same conclusion myself. But I ask your permission, in justice to artists who have at least given much time and toil to their pictures, to institute some more serious inquiry into their merits and faults than your general notice of the Academy could possibly have admitted.

Let me state, in the first place, that I have no acquaintance with any of these artists, and very imperfect sympathy with them. No one who has met with any of my writings will suspect me of desiring to encourage them in their Romanist and Tractarian tendencies. I am glad to see that Mr. Millais' lady in blue ["Mariana," Sir Roger Makins] is heartily tired of her painted window and idolatrous toilet table; and I have no particular respect for Mr. [C. A.] Collins' lady in white, because her sympathies are limited by a dead wall, or divided between some gold fish and a tadpole—(the latter Mr. Collins may, perhaps, permit me to suggest *en passant*, as he is already half a frog, is rather too small for his age). But I happen to have a special acquaintance with the water plant, *Alisma Plantago*, among which the said gold fish are swimming; and as I never saw it so thoroughly or so well drawn, I must take leave to remonstrate with you, when you say sweepingly that these men "sacrifice *truth* as well as feeling to eccentricity." For as a mere botanical study of the water lily and *Alisma*, as well as of the common lily and several other garden flowers, this picture would be invaluable to me, and I heartily wish it were mine.

But, before entering into such particulars, let me correct an impression which your article is likely to induce in most minds, and which is altogether false. These pre-Raphaelites (I cannot compliment them on common sense in choice of a *nom de guerre*) do *not* desire nor pretend in any way to imitate antique painting as such. They know very little of ancient paintings who suppose the works of these young artists to resemble them. As far as I can judge of their aim —for, as I said, I do not know the men themselves—the Pre-Raphaelites intend to surrender no advantage which the knowledge or inventions of the present time can afford to their art. They intend to return to early days in this one point only—that, as far as in them lies, they will draw either what they see, or what they suppose might have been the actual facts of the scene they desire to represent, irrespective of any conventional rules of picture-making; and they have chosen their unfortunate though not inaccurate name because all artists did this before Raphael's time, and after Raphael's time did *not* this, but sought to paint fair pictures, rather than represent stern facts; of which the consequence has been that, from Raphael's time to this day, historical art has been in acknowledged decadence.

Now, Sir, presupposing that the intention of these men was to return to archaic *art* instead of to archaic *honesty,* your critic borrows Fuseli's expression respecting ancient draperies "snapped instead of folded," and asserts that in these pictures there is a "*servile* imitation of *false* perspective." To which I have just this to answer:—

That there is not one single error in perspective in four out of the five pictures in question; and that in Millais' "Mariana" there is but this one—that the top of the green curtain in the distant window has too low a vanishing-point; and that I will undertake, if need be, to point out and prove a dozen worse errors in perspective in any twelve pictures, containing architecture, taken at random from among the works of the popular painters of the day.

Secondly: that, putting aside the small Mulready, and the works of Thorburn and Sir W. Ross, and perhaps some others of those in the miniature room which I have not examined, there is not a single study of drapery in the whole Academy, be it in large works or small, which for perfect truth, power, and finish could be compared for an instant with the black sleeve of the Julia, or with the velvet on the breast and the chain mail of the Valentine, of Mr. Hunt's picture ["Valentine receiving Sylvia," Birmingham] or with the white draperies on the table of Mr. Millais' "Mariana," and of the right-hand figure in the same painter's "Dove returning to the Ark" [Oxford].

And further: that as studies both of drapery and of every minor detail, there has been nothing in art so earnest or so complete as these pictures since the days of Albert Dürer. This I assert generally and fearlessly. On the other hand, I am perfectly ready to admit that Mr. Hunt's "Sylvia" is not a person whom Proteus or any one else would have been likely to fall in love with at first sight; and that one cannot feel very sincere delight that Mr. Millais' "Wives of the Sons of Noah" [i.e., "Dove returning"] should have escaped the Deluge; with many other faults besides on which I will not enlarge at present, because I have already occupied too much of your valuable space, and I hope to enter into more special criticism in a future letter.[90]

SIR,—Your obliging insertion of my former letter encourages me to trouble you with one or two further notes respecting the pre-Raphaelite pictures. I had intended, in continuation of my first letter, to institute as close an inquiry as I could into the character of the morbid tendencies which prevent these works from favourably arresting the attention of the public; but I believe there are so few pictures in the Academy whose reputation would not be grievously diminished by a deliberate inventory of their errors, that I am disinclined to undertake so ungracious a task with respect to this or that particular work. These points, however, may be noted, partly for the consideration of the painters themselves, partly that forgiveness of them may be asked from the public in consideration of high merits in other respects.

The most painful of these defects is unhappily also the most prominent—the commonness of feature in many of the principal figures. In Mr. Hunt's "Valentine defending Sylvia," this is, indeed, almost the only fault. Further examination of this picture has even raised the estimate I had previously formed of its marvellous truth in detail and splendour in colour; nor is its general conception less deserving of praise: the action of Valentine, his arm thrown round Sylvia, and his hand clasping hers at the same instant as she falls at his feet, is most faithful and beautiful, nor less so the contending of doubt and distress with awakening hope in the half-shadowed, half-sunlit countenance of Julia. Nay, even the momentary struggle of Proteus with Sylvia just past, is indicated by the trodden grass and broken fungi of the foreground. But all this thoughtful conception, and absolutely inimitable execution, fail in making immediate appeal to the feelings, owing to the un-

[90] From the *Times*, May 13, 1851, in *Works*, vol. XII, 319–23

fortunate type chosen for the face of Sylvia. Certainly this cannot be she whose lover was

> "As rich in having such a jewel,
> As twenty seas, if all their sands were pearl."[91]

Nor is it, perhaps, less to be regretted that, while in Shakspeare's play there are nominally "Two Gentlemen," in Mr. Hunt's picture there should only be one,—at least, the kneeling figure on the right has by no means the look of a gentleman. But this may be on purpose, for any one who remembers the conduct of Proteus throughout the previous scenes will, I think, be disposed to consider that the error lies more in Shakspeare's nomenclature than in Mr. Hunt's ideal.

No defence can, however, be offered for the choice of features in the left-hand figure of Mr. Millais' "Dove returning to the Ark." I cannot understand how a painter so sensible of the utmost refinement of beauty in other objects should deliberately choose for his model a type far inferior to that of average humanity, and unredeemed by any expression save that of dull self-complacency. Yet let the spectator who desires to be just turn away from this head, and contemplate rather the tender and beautiful expression of the stooping figure, and the intense harmony of colour in the exquisitely finished draperies; let him note also the ruffling of the plumage of the wearied dove, one of its feathers falling on the arm of the figure which holds it, and another to the ground, where, by-the-bye, the hay is painted not only elaborately, but with the most perfect ease of touch and mastery of effect, especially to be observed because this freedom of execution is a modern excellence, which it has been inaccurately stated that these painters despise, but which, in reality, is one of the remarkable distinctions between their painting and that of Van Eyck or Memling, which caused me to say in my first letter that "those knew little of ancient painting who supposed the works of these men to resemble it."

[91] (*Two Gentlemen of Verona*, ii, sc. 4; the painting itself refers to Act v, sc. 4.)

Next to this false choice of feature, and in connection with it, is to be noted the defect in the colouring of the flesh. The hands, at least in the pictures in Millais, are almost always ill painted, and the flesh tint in general is wrought out of crude purples and dusky yellows. It appears just possible that much of this evil may arise from the attempt to obtain too much transparency—an attempt which has injured also not a few of the best works of Mulready. I believe it will be generally found that close study of minor details is unfavourable to flesh painting; it was noticed of the drawing ["The Harem"] by John Lewis, in the old water-colour exhibition of 1850, (a work which, as regards its treatment of detail, may be ranged in the same class with the pre-Raphaelite pictures,) that the faces were the worst painted portions of the whole.

The apparent want of shade is, however, perhaps the fault which most hurts the general eye. The fact is, nevertheless, that the fault is far more in the other pictures of the Academy than in the pre-Raphaelite ones. It is the former that are false, not the latter, except so far as every picture must be false which endeavours to represent living sunlight with dead pigments. I think Mr. Hunt has a slight tendency to exaggerate reflected lights; and if Mr. Millais has ever been near a piece of good painted glass, he ought to have known that its tone is more dusky and sober than that of his Mariana's window. But for the most part these pictures are rashly condemned because the only light which we are accustomed to see represented is that which falls on the artist's model in his dim painting-room, not that of sunshine in the fields.

I do not think I can go much further in fault-finding. I had, indeed, something to urge respecting what I supposed to be the Romanizing tendencies of the painters; but I have received a letter assuring me that I was wrong in attributing to them anything of the kind; whereupon, all I can say is that, instead of the "pilgrimage" of Mr. Collins' maiden over a plank and round a fish-pond, that old pilgrimage of Christiana and her children towards the place where they should "look the Fountain of Mercy in the face,"[92] would have been more to the purpose in these times. And so I wish them all heartily good speed, believing in sincerity that if they temper the courage and energy which they have shown in the adoption of their systems with patience and discretion in framing it, and if they do not suffer themselves to be driven by harsh or careless criticism into rejection of the ordinary means of obtaining influence over the minds of others, they may, as they gain experience, lay in our England the foundations of a school of art nobler than the world has seen for three hundred years.[93]

"Pre-Raphaelitism," 1851

[B]ut it being required to produce a poet on canvas, what is our way of setting to work? We begin, in all probability, by telling the youth of fifteen or sixteen, that Nature is full of faults, and that he is to improve her; but that Raphael is perfection, and that the more he copies Raphael the better; that after much copying of Raphael, he is to try what he can do himself in a Raphaelesque, but yet original manner: that is to say, he is to try to do something very clever, all out of his own head, but yet this clever something is to be properly subjected to Raphaelesque rules, is to have a principal light occupying one-seventh of its space, and a principal shadow occupying one-third of the same; that no two people's heads in the picture are to be turned the same way, and that all the personages represented are to possess ideal beauty of the highest order, which ideal beauty consists partly in a Greek outline of nose, partly in proportions expressible in decimal fractions between the lips and chin; but mostly in that degree of improvement which the youth of sixteen is to bestow upon God's work in general. This I say is the kind of teaching which through various channels, Royal Academy lecturings, press criticisms, public enthusiasm, and not least by solid weight of gold, we give to our young men. And we wonder we have no painters!

[92] (*Pilgrim's Progress*, Part ii.)
[93] From the *Times*, May 30, 1851, in *Works*, vol. XII, 324–27

That two youths [Millais and Hunt] of the respective ages of eighteen and twenty, should have conceived for themselves a totally independent and sincere method of study, and enthusiastically persevered in it against every kind of dissuasion and opposition, is strange enough; that in the third or fourth year of their efforts they should have produced works in many parts not inferior to the best of Albert Dürer, this is perhaps not less strange. But the loudness and universality of the howl which the common critics of the press have raised against them, the utter absence of all generous help or encouragement from those who can both measure their toil and appreciate their success, and the shrill, shallow laughter of those who can do neither the one nor the other—these are strangest of all—unimaginable unless they had been experienced.

Yet let me not be misunderstood. I have adduced [the Pre-Raphaelite paintings] only as examples of the kind of study which I would desire to see substituted for that of our modern schools, and of singular success in certain characters, finish of detail, and brilliancy of colour. What faculties, higher than imitative, may be in these men, I do not yet venture to say; but I do say, that if they exist, such faculties will manifest themselves in due time all the more forcibly because they have received training so severe.

For it is always to be remembered that no one mind is like another, either in its powers or perceptions; and while the main principles of training must be the same for all, the result in each will be as various as the kinds of truth which each will apprehend; therefore, also, the modes of effort, even in men whose inner principles and final aims are exactly the same. Suppose, for instance, two men, equally honest, equally industrious, equally impressed with a humble desire to render some part of what they saw in nature faithfully; and, otherwise, trained in convictions such as I have above endeavoured to induce. But one of them is quiet in temperament, has a feeble memory, no invention, and excessively keen sight. The other is impatient in temperament, has a memory which nothing escapes, an invention which never rests, and is comparatively nearsighted.

Set them both free in the same field in a mountain valley. One sees everything, small and large, with almost the
same clearness; mountains and grasshoppers alike; the
leaves on the branches, the veins in the pebbles, the bubbles in the stream; but he can remember nothing, and invent nothing. Patiently he sets himself to his mighty task;
abandoning at once all thoughts of seizing transient effects,
or giving general impressions of that which his eyes present
to him in microscopical dissection, he chooses some small
portion out of the infinite scene, and calculates with courage the number of weeks which must elapse before he can
do justice to the intensity of his perceptions, or the fulness
of matter in his subject.

Meantime, the other has been watching the change of
the clouds, and the march of the light along the mountain sides; he beholds the entire scene in broad, soft masses
of true gradation, and the very feebleness of his sight is in
some sort an advantage to him, in making him more sensible of the aerial mystery of distance, and hiding from him
the multitudes of circumstances which it would have been
impossible for him to represent. But there is not one change
in the casting of the jagged shadows along the hollows
of the hills, but it is fixed on his mind for ever; not a flake
of spray has broken from the sea of cloud about their
bases, but he has watched it as it melts away, and could
recall it to its lost place in heaven by the slightest effort
of his thoughts. Not only so, but thousands and thousands
of such images, of older scenes, remain congregated in his
mind, each mingling in new associations with those now
visibly passing before him, and these again confused with
other images of his own ceaseless, sleepless imagination,
flashing by in sudden troops. Fancy how his paper will be
covered with stray symbols and blots, and undecipherable
shorthand:—as for his sitting down to "draw from Nature,"
there was not one of the things which he wished to represent, that stayed for so much as five seconds together: but
none of them escaped for all that: they are sealed up in
that strange storehouse of his; he may take one of them
out perhaps, this day twenty years, and paint it in his dark
room, far away. Now, observe, you may tell both of these

men, when they are young, that they are to be honest, that they have an important function, and that they are not to care what Raphael did. This you may wholesomely impress on them both. But fancy the exquisite absurdity of expecting either of them to possess any of the qualities of the other.

I have supposed the feebleness of sight in the last, and of invention in the first painter, that the contrast between them might be more striking; but, with very slight modification, both the characters are real. Grant to the first considerable inventive power, with exquisite sense of colour; and give to the second, in addition to all his other faculties, the eye of an eagle; and the first is John Everett Millais, the second Joseph Mallord William Turner.

They are among the few men who have defied all false teaching, and have therefore, in great measure, done justice to the gifts with which they were intrusted. They stand at opposite poles, marking culminating points of art in both directions; between them, or in various relations to them, we may class five or six more living artists who, in like manner, have done justice to their powers. I trust that I may be pardoned for naming them, in order that the reader may know how the strong innate genius in each has been invariably accompanied with the same humility, earnestness, and industry in study.[94]

It is not, however, only in invention that men overwork themselves, but in execution also; and here I have a word to say to the Pre-Raphaelites specially. They are working too hard. There is evidence in failing portions of their pictures, showing that they have wrought so long upon them that their very sight has failed for weariness, and that the hand refused any more to obey the heart. And, besides this, there are certain qualities of drawing which they miss from over-carefulness. For, let them be assured, there is a great truth lurking in that common desire of men to see things done in what they call a "masterly," or "bold," or "broad," manner: a truth oppressed and abused, like almost every other in this world, but an eternal one nevertheless; and

[94] PRB, 353–61, omit.

whatever mischief may have followed from men's looking
for nothing else but this facility of execution, and supposing that a picture was assuredly all right if only it were
done with broad dashes of the brush, still the truth remains
the same:—that because it is not intended that men shall
torment or weary themselves with any earthly labour, it is
appointed that the noblest results should only be attainable
by a certain ease and decision of manipulation. I only
wish people understood this much of sculpture, as well as
of painting, and could see that the finely finished statue
is, in ninety-nine cases out of a hundred, a far more vulgar
work than that which shows rough signs of the right hand
laid to the workman's hammer: but at all events, in painting it is felt by all men, and justly felt. The freedom of
the lines of nature can only be represented by a similar
freedom in the hand that follows them; there are curves
in the flow of the hair, and in the form of the features,
and in the muscular outline of the body, which can in no
wise be caught but by a sympathetic freedom in the stroke
of the pencil. I do not care what example is taken; be it
the most subtle and careful work of Leonardo himself, there
will be found a play and power and ease in the outlines,
which no *slow* effort could ever imitate. And if the Pre-
Raphaelites do not understand how this kind of power, in
its highest perfection, may be united with the most severe
rendering of all other orders of truth, and especially of
those with which they themselves have most sympathy,
let them look at the drawings of John Lewis.[95]

1853

The great mistake which has hitherto prevented the
public mind from fully going with [the Pre-Raphaelites]
must soon be corrected. That mistake was the supposition
that, instead of wishing to recur to the *principles* of the
early ages, these men wished to bring back the *ignorance*
of the early ages. This notion, grounded first on some hardness in their earlier works, which resulted—as it must al-

[95] PRB, 388 f

ways result—from the downright and earnest effort to paint nature as in a looking-glass, was fostered partly by the jealousy of their beaten competitors, and partly by the pure, perverse, and hopeless ignorance of the whole body of art-critics, so called, connected with the press. No notion was ever more baseless or more ridiculous. It was asserted that the Pre-Raphaelites did not draw well, in the face of the fact, that the principal member of their body, from the time he entered the schools of the Academy, had literally encumbered himself with the medals given as prizes for drawing.[96] It was asserted that they did not draw in perspective, by men who themselves knew no more of perspective than they did of astrology; it was asserted that they sinned against the appearances of nature, by men who had never drawn so much as a leaf or a blossom from nature in their lives. And, lastly, when all these calumnies or absurdities would tell no more, and it began to be forced upon men's unwilling belief that the style of the Pre-Raphaelites *was* true and was according to nature, the last forgery invented respecting them is, that they copy photographs. You observe how completely this last piece of malice defeats all the rest. It admits they are true to nature, though only that it may deprive them of all merit in being so. But it may itself be at once refuted by the bold challenge to their opponents to produce a Pre-Raphaelite picture, or anything like one, by themselves copying a photograph.

Let me at once clear your minds from all these doubts, and at once contradict all these calumnies.

Pre-Raphaelitism has but one principle, that of absolute, uncompromising truth in all that it does, obtained by working everything, down to the most minute detail, from nature, and from nature only.[97] Every Pre-Raphaelite land-

[96] (Millais, admitted to the Academy schools at the age of ten, won a medal when thirteen and the gold medal for painting when seventeen.) LAP 156 f

[97] (Ruskin note: "Or, where imagination is necessarily trusted to, by always endeavouring to conceive a fact as it really was likely to have happened, rather than as it most prettily *might* have happened. The various members of the school are not all

scape background is painted to the last touch, in the open
air, from the thing itself. Every Pre-Raphaelite figure, however studied in expression, is a true portrait of some living
person. Every minute accessory is painted in the same
manner. And one of the chief reasons for the violent opposition with which the school has been attacked by other
artists, is the enormous cost of care and labour which such
a system demands from those who adopt it, in contradis-
tinction to the present slovenly and imperfect style.

This is the main Pre-Raphaelite principle. But the battle
which its supporters have to fight is a hard one; and for
that battle they have been fitted by a very peculiar character.

You perceive that the principal resistance they have to
make is to that spurious beauty, whose attractiveness had
tempted men to forget, or to despise, the more noble quality of sincerity: and in order at once to put them beyond
the power of temptation from this beauty, they are, as a
body, characterised by a total absence of sensibility to the
ordinary and popular forms of artistic gracefulness; while,
to all that still lower kind of prettiness, which regulates
the disposition of our scenes upon the stage, and which
appears in our lower art, as in our annuals, our commonplace portraits, and statuary, the Pre-Raphaelites are not
only dead, but they regard it with a contempt and aversion
approaching to disgust. This character is absolutely necessary to them in the present time; but it, of course, occasionally renders their work comparatively unpleasing. As
the school becomes less aggressive, and more authoritative
—which it will do—they will enlist into their ranks men who
will work, mainly, upon their principles, and yet embrace
more of those characters which are generally attractive,
and this great ground of offence will be removed.

Again: you observe that as landscape painters, their
principles must, in great part, confine them to mere fore-

equally severe in carrying out its principles, some of them trust-
ing their memory or fancy very far; only all agreeing in the effort to make their memories so accurate as to seem like portraiture, and their fancy so probable as to seem like memory.")
LAP 157

ground work; and singularly enough, that they may not be tempted away from this work, they have been born with comparatively little enjoyment of those evanescent effects and distant sublimities which nothing but the memory can arrest, and nothing but a daring conventionalism portray. But for this work they are not now needed. Turner, the first and greatest of the Pre-Raphaelites, has done it already; he, though his capacity embraced everything, and though he would sometimes, in his foregrounds, paint the spots upon a dead trout, and the dyes upon a butterfly's wing, yet for the most part delighted to begin at that very point where the other branches of Pre-Raphaelitism become powerless.

Lastly. The habit of constantly carrying everything up to the utmost point of completion deadens the Pre-Raphaelites in general to the merits of men who, with an equal love of truth up to a certain point, yet express themselves habitually with speed and power, rather than with finish, and give abstracts of truth rather than total truth. Probably to the end of time artists will more or less be divided into these classes, and it will be impossible to make men like Millais understand the merits of men like Tintoret; but this is the more to be regretted because the Pre-Raphaelites have enormous powers of imagination, as well as of realisation, and do not yet themselves know of how much they would be capable, if they sometimes worked on a larger scale, and with a less laborious finish.

With all their faults, their pictures are, since Turner's death, the best—incomparably the best—on the walls of the Royal Academy; and such works as Mr. Hunt's "Claudio and Isabella" [Tate Gallery] have never been rivalled, in some respects never approached, at any other period of art.[98]

1856

If the reader, before fixing his attention on any particular work, will glance generally round any of the rooms [of

[98] LAP 157–60

the Royal Academy], he will be struck by a singular change in the character of the entire exhibition. He will find that he can no longer distinguish the Pre-Raphaelite works as a separate class, but that between them and the comparatively few pictures remaining quite of the old school, there is a perfectly unbroken gradation, formed by the works of painters in various stages of progress, struggling forward out of their conventionalism to the Pre-Raphaelite standard. The meaning of this is simply that the battle is completely and confessedly won by the latter party; that animosity has changed into emulation, astonishment into sympathy, and that a true and consistent school of art is at last established in the Royal Academy of England.[99]

1857

As year by year, in the Royal Academy, the principles established by the Pre-Raphaelites are more frankly accepted, and more patiently put in practice, I observe that, notwithstanding all the substantial advantage derived from them, two results must necessarily follow, involving some disappointment to the public and great mortification to the artist. I see that we shall have more wayside nooks, corners of green fields, pools of watercress streams, and the like, than can, in the aggregate, contribute much to the amusement of the restless and over-excited crowd of London spectators; and I see also that there will be so high an average of perseverance and care brought to bear on every subject, that both will pass unnoticed unless recommended by more brilliant qualities; and painters who flattered themselves that the devotion of a year's honest labour could not but make their pictures conspicuous, and their names illustrious, will find, with bitter disappointment, that patience and sincerity are no longer distinctive, and that industry will soon be less notable than sloth.[100]

[99] Acad 1856, 47
[100] Acad 1857, 91

1858

[T]he pictures of the rising school will in a few years be much more interesting than they are now. In learning to work carefully from Nature, everybody has been obliged to paint what will stay to be painted; and the best of Nature will not wait. Moreover, a subject which must be returned to every day for a couple of months must necessarily be near the house door; and artists cannot always have their lodgings where they choose: many of them, unable to quit their usual residences, must paint the best thing they can find in their neighbourhood; and this best accessible bit, however good as a study—(anything will do for that)—will usually be uninteresting to the public. The evil is increased by affectations of Wordsworthian simplicity; also by a good deal of genuine simplicity; and of more or less foolish sentiment.

But what shall we say when the power of painting, which makes even these so interesting, begins to exert itself, with the aid of imagination and memory, on the splendid transience of Nature, and her noblest continuance; when we have the courses of heaven's golden clouds instead of squares of blue through cottage casements; and the fair river mists and mountain shrouds of vapour instead of cottage smoke—pine forests as well as banks of grass, and fallen precipices instead of heaps of flints.[101]

1878

Rossetti's "Annunciation" [Tate Gallery] differs from every previous conception of the scene known to me, in representing the angel as waking the Virgin from sleep to give her his message. The Messenger himself also differs from angels as they are commonly represented, in not depending, for recognition of his supernatural character, on the insertion of bird's wings at his shoulders. If we are to know him for an angel at all, it must be by his face, which

[101] Acad 1858, 152–54, omit.

is that simply of youthful, but grave, manhood. He is neither transparent in body, luminous in presence, nor auriferous in apparel;—wears a plain, long, white robe,—casts a natural and undiminished shadow,—and, although there are flames beneath his feet, which upbear him, so that he does not touch the earth, these are unseen by the Virgin.

She herself is an English, not a Jewish girl, of about sixteen or seventeen, of such pale and thoughtful beauty as Rossetti could best imagine for her; concerning which effort, and its degree of success, we will inquire farther presently.

She has risen half up, not *started* up, in being awakened; and is not looking at the angel, but only thinking, it seems, with eyes cast down, as if supposing herself in a strange dream. The morning light fills the room, and shows at the foot of her little pallet-bed, her embroidery work, left off the evening before,—an upright lily.

Upright, and very accurately upright, as also the edges of the piece of cloth in its frame,—as also the gliding form of the angel,—as also, in severe fore-shortening, that of the Virgin herself. It has been studied, so far as it has been studied at all, from a very thin model; and the disturbed coverlid is thrown into confused angular folds, which admit no suggestion whatever of ordinary girlish grace. So that, to any spectator little inclined towards the praise of barren "uprightnesse," and accustomed on the contrary to expect radiance in archangels, and grace in Madonnas, the first effect of the design must be extremely displeasing, and the first is perhaps, with most art-amateurs of modern days, likely to be the last.

The background of the second picture (Millais' "Blind Girl" [Birmingham]), is an open English common, skirted by the tidy houses of a well-to-do village in the cockney rural districts. I have no doubt the scene is a real one within some twenty miles from London, and painted mostly on the spot.

The common is a fairly spacious bit of ragged pasture, with a couple of donkeys feeding on it, and a cow or two, and at the side of the public road passing over it, the blind girl has sat down to rest awhile. She is a simple beggar, not a poetical or vicious one;—being peripatetic with musical instrument, she will, I suppose, come under the general term of tramp; a girl of eighteen or twenty, extremely plain-featured, but healthy, and just now resting, as any one of us would rest, not because she is much tired, but because the sun has but this moment come out after a shower, and the smell of the grass is pleasant.

The shower has been heavy, and is so still in the distance, where an intensely bright double rainbow is relieved against the departing thunder-cloud. The freshly wet grass is all radiant through and through with the new sunshine; full noon at its purest, the very donkeys bathed in the raindew, and prismatic with it under their rough breasts as they graze; the weeds at the girl's side as bright as a Byzantine enamel, and inlaid with blue veronica; her upturned face all aglow with the light that seeks its way through her wet eyelashes (wet only with the rain). Very quiet she is,—so quiet that a radiant butterfly has settled on her shoulder, and basks there in the warm sun. Against her knee, on which her poor instrument of musical beggary rests (harmonium), leans another child, half her age —her guide;—indifferent, this one, either to sun or rain, only a little tired of waiting. No more than a half profile of her face is seen; and that is quite expressionless, and not the least pretty.

Both of these pictures are oil-paintings. This drawing ["The King's Wedding," of 1870, The Hon. Mrs. George Lambton] of Mr. [Burne-] Jones's, however, is far less representative of his scale of power than either of the two pieces already described, which have both cost their artists much care and time; while this little water-colour has been perhaps done in the course of a summer afternoon. It is only about seven inches by nine: the figures of the average size of Angelico's on any altar predella; and the heads, of those on an average Corinthian or Syracusan coin. The bride and bridegroom sit on a slightly raised throne at the side of the picture, the bride nearest us; her head seen in profile, a little bowed. Before them, the three bridesmaids and their groomsmen dance in circle, holding each other's hands, barefooted, and dressed in long dark blue robes. Their figures are scarcely detached from the dark background, which is a wilful mingling of shadow and light, as the artist chose to put them, representing, as far as I remember, nothing in particular. The deep tone of the picture leaves several of the faces in obscurity, and none are drawn with much care, not even the bride's; but with enough to show that her features are at least as beautiful as those of an ordinary Greek goddess, while the depth of the distant background throws out her pale head in an almost lunar, yet unexaggerated, light; and the white and blue flowers of her narrow coronal, though *merely* white and blue, shine, one knows not how, like gems. Her bridegroom stoops forward a little to look at her, so that we see his front face, and can see also that he loves her.

I believe the reader will discover, on reflection, that there is really only one quite common and sympathetic impulse shown in these three works, otherwise so distinct in aim and execution. And this fraternal link he will, if careful in reflection, discover to be an effort to represent, so far as in these youths lay either the choice or the power, things as they are or were, or may be, instead of, according to the practice of their instructors and the wishes of their public, things as they are *not*, never were, and never can be: this effort being founded deeply on a conviction that it is at first better, and finally more pleasing, for human minds to contemplate things as they are, than as they are not.[102]

The central branch of the school, represented by the central picture above described:—"The Blind Girl"—was essentially and vitally an uneducated one. It was headed, in literary power, by Wordsworth; but the first pure example of its mind and manner of Art, as opposed to the erudite and *artificial* schools, will be found, so far as I know, in Molière's song: *j'aime mieux ma mie.*

Its mental power consisted in discerning what was lovely in present nature, and in pure moral emotion concerning it.

Its physical power, in an intense veracity of direct realization to the eye.

[102] Colours 149–55, omit.

So far as Mr. Millais saw what was beautiful in vagrants, or commons, or crows, or donkeys, or the straw under children's feet in the Ark (Noah's or anybody else's does not matter),—in the Huguenot and his mistress, or the ivy behind them,—in the face of Ophelia [Tate Gallery] or in the flowers floating over it as it sank;—much more, so far as he saw what instantly comprehensible nobleness of passion might be in the binding of a handkerchief,—in the utterance of two words, "Trust me" or the like: he prevailed, and rightly prevailed, over all prejudice and opposition; to that extent he will in what he has done, or may yet do, take, as a standard-bearer, an honourable place among the reformers of our day.

So far as he could not see what was beautiful, but what was essentially and for ever common (in that God had not cleansed it), and so far as he did not see truly what he thought he saw; (as for instance, in this picture, under immediate consideration, when he paints the spark of light in a crow's eye a hundred yards off, as if he were only painting a miniature of a crow close by,)—he failed of his purpose and hope; but how far, I have neither the power nor the disposition to consider.

The school represented by Mr. Rossetti's picture and adopted for his own by Mr. Holman Hunt, professed, necessarily, to be a learned one; and to represent things which had happened long ago, in a manner credible to any moderns who were interested in them. The value to us of such a school necessarily depends on the things it chooses to represent, out of the infinite history of mankind. For instance, David, of the first Republican Academe, was a true master of this school; and, painting the Horatii receiving their swords [Louvre], foretold the triumph of that Republican Power. Gérome, of the latest Republican Academe, paints the dying Polichinelle, and the *morituri* gladiators: foretelling, in like manner, the shame and virtual ruin of modern Republicanism. What our own painters have done for us in this kind has been too unworthy of their real powers, for Mr. Rossetti threw more than half his strength into literature, and, in that precise measure, left himself unequal to his appointed task in painting; while

Mr. Hunt, not knowing the necessity of masters any more than the rest of our painters, and attaching too great importance to the externals of the life of Christ, separated himself for long years from all discipline by the recognized laws of his art; and fell into errors which wofully shortened his hand and discredited his cause—into which again I hold it no part of my duty to enter. But such works as either of these painters have done, without antagonism or ostentation, and in their own true instincts; as all Rossetti's drawing from the life of Christ, more especially that of the Madonna gathering the bitter herbs for the Passover when He was twelve years old; and that of the Magdalen leaving her companions to come to Him; these, together with all the mythic scenes which he painted from the *Vita Nuova* and *Paradiso* of Dante, are of quite imperishable power and value: as also many of the poems to which he gave up part of his painter's strength. Of Holman Hunt's "Light of the World" [Oxford] and "Awakening Conscience" [Sir Colin Anderson], I have publicly spoken and written, now for many years, as standard in their kind: the study of sunset on the Egean, lately placed by me in the schools of Oxford, is not less authoritative in landscape, so far as its aim extends.

But the School represented by the third painting, "The Bridal," is that into which the greatest masters of *all* ages are gathered, and in which they are walled round as in Elysian fields, unapproachable but by the reverent and loving souls, in some sort already among the Dead.[103]

[103] Colours 166–69

21

ROSSETTI AND HOLMAN HUNT

I may be permitted, in the reverence of sorrow, to speak first of my much loved friend, Gabriel Rossetti. But, in justice, no less than in the kindness due to death [in 1882], I believe his name should be placed first on the list of men, within my own range of knowledge, who have raised and changed the spirit of modern Art: raised, in absolute attainment; changed, in direction of temper. Rossetti added to the before accepted systems of colour in painting, one based on the principles of manuscript illumination, which permits his design to rival the most beautiful qualities of painted glass, without losing either the mystery or the dignity of light and shade. And he was, as I believe it is now generally admitted, the chief intellectual force in the establishment of the modern romantic school in England.

I trust that Mr. Holman Hunt will not think that in speaking of him as Rossetti's disciple I derogate from the respect due to his own noble and determined genius.

But when Holman Hunt, under such impressive influence, quitting virtually for ever the range of worldly subjects, to which belonged the pictures of Valentine and Sylvia, of Claudio and Isabel [Tate Gallery] and of the "Awakening Conscience," rose into the spiritual passion which first expressed itself in "The Light of the World," an instant and quite final difference was manifested between his method of conception, and that of his forerunner. To Rossetti, the Old and New Testaments were only the greatest poems he knew; and he painted scenes from them with no more actual belief in their relation to the present life and business of men than he gave also to the "Morte d'Arthur" and the "Vita Nuova." But to Holman Hunt, the story of the New Testament, when once his mind entirely fastened on it, became what it was to an old Puritan, or an old Catholic of true blood,—not merely a Reality, not merely the greatest of Realities, but the only Reality.

Beyond calculation, greater, beyond comparison, happier, than Rossetti, in this sincerity, he is distinguished also from him by a respect for physical and material truth which renders his work far more generally, far more serenely, exemplary.

The specialty of colour-method which I have signalized in Rossetti, as founded on missal painting, is in exactly that degree conventional and unreal. Its light is not the light of sunshine itself, but of sunshine diffused through coloured glass. And in object-painting he not only refused, partly through idleness, partly in the absolute want of opportunity for the study of nature involved in his choice of abode in a garret at Blackfriars,—refused, I say, the natural aid of pure landscape and sky, but wilfully perverted and lacerated his powers of conception with Chinese puzzles and Japanese monsters, until his foliage looked generally fit for nothing but a fire-screen, and his landscape distances like the furniture of a Noah's Ark from the nearest toy-shop. Whereas Holman Hunt, in the very beginning of his career, fixed his mind, as a colourist, on the true representation of actual sunshine, of growing leafage, of living rock, of heavenly cloud . . .

The apparently unimportant picture by Holman Hunt, "The Strayed Sheep," which—painted thirty years ago [1853; Tate Gallery]—you may perhaps have seen last autumn in the rooms of the [Fine] Art Society in Bond Street, at once achieved all that can ever be done in that kind: it will not be surpassed—it is little likely to be rivalled —by the best efforts of the times to come. It showed to us, for the first time in the history of art, the absolutely faithful balances of colour and shade by which actual sunshine might be transposed into a key in which the harmonies possible with material pigments should yet produce the same impressions upon the mind which were caused by the light itself. [A]nd this picture, were it only the first that cast true sunshine on the grass, would have been in that virtue sacred: but in its deeper meaning, it is, actually, the first of Hunt's sacred paintings—the first in which, for those who can read, the substance of the conviction and the teaching of his after life is written, though not distinctly told till afterwards in the symbolic picture of "The Scapegoat."[104]

It may have been observed, and perhaps with question of my meaning, by some readers, that . . . I used the word "materialistic" of the method of conception common to Rossetti and Hunt, with the greater number of their scholars. I used that expression to denote their peculiar tendency to feel and illustrate the relation of spiritual creatures to the substance and conditions of the visible world; more especially, the familiar, or in a sort humiliating, accidents or employments of their earthly life;—as, for instance, in the picture I referred to, Rossetti's Virgin in the house of St. John, the Madonna's being drawn at the moment when she rises to trim their lamp. In many such cases, the incidents may of course have symbolical meaning, as, in the unfinished drawing by Rossetti of the Passover [National Gallery, London], the boy Christ is watching the blood struck on the doorpost;—but the peculiar value and character of the treatment is in what I called its *material* veracity, compelling the spectator's belief, if he have the instinct of belief in him at all, in the thing's having verily happened; and not being a mere poetical fancy. If the spectator, on the contrary, have no capacity of belief in him, the use of such representation is in making him detect his own incredulity; and recognize, that in his former dreamy acceptance of the story, he had never really asked himself whether these things were so.[105]

[104] ArtEng 269–74, omit.
[105] ArtEng 287 f

22

HOLMAN HUNT

"The Light of the World"

I speak of the picture called "The Light of the World"
[Oxford], by Mr. Holman Hunt. Standing by it yesterday
for upwards of an hour, I watched the effect it produced
upon the passers-by. Few stopped to look at it, and those
who did almost invariably with some contemptuous expression, founded on what appeared to them the absurdity
of representing the Saviour with a lantern in his hand. Now,
it ought to be remembered that, whatever may be the
faults of a Pre-Raphaelite picture, it must at least have
taken much time; and therefore it may not unwarrantably
be presumed that conceptions which are to be laboriously
realized are not adopted in the first instance without some
reflection.

Mr. Hunt has never explained his work to me. I give
what appears to me its palpable interpretation. The legend
beneath it is the beautiful verse,—"Behold, I stand at the
door and knock. If any man hear my voice, and open the
door, I will come in to him, and will sup with him, and he
with me."—Rev. iii. 20. On the left-hand side of the picture
is seen this door of the human soul. It is fast barred: its bars
and nails are rusty; it is knitted and bound to its stanchions
by creeping tendrils of ivy, showing that it has never been
opened. A bat hovers about it; its threshold is overgrown
with brambles, nettles, and fruitless corn,—the wild grass
"whereof the mower filleth not his hand, nor he that
bindeth the sheaves his bosom." Christ approaches it in
the night-time,—Christ, in his everlasting offices of prophet,
priest, and king. He wears the white robe, representing the
power of the Spirit upon him; the jewelled robe and breast-

plate, representing the sacerdotal investiture; the rayed crown of gold, inwoven with the crown of thorns; not dead thorns, but now bearing soft leaves, for the healing of the nations.

Now, when Christ enters any human heart, he bears with him a twofold light: first, the light of conscience, which displays past sin, and afterwards the light of peace, the hope of salvation. The lantern, carried in Christ's left hand, is this light of conscience. Its fire is red and fierce; it falls only on the closed door, on the weeds which encumber it, and on an apple shaken from one of the trees of the orchard, thus marking that the entire awakening of the conscience is not merely to committed, but to hereditary guilt.

The light is suspended by a chain, wrapt about the wrist of the figure, showing that the light which reveals sin appears to the sinner also to chain the hand of Christ. The light which proceeds from the head of the figure, on the contrary, is that of the hope of salvation; it springs from the crown of thorns, and, though itself sad, subdued, and full of softness, is yet so powerful that it entirely melts into the glow of it the forms of the leaves and boughs, which it crosses, showing that every earthly object must be hidden by this light, where its sphere extends.

I believe there are very few persons on whom the picture, thus justly understood, will not produce a deep impression. For my own part, I think it one of the very noblest works of sacred art ever produced in this or any other age. It may, perhaps, be answered, that works of art ought not to stand in need of interpretation of this kind. Indeed, we have been so long accustomed to see pictures painted without any purpose or intention whatsoever, that the unexpected existence of meaning in a work of art may very naturally at first appear to us an unkind demand on the spectator's understanding. But in a few years more I hope the English public may be convinced of the simple truth, that neither a great fact, nor a great man, nor a great poem, nor a great picture, nor any other great thing, can be fathomed to the very bottom in a moment of time; and that no high enjoyment, either in picture-seeing or any other occupation, is consistent with a total lethargy of the powers of the understanding.

As far as regards the technical qualities of Mr. Hunt's painting, I would only ask the spectator to observe this difference between true Pre-Raphaelite work and its imitations. The true work represents all objects exactly as they would appear in nature in the position and at the distances which the arrangement of the picture supposes. The false work represents them with all their details, as if seen through a microscope. Examine closely the ivy on the door in Mr. Hunt's picture, and there will not be found in it a single clear outline. All is the most exquisite mystery of colour; becoming reality at its due distance. In like manner examine the small gems on the robe of the figure. Not one will be made out in form, and yet there is not one of all those minute points of green colour, but it has two or three distinctly varied shades of green in it, giving it mysterious value and lustre.

The spurious imitations of Pre-Raphaelite work represent the most minute leaves and other objects with sharp outlines, but with no variety of colour, and with none of the concealment, none of the infinity of nature.[106]

"Awakening Conscience"

SIR,—Your kind insertion of my notes on Mr. Hunt's principal picture encourages me to hope that you may yet allow me room in your columns for a few words respecting his second work in the Royal Academy, the "Awakening Conscience" [Sir Colin Anderson]. Not that this picture is obscure, or its story feebly told. I am at a loss to know how its meaning could be rendered more distinctly, but assuredly it is not understood. People gaze at it in a blank wonder, and leave it hopelessly; so that, though it is almost an insult to the painter to explain his thoughts in this instance, I cannot persuade myself to leave it thus misunderstood. The poor girl has been sitting singing with

[106] Letter to the *Times,* May 5, 1854, in *Works,* vol. XII, 328–32, omit.

her seducer; some chance words of the song, "Oft in the stilly night," have struck upon the numbed places of her heart; she has started up in agony; he, not seeing her face, goes on singing, striking the keys carelessly with his gloved hand.

I suppose that no one possessing the slightest knowledge of expression could remain untouched by the countenance of the lost girl, rent from its beauty into sudden horror; the lips half open, indistinct in their purple quivering; the teeth set hard; the eyes filled with the fearful light of futurity, and with tears of ancient days. But I can easily understand that to many persons the careful rendering of the inferior details in this picture cannot but be at first offensive, as calling their attention away from the principal subject. It is true that detail of this kind has long been so carelessly rendered, that the perfect finishing of it becomes a matter of curiosity, and therefore an interruption to serious thought. But, without entering into the question of the general propriety of such treatment, I would only observe that, at least in this instance, it is based on a truer principle of the pathetic than any of the common artistical expedients of the schools. Nothing is more notable than the way in which even the most trivial objects force themselves upon the attention of a mind which has been fevered by violent and distressful excitement. They thrust themselves forward with a ghastly and unendurable distinctness, as if they would compel the sufferer to count, or measure, or learn them by heart. Even to the mere spectator a strange interest exalts the accessories of a scene in which he bears witness to human sorrow. There is not a single object in all that room—common, modern, vulgar (in the vulgar sense, as it may be), but it becomes tragical, if rightly read. That furniture so carefully painted, even to the last vein of the rosewood—is there nothing to be learnt from that terrible lustre of it, from its fatal newness; nothing there that has the old thoughts of home upon it, or that is ever to become a part of home? Those embossed books, vain and useless—they also new—marked with no happy wearing of beloved leaves; the torn and dying bird upon the floor; the gilded tapestry, with the fowls of the air feeding on the ripened corn; the picture above the fireplace, with its single drooping figure—the woman taken in adultery; nay, the very hem of the poor girl's dress, at which the painter has laboured so closely, thread by thread, has story in it, if we think how soon its pure whiteness may be soiled with dust and rain, her outcast feet failing in the street . . .

I surely need not go on. Examine the whole range of the walls of the Academy,—nay, examine those of all our public and private galleries,—and while pictures will be met with by the thousand which literally tempt to evil, by the thousand which are directed to the meanest trivialities of incident or emotion, by the thousand to the delicate fancies of inactive religion, there will not be found one powerful as this to meet full in the front the moral evil of the age in which it is painted; to waken into mercy the cruel thoughtlessness of youth, and subdue the severities of judgment into the sanctity of compassion.[107]

"The Scapegoat"

Of all the scenes in the Holy Land there are none whose present aspect tends so distinctly to confirm the statements of Scripture as this condemned shore [in "The Scapegoat," Lady Lever Art Gallery, Port Sunlight]. It is therefore exactly the scene of which it might seem most desirable to give a perfect idea to those who cannot see it for themselves; it is that also which fewest travellers are able to see; and which, I suppose, no one but Mr. Hunt himself would ever have dreamed of making the subject of a close pictorial study. The work was therefore worth his effort; and he has connected it in a simple, but most touching way, with other subjects of reflection, by the figure of the animal upon its shore. It is necessary, in this present instance, only to remember that the view taken by the Jews of the appointed sending forth of the scapegoat into the Wilderness was that it represented the carrying away of their sin into a place uninhabited and forgotten; and that the ani-

[107] Letter to the *Times*, May 25, 1854, in *Works*, vol. XII, 333–35, omit.

mal on whose head the sin was laid became accursed . . .
The goat, thus tormented, and with a scarlet fillet bound
about its brow, was driven by the multitude wildly out of
the camp, and pursued into the Wilderness. The painter
supposes it to have fled towards the Dead Sea, and to be
just about to fall exhausted at sunset—its hoofs entangled
in the crust of salt upon the shore. The opposite mountains, seen in the fading light, are that chain of Abarim on
which Moses died.

Now, we cannot, I think, esteem too highly, or receive
too gratefully, the temper and the toil which have produced this picture for us. Consider for a little while the
feelings involved in its conception, and the self-denial and
resolve needed for its execution; and compare them with
the modes of thought in which our former painters used
to furnish us annually with their "Cattle pieces" or "Lake
scenes," and I think we shall see cause to hold this picture as one more truly honourable to us, and more deep
and sure in its promise of future greatness in our schools
of painting, than all the works of "high art" that since the
foundation of the Academy have ever taxed the wonder,
or weariness, of the English public. But, at the same time,
this picture indicates a danger to our students of a kind
hitherto unknown in any school—the danger of a too great
intensity of feeling, making them forget the requirements of
painting as an *art*. This picture regarded merely as a landscape, or as a composition, is a total failure. The mind of
the painter has been so excited by the circumstances of the
scene, that, like a youth expressing his earnest feeling by
feeble verse (which seems to him good, because he *means*
so much by it), Mr. Hunt has been blinded by his intense
sentiment to the real weakness of the pictorial expression;
and in his earnest desire to paint the Scapegoat, has forgotten to ask himself first, whether he could paint a goat
at all.

I am not surprised that he should fail in painting the
distant mountains; for the forms of large distant landscape
are a quite new study to the Pre-Raphaelites, and they
cannot be expected to conquer them at first: but it is a
great disappointment to me to observe, even in the painting

of the goat itself, and of the fillet on its brow, a nearly total want of all that effective manipulation which Mr. Hunt displayed in his earlier pictures. I do not say that there is absolute want of skill—there may be difficulties encountered which I do not perceive—but the difficulties, whatever they may have been, are not conquered: this may be very faithful and very wonderful painting—but it is not *good* painting; and much as I esteem feeling and thought in all works of art, still I repeat, again and again, a painter's business is first to *paint*. No one could sympathize more than I with the general feeling displayed in the "Light of the World"; but unless it had been accompanied with perfectly good nettle painting, and ivy painting, and jewel painting, I should never have praised it; and though I acknowledge the good purpose of this picture, yet, inasmuch as there is no good hair painting, nor hoof painting in it, I hold it to be good only as an omen, not as an achievement; and I have hardly ever seen a composition, left apparently almost to chance, come so unluckily: the insertion of the animal in the exact centre of the canvas making it look as if it were painted for a sign. I can only, therefore, in thanking Mr. Hunt heartily for his work, pray him, for practice' sake, now to paint a few pictures with less feeling in them, and more handling.[108]

[108] Acad 1856, 63–66, omit.

23

MILLAIS

["The Rescue," National Gallery of Victoria, Melbourne] is the only *great* picture exhibited this year [1855]; but this is *very* great. The immortal element is in it to the full. It is easily understood, and the public very generally understand it. Various small cavils have been made at it, chiefly by conventionalists, who never ask how the thing is, but fancy for themselves how it ought to be. I have heard it said, for instance, that the fireman's arm should not have looked so black in the red light. If people would only try the experiment, they would find that near black, compared with other colours, is always black. Coals do not look red in a fire, but where they are red hot. In fact, the contrast between any dark colour and a light one, is always nearly the same, however high we raise the light that falls on both. Paul Veronese often paints local colour darker in the lights than in the shadow, generally equal in both. The glow that is mixed with the blackness is here intensely strong; but, justly, does not destroy the nature of the blackness.

The execution of the picture is remarkably bold—in some respects imperfect. I have heard it was hastily finished; but, except in the face of the child kissing the mother, it could not be much bettered. For there is a true sympathy between the impetuousness of execution and the haste of the action.[109]

[109] Acad 1855, 22 f

1857

And this promise was very visible in the works of Millais last year; a new power of conception being proved in them —to instance two things among many—by the arrangement of the myrtle branches in the "Peace" [T. P. Miller until 1946], and the play of the colours in the heap of "Autumn Leaves" [Manchester]. There was a slovenliness and imperfection in many portions, however, which I did not speak of, because I thought them accidental—consequent, probably, on too exulting a trial of his new powers, and likely to disappear as he became accustomed to them. But, as it is possible to stoop to victory, it is also possible to climb to defeat; and I see with consternation that it was not the Parnassian rock which Mr. Millais was ascending, but the Tarpeian. The change in his manner, from the years of "Ophelia" and "Mariana" to 1857, is not merely Fall—it is Catastrophe . . .[110]

[Of "Sir Isumbras at the Ford," (Lady Lever Art Gallery, Port Sunlight)] I say, first, an irregularity of conception. Thus, it seems only to have struck the painter suddenly, as he was finishing the knight's armour, that it ought to be more or less reflective; and he gives only one reflection in it—of the crimson cloth of the saddle, that one reflection being violently exaggerated: for though, from a golden surface, it would have been, as he has rendered it, warmer than the crimson, no reflection is ever *brighter* than the thing reflected. But all the rest of the armour is wholly untouched by the colour of the children's dresses, or of their glowing faces, or of the river or sky. And if Mr. Millais meant it to be old armour, rough with wear, it ought to have been deadened and darkened in colour, hacked with edges of weapons, stained with stains of death; if he meant it merely to be dusty, the dust should have lain white on some of the ridges, been clearly absent from others, and should have been dark where it was wet by the splashing of the horse. The ripple of the water against the horse it-

[110] Acad 1857, 107

self, however, being unnoticed, it is little wonder if the dash of the chance spray is missed. A more manifest sign still of this irregular appliance of mind is in the fact that the peacock's plume, the bundle of wood, and the stripes of the saddle-cloth are painted with care; while the children's faces, though right in expression, are rudely sketched, with unrounded edges, half in rose colour and half in dirty brown. Vestiges of his old power of colouring, still unattainable by any other man, exist, however, in that saddlecloth and in the peacock's feather. But the second sign, the warping of feeling, is a still more threatening one.[111]

[111] Acad 1857, 110

24

BURNE-JONES

His work, first, is simply the only art-work at present produced in England which will be received by the future as "classic" in its kind,—the best that has been, or could be. I think those portraits by Millais may be immortal (if the colour is firm), but only in such subordinate relation to Gainsborough and Velasquez, as Bonifazio, for instance, to Titian. But the action of imagination of the highest power in Burne-Jones, under the conditions of scholarship, of social beauty, and of social distress, which necessarily aid, thwart, and colour it, in the nineteenth century, are alone in art,—unrivalled in their kind; and I *know* that these will be immortal, as the best things the mid-nineteenth century in England could do, in such true relations as it had, through all confusion, retained with the paternal and everlasting Art of the world.

Secondly. Their faults are, so far as I can see, inherent in them as the shadow of their virtues;—not consequent on any error which we should be wise in regretting, or just in reproving. With men of consummately powerful imagination, the question is always, between finishing one conception, or partly seizing and suggesting three or four: and among all the great inventors, Botticelli is the only one who never allowed conception to interfere with completion. All the others,—Giotto, Masaccio, Luini, Tintoret, and Turner, permit themselves continually in slightness; and the resulting conditions of execution ought, I think, in every case to be received as the best possible, under the given conditions of imaginative force. To require that any one of these Days of Creation should have been finished as Bellini or Carpaccio would have finished it, is simply to require that the other Days should not have been begun.

Lastly, the mannerisms and errors of these pictures, whatever may be their extent, are never affected or indolent. The work is natural to the painter, however strange to us; and it is wrought with utmost conscience of care, however far, to his own or our desire, the result may yet be incomplete. Scarcely so much can be said for any other pictures of the modern schools: their eccentricities are almost always in some degree forced; and their imperfections gratuitously, if not impertinently, indulged. For Mr. Whistler's own sake, no less than for the protection of the purchaser, Sir Coutts Lindsay ought not to have admitted works into the gallery in which the ill-educated conceit of the artist so nearly approached the aspect of wilful imposture. I have seen, and heard, much of Cockney impudence before now; but never expected to hear a coxcomb ask two hundred guineas for flinging a pot of paint in the public's face.[112]

I must delay you a little, though perhaps tiresomely, to make myself well understood on this point; for the first celebrated pictures of the pre-Raphaelite school having been extremely minute in finish, you might easily take minuteness for a speciality of the style,—but it is not so in the least. Minuteness I *do* somewhat claim, for a quality insisted upon by myself, and required in the work of my own pupils; it is—at least in landscape—Turnerian and Ruskinian—not pre-Raphaelite at all:—the pre-Raphaelism common to us all is in the frankness and honesty of the touch, not in its dimensions.

Now then, I think I have got the manner of Pre-Raphaelite "Realization" — "Verification" — "Materialization" —or whatever else you choose to call it, positively enough asserted and defined: and hence you will see that it follows, as a necessary consequence, that Pre-Raphaelite subjects must usually be of real persons in a solid world—not of personifications in a vaporescent one.

Nevertheless, we find one of the artists whose close

[112] Fors 1877, 159 f

friendship with Rossetti, and fellowship with other members of the Pre-Raphaelite brotherhood, have more or less
identified his work with theirs, yet differing from them all
diametrically in this, that his essential gift and habit of
thought is *in* personification, and that,—for sharp and brief
instance,—had both Rossetti and he been set to illustrate
the first chapter of Genesis, Rossetti would have painted
either Adam or Eve; but Edward Burne-Jones, a Day of
Creation.

And in this gift, he becomes a painter, neither of Divine
History, nor of Divine Natural History, but of Mythology,
accepted as such, and understood by its symbolic figures to
represent only general truths, or abstract ideas.

It should be a ground of just pride to all of us here in
Oxford, that out of this University came the painter whose
indefatigable scholarship and exhaustless fancy have together fitted him for this task, in a degree far distinguishing him above all contemporary European designers. It is
impossible for the general public to estimate the quantity
of careful and investigatory reading, and the fine tact of
literary discrimination, which are signified by the command
now possessed by Mr. Burne-Jones over the entire range
both of Northern and Greek Mythology, or the tenderness
at once, and largeness, of sympathy which have enabled
him to harmonize these with the loveliest traditions of
Christian. His outline is the purest and quietest that is possible to the pencil; nearly all other masters accentuate
falsely, or in some places, as Richter, add shadows which
are more or less conventional. But an outline by Burne-
Jones is as pure as the lines of engraving on an Etruscan
mirror; and I placed the series of drawings from the story
of Psyche in your school as faultlessly exemplary in this
kind. Whether pleasing or displeasing to your taste, they
are entirely masterful; and it is only by trying to copy
these or other such outlines, that you will fully feel the
grandeur of action in the moving hand, tranquil and swift
as a hawk's flight, and never allowing a vulgar tremor, or a
momentary impulse, to impair its precision, or disturb its
serenity.

Again, though Mr. Jones has a sense of colour, in its

kind, perfect, he is essentially a chiaroscurist. Diametrically opposed to Rossetti, who could conceive in colour only, he prefers subjects which can be divested of superficial attractiveness; appeal first to the intellect and the heart; and convey their lesson either through intricacies of delicate line, or in the dimness or coruscation of ominous light.[113]

[113] ArtEng 289–301, omit.

25

JOHN BRETT

This ["Stonebreaker," Liverpool] after John Lewis's, is simply the most perfect piece of painting with respect to touch in the Academy this year [1858]; in some points of precision it goes beyond anything the Pre-Raphaelites have done yet. I know no such thistledown, no such chalk hills, and elm-trees, no such natural pieces of far-away cloud, in any of their works.

The composition is palpably crude and wrong in many ways, especially in the awkward white cloud at the top; and the tone of the whole a little too much as if some of the chalk of the flints had been mixed with all the colours. For all that, it is a marvellous picture, and may be examined inch by inch with delight; though nearly the last stone I should ever have thought of any one's sitting down to paint would have been a chalk flint. If he can make so much of that, what will Mr. Brett not make of mica slate and gneiss! If he can paint so lovely a distance from the Surrey downs and railway-traversed vales, what would he not make of the chestnut groves of the Val d'Aosta! I heartily wish him good-speed and long exile.[114]

"Val d'Aosta"

Yes, here ["Val d'Aosta," Sir William Cooper] we have it at last—some close-coming to it at least—historical landscape, properly so called—landscape painting with a meaning and a use. We have had hitherto plenty of industry, precision quite unlimited; but all useless, or nearly so, be-

[114] Acad 1858, 171 f

ing wasted on scenes of no majesty or enduring interest. Here is, at last, a scene worth painting—painted with all our might (not quite with all our heart, perhaps, but with might of hand and eye). And here, accordingly, for the first time in history, we have, by help of art, the power of visiting a place, reasoning about it, and knowing it, just as if we were there, except only that we cannot stir from our place, nor look behind us. For the rest, standing before this picture is just as good as standing on that spot in Val d'Aosta, so far as gaining of knowledge is concerned; and perhaps in some degree pleasanter, for it would be very hot on that rock to-day, and there would probably be a disagreeable smell of juniper plants growing on the slopes above.

So if any simple-minded, quietly-living person, indisposed towards railroad stations or crowded inns, cares to know in an untroublous and uncostly way what a Piedmontese valley is like in July, there it is for him. Rocks overlaid with velvet and fur to stand on in the first place: if you look close into the velvet you will find it is jewelled and set with stars in a stately way. White poplars by the roadside, shaking silvery in the wind: I regret to say the wind is apt to come up the Val d'Aosta in an ill-tempered and rude manner, turning leaves thus the wrong side out; but it will be over in a moment. Beyond the poplars you may see the slopes of arable and vineyard ground, such as give the wealth and life to Italy which she idly trusts in—ground laid ages ago in wreaths, like new cut hay by the mountain streams, now terraced and trimmed into all gentle service. If you want to know what vines look like under Italian training (far from the best), *that* is the look of them—the dark spots and irregular cavities, seen through the broken green of their square-set ranks, distinguishing them at any distance from the continuous pale fields of low-set staff and leaf, divided by no gaps of gloom, which clothe a true vine country. There, down in the mid-valley, you see what pasture and meadow land we have, we Piedmontese, with our hamlet and cottage life, and groups of glorious wood. Just beyond the rock are two splendid

sweet chestnut trees, with forming fruit, good for making
bread of, no less than maize; lower down, far to the left, a
furlong or two of the main stream with its white shore and
alders: not beautiful, for it has come down into all this fair
country from the Courmayeur glaciers, and is yet un-
tamed, cold, and furious, incapable of rest. But above,
there is rest, where the sunshine streams into iridescence
through branches of pine, and turns the pastures into
strange golden clouds, half grass, half dew; for the shadows
of the great hills have kept the dew there since morning.
Rest also, calm enough, among the ridges of rock and
forest that heap themselves into that purple pyramid high
on the right. Look well into the making of it—it is indeed
so that a great mountain is built and bears itself, and its
forest fringes, and village jewels—for those white spots far
up the ravine are villages—and peasant dynasties are hidden among the film of blue. And above all are other more
desolate dynasties—the crowns that cannot shake—of jagged
rock; they also true and right, even to their finest serration.
So it is that the snow lies on those dark diadems for ever.
A notable picture truly; a possession of much within a few
feet square.

Yet not, in the strong, essential meaning of the word, a
noble picture. It has a strange fault, considering the school
to which it belongs—it seems to me wholly emotionless.
I cannot find from it that the painter loved, or feared, anything in all that wonderful piece of the world. There seems
to me no awe of the mountains there—no real love of the
chestnuts or the vines. Keenness of eye and fineness of hand
as much as you choose; but of emotion, or of intention,
nothing traceable. Not but that I believe the painter to be
capable of the highest emotion: any one who can paint
thus must have passion within him; but the passion here is
assuredly not out of him. He has cared for nothing, except
as it was more or less pretty in colour and form. I never
saw the mirror so held up to Nature; but it is Mirror's
work, not Man's.

Historical landscape it is, unquestionably; meteorological
also; poetical—by no means: yet precious, in its patient

way; and, as a wonder of toil and delicate handling, un-impeachable. There is no such subtle and precise work on any other canvas here.[115]

[115] Acad 1859, 234–37, omit.

26

CARICATURE AND ILLUSTRATION

I believe . . . whatever wit, delicate appreciation of ordinary character, or other intellectual power may belong to the modern masters of caricature, their method of study for ever incapacitates them from passing beyond a certain point, and either reaching any of the perfect forms of art themselves, or understanding them in others. Generally speaking, their power is limited to the use of the pen or pencil—they cannot touch colour without discomfiture; and even those whose work is of higher aim, and wrought habitually in colour, are prevented by their pursuit of *piquant* expression from understanding noble expression.

On the other hand, all the real masters of caricature deserve honour in this respect, that their gift is peculiarly their own—innate and incommunicable. No teaching, no hard study, will ever enable other people to equal, in their several ways, the works of Leech or Cruikshank; whereas, the power of pure drawing is communicable, within certain limits, to every one who has good sight and industry. I do not, indeed, know how far, by devoting the attention to points of character, caricaturist skill may be laboriously attained; but certainly the power is, in the masters of the school, innate from their childhood.

Farther. It is evident that many subjects of thought may be dealt with by this kind of art which are inapproachable by any other, and that its influence over the popular mind must always be great; hence it may often happen that men of strong purpose may rather express themselves in this way (and continue to make such expression a matter of earnest study), than turn to any less influential, though more dignified, or even more intrinsically meritorious, branch of art. And when the powers of quaint fancy are associated (as is frequently the case) with stern understanding of the nature of evil, and tender human sympathy, there results a bitter, or pathetic spirit of grotesque to which mankind at the present day owe more thorough moral teaching than to any branch of art whatsoever.[116]

Punch

Although I have headed my lecture only with the names of Leech and Tenniel, as being the real founders of *Punch*, and by far the greatest of its illustrators, both in force of art and range of thought, yet in the precision of the use of his means, and the subtle boldness to which he has educated the interpreters of his design, Mr. Du Maurier is more exemplary than either; and I have therefore had enlarged by photography,—your thanks are due to the brother of Miss Greenaway for the skill with which the proofs have been produced,—for first example of fine woodcutting, the heads of two of Mr. Du Maurier's chief heroines, Mrs. Ponsonby de Tomkyns, and Lady Midas, in the great scene where Mrs. Ponsonby takes on herself the administration of Lady Midas's "at home."[117]

You see at once how the effect in both depends on the coagulation and concretion of the black touches into masses relieved only by interspersed sparkling grains of incised light, presenting the realistic and vital portraiture of both ladies with no more labour than would occupy the draughtsman but a few minutes, and the engraver perhaps an hour or two. It is true that the features of the elder of the two friends might be supposed to yield themselves without difficulty to the effect of the irregular and blunt lines which are employed to reproduce them; but it is a matter of no small wonderment to see the delicate profile and softly rounded features of the younger lady suggested by an outline which must have been drawn in

[116] MP IV, 470 f, omit.
[117] (*Punch*, July 7, 1883.) ArtEng 356 f

the course of a few seconds, and by some eight or ten firmly swept parallel penstrokes right across the cheek.

The rule ["that all the white in the picture is precious, and all the black, conspicuous"] is just as true for wood-cutting. In fine examples of it, the black is left for local colour only—for dark dresses, or dark patterns on light ones, dark hair, or dark eyes; it is never left for general gloom, out of which the figures emerge like spectres.

When, however, a number of Mr. Du Maurier's compositions are seen together, and compared with the natural simplicity and aerial space of Leech's, they will be felt to depend on this principle too absolutely and undisguisedly; so that the quarterings of black and white in them sometimes look more like a chess board than a picture. But in minor and careful passages, his method is wholly exemplary, and in the next example I enlarge for you,—Alderman Sir Robert admiring the portraits of the Duchess and the Colonel,[118]—he has not only shown you every principle of woodcutting, but abstracted for you also the laws of beauty, whose definite and every year more emphatic assertion in the pages of *Punch* is the ruling charm and most legitimate pride of the immortal periodical. Day by day the search for grotesque, ludicrous, or loathsome subject which degraded the caricatures in its original, the *Charivari,* and renders the dismally comic journals of Italy the mere plagues and cancers of the State, became, in our English satirists, an earnest comparison of the things which were graceful and honourable, with those which were graceless and dishonest, in modern life. Gradually the kind and vivid genius of John Leech, capable in its brightness of finding pretty jest in everything, but capable in its tenderness also of rejoicing in the beauty of everything, softened and illumined with its loving wit the entire scope of English social scene; the graver power of Tenniel brought a steady tone and law of morality into the licence of political contention; and finally the acute, highly trained, and accurately physiologic observation of Du Maurier traced for us, to its true origin in vice or virtue, every or-

[118] (*Punch,* August 25, 1883.) ArtEng 357–59, omit.

der of expression in the mixed circle of metropolitan rank and wealth: and has done so with a closeness of delineation the like of which has not been seen since Holbein, and deserving the most respectful praise in that, whatever power of satire it may reach by the selection and assemblage of telling points of character, it never degenerates into caricature. Nay, the terrific force of blame which he obtains by collecting, as here in the profile of the Knight-Alderman, features separately faultful into the closest focus, depends on the very fact that they are *not* caricatured.

The "liking for ugliness"

It seems to have been hitherto impossible, when once the zest of satirical humour is felt, even by so kind and genial a heart as John Leech's, to restrain it, and to elevate it into the playfulness of praise. In the designs of Richter, of which I have so often spoken, among scenes of domestic beauty and pathos, he continually introduces little pieces of play,—such, for instance, as that of the design of the "Wide, Wide World," in which the very young puppy, with its paws on its—relatively as young—master's shoulder, looks out with him over the fence of their cottage garden. And it is surely conceivable that some day the rich power of a true humorist may be given to express more vividly the comic side which exists in many beautiful incidents of daily life, and refuse at last to dwell, even with a smile, on its follies.

This, however, must clearly be a condition of future human development, for hitherto the perfect power of seizing comic incidents has always been associated with some liking for ugliness, and some exultation in disaster. The law holds—and holds with no relaxation—even in the instance of so wise and benevolent a man as the Swiss schoolmaster, Töpffer, whose death, a few years since, left none to succeed him in perfection of pure linear caricature. He can do more with fewer lines than any draughtsman known to me, and in several plates of his *Histoire d'Albert*, has succeeded in entirely representing the tenor of con-

versation with no more than half the profile and one eye
of the speaker.

He generally took a walking tour through Switzerland,
with his pupils, in the summer holidays, and illustrated his
exquisitely humorous diary of their adventures with pen
sketches,[119] which show a capacity of appreciating beautiful landscape as great as his grotesque faculty; but his
mind is drawn away from the most sublime scene, in a
moment, to the difficulties of the halting-place, or the ras-
calities of the inn; and his power is never so marvellously
exerted as in depicting a group of roguish guides, shame-
less beggars, or hopeless cretins.[120]

Tenniel

You no doubt have at the Union the most interesting
and beautiful series of the Tenniel cartoons which have
been collectively published, with the explanation of their
motives.[121] If you begin with No. 38, you will find a consecutive series of ten extremely forcible drawings, casting
the utmost obloquy in the power of the designer upon
the French Emperor, the Pope, and the Italian clergy, and
alike discourteous to the head of the nation which had
fought side by side with us at Inkerman, and impious in
its representation of the Catholic power to which Italy
owed, and still owes, whatever has made her glorious
among the nations of Christendom, or happy among the
families of the earth.

Among them you will find other two, representing our
wars with China, and the triumph of our missionary manner of compelling free trade at the point of the bayonet:
while, for the close and consummation of the series, you
will see the genius and valour of your country figuratively
summed in the tableau, subscribed,—

"John Bull defends his pudding."

[119] (Rodolphe Töpffer's *Voyages en Zigzag*, Paris, 1843 and
1853.) ArtEng 359–63, omit.

[120] ArtEng 363

[121] (*Cartoons from Punch*, by John Tenniel, First Series.)
ArtEng 366

Is this indeed then the final myth of English heroism, into which King Arthur, and St. George, and Britannia, and the British Lion are all collated, concluded, and perfected by Evolution, in the literal words of Carlyle, "like four whale cubs combined by boiling"?

For, indeed, in many a past year, it has every now and then been a subject of recurring thought to me, what such a genius as that of Tenniel would have done for us, had we asked the best of it, and had the feeling of the nation respecting the arts, as a record of its honour, been like that of the Italians in their proud days.

Tenniel has much of the largeness and symbolic mystery of imagination which belong to the great leaders of classic art: in the shadowy masses and sweeping lines of his great compositions, there are tendencies which might have won his adoption into the school of Tintoret; and his scorn of whatever seems to him dishonest or contemptible in religion, would have translated itself into awe in the presence of its vital power.

I gave you, when first I came to Oxford, Tintoret's picture of the Doge Mocenigo, with his divine spiritual attendants, in the cortile of St. Mark's. It is surely our own fault, more than Mr. Tenniel's, if the best portraits he can give us of the heads of our English government should be rather on the occasion of their dinner at Greenwich than their devotion at St. Paul's.[122]

John Leech

It is merely and simply a matter of public concern that the value of [John Leech's] drawings should be known and measures taken for their acquisition, or, at least, for obtaining a characteristic selection from them, as a National property. It cannot be necessary for me, or for any one now to praise the work of John Leech. Admittedly it contains the finest definition and natural history of the classes of our society, the kindest and subtlest analysis of its foibles, the tenderest flattery of its pretty and well-bred ways, with which the modesty of subservient genius ever

[122] ArtEng 366–69, omit.

amused or immortalized careless masters. But it is not generally known how much more valuable, as art, the first sketches for the woodcuts were than the finished drawings, even before those drawings sustained any loss in engraving.

John Leech was an absolute master of the elements of character—but not by any means of those of *chiaroscuro,*— and the admirableness of his work diminished as it became elaborate. The first few lines in which he sets down his purpose are invariably of all drawing that I know the most wonderful in their accurate felicity and prosperous haste. It is true that the best possible drawing, whether slight or elaborate, is never hurried. Holbein or Titian, if they lay only a couple of lines, yet lay them quietly, and leave them entirely right. But it needs a certain sternness of temper to do this.

Most, in the prettiest sense of the word, *gentle* artists indulge themselves in the ease, and even trust to the felicity of rapid—and even in a measure inconsiderate—work in sketching, so that the beauty of a sketch is understood to be consistent with what is partly unintentional. There is, however, one condition of extreme and exquisite skill in which haste may become unerring. It cannot be obtained in completely finished work; but the hands of Gainsborough, Reynolds, or Tintoret often nearly approach completion at full speed, and the pencil sketches of Turner are expressive almost in the direct ratio of their rapidity. But of all rapid and condensed realization ever accomplished by the pencil, John Leech's is the most dainty, and the least fallible, in the subjects of which he was cognizant. Not merely right in the traits which he seizes, but refined in the sacrifice of what he refuses.

The drawing becomes slight through fastidiousness, not indolence, and the finest discretion has left its touches rare. In flexibility and lightness of pencilling, nothing but the best outlines of Italian masters with the silver point can be compared to them. That Leech sketched English squires instead of saints, and their daughters instead of martyrs, does not in the least affect the question respecting skill of pencilling; and I repeat deliberately that nothing but the best work of sixteenth-century Italy with the silver point exists in art, which in rapid refinement these playful English drawings do not excel. There are too many of them (fortunately) to be rightly exemplary—I want to see the collection divided, dated carefully, and selected portions placed in good light, in a quite permanent arrangement, in each of our great towns in connection with their drawing schools.[123]

Art for children

It is only in recent times that pictures have become familiar means of household pleasure and education: only in our own days—nay, even within the last ten years of those,—that the means of illustration by colour-printing have been brought to perfection, and art as exquisite as we need desire to see it, placed, if our school-boards choose to have it so, within the command of every nursery governess.

Having then the colour-print, the magic-lantern, the electric-light, and the—to any row of ciphers—magnifying lens, it becomes surely very interesting to consider what we may most wisely represent to children by means so potent, so dazzling, and, if we will, so faithful. For it is quite an inexorable law of this poor human nature of ours, that in the development of its healthy infancy, it is put by Heaven under the absolute necessity of using its imagination as well as its lungs and its legs;—that it is forced to develop its power of invention, as a bird its feathers of flight; that no toy you can bestow will supersede the pleasure it has in fancying something that isn't there; and the most instructive histories you can compile for it of the wonders of the world will never conquer the interest of the tale which a clever child can tell itself, concerning the shipwreck of a rose-leaf in the shallows of a rivulet.

You must, however, always carefully distinguish these states of gloomy fantasy, natural, though too often fatal, to men of real imagination,—the spectra which appear,

[123] *Catalogue of the Exhibition of Outlines by the late John Leech,* London, 9 Conduit Street and Regent Street, 1872, in *Works,* vol. XIV, 332–34

whether they desire it or not,—to men like Orcagna, Dürer, Blake, and Alfred Rethel,—and dwelt upon by them, in the hope of producing some moral impression of salutary awe by their record—as in Blake's Book of Job, in Dürer's Apocalypse, in Rethel's Death the Avenger and Death the Friend,—and more nobly in his grand design of Barbarossa entering the grave of Charlemagne;—carefully, I say, you must distinguish this natural and lofty phase of visionary terror, from the coarse delight in mere pain and crisis of danger, which, in our infidel art and literature for the young, fills our books of travel with pictures of alligators swallowing children, hippopotami upsetting canoes full of savages, bears on their hind-legs doing battle with northern navigators, avalanches burying Alpine villages, and the like . . .

Kate Greenaway

I have brought with me to-day in the first place some examples of [Miss Greenaway's] pencil sketches in primary design. These in general the public cannot see, and these, as is always the case with the finest imaginative work, contain the best essence of it,—qualities never afterwards to be recovered, and expressed with the best of all sensitive instruments, the pencil point.

You have here, for consummate example, a dance of fairies under a mushroom, which she did under challenge to show me what fairies were like. "They'll be very like children," she said; I answered that I didn't mind, and should like to see them, all the same;—so here they are, with a dance, also of two girlies, outside of a mushroom; and I don't know whether the elfins or girls are fairy-footedest: and one or two more subjects, which you may find out;—but, in all, you will see that the line is ineffably tender and delicate, and can't in the least be represented by the lines of a woodcut.

First, her own design has been greatly restricted by being too ornamental, or, in your modern phrase, decorative; —contracted into any corner of a Christmas card, or stretched like an elastic band round the edges of an almanack. Now, her art is much too good to be used merely for illumination; it is essentially and perfectly that of true colour-picture, and that the most naïve and delightful manner of picture, because, on the simplest terms, it comes nearest reality. No end of mischief has been done to modern art by the habit of running semi-pictorial illustration round the margins of ornamental volumes, and Miss Greenaway has been wasting her strength too sorrowfully in making the edges of her little birthday books, and the like, glitter with unregarded gold, whereas her power should be concentrated in the direct illustration of connected story, and her pictures should be made complete on the page, and far more realistic than decorative. There is no charm so enduring as that of the real representation of any given scene; her present designs are like living flowers flattened to go into an herbarium, and sometimes too pretty to be believed. We must ask her for more descriptive reality, for more convincing simplicity, and we must get her to organize a school of colourists by hand, who can absolutely facsimile her own first drawing.

There are no railroads in [Miss Greenaway's landscape] to carry the children away with, are there? no tunnel or pit mouths to swallow them up, no league-long viaducts— no blinkered iron bridges? There are only winding brooks, wooden foot-bridges, and grassy hills without any holes cut into them!

And more wonderful still,—there are no gasworks! no waterworks, no mowing machines, no sewing machines, no telegraph poles, no vestige, in fact, of science, civilization, economical arrangements, or commercial enterprise! ! !

Would you wish me, with professional authority, to advise her that her conceptions belong to the dark ages, and must be reared on a new foundation? Or is it, on the other hand, recommendably conceivable by *you*, that perhaps the world we truly live in may not be quite so changeable as you have thought it;—that all the gold and silver you can dig out of the earth are not worth the kingcups and the daisies she gave you of her grace . . .[124]

[124] ArtEng 327–47, omit.

INDEX